THE VIEW FROM THE MASTHEAD

The VIEW *from the* MASTHEAD

MARITIME IMAGINATION
AND ANTEBELLUM AMERICAN
SEA NARRATIVES

HESTER BLUM

The University of North Carolina Press

Chapel Hill

© 2008 THE UNIVERSITY
OF NORTH CAROLINA PRESS
All rights reserved

Designed by Amy Ruth Buchanan
Set in Bembo by Keystone Typesetting.
Manufactured in the United States of
America

This book was published with the
assistance of the Anniversary Endowment Fund of the University of North
Carolina Press.

The paper in this book meets the guidelines for permanence and durability of
the Committee on Production Guidelines
for Book Longevity of the Council on
Library Resources.

Library of Congress Cataloging-in-
Publication Data
Blum, Hester.
The view from the masthead : maritime
imagination and antebellum American sea
narratives / by Hester Blum.
p. cm.
Includes bibliographical references and index.
ISBN 978-0-8078-3169-4 (cloth: alk. paper)
ISBN 978-0-8078-5855-4 (pbk.: alk. paper)
1. Sea stories, American—History and
criticism. 2. American literature—19th
century—History and criticism. 3. Sailors in
literature. 4. Seafaring life in literature.
5. Labor in literature. 6. Self in literature.
7. National characteristics, American, in
literature. 8. Knowledge, Theory of, in
literature. I. Title.
PS217.S4B68 2008
810.9'32—dc22   2007022090

A portion of Chapter 2 appeared in Early
American Studies 1, no. 2 (Fall 2003): 133–58,
and is reprinted here by permission of the
University of Pennsylvania Press, copy-
right © 2003 The McNeil Center for Early
American Studies.

cloth   12 11 10 09 08   5 4 3 2 1
paper   12 11 10 09 08   5 4 3 2 1

CONTENTS

ILLUSTRATIONS

ACKNOWLEDGMENTS

I am not a sailor. My interest in sea literature emerges not from nautical experience but from a particular literary archive: the Extracts section found at the beginning of *Moby-Dick*. When I first read Melville's novel in high school, I wondered about the sources of its references to whales, many of which are drawn, naturally enough, from writing by and about sailors. My curiosity about the cited narratives   some of whose titles remain in literary circulation only in *Moby-Dick*'s front matter—led eventually to this book.

I thus wish to acknowledge, first and foremost, the libraries and archives from which the material of my work has been extracted. My primary research was conducted at the American Antiquarian Society, with the support of a Reese Research Fellowship; Mystic Seaport's G. W. Blunt White Library, in conjunction with the Frank C. Munson Institute of American Maritime Studies; the Library Company of Philadelphia; the Annenberg Rare Book and Manuscript Library at the University of Pennsylvania; and the Houghton Library at Harvard University. I am grateful for the invaluable assistance of the librarians of these institutions and wish to thank Joanne Chaison, Jim Hench, Marie Lamoureux, and Caroline Sloat of the AAS; Paul O'Pecko of the Blunt White Library; Jim Green of the Library Company; and John Pollock at Penn. I am also grateful to the National Endowment for the Humanities for an NEH Summer Stipend in support of my completion of the book.

I first learned the pleasures of archival work from Christopher Looby, whose inventiveness and judiciousness have been models for my own attempts to approach canonical and noncanonical literature. Elisa New believed in this project from its earliest conception; indeed, the example of her keen and imaginative eye was fundamental to conceiving it in the first place. Nancy Bentley's intellectual breadth and professional grace have been a strong influence on me, and I am thankful to have had her guidance. Chris, Lisa, and

Nancy were this project's first readers, and my admiration of them is exceeded only by my gratitude for their help and friendship.

My graduate study at the University of Pennsylvania introduced me to the importance of conversations across the disciplines of literature, American studies, and history. The American Literature Seminar at Penn was a model of collegiality and incisiveness, and I thank its members for their responses to preliminary versions of portions of this book. A Marguerite Bartlett Hamer Dissertation Fellowship at the McNeil Center for Early American Studies was transformative for my scholarship, and I am very grateful to Dan Richter for his support and for his smart comments on an earlier version of Chapter 2, as well as on an early draft of this book. Rosalind Remer and the members of the McNeil Center Seminar also provided vital feedback on this score. At Penn I enjoyed, and continue to learn from, conversations with Kendall Johnson, Jeannine DeLombard, Max Cavitch, Peter Conn, Jim English, and especially Martha Schoolman, my best Americanist comrade.

I have had the privilege of interacting with other communities of scholars whose wisdom and generosity have animated these pages. My work has been enhanced by the methodological instruction I received from Michael Winship at Rare Book School at the University of Virginia. At the American Antiquarian Society's Summer Seminar in the History of the Book in American Culture I found similarly invaluable training and a great network of friends. I am indebted to the University of Tennessee for granting me a Professional Development and Research Award in support of my research, making possible my attendance at Rare Book School and the AAS Summer Seminar. A National Humanities Center Summer Institute in Literary Studies on *Moby-Dick*, led by Richard Brodhead, was a fine exercise in fellowship, and I have been glad to continue the exchanges I began there with Jeff Clymer, Ivy Wilson, and the other members of the seminar. In its earliest stages, my work profited from astute feedback from Don Pease, Carl Gutierrez-Jones, and the other members of Dartmouth College's Futures of American Studies Institute. A fortuitous conversation about Barbary piracy with Gillian Weiss in Paris in 1999 was the formative influence on Chapter 2; I owe her my gratitude. I also thank Wyn Kelley, Paul Gilje, my former colleagues at the University of Tennessee, and participants in the seminars, conferences, and symposia in which I have taken part for their contributions, direct and indirect, to this book. I owe Robert Levine extra thanks for his estimable generosity and mentorship. The personal and intellectual fellowship I have found among these diverse groups of scholars has aided my own work on literary communities in more ways than I can describe.

My colleagues at the Pennsylvania State University are terrific, and I thank them all. I will take special notice here of Michael Bérubé, Scott Herring, Kit Hume, Julia Kasdorf, Mark Morrisson, Carla Mulford, Janet Lyon, Laura Reed-Morrisson, Aldon Nielsen, Robin Schulze, Susan Squier, Sandy Stelts, Lisa Surwillo, Rachel Teukolsky, Steven Thomas, Jim West, the members of the American Women Writers Workshop, the staff, and my students. I am grateful to Penn State's English Department, the College of Liberal Arts, and Deans Susan Welch and Ray Lombra for giving me abundant research support and a semester of leave from teaching. I wish to single out Robert Caserio, who reads more—and more attentively—than anyone I've ever met; I am very glad to have him as a reader of my work.

My experience with the University of North Carolina Press has been a delight, and I thank the editorial and production staff, especially Stephanie Wenzel and the excellent Sian Hunter. Working with Sian has been a pleasure and a privilege. I am most grateful to Sam Otter and to Shelley Streeby, whose exemplary rigor and intelligence in reviewing the manuscript have immeasurably improved this book. Christine Cuccio Radlmann provided expert proofreading; Anne Marie Houppert did an outstanding job in preparing the index.

I am lucky to have such clever and curious friends as Mike Barsanti, Jeremy Braddock, Rayna Kalas, Damien Keane, Jim Kearney, Ben Lee, Elizabeth Scanlon, Lisi Schoenbach, Martha Schoolman, Jamie Taylor, Caitlin Wood, Emily Zinn, and Gabriela Zoller. Amy Elias has been as good a friend as she has been a mentor. In the final stages of this book, Alex and Katie Novak shared their friendship and publishing expertise.

I owe the largest debts to my family. My parents, Carl and Maureen Blum, and my brother, Jonah Blum, have given me continual support and love: excellent job by them. Adelaide Blum Eburne was born as I was finishing this book, and every day with her brings freshness and wonder. Above all else I thank Jonathan Eburne, my ideal reader in all things; there are no words for the marvelousness he produces in our life together.

THE VIEW FROM THE MASTHEAD

INTRODUCTION

For sailors, though they have their jokes,
Still feel and think like other folks.
—BENJAMIN MORELL JR.

When Ishmael ascends the ship's mast to sight whales in *Moby-Dick*, he admits that he is a poor lookout. He views his time in the masthead as an opportunity for contemplation rather than vigilance, for when sent to such a "thought-engendering altitude," Ishmael claims he cannot help but consider what he calls the "problem of the universe." Yet the risks he faces in contemplating metaphysical questions too deeply are not simply disciplinary measures from officers who might feel that a meditative sailor does not take a proper interest in the economic demands of a whaleship. More immediately, Ishmael's philosophizing puts him in mortal danger. Part of the attraction of standing in the masthead is the lure of losing his "identity" while lulled into a reverie by the "elusive thoughts" that come to the solitary man on a watch. But the lookout must never forget the tenuous physical position he occupies when absorbed by such thoughts. Herman Melville's novel cautions a sailor dreaming aloft not to "move your foot or hand an inch; slip your hold at all," lest "your identity comes back in horror."[1] If he is not attentive to his job, in other words, the sailor will fall from the masthead and drown. In this scene the sailor's productivity and survival seem to depend on his working body, not his thinking body. Yet labor and contemplation can be productively aligned, Melville suggests. Metaphysical questioning—Ishmael's "problem of the universe"—is in fact the result of a tension between the thinking body and the material conditions of labor.[2]

In its attention to the risks a workingman faces in striving to maintain both his working and thinking selves while at sea, *Moby-Dick* is the best known analogue to the sizable and critically untapped archive of narratives written by laboring sailors. This vibrant body of American popular sea writing concerns itself with a broader question in intellectual and cultural history: how can a place of labor serve simultaneously as a site for contemplation? The first-person narratives produced by working sailors in the first half of the long nineteenth century seek to represent the facts of labor. American maritime writing, both fictional and nonfictional, includes for nonspecialist readers such details as latitude and longitude notation and meticulous descriptions of ship labor. These experiential practices receive a special textual emphasis and carry an unexpected rhetorical and cultural burden: they become the mechanism for a larger effort to reimagine the maritime world as a sphere of both manual and intellectual labor. Nineteenth-century sailors were jarringly anomalous wage laborers. They had no viable egress from their job site, and the capriciousness of nature made the regulation of their hours erratic; yet such conditions were precisely the reason why maritime writing could conjoin labor and contemplation. Periods of idleness, and thus the opportunity for reading and writing, were part of the job.[3] The sailor narrative became both the artistic product of natural observation and a commodity produced by maritime industry.

This book is about sailors' literary culture and the epistemology of maritime narratives. As both producers and consumers, seamen were important figures in the nineteenth-century American literary public sphere, although their contributions have been little recognized in literary history. The genre of sea writing, which continually increased in popularity with a land-based readership in the first half of the nineteenth century, has been marginalized in critical discourse as low or rough, much as sailors themselves were typed. Sailors, however, did not devalue their contributions to literary culture. Their narratives, which explicitly and implicitly engaged with contemporary crises of nation- and selfhood, stipulate a process of moving from a state of physical competence to one of imaginative confidence that has wider implications for literary and cultural history. The model of knowledge put forward by sailor narratives helps to reconfigure our understanding of larger critical and historical issues in antebellum American literature and culture, from transcendental modes of understanding to the emergence of slave and captivity narratives and the rise of the American novel. Sea narratives, for example, anticipate and contextualize the overlooked fact that Emerson's transparent eyeball—one of the organizing metaphors of nineteenth-century American visionary practice—must operate from a position "standing on the bare ground," that is, rooted in the material world.[4] In a period that saw increasing attention to the idea of writing as work, sailor narratives offer a remarkable example of what can be produced when the work of writing and the work of manual labor are concurrent. The epistemology developed in sea writing stresses the interpenetration of the spheres of manual and intellectual labor, finding an empirical basis for imagination.

Maritime knowledge emerges from the mechanics of nautical experience, or the "plain matters of fact" that find articulate expression in sailor writing. As Richard Henry Dana Jr. explains of his narrative in his preface to *Two Years before the Mast* (1840), "There may be in some parts a good deal that is unintelligible to the general reader; but I have found from my own experience, and from what I have heard from others, that plain matters of fact in relation to customs and habits of life new to us, and descriptions of life under new aspects, act upon the inexperienced through imagination, so that we are hardly aware of our want of technical knowledge."[5] In Dana's narrative, like those of common seamen, the mechanical specificity of life at sea is presented as an invitation to nonspecialist readers, who are encouraged to make legible the experience of a class of laborers whose work was geographically distant and obscure. The truth of plain matters of fact, for Dana, is in part rhetorical and helps to construct a reading community of those to whom such truths might otherwise seem "unintelligible."

I call the type of vision that encompasses both labor and contemplation the sea eye. This term derives from maritime narratives themselves, and I adapt it to denote an experiential vision whose attainment forms the organizing principle of many such narratives. The sea eye has two principal applications in maritime writing. For one, it describes the experiential view from the masthead, which in nautical parlance refers to the sailor's vantage point while on lookout duty, high above the decks (and away from officers or passengers). The view from the masthead is figurative as well, as the sea eye reflects the analytical perspective offered by the common laboring sailor. Thus for seamen, to adapt Jesse Lemisch's influential conception of "history from the bottom up," the view from above is also a view from below. This perspective is frequently associated with book knowledge, remarkably, as seasoned mariners are said to be able to "read" the ocean or the weather, while inexperienced hands have no "eye" for such texts. In their narratives, sailors consistently justify the value of their labor—as well as the value of their cultural perspective—to their land-based readers.

While the first aspect of the sea eye is perspectival, the second is theoretical, as it comprehends the coextensive nature of labor and contemplation described in seamen's narratives. Neither crude, unthinking drones nor disembodied transcendental eyeballs, sailors propose a method for aligning reflection and literary production with labor practice. The epistemology of sea narratives, in turn, has applications that extend beyond the maritime world. By paying attention to the literary work of seaman authors, this book chronicles the vital and historically undervalued participation of sailor narratives in nineteenth-century American literature and culture. Taking my cue from the two functions of the sea eye, in the first half of this book I study sailor narratives from the vantage points of their historical and formal qualities, while in the second half I turn to sailors' theoretical exploration of what might be called maritime epistemology. The knowledge system described by sailor writing requires that the material practices of nautical labor serve as the experiential and rhetorical foundation for imaginative speculation.

To this end, I examine the first-person accounts of life at sea (primarily nonfictional) written by working American sailors in the decades between the Revolution and the Civil War. For the most part, these seamen were on long-voyaging ships whose one- to four-year voyages took them to the Pacific and Indian Oceans as well as throughout the Atlantic. Whereas some literary-minded sailors went on to other careers in print—William Leggett and Hawser Martingale [John Sherburne Sleeper] became successful newspaper editors, for example, and other former seamen contributed work to periodicals—many sailor authors produced little beyond narratives of their experiences. While there may be a variance in the course of their lives before and after going to sea, the sailors I discuss in this book composed narratives whose striking generic awareness and rhetorical affinity argues for their consideration in common. Their writing appeared in an interval delimited by the beginning of the Barbary piracy crises (which affected American seamen after the Revolution) and the end of the so-called golden age of American shipping (1815–50), after which the commercial and popular imaginations of the nation were increasingly directed along overland western routes.[6] From the earliest colonial settlement of North America, the sea had figured prominently in literary and historical accounts; but this sea was a place of danger and wonder, the realm of monsters and the crucible of God's judgment.[7] In eighteenth-century British and American popular culture sailors appeared as romantic figures in the Byronic mode. By the nineteenth century, however, sailors were acknowledged as skilled laborers whose wages and working conditions merited attention and whose acquisition of literacy and religious training was of humanitarian interest.[8] This interest coincided with the increasing urbanization of the American population and workforce in the early nineteenth century as well as the growth of reform movements more generally. The position of sailors, both socially and geographically, became of national importance in a time when broader social and economic questions found expression in periodical publication. The world of print helped sustain sailors intellectually and financially during the crises of impressment and Barbary piracy, when their narratives of captivity were published, reviewed, and taken up by the popular press. The expansion of the print public sphere in America, and especially the technological innovations in the 1830s that helped fuel an explosion of magazines and cheap editions of books, created readers and writers.[9] Sailors were both.

Seamen were literate to a degree unusual among laboring classes—the best estimates place sailor literacy in a range from 75 percent to as high as 85–90 percent—and they engaged in a lively system of exchange of books and other reading materials among ships.[10] Their literary practices were likewise collective, for as seaman George Little recalls of Sunday afternoons at sea, "On one side of the forecastle might be seen some engaged in painting vessels, landscapes, &c.; on the other were a group writing their journals; while a third set were learning navigation, taught by a young shipmate who had graduated at Cambridge."[11] Sea narratives pay close attention to what seamen were reading and document what especially appealed to their interests. Indeed, sailors' reading practices became an explicit target of reform movements in the 1820s and 1830s, which were particularly concerned with raising literacy rates and promoting Bible reading among seamen.[12] Sailors benefited from these religious and secular reform movements to a great extent but affirmed their literary preference for the *Pirates Own Book*, say, over pious tracts. What is more, as their narratives of their experiences became more popular with a land-based audience, sailors became more and more canny about the requirements of the literary marketplace in the antebellum period.

The picture of American literature presented in this book is composed of the scores of now-neglected sea narratives that influenced—and jostled for shelf space with—the canonical writings of Dana, Melville, James Fenimore Cooper, and Edgar Allan Poe, which also receive my attention. These mariner authors include Robert Adams, Nathaniel Ames, J. Ross Browne, Joseph G. Clark, Jacob Hazen, Nicholas Isaacs, Samuel Leech, William Leggett, George Little, Hawser Martingale, William Nevens, David Porter, James Riley, and William Whitecar, to name a few. Almost none of their narratives remain in print. I read the more canonical sea texts of Melville and Cooper in their own terms—that is, within the context of narrative maritime writing, a genre to which the works of these familiar authors contributed and from which they did not distinguish themselves. By this I mean that Melville and Cooper consistently located the value of their works in their individual experiences as working sailors, and I take them at their word. Sea writing took a profusion of forms in the nineteenth century, including popular broadsides and shipwreck pamphlets, racy pirate novels and widely printed ballads, and nationalistic naval hymns and sea chanteys. I concentrate, however, on narratives related in the first person, by authors who had been to sea as working seamen, as these comprise the largest and most coherent form of sea writing and have been the most critically overlooked.[13] That is, pamphlet sea novels and pirate stories are part of a broader genre of popular fiction best described by Michael Denning (who does not, however, mention sea literature as mechanic writing); but the first-person nonfictional narratives by actual seamen constitute a literary class unto themselves.[14] Significantly, while sailor authors retained their status as seamen, they demonstrated a keen interest in the book trades and negotiated their writerly position, often cannily, in a publication industry whose codes and expectations sailors both adopted and defied.

The genealogy of the form of the sea narrative in America is detailed in the first half of this book, but an outline of the typical antebellum narrative is appropriate here. It should be noted that sailor writing is distinct from the standard forms of contemporary travel writing in the sense that sailors are concerned with describing the places and people they encounter only to a secondary degree; the main impetus of their narratives is to describe the local culture of the ship, as well as its material demands. Whether describing a single voyage or a lifetime spent on the main, a sailor's first-person account of maritime experience traditionally spends little time on land prior to the first voyage, establishing briefly the conditions that made nautical life attractive (or a refuge of last resort). A young man determines to go to sea either for personal benefit or to escape from domestic responsibility; often, the impetus for this choice lies in hearing or reading tales of maritime adventure. As Martingale writes, in a representative recollection, "From my earliest years I manifested a strong attachment to reading; and as matters relating to ships and sailors captivated my boyish fancy, and exerted a magic influence on my mind, the 'Adventures of Robinson Crusoe,' 'Peter Wilkins,' 'Philip Quarle,' and vagabonds of a similar character, were my favorite books."[15] The novice seaman finds that his romantic ideas of seeing the world from a ship are betrayed, however, by the difficulty and monotony of nautical labor. One labor advocate for seamen worries that in such circumstances a boy "would soon become disgusted with the absence of that poetry of the sea, about which he had heard so much."[16] Some even feel "deceived," as George Little recalls, for supposing that "there would be no work on board of a ship, after leaving port, until her arrival at the place of destination." What Little and others find is that the "very reverse, however, is the fact; for, during the three years' cruise, I never knew, except in bad weather, any man belonging to the watch on deck to spend an idle moment."[17]

The sailor responds to these conditions by embracing the minutiae of maritime labor, which receive extensive textual enumeration. Sea narratives' emphasis on nautical activity is rarely glossed for the nonspecialist reader, though; sailors' jargon is left intact and unmediated. One sailor's account of a violent storm, for instance, focuses its descriptive energies entirely on the technical response of the mariners: "The studding sails were soon on her and the wind soon increased to a gale attended with a heavy hail squall, her upper works were very rotten and both pumps were soon going. . . . Privately the mate gave the order to take in the main top gallant sail; this was done unperceived, by the old sea dog although it took three of us to pull it in, a heavy squall of hail, the sea run so high that our staboard quarter boat was washed down from our cranes and at the same moment the fore topmast studding sail tack gave way taking nine feet of the weather vail with it."[18] Such attention to the material details of work at sea is the keynote for whatever adventures follow in the account, whether in whaling, the merchant trades, or the navy. Novice sailors endure initiation rituals, the narratives document. As a consequence, in nautical argot, the sailor loses his "green hands" (denoting an inexperienced worker and sometimes specifically a boy straight from the farm) and finds his "sea legs" (the ability to keep balance on a pitching deck); finally, the newly constituted "Jack Tar" (the generic appellation for a sailor, referring both to the tarry substance with which ships' ropes were fortified and to the tarpaulin fabric from which sails and clothing were made) can move through the world with the practiced seaman's swagger. Many narratives were written at sea, in journal format, and those that were commenced thereafter frequently preserve the rhetoric of a journal. William Whitecar, for example, derives his narrative from his "log-book or journal, in which, at the expiration of each nautical day, I noted the different employments of the crew, manner of sailing the vessel, incidents arising in the capturing of whales, general personal treatment, amount and quality of provisions, and the phases of the weather in different latitudes."[19] The structure of sea writing is circular, as the narratives end, naturally enough, where they begin: in port. And while sea writing is far from monolithic, sailors themselves recognize that most of their narratives display common features—indeed, when an individual mariner's work deviates from these shared characteristics, he often notes the fact.[20]

The first-person narratives of antebellum sailors are part of a longer textual history of the sea and its relationship to America.[21] Yet while the Atlantic has always figured prominently in American literature and history, the seamen's narratives of the first half of the nineteenth century occupy a special and anomalous place in literary history. Rather than experiencing the sea as a nautical version of the puritanical howling wilderness, or as an inspiration for metaphor, nineteenth-century sailors saw the ocean instrumentally. By this I mean that the ocean primarily functioned for sailors as a site of labor. Their writings reflect their manual engagement with the ocean for reasons specific to the period. Indeed, after the Civil War, the age of sail was largely relegated to the nostalgic past in the advent of steamships and westward expansion by railroad. Furthermore, American sea narrative writing of the nineteenth century was distinct from British maritime writing, which has a longer history, one I do not address in this book. British sea novels were generally concerned with the Royal Navy and the island nation's long history of maritime prowess. As a consequence of this ideological and historical difference, fewer British works of the nineteenth century were first-person narratives of personal experience, which was the form most often taken by American sea writing.[22]

For the Europeans who colonized North America, the sea was the first point of encounter with what they saw as a new world, and in their writings the Atlantic, and later the Pacific, figured as both the medium for and impediment to their imperial projects. The sea operates in the literature of contact and settlement as a place of danger, a forbidding element controlled by divine power and thus either placid or furious depending on the will of God. Narratives set in part on the ocean during this period concerned deliverance, whether described in impious and sensational pamphlets or in didactic collections of examples of divine judgment and mercy.[23] As the maritime trades began to expand in the eighteenth century, narratives of shipwreck and captivity became increasingly popular with British and colonial audiences; *Robinson Crusoe* is the most prominent example of this genre. Daniel Defoe's novel anticipated many of the terms of the form: it was presented as fact, and it paid fastidious attention to the minute tasks of everyday survival.[24] Furthermore, *Robinson Crusoe* featured the transatlantic concerns of Barbary captivity, slavery, shipwreck, and providential rescue.

American sailor writing came into being, this book argues, when U.S. ships fell victim to Barbary piracy in the absence of British protection after the Revolutionary War. Although European narratives of captivity in the hands of the North African Barbary States had been published since the sixteenth century, the captive American sailors wrote accounts that invoked nautical experience as a strategy for responding to the demands of survival in North Africa. Both seamen (such as James Riley) and nonsailors (such as Royall Tyler) used the public distress over American slaves in Africa to promote abolitionist arguments. Sea writing was also employed to record the monstrosity of the Atlantic slave trade, primarily in narratives of the Middle Passage, most notably Olaudah Equiano's *Interesting Narrative* (1791).[25] Black mariners (and former slaves) such as Venture Smith and John Jea also wrote narratives of their fraught circulation throughout the Atlantic world.[26] The sea genre was marshaled to serve the ends of U.S. nationalism as well, when late-eighteenth-century dramatists such as Susanna Rowson and poets such as

Philip Freneau used the Atlantic as a space for poetic and national self-definition.

In the aftermath of the Revolution and the War of 1812, James Fenimore Cooper produced the first American sea novels, writing that could for the first time comfortably look back to a maritime world in which American sea sovereignty had been far from assumed.[27] It is significant that Cooper's sea novels, which of his oeuvre were particularly fine sellers, are mostly set in the nation's colonial past in the manner of historical romance. For Cooper, the sea became an instructive space in which national history could be identified and described retroactively, not unlike the early colonial deliverance tales. His maritime romances helped inspire the cheap fictions of popular writers such as Joseph Holt Ingraham and Ned Buntline (nautical nom de plume of Edward C. Z. Judson), increasing the audience for sea tales. A fundamental shift in sea literature came as American shipping entered its most productive years, from roughly 1815 to 1850. Freed from restrictive British policies and expanding at a prodigious rate, the maritime trades became safer, more profitable, and more glamorous. The voyages themselves became faster, better regulated, and more certain, thanks to innovations in ship design, navigational science, and later, the use of steam. While the common seaman was still regarded as a marginal character, the responsibilities of an ever more complex American economy and society nevertheless made the option of going to sea more alluring.

A newly energized body of sea writing helped fuel the maritime boom, and a diverse array of other textual productions took the sea as their subject, seeking readership among land-based readers as well as sailors themselves. Ephemeral printed materials, such as pamphlet novels and pirate tales, sea chanteys and ballads, broadsides, and religious tracts directed at seamen, appeared in profusion as new technologies permitted the inexpensive production of masses of printed matter. This material was widely available at dockside newsstands, as sailor writing documents with enthusiasm (and seamen's charities report with regret). To counter the appeal of such ephemera, benevolent associations advocated the sponsorship of shipboard libraries as well as portside seamen's reading rooms. In promoting the Sailor's Reading Room, for instance, the Seaman's Friend Society recommended stocking the free library with "History, Biography, Voyages, and Travels, and any others that are *good* and *true*."[28] A religious magazine for seamen called *The Life Boat*, in another example, lamented the presence aboard one ship of a young sailor who was "a constant reader, but rather obstinate in his adherence to the light trash in the form of cheap literature which floods our land, and is generally found in our forecastle, and often in the cabin also." *The Life Boat* records with a sense of triumph, though, how the presence of a formal library of "good" books could transform the hungry reader: "His stock on hand was soon exhausted, and he began to look quite attentively at our chaste little collection, and soon commenced reading aloud to his shipmates."[29] Observe that the "chaste" collection of books finds a collective public audience, while the sailor's "trash" reading is presumed to be done covertly.

Most notably, scores of narratives were published about the experiences of tyros accustoming themselves to life "before the mast," or as common sailors. The phrase refers to the fact that nonofficers were communally housed in a small area known as the forecastle, which was located in the forward part of a ship, in front of the main mast. The most influential such account was Dana's *Two Years before the Mast*, which has been seen as the exemplar of the form of the first-person American sea narrative, even though Dana's family background was anomalous.[30] It was especially influential for the value it placed on the common seaman's life, as opposed to previous memoirs of sail, which generally had been composed by officers or passengers who did not labor as the hired hand did.[31] Dana's narrative, which will be referenced throughout this book, describes a merchant voyage from Boston to the California coast, where Dana participates in the trade in hides until his return around Cape Horn. What he finds, and documents in *Two Years before the Mast*, is that there is little romance in the life of the common sailor. Dana's narrative casts itself, ultimately, as a work of advocacy for working sailors, as he condemns flogging (the disciplinary whipping of seamen) and endorses charitable efforts on behalf of mariners. Such was the popularity of *Two Years before the Mast* that a wave of Dana imitators advertised their own intimacy with the experience of ship labor and titled their works accordingly: examples include Nicholas Isaacs's *Twenty Years before the Mast* (1845), Samuel Leech's *Thirty Years from Home; or, A Voice from the Main Deck* (1843), and William Nevens's *Forty Years at Sea* (1845). The early sea novels of Herman Melville, a great admirer of Dana's, appeared in this period.

This narrative form remained more or less intact throughout the 1840s and 1850s; after the 1848–49 Gold Rush and the Civil War, however, when the nation's arena for adventure and growth shifted to the West, popular fictions focused on the expanses of the land rather than of the sea. In fact, one of the most prolific nineteenth-century pamphlet novelists, Ned Buntline, adroitly made the transition from pirate fictions to cowboy tales.[32] And as the nation industrialized and pushed westward, the importance of Atlantic coastal sea communities changed as well; the whaling industry, for example, collapsed after 1859, when petroleum was first manufactured, obviating the need for whale oil. The literary age of realism, which began in part as a response to an increasingly mechanized world, found the sea trades dominated by brisk yet noxious steamships instead of the masted ships of the earlier part of the century. Sea literature, while no longer the popular sensation it had been, was nevertheless marshaled in response to these mechanical and economic changes. Regional writers documented the effect of the economic decline of coastal trades on their communities, such as in the case of Sarah Orne Jewett's representation of Captain Littlepage in *Country of the Pointed Firs* (1896). Jack London's sea tales, which eulogized wooden sailing ships even as they updated the sea as a space for social realism, revitalized popular interest in nautical writing. Most recently, the revival of interest in sea writing has made best sellers of the late-twentieth-century novels of Patrick O'Brian. Furthermore, natural disaster narratives such as Sebastian Junger's *The Perfect Storm* (1997)—which spawned a huge number of new sea disaster tales as well as the reprinting of neglected sea texts—have captivated a broad American reading audience.

When scholars have devoted attention to sea writing in the past few decades, they have been keenly aware of the historical scarcity of interest in the genre, as well as the difficulty in locating largely out-of-print texts. As such, these scholarly works have been mostly concerned with providing a broad overview of what constitutes sea writing in America. In an essay collection titled *America and the Sea* (1995), for one, editor Haskell Springer explains that while "the vanished western frontier has been repeatedly so studied and invoked as to make it a hoary cliché, that other, and permanent, American frontier, the sea, hardly registers today in our cultural consciousness as setting, theme, metaphor, symbol, or powerful shaper of literary history."[33] Thomas Philbrick's earlier landmark work, *James Fenimore Cooper and the Development of American Sea Fiction* (1961), cast a more comprehensive eye on American maritime fiction, one directed through the lens of James Fenimore Cooper's novels. Philbrick, however, maintains a status distinction between the sea novel as modeled after Cooper's early efforts, *The Pilot* (1823) and *The Red Rover* (1828), and the narratives written by laboring seamen. For example, Philbrick's discussion of *Ned Myers*, the narrative of a former shipmate edited by Cooper, praises the established author's success in "preserving the idioms and intonation of the seaman and in imposing, at the same time, the order and control which are so conspicuously lacking in the narratives of the other literary tars." Philbrick's evaluative choices privilege "artistic merit" even though he remarks that he is "forced occasionally to deal with inferior works."[34] It is my aim in this book, however, to credit the textual organization and literary achievements of the narratives of the "literary tars" devalued by Philbrick. Sailor narratives are invested in book culture, from reading practices to textual materiality, and, as such, are important to any study of print and the material text in American literature.

The growing fields of Atlantic and Black Atlantic studies, globalism, transatlantic print culture, and Pacific studies suggest new ways to think about maritime literature in America. In literary and historical criticism to date, sea narratives have been most cited by naval or maritime historians. There has been an ideological discrepancy, however, between traditional naval historians and those who locate their work in the newer fields of the Atlantic or Black Atlantic world. Whereas Atlantic world scholars seek to dissolve the national affiliations that become less relevant, they contend, in the broader oceanic sphere, maritime or naval historians have generally relied on national structures in order to describe the sea and its literature. American sailor narratives present a challenge at the intersection of the established and newer fields. For one, U.S. sailors have been seen by naval and maritime historians as agents in the project of early American nation building, even though seamen faced historically specific problems that frustrated the benefits of national affiliation (most directly, Barbary piracy and British impressment). The importance of their status as American citizens would fade in sailor writing after the early decades of the nineteenth century, in fact, when the threats of piracy and impressment were largely eliminated. International by definition, sailors and their multinational crewmates would appear to be the perfect subjects for the study of the global political economy, and indeed, scholars in Atlantic and related studies have discussed their position as collective laborers in an international setting. Yet sailors' actual writings have not significantly factored in such criticism.[35] And although sea narratives have been frequently invoked as primary evidence by maritime, labor, social, and political historians, nonfictional sailor writing has not to this point received any sustained analysis as literature. Nevertheless, scholars who have studied narrative and popular writing of the nineteenth century have shown how such work can be accomplished through a synthesis of the methodologies of book history, print culture, literary recovery, and cultural studies.[36] *The View from the Masthead* is the first book to describe seamen's vital yet undervalued participation in literary culture, as both producers and consumers of intellectual as well as manual labor.

This book attends to sailors as professionals, as authors, and as professional authors, designations they have seldom been granted. Sailors used the form of the narrative as a record of their experience in a landscape singularly unfriendly to poetic and political inscription. In Barbary captivity narratives, sailors directed their writing explicitly to an audience of their fellow mariners, providing navigational suggestions and concrete strategies for responding to the threat of captivity. In the boom years of nautical writing and trade that followed, however, sailors moved beyond that narrow reading community and addressed their narratives to a broader audience. Sea literature remained invested in maritime experience, but its instructive purpose was newly concerned with the landed reading community, which it strongly encouraged to assimilate technical nautical language and practice through comparative reading practices.

The two parts of this book address American maritime literature of the federal and antebellum periods from historical and theoretical perspectives. The first three chapters address sailors' literary culture and the development of the form of the sea narrative; the final three chapters analyze the structure of maritime epistemology. This twofold attention to both the generic and conceptual stakes of maritime narratives reflects a need to describe the terms and content of sea writing for a readership unfamiliar with an overlooked genre in order to argue, in turn, for the value of the critical and theoretical work done by sailor writing in its broader applications. In the first half of the book, then, I stipulate a new genealogy for sea writing, one that places it in conversation with broader literary and historical developments; in the second half I explore the experiential methodology proposed by sailors and discuss what happens when that methodology proves inadequate in the face of death and other crises of meaning.

To this end, Chapter 1, "The Literati of the Galley," documents sailors' literacy rates, literary tastes, and participation in U.S. print culture. Shipboard libraries were assembled using a subscription method initiated by common seamen, and sailors also took advantage of the ministrations of the many charitable and religious organizations interested in seamen's welfare in order to furnish themselves with reading materials. Sailors wished to demonstrate that the typical "Jack" was more than "a mere machine,—a mass of bone and muscle," as one advocate put it.[37] Seamen's access to and participation in a transoceanic literary circulation positioned them as crucial although historically marginalized figures in a world that was witnessing democratic revolution, industrial revolution, the next great age of exploration, and the expansion of the print public sphere.

In the second chapter, "Barbary Captivity and Intra-Atlantic Print Culture," I focus on what I argue is the first coherent body of American sea literature: Barbary captivity narratives, which were produced by sailors who had been held captive or enslaved in Africa, particularly in the North African Barbary States. The eighteenth-century Atlantic was a marketplace of oppositional freedoms and fetters: sailors were participants in and victims of the slave trade, impressment, privateering, and piracy. In the face of Barbary captivity, American seamen did more to resist these forces than simply to pass around the histories of their violations. Significantly, sailors participated in and took narrative control over their own circulation by producing narratives that offered concrete strategies for response to physical, cultural, and national threats.

"Naval Memoirs and the Literary Marketplace," the third chapter, concentrates on the period of transition (roughly dated 1815–40) in which sea narratives, particularly naval memoirs and the early sea novels of James Fenimore Cooper, began to explore how the sea could be more than a site for national contestations. One of the narratives that receives sustained attention in this chapter is *Ned Myers; or, A Life before the Mast* (1843), arguably Cooper's least-known publication. *Ned Myers* is the narrative biography of a common sailor, "edited" by Cooper, who offered himself as amanuensis for Myers's reform narrative of his adventures with war, impressment, tyranny, and riotous port life. *Ned Myers*'s unusual form—neither strictly first-person account nor biography, neither wholly Cooper's own imaginative work nor his editorial production—helps to illustrate the pressures on Cooper's later authorial career, as well as the status of sailors as authors in a literary marketplace.

The second half of the book synthesizes this reading of maritime literature in order to propose a theory of the sea narrative genre. In the fourth chapter, "The Sea Eye," I turn to the interpenetration of the spheres of manual and intellectual labor in sea narratives and describe the concept of an experiential eye. Chapter 4 concludes with a reading of *Moby-Dick*, which I understand as a commonplace book of experiential and reading knowledge. In its extracts and citations, Melville's novel reveals that all sea narratives are composites of sailors' collective literary and labor knowledge. Sailors frequently describe their work by means of metaphors of reading, especially when their narratives depict a seaman's turn on lookout duty in a ship's masthead. *Moby-Dick*, which is mindful of this figuration of maritime vision, theorizes in turn how book knowledge is translated into modes of vision that are materially embodied.

The fifth and sixth chapters look at the boom years of American nautical writing (1840–60), when the accounts of a sailor's life at sea proposed a more technically and imaginatively specific method of writing about nature. Chapter 5, "The Galapagos and the Evolution of the Maritime Imagination," explores the way certain sailors, such as James Colnett, Amasa Delano, David Porter, Charles Darwin, and Herman Melville, employed the volcanic Galapagos Islands as a productive site for both maritime and intellectual labor. Nautical science and other forms of statistical accounting practices provide a way of imagining facts, an interpretive process that Melville derives from his reading of Darwin's *Journal of Researches* and other sea narratives and that he employs in *Putnam's Monthly Magazine* in order to address sea writing's ideological investment in a rigorously empiricist imaginative project.

The sixth and final chapter, "From Preface to Postscript: Death and Burial at Sea," analyzes the theoretical problem that death and burial at sea posed for the sailor and for the sea narrative genre. The standard method of burial at sea invited a metaphysical crisis for sailors, especially since it differed so radically from the burial practices of a rural cemetery-era America that preferred its dead bodies tidily memorialized and preserved. Disposing both of the physical body and of the possibility for any tangible grave marker, burial at sea threatened a sailor's understanding of his place in a broader world usually defined in sea literature in terms of its regular industrial practices. But long-voyaging sailors discovered that Pacific islands provided terrestrial graves to a few relatively fortunate sailors. These Pacific plots raise questions about the imaginative geography of burial spaces and ask what kind of territorial claims can be made by the dead.

A brief conclusion considers the afterlife of the genre of sailor writing. It notes the multiple iterations of the story of the 1819 wreck of the whaleship *Essex* in narratives written by the ship's survivors, in *Moby-Dick* and other nineteenth-century works, and in the shipwreck's recent retelling in a best-selling and National Book Award–winning work of popular history, Nathaniel Philbrick's *In the Heart of the Sea* (2000). The afterword contemplates the legacy of maritime custom.

The "view from the masthead" offered by this book is one that comprehends a sailor's complex relationship to the work, in all senses of the term, of nineteenth-century American literature. Sea narratives argue for sailors' inclusion in American literary culture, as well as their fitness as public citizens. At the same time, however, sea writing maintains that labor—in its mechanics, its dangers, its products—must be the foundation to the formulation of a literary identity. That is, sea narratives disallow imaginative output that is not based on the material and experiential specificity of work.

Part I   THE SEA NARRATIVE

AND SAILORS' LITERARY

CULTURE

1 THE LITERATI OF THE GALLEY

The naval memoir *Life in a Man-of-War*, published anonymously in 1841, provides a witty account of a cruise in "Old Ironsides," or the legendary warship *Constitution*. Rather than an account of military exercises or engagements, though, *Life in a Man-of-War* presents a cultural history of shipboard life in the American navy. The narrator, working in a self-described "scribbling vein," aims to document—in "the rude, unpretending, and unpolished style" of a common sailor—the "disquietudes, delights, sorrows, joys, troubles, and perplexities" of the naval service.[1] The narrator's avowed lack of literary pretension is a conventional move, certainly. His confession to a "scribbling" urge aligns him with other nineteenth-century would-be authors who felt the itch to write in a market that could newly accommodate literary amateurs.[2] Yet his self-deprecating gesture toward the conventions of narrative writing does not deny this sailor literary authority. "Nothing is lost on him that sees / With an eye that feeling gave," the epigraph to *Life in a Man-of-War* reads; "For him there's a story in every breeze, / A picture in every wave."[3] Sailors may joke and lark, the narrative suggests, but they still are part of a broader fraternity of feeling.

Early in *Life in a Man-of-War*, the reader is invited to survey the groups of sailors who congregate on the decks in their time of leisure. The narrator is presumably a member of this crew, for the memoir is credited only to "a foretop-man," or a common sailor who works high in the foremost mast. Among those engaged in sewing or napping, one group of idlers in particular stands out. The narrator, shifting his prose account into verse form, calls attention to

> A literary group of three or four,
> Discussing the merits of some novel o'er
> "Have you read Marryatt's *Phantom Ship* all through?"

Eagerly asks one of this book-learned crew:
"I have," is the reply, "and I must own,
In my opinion it has not that tone
Of interest—nor the language half the zest
Of Simple, Faithful, Easy, or the rest."[4]

This discriminating sailor critiques the work of the popular British sea novel-ist Frederick Marryat (or Marryatt, in its common misspelling), whose best-known novels *Jacob Faithful*, *Peter Simple*, and *Midshipman Easy* are referenced here. But a fellow member of what the narrator elsewhere calls "*the literati of the galley*" becomes indignant at the sailor's analysis and replies with spirit: "I'm sure I never thought 'twould come to pass / Have Marryatt's works reviewed by such an ass."[5] What is notable about the literary debate staged in *Life in a Man-of-War* is that the terms of the conflict lie not in questions about the novels' accuracy or seamanship but instead in their literary value: their tone, their use of language, their aesthetic concerns. The literary taste dis-played by the sailors functions as a comic element of the memoir, in part, since seamen have traditionally been overlooked in the broader community of readers. But the joke is not wholly on this "book-learned crew." *Life in a Man-of-War* is one of scores of seamen's narratives that assiduously cataloged the ways in which sailors participated in the production and dissemination of literature, as well as its consumption.

Indeed, the reading communities of nineteenth-century American sea-men were lively yet discriminating. The books they read at sea, the methods they used to acquire books, and sailors' own engagement with the print public sphere constitute the focus of this chapter. What follows serves as an overview of seamen's literary culture in antebellum America, one that aims to contextualize the more specific focuses of subsequent chapters. Instrumental in a vibrant circulation of books in the oceanic world in the eighteenth and nineteenth centuries, sailors produced, traded, gambled for, and retold a diverse body of printed works. This market was well documented in, and in part constituted by, the sailors' own writing. Their narratives detail what their fellow seamen were reading and which books especially appealed to their interests. Forming their own literary coteries, sailors were attentive to the popular books of the day. These works—including the novels of Cooper, Scott, Bulwer-Lytton, Marryat, and Godwin as well as travel narratives, con-duct manuals, reform tracts, "flash" papers, pamphlet novels, and other ephemeral works—were invoked and analyzed within sailors' narrative ac-counts of their maritime experience. In citing works that would likely be familiar to nonspecialist readers of sea narratives, too, sailors were able to stake out their relative interests, terms, and circulation within the broader literary world. Books at sea were not only designated for private use but shared among fellow crewmen and exchanged with other ships. Many sailors recount such trades, such as when Richard Henry Dana describes a typical visit with another ship's crew: "We exchanged books with them—a practice very common among ships in foreign ports."[6]

Sailors' participation in broader literary culture was peculiar, however, in the same way that sailors' status as wage laborers was peculiar: both were in thrall to old and new orders of production.[7] Historians of reading practices have argued that early American reading was intensive—that is, households owned few books, but those books were read again and again. As advancements in book production and circulation made printed works more affordable and more widely available, reading became extensive—readers might read a far greater number of works but would know each work less intimately.[8] By necessity, American sailors were engaged in intensive reading practices, even though they lived in an age of rapidly expanding print possibilities. J. Ross Browne's narrative of his whaling voyage mentions on several occasions that he "read and re-read" the stock of books on board ship "till I almost had them by heart."[9] Dana's narrative confirms that the opportunity to trade books with sailors on other ships is eagerly seized because of the chance to "get rid of the books you have read and re-read, and a supply of new ones in their stead, and Jack is not very nice as to their comparative value."[10] Given the limited stock of books aboard ship, reading became automatically intensive and collective, as literate sailors shared a common body of texts.

Yet despite the fact that sailors' reading practices tended to reflect older modes of consumption, reading at sea nevertheless was encouraged by technological and economic advancements in the world of print in the first half of the nineteenth century. Transformations in the mechanics of printing made mass production of literature possible, lowering costs and making a broad array of published works available to the reading public. The diversity of works aboard any given ship, both in content and in class, testifies to this effect of modernization. A list of the books Browne read while at sea, for example, includes his shipmates' hoards: "The cooper's stock of literature consisted of a temperance book, a few Mormon tracts, and Lady Dacre's Diary of a Chaperon." Further, Browne records, "one of my shipmates had a Bible; another, the first volume of Cooper's Pilot; a third, the Songster's own Book; a fourth, the Complete Letter Writer; and a fifth claimed, as his total literary stock, a copy of the Flash newspaper, published in New York, in which he cut a conspicuous figure as the 'Lady's Fancy Man.' I read and re-read all these."[11] Ranging from etiquette books to religious writing, from racy flash papers of the urban underworld to Cooper's popular sea novel, this catalog shows both the hunger and the range of seamen's participation in literary culture, as well as their class aspirations. Furthermore, the presence of temperance materials and religious tracts reflects the influence of charitable reform movements, many of which saw mariners as a special object of attention after the 1820s. Other sailors recall similarly extensive shipboard libraries, whether collected centrally or passed around informally. C. S. Stewart appreciated having an official ship's library "for the recreation and improvement of the crew." In the first month of his naval service, Stewart records having read "Irving's Life of Columbus, Scott's Napoleon, the Lady of the Manor, Erskine's Freeness of the Gospel, Weddell's Voyages, Payson's Sermons, and Martyn's Life."[12] A comparable range of reading interests is displayed in the list of books read by James C. Osborn, the second mate of the whaleship *Charles W. Morgan*, as recorded in the ship's log. It includes many popular novels such as *Pamela, Humphrey Clinker, The Pathfinder, The Pilot*, and twelve volumes of Bulwer; travel narratives identified as *Steam Voyage down the Danube, Travels in Egypt and Arabia*, and Morell's *Voyages*; and temperance tracts and conduct manuals, including "Tracks on Disapation" [*sic*], "Husbands Duty to Wife," "Health Adviser," and Alcott's "Young Man's Guide" (see fig. 1.1).[13]

While Browne, Stewart, and Osborn faced limitations in the total amount of written material available to them at sea, it should be clear from the above examples that they were not limited in terms of the variety of genres of reading material. The range and diversity of materials to which sailors had access reflect the contingencies of shipboard reading, as well as its expansive possibilities. For the democratization of reading and writing should include sailors, their own works argued. When the narrator of *Life in a Man-of-War*, for one, announces that he will describe his fellow shipmates as "Literary Tars," he anticipates that the title would generate some criticism:

> Methinks I hear you with a *pish* exclaim, "Literary Tars—quotha, upon my word the Belles Lettres are becoming fearfully defiled, when the wild, reckless sailor, ruffles the leaves with his clumsy and tar-besmeared fingers." But the bard of Avon says . . . that "there are water rats as well as land rats;" why then should it be considered a strange or unaccountable coincidence if we had our book-worms on the forecastle of a tight Yankee frigate, as well as in the boudoir or the drawing-room.—The "march of mind" is abroad, and making rapid strides in both the hemispheres; why then should it not on its journey take a sly peep amongst the worthies of a man-of-war?[14]

Literary practices are staged in the forecastle as well as in the drawing room, the narrator insists. And as recruits in the "march of mind," he further implies, sailors should write and circulate their own works, not merely consume the works of others.

Sailors were keen to show that the typical Jack Tar should not be thought of as "a mere machine,—a mass of bone and muscle."[15] As the whaling voyager William Whitecar found, his fellow crew members were not reflexive machines but were instead "thoroughly conversant with the leading topics of the day, and each, like every true American, had his individual opinion of the merits of newspaper notorieties, politics, and other matters that engross the American mind."[16] The "matters" that engage opinionated sailors, Whitecar stresses, are not particular to their trade. Reformers took up this line in their mission to improve the moral and spiritual condition of sailors; as one wrote, "The class of youth from which it is proposed to raise up an efficient marine, are imbued with a passion for the sea, and are generally above the average of mind, education and social position. . . . The ocean *is* adapted to high intellectual, social and moral development. First, the employments of the sea demand skill, ingenuity and intellectual ability, in a far greater degree than the purely mechanical employments on shore. Next, a well regulated ship affords ample opportunity for intellectual and social culture."[17] Both sailors and the reformers who targeted them benefited from this approach. The charitable attention devoted to seamen complemented the broader culture of reform that characterized antebellum society, in its interest in increasing literacy, sobriety, and piety among workingmen. In turn, sailors were esteemed for their "skill, ingenuity and intellectual ability," which fit within their own conception of their mechanical and imaginative facility.

Still, the Atlantic and Pacific worlds of the late eighteenth and nineteenth centuries presented much for sailors to think about. While maritime laborers were, by definition, itinerant agents in international trade, the immediate circumstances of their work aboard ship meant that their daily lives were characterized by confinement and circumscription rather than mobility. Furthermore, the "imaginative communities" created by the rise of nations and of nationalism in the Ages of Enlightenment and Revolution, to use Benedict Anderson's familiar description, did not always encompass sailors. That is, in an era of impressment and state-sponsored and renegade piracy, sailors who claimed national affiliation or protection found their appeals routinely disappointed or disavowed.[18] Paul Gilje takes up one aspect of this paradox in his illuminating meditation on the meaning of "liberty" to antebellum American sailors. Although sailors accepted revolutionary ideals of freedom, the notion

A List of Books that I have read on the Voyage.

1 Vol. Goods Book of Nature.   The American Longer — 1 Vol
1 = Vol Self Knowledg.   Ben: Han   1 - Vol
1 = Vol Morrels Voyages.   Pelham Bulwer   2 - Vol
2 = Vol Made De Stacy.   Rolans History —   3 - Vol
2 = Vol Quadroon.   Napolians Aniedotes 1 - Vol
2 = Vol Pathfinder.   Bulwers Novels — 12 Vols
1 = Vol Pilot.   The Prince & Pedler — 2 Vol
1 = Vol Beuenza or the Coast of the Trybunes.
1 = Vol Numia or Pompei.   Jack Adams   — 1 Vol
1 = Vol Book of Beauty.   May you like it — 1 Vol
1 = Vol Tracks in Disaration.   Kings High way — 2 Vol
1 = Vol Gray Hams Lectures.   The Young mans Guide 1 - Vol
1 = Vol Husbands Duty to Wife.
1 = Vol Ladys Medical Guide.
1 =   Madam Tusades History of the French Revolution.

James C Osborn at Sea Jun 9th 1841.

1 = Vol Pamelia   1842.
2 — Vol Meriam Coffin   Edgartown is my native pl
1 = Vol Ten Thousands a Year.
1 = Vol Humphrey Clinker.

Journal of a Voyage to the Pacifick Ocean in the

Good Ship, Chas W Morgan. Thomas A Norton Master 1841
2 = Vol Bracebridge Hall.   1842
1 = Vol Travels in Egypt & Arabia Felix   Arived Jan 5th 1843
2 = Vol Elizabeth De Bruce.   1844
2 - Vol Bravo.
2 = Vol Repealers.
2 Vol Steam Voyage Down The Danube.
1 - Vol Memoirs of Dr Edward Young.
1 - Vol Health Advisor.
1 — Vol Female Wanderer.
1 — Vol Female Horse Thief.
1 - Vol Holdens Narative.
1 — Vol Bexamonds Narative of the Reoman Catholic Priest &c
2 — Vol Mercedes of Castile
22 = Vol Of Marryatts Works.

of liberty that had the most immediate relevance for them was the concept of liberty as shore leave, which translated as the freedom to drink, carouse, and burn their wages.[19] Both Gilje's work on sailors in the Revolutionary War and Michael J. Bennett's examination of Union sailors in the Civil War find that the multiracial and multinational crews aboard U.S. ships made national ideology and identification more the work of commercial or personal advantage than of patriotism.[20] When sailors did take a more explicit interest in political or national affairs, they focused on causes near to them. Barbary captive William Ray, for one, compared American sea captains to the despots of North Africa, while other sailors protested the practice of flogging by invoking American chattel slavery.

Nevertheless their class status was the issue of most concern to sailors, as Marcus Rediker, in his influential study of early-eighteenth-century Anglo-American seamen, *Between the Devil and the Deep Blue Sea*, has most ably demonstrated in his labor history of maritime collectivity.[21] And their literary efforts, sailors were aware, would be evaluated in terms of their position as laborers. Indeed, seamen were conscious of their standing to a notable degree. George Little, for one, much lamented the fact that few of his countrymen considered "the relative importance of seamen, either for the advancement of commercial pursuits, or for the protection of our country's rights, or for the maintenance of our national honor." Little found that most did not realize that "seamen are the great links of the chain which unites nation to nation, ocean to ocean, continent to continent, and island to island."[22] Little's conclusion here may seem perverse: he stresses the exemplary nationalism of sailors while simultaneously dissolving their national identification in favor of an affiliative chain that could figuratively link continents, seas, and countries. Yet he salutes seamen's position as workers whose value was both material and symbolic. That is, sailors had two functions in the nineteenth-century maritime world: for one, in the time before steamships, sailors' bodies were the engines that propelled both sailing ships and the global economy. Little wishes the readers of his sea narrative to be mindful always of sailors' actual labor. The second function of the figure of the sailor, Little recognized, was as

FIGURE 1.1: "A List of Books that I have read on the Voyage."
This list is included in the logbook of the whaleship *Charles W. Morgan* by James C. Osborn, the twenty-six-year-old second mate of the ship; Osborn recorded the books he had read in the course of the *Morgan*'s multiyear cruise. (Log 143; Logbook, 1841–1845, *Charles W. Morgan* [Ship: 1841], 185; © G. W. Blunt White Library, Mystic Seaport, Mystic, Conn.)

a symbolic representation of a romantic (or sordid) life of adventure, indulgence, and freedom from responsibility. In their own writing, then, sailors strove to represent their labor as fundamental to the pictures of life under new aspects promised by their narratives. Rather than argue that their labor had value because it enabled their literary and imaginative productions, sailors instead located the value of their narratives in their presentation of the working and thinking lives of maritime laborers.

LITERACY ASEA

Sailors were a class of workers who attained an above-average degree of literacy and who participated in a robust culture of reading and writing. Yet the fact that seamen of the late eighteenth and early nineteenth centuries were intimately involved with book culture is scarcely a matter of prominent literary historical record, and the difficulty in general in fixing early American literacy patterns across social categories accounts for this underexposure in part. Literacy rates for American sailors—and for all Americans in the late colonial, federal, and antebellum periods—are impossible to state definitively but can be estimated with some confidence using several means. Some of these methods, such as signature estimates and charitable organization surveys, are used to determine literacy rates for the general population; others, such as naval library records and laborers' subscription library histories, are more specific to mariners' reading habits.

The various methods are variously satisfying or accurate. The signature standard, used widely by scholars of early America for lack of better methods, is primarily judged using last wills and testaments: those able to sign are presumed literate to some degree. Studying probate records to see which households owned books is a related approach. Sailors' signatures can be collected from port records and ship registers, and Marcus Rediker's pioneering work on the eighteenth-century Anglo-American Atlantic as well as Ira Dye's quantitative work on American seamen base their literacy statistics on this method. Rediker's statistics, derived from the admiralty records of thirty ships (rather a small sampling), are broken down by occupational categories: for example, captains, mates, cooks, quartermasters, and surgeons attained 100 percent literacy; for common seamen, the number drops to mid-60 percent. The combined percentage of literate men in the sample of 394 employed by the merchant shipping industry studied by Rediker is 75.4. He assumes that "the ability to sign one's name indicates a minimal and functional degree of literacy."[23]

At the beginning of the nineteenth century, the common sailor, as the profane, immoral Jack Tar of popular fancy, became the special target of Christian organizations whose promotion of Bible distribution and study in turn promoted literacy. Many of these organizations took note of the percentage of literate sailors in the collective body they served, and so the records of such charitable organizations (which flourished in the 1820s–40s) provide a second basis on which to ground estimates of shipboard literacy. Naval vessels historically have kept more complete records than merchant ships of their crews' habits and specifications, and while literacy is not a statistic maintained by the navy, the contents of shipboard libraries do to some extent make their appearance in naval history and therefore serve as a third means to estimate sailor literacy. Books in naval libraries, which range from manuals of practical seamanship to histories to travel and adventure narratives, would have appealed to common sailors as much as to the ships' educated officers, who customarily kept their own private libraries. Further, the early-nineteenth-century rise of workingmen's subscription libraries, patterned after the eighteenth-century Franklinian model, had an impact on how sailors provisioned themselves with books and demonstrate an identifiable demand for certain kinds of literature.

These four types of literacy sources—signature estimates, charitable organization surveys, naval library records, and mechanics' library histories—serve Harry R. Skallerup in his study *Books Afloat and Ashore*, which constitutes the only attempt to describe sailors' reading practices on both sides of the Atlantic, beginning in the Early Modern era.[24] I am indebted to Skallerup's quantitative work for my claims about seamen's reading culture. Throughout this book, however, I rely principally on a fifth indicator of mariner literacy: the written narratives of sailors themselves. The range and vibrancy of their writings, which repeatedly document the larger cultures of reading in which each narrator participates aboard ship, testify to the pervasive and powerful cultures of reading and writing at sea. Sailors on individual ships had their own small literary circles, and even those who could not read had access to books through the oral performance of texts. Furthermore, the impact of the closed community of a given ship extended beyond its center of readerly interest. Books and libraries at sea became part of broader exchanges among ships and in ports, as books were not only designated for private use. Indeed, as Skallerup notes, "Mariners as individuals had traditionally engaged in their own private trading operations in order to supplement their wages. . . . Books, by virtue of their intrinsic and physical properties, were ideal goods to trade in."[25]

Many sailors recognized that their term of maritime service could be an opportunity for knowledge and learning. For some, this prospect for education offset the difficulties of their service on board ship. Reading and writing were skills not divorced from maritime success; indeed, they were necessary for advancement. Even the lowest class of mate had to be literate, and navigational skill required letters and mathematical ability. Robert Boyle, later a Barbary captive skilled enough in navigation to be offered the opportunity to "turn Turk" (convert to Islam and therefore be made an officer on a Barbary ship as a renegado), acquired his nautical skills after he was tricked into sailing service by a cruel uncle. Boyle, despite feeling the "Dread" of being treated as a "Slave" as an unskilled seaman, figures out how to upgrade his position: "I set myself with all my Diligence to learn the Mathematicks, as also the Work of a Sailor, and quickly attain'd to some Knowledge I soon ingratiated my self with most of the Crew, who instructed me in all they knew."[26] The kind of specialized knowledge that sea life required—"the language of the sea"— could create a community in which learning was valued across the boundaries of hierarchy. A popular anthology of sea voyages encouraged such pursuits, noting that many "serving in subordinate and laborious situations . . . on shipboard, have attained to great familiarity with books, and sometimes risen to considerable literary or scientific distinction."[27]

Merchant seaman George Little participated in this process as both a student and a teacher. Little himself learned aboard ship from a well-schooled fellow sailor who had been to Harvard: "The forecastle was more like a school than any thing else; the elementary branches of education were taught, as well as the sciences of navigation and mathematics, by our young shipmate, Wm. Harris, who . . . was an under-graduate of Harvard University." In turn, Little passes on his own learning to an older sailor who had never learned to read. Little is delighted to find that his messmate makes "rapid progress in learning to read," which is "the height of his ambition." As a result, the sailor becomes a "different man."[28] Indeed, as Marcus Rediker points out about this fraternity, "Masters and chief mates, who were frequently the most knowledgeable about the technicalities of language and labor, were often the dominant figures in this community, though seamen learned much of the language of the sea from their peers. The 'speech community' contained within it a set of bonds, the basis for a consciousness of kind and a collectivism among all those who lived by the sea."[29]

How many sailors could read and write, in the best possible estimation? Rediker reports that "as many as three-quarters of the sailors employed in the merchant shipping industry between 1700 and 1750 were literate if judged by the standard of the ability to sign one's own name."[30] Although Rediker contends that this signature standard falsely inflates the number of those able to read, many historians of early American literacy now believe that evaluating literacy by the ability to sign one's name actually underestimates the tally of the literate population.[31] Such scholars have pointed out that the standard education models in early America taught reading before writing in order to facilitate Bible reading; therefore, someone unable to sign his or her name conceivably could be an adequate reader.[32] Also potentially misleading are the estimates of literacy based on probate inventories of books owned, since as David D. Hall points out in *Cultures of Print*, these estimates overlook those who had access to circulating books they need not have owned as well as overlooking those printed materials that had either been worn out or discarded.[33] In *Revolution and the Word*, Cathy Davidson relates the example of Ethan Allen Greenwood, who "read nearly a volume a day even during his poorest student days. But he largely borrowed these books by joining three libraries—a fraternity library, a social library, and a circulating library—and literally thousands of other readers (especially novel readers) did essentially the same."[34] By circumstance, sailors had a similar culture of circulation. Furthermore, a great portion of eighteenth- and nineteenth-century sailors came from New England, which boasted extraordinarily high rates of literacy. the figures most cited set the rate of white male literacy at 90 percent by the end of the eighteenth century, with the figure rising throughout the nineteenth century.[35]

And Rediker's 75 percent figure for literate sailors in the first half of the eighteenth century would naturally rise in the next 100 years, aided by the concurrent rise of benevolent Christian organizations, whose mission it was to distribute Bibles for poor or working people to own and read. Although Christian organizations had long lamented what they saw as the degenerate state of maritime life, replete with cursing, carousing, and nonobservance of the Sabbath, the situation of the American captives in Barbary, as Christians beset by "infidels," helped spur the targeted activities of seamen's Bible societies. Indeed, the literacy rates usually cited for sailors of the early nineteenth century are those calculated by such charitable Christianizing organizations as the Seamen's Friend Society, the American Tract Society, and the Merchant Seamen's Bible Society, among others, which distributed Bibles and carefully noted the relative proportions of literate men at sea. One agent of the Merchant Seamen's Bible Society, a British distributor of Bibles to sailors, recorded that of 24,765 men visited on a total of 1,681 ships, "21,671 were stated to be able to read." A survey of another 590 ships discovered 5,490 purported literate sailors out of 6,149 seamen; the general rate of literacy in these and similar religious society surveys is 80 to 90 percent.[36]

Christian charities attentive to the needs of sailors were part of a larger wave of reform in antebellum America inspired by the Second Great Awakening and given special urgency within the context of the growth of both the middle class and cities. Efforts on behalf of seamen joined other charitable efforts in targeting intemperance, impiety, and illiteracy, problems whose amelioration, it was hoped, would improve workers' production and satisfaction and thus society more broadly. Campaigns against corporal punishment, furthermore, incorporated sailors' opposition to the practice of flogging.[37] Sailor vice had a special visibility, for as Paul Gilje astutely recognizes, most Americans saw sailors while debauched in port rather than at the relatively more sober scene of their actual labor; this circumstance also caused the middle class to romanticize the work of the sailor.[38] To counter the stereotype of sailors as profane drunks or as carefree and thoughtless wanderers, many agents for reform cited seamen's potential for advancement. Reformers flattered their intellectual potential in a drive to distribute Bibles and thus promote good reading amongst seamen: "There is no small share of mental power concealed beneath the weather-beaten forms of our hardy tars," a report in the religious periodical *Sheet Anchor* argued; "This talent will remain unknown and unacknowledged, if it remains uncultivated; but give to sailors the opportunity, while at sea, to expand their powers by a course of profitable reading, and they will present to the world the evidence, that they need only the requisite education to exhibit energies which it has hardly been imagined they possess."[39]

The American Seamen's Friend Society, perhaps the most prominent and active charitable association, sought to increase the amount of books in circulating sea libraries. The *Sailor's Magazine* reported that the American Seamen's Friend Society "carefully prepared" ship libraries, "containing each sixty volumes in a neat and substantial case," for the benefit of subscribing crews. "The cost of a library is $25, or $1 each to a crew of twenty-five men," the report continued and asked, "And what sailor, who is to be away from the world where to the making of books there is no end, would not give $25 for such a library during his voyage."[40] The number of loan libraries, as they were called, expanded so rapidly that the magazine's index began a separate monthly category for "Ships' Libraries' Reports." In one such report, on the origins of the loan library, a correspondent writes, "Seventy-five dollars were appropriated at the beginning, and neat wooden cases, 16 by 20 inches, prepared, (one of which now stands before the writer,) each with a good lock, and painted for better preservation. By referring to the entries then made, it appears that Baxter's Call, Pilgrim's Progress, Alleine's Alarm, Boatswain's Mate, Beecher on Intemperance, Newton's Life, Harlan Page, Saints' Rest, Flavel's Touchstone, Temperance Volume, and a variety of Tracts, formed the staple of study."[41] Religious reformers, understandably, stocked these loan libraries with volumes reflecting their cause. In promoting such libraries, the Boston Seaman's Friend Society underlined their popularity: "Nearly all the books which belong to the circulating library are upon the waters," an 1839 report claims; "Few remain at home, for they are called for as fast as they are returned."[42]

The American Seamen's Friend Society testified to the "good effects which have resulted from their depository of books for circulating sea librar- ies." The Register Office recorded that "1426 seamen entered their names during the year 1830, of whom 45 appeared to be pious; and 130 vessels were recorded as being navigated without the use of spirituous liquors."[43] While the number of dry vessels would indeed be encouraging, note that the per- centage of apparently "pious" sailors is about 3 percent. The solution to this low rate, many charities believed, would be to make more religious books available to sailors. Since it was clear that sailors did read, and read avidly, many reformers thought that proximity to appropriate reading material would accomplish the desired "good effects." A religious but nonsectarian paper for seamen titled the *Sheet Anchor* expresses the general sentiment:

> It is highly important that books, or other publications of the right kind, such as are *interesting*, and convey accurate knowledge, or correct moral sentiments, should be placed within their reach. And we learn with pleasure that plans have been devised for arranging "Seaman's Libraries," to consist of forty or fifty volumes, judiciously selected, and which can be furnished at a low price. If a library of this description should be placed on board a vessel by the owner, and made free to all, or should be purchased by the crew before sailing—and a steady ship's company can always muster ten or twelve dollars for such a purpose—it will afford a fund of entertainment, and information during the voyage, which will exert a most happy effect on the character of the sailors, by giving them a thirst for knowledge, and stimulating their ambition and self-respect, as well as by directly improving their moral characters.[44]

While the *Sheet Anchor* would be understandably concerned with sailors' "moral characters," the paper places an equal if not greater emphasis on stimulating seamen's "ambition and self-respect" through a "thirst for knowl- edge." This has a very different charitable effect than simply designating sailors as objects of pity or compassion. Instead, this charitable impulse invites maritime workers to participate in the world of letters. "What shall we do for the sailor?" a later article in the *Sheet Anchor* asks; "See that he is provided with good books."[45]

And charities did provide sailors with books, in abundance. The records of such donations are found not just in the reports of the reform organizations but in sailor narratives as well. In *Deck and Port*, an 1850 account of a naval cruise, Walter Colton is pleased that his shipmates will be amply supplied with books—the frigate boasts "a library comprising between three and four hundred volumes." Colton takes care to credit the charitable sources of many of the volumes: "For many of the miscellaneous and religious books in this library I am indebted to the Presbyterian Board of Publication, to the Sunday School Union, to the American Tract Society, and to the liberality of Commodore Stockton. My acknowledgements are also due to the American Bible Society for a donation of Bibles adequate to the wants of the crew."[46] Yet such efforts were not always to sailors' tastes. One reformer, who urged the creation of both a Marine Free Circulating Library and a Nautical Free School, recognized that gifts of books to sailors were not always well chosen. In his 1853 report on the efforts on behalf of seamen, the reformer included a testimonial from a captain who regretted that "the selection of books usually made for sailors are not wisely selected." The captain reported that the usual selections "consist almost entirely of Bibles, Testaments, Prayer Books, and Tracts, all of which are invaluable treasures. But sailors are like other folks, at least not more religious, and they want useful reading matter that will enlist them."[47]

The issue is taken up less charitably by Nathaniel Ames, author of the popular *Mariner's Sketches* (1830), when he laments the efforts of reformers who "have volunteered a feeble crusade against the vices and sins of seamen and have accordingly stuffed ships full of tracts which have entirely defeated their own object."[48] While the efforts of charitable associations were instrumental in encouraging literacy, charitable interest in sailors' reading habits rarely reflected sailors' reading tastes. Mariners did have options, though, when it came to choosing what to read at sea. Organizations that supported laborers become involved in furnishing workers with practical and entertaining reading materials, books that seamen helped choose and that better reflected their tastes. The benefits would extend beyond mariners' present circumstance, reformers promised. In a lecture series titled "Words for the Workers," one labor advocate describes a lifetime of guidance from reading: "A good library is an anchor to keep a young man from roving, and a helm to aid an old man to gain the greatest possible benefit from what remains of the breeze."[49]

CARGOES OF BOOKS

Labor associations that provided books to sailors continued the legacy of Benjamin Franklin, who in his formation of the first American circulating library stressed its value to tradesmen.[50] For example, the New York Mercantile Library Association, which was chartered in 1820 as a means for workingmen to have access to books, quickly decided to expand its efforts on behalf of the laboring class to include sailors; the resultant Committee for the Distribution of Books to Seamen formed seamen's libraries and solicited public support for additional ones using the same methods as the workingmen's organizations. The association's appeal to a generous public was advertised in 1821 in the *Boston Commercial Gazette*: "It is the intention of some individuals to procure, by gift, for the exclusive use of *Seamen*, a *Library*, of 20 to 25 vols. for every ship belonging to the port."[51] The success of the Committee for the Distribution of Books to Seamen was celebrated in the press, and the library on one ship, the seventy-four-gun USS *Franklin*, received wide notice. A letter of thanks from an officer of the *Franklin* was published in newspapers from South Carolina to Massachusetts:

> Gentlemen of the Committee for the distribution of books to seamen—
>
> I have the honor to acknowledge the reception of the present of books★ you have been pleased to make to the seamen of the Franklin. Allow me to return my thanks with those of the crew for your generous kindness.
>
> The sailors of this ship could not witness our exertions for the diffusion of knowledge among them unmoved. When your letter was read to them, they requested unanimously that one dollar may be appropriated from the pay of each, towards the increase of the Seamen's Library on board. This fund I will take an early opportunity of placing at the disposal of the Committee, from whose philanthropy originated the laudable design, tending so much to ameliorate the condition of seamen.
>
> ★One hundred and fifty volumes of Voyages, Travels, History, Geography and Navigation.[52]

Another paper out of the New England port of Salem reported that "the Seamen's Library Company of N.Y. have presented 150 valuable volumes to the crew [of the *Franklin*], and the 600 seamen of the ship have subscribed each 1 dollar for the increase of their library."[53]

The U.S. Navy, too, made a practice of providing libraries to its sailors, and the contents of such libraries likewise spoke to the organization's mission. A naval list from 1839, for example, heavily featured histories, travel narratives, and Cooper's sea novels (see fig. 1.2).[54] The library catalog for the U.S. steam sloop *Narragansett* survives in pamphlet form—a rare artifact—and suggests that other ships might have had printed catalogs for browsing (see fig. 1.3). The library aboard the *Narragansett* held 392 volumes, and its rules dictated, "Only one volume can be taken at a time. Books may be kept out fourteen days. A fine of two cents a volume will be incurred for each day a book is detained more than fourteen days." All classes aboard ship subscribed to the library; the list of members includes the commodore, captains, mates, cooks, armorers, firemen, landsmen, corporals, and privates. Of nearly 100 subscribers, 30 are common seamen and coal heavers. The books are listed in the order they were acquired, and a few items are worthy of note. The library was first stocked with the novels of Cooper, Marryat, Scott, and the other popular fiction writers of the day; late additions to the library fell into a different category, as twelve school readers were clustered on the most recent list of arrivals.[55] Later in the century, however, a different naval library segregated its contents. Officers had access to one set of books, and enlisted men another, composed "of the lighter literature and of primary text-books," even though the officers had privileges at both libraries.[56]

While there is a historical record of the contents of certain official naval libraries and of the portable loan libraries provided by charities, few catalogs of the contents of merchant or whaling ship libraries have survived. One rare example can be found in the logbook of the whaleship *Charles W. Morgan*, in which a mate recorded the contents of the ship's library (see fig. 1.1). His list heavily features travel narratives, conduct books, and novels (particularly those of Cooper, Bulwer, and Marryat, although *Pamela* and *Humphrey Clinker* also make the list).[57] While the *Morgan* was but one ship, reasonable assumptions can be made that its library was not the only of its kind in the whaling fleet. Most sailor narratives, for one, confirm the presence of a variety of books aboard ship. A methodological model, furthermore, is provided by the example of a reading diary kept by a young cabinetmaker's apprentice, Edward Jenner Carpenter, in Massachusetts in 1844–45. Carpenter's journal has been used by scholars to suggest the range and diversity of the reading habits of a relatively isolated workingman, and similar conclusions can be derived from the list aboard the whaleship *Morgan*.[58]

The books read aboard the *Morgan* were most likely donated or communally purchased. This is especially probable given the presence of multi-volume works aboard ship (twenty-two volumes of Marryat's works, twelve of Bulwer's), which one sailor would be unlikely to purchase. While few analogous records remain, it is possible to gauge with reasonable accuracy what kinds of books most appealed to sailors, for accounts of maritime life specify what books were read and valued. It is important to reiterate that these unofficial seamen's libraries, while containing some religious tracts and instructional manuals, were primarily composed of travel narratives, histories of voyages, and other adventurous fare, which more appealed to the tastes of most sailors. This taste could be subversive and even dangerous. In one case, Philip Spencer, the accused ringleader of the notorious *Somers* mutiny against

Captain Alexander Slidell MacKenzie in 1842, was presumed to be influenced in his capital offense by reading the *Pirates Own Book*, an anthology of buccaneer tales, and James Fenimore Cooper's piracy novel *The Red Rover*. An article titled "Life at Sea" published in a religious seamen's newspaper confirms that "among the various kinds of books found in the seaman's chest, Narratives form a conspicuous, and we had almost said the largest portion.— Among these, tales of the sea have, from the earliest period of book making and story telling, to the present time, been found capable of exciting a deep interest."[59]

In time, most ships provisioned themselves with libraries prior to their voyages, and mariners continued to participate in the selection of the texts. In *Life in a Man-of-War*, the distribution of the library is attended with great interest. Some "three or four hundred volumes" comprise the library, which includes the works of Scott, Marryat, Cooper, Irving, and Bulwer. When the crew learns of this acquisition, the narrator writes, "the greater part of our jolly tars came forward with avidity and subscribed their mites towards repaying the purchase money, and felt pleased to think that they had now in their possession a stock of intellectual food to beguile the heavy tediousness of the cruise, or to refresh their thirst for mental acquirements."[60] The crew's choices are dramatized to punning effects, as the cook "always like[s] something *heavy* to digest," and the ship's barber, razor in hand, finds his allotted book "too *dull* altogether for me."[61] After the books have been distributed, they are visibly enjoyed, in this instance collectively:

> Who will say then, that some of the inmates of a vessel-of-war do not thirst after literature? To illustrate the fact, just glance your eye along our ships' decks when lying in port; under the break of the poop you may observe a group of mizen-topmen, eagerly listening to some more talented shipmate, who, with voice and effect worthy of the subject, is reading aloud passages from one of the splendid and romantic poems of the celebrated Byron:—in the larboard gangway are assembled, distorting their risible muscles at the trying through ludicrous scenes in Marryat's Jacob Faithful or Midshipman Easy:—Again, on the starboard side amongst the main-topmen, a little *coterie* are gathered together, wrapped in profound silence, every ear intent, with open mouth, swallowing some of Cooper's thrilling descriptions of nautical life, or digesting the eccentricities of Scott's liquor-loving Peter Peebles, or the original and trite remarks of Boz's inimitable Sam Weller.[62]

While the poems, popular adventures, and romances listed in *Life in a Man-of-War* remained staples in the ship cabins as well as in drawing rooms, sailor

The following books will be furnished for the use of Vessels of War when on a cruise, and for the use of Navy Yards, until otherwise ordered.

Navy Department June 10th 1830.

Nicholsons Mathematics

Euclids Elements

Bowditchs Navigation

Maurys   do

Ramsays Universal History

Gibbons History — Decline & Fall of Rome

Fergusons History of Roman Republic

Gillies History of Greece

Rollins ancient History

Lingards History of England

Constitution of the U.S. & the different States

Marshall's Life of Washington

Bottas American Revolution (until Bancrofts is compiled)

Hallams constitutional History

Vattels Law of Nations

★ Bradfords Atlas

Jacobson's Sea Laws

Gordons Digest, or Ingersolls abridgement of U.S. Laws

Treaties with foreign Powers

Federalist

Ledyards Travels

Astoria

Voyage of the Potomac

Porter's Voyage, 2d Edtn published by Wiley. N.Y.

Ross, Parry's & Franklins Voyages

Life & Voyages of Columbus

Bancrofts History of the U. States

Prescott's Ferdinand & Isabella

Cooper's Naval History of the U.S.

   do   Pilot

   do   Red Rover

   do   Water Witch

   do   Homeward Bound

Encyclopedia Britannica

Hutton's Tracts

Arnotts Natural Philosophy

Wood & Baches Dispensary

Walsh's Appeal

Kents Commentaries

Incidents of Travel in Egypt, Arabia & the Holy Land

A year in Spain

Lives & Voyages of Drake Cavendish & Dampier

Historical account of the Circumnavigation of the Globe &c from the Voyage of Magellan to the death of Cook

Plutarch's Lives

Bible & Prayer book

Note.— In the foregoing list are comprised, with a few exceptions, the works authorised for Vessels on a cruise & for Navy Yards, by the order of 23d Feby 1831 and such as have been since added.—

★ "Illustrated Atlas of the United States"— See Secty letter of 19 Oct. 1839.

"Akins Naval Battles"

"Pere de Hostes Naval Tactics and Naval Actions   English translation"   } See Secys letters of 8th Feby 1841 & 23d Feby "

"Gen Alexr Macombs work on Courts Martial"— See Secs letter of 15 Feb 1841.

reading habits did take other forms. As the *Sheet Anchor* observed with regret, "Sailors are readers, and in many cases supply themselves with licentious books, the evil influence of which is incalculable."[63]

The evolution of the taste of Richard Marks, who served in the U.S. Navy during its battles against Barbary piracy and British impressment and later became a model Christian, is a telling example. The types of reading material preferred by sailors are reflected in the early and self-avowedly sinful tastes of the American naval officer, who notes of his reckless pre-reform years that he embraced "the most vile and infamous writings that ever appeared," which Marks remembers reading "again and again" and "making extracts from them." However, he continues, he had "not the smallest recollection, while belonging to this ship, of ever seeing a Bible, though I once endeavoured to call to mind that sacred volume; not with the view of remembering and applying any of its sublime and awful contents to my heart, but to dress up a ludicrous account of some late adventures among the midshipmen in its peculiar language and solemn phraseology!"[64] It is striking to mark here not only the attractively "vile" writings but also the playful literary dexterity of Marks and his fellow sailors, who enjoy parodies of biblical language and writings. These sailors demonstrate a certain awareness of the current literary marketplace, such as when a lieutenant procures for the frigate a new book, "one of the most popular and sensible novels ever published in England." As Marks reports (with some personal regret), the purchaser of this "famous new novel" does not know what to think of it: "There is too much of religion in it. I have read but a few pages."[65] The will sailors displayed in choosing and circulating the kinds of printed matter they preferred was strong. As Skallerup notes, "A large portion of the reading diet of seamen was doubtlessly comprised of the cheap, ephemeral literature of the streets which consisted of bizarre, lurid and sensational stories, political pamphlets, and books of amusement. Indeed, some of it might have been especially prepared for the seamen's consumption."[66] Herman Melville's *White Jacket* (which draws heavily from *Life in a Man-of-War*) intimates the pornographic nature of these choices, highlighting those "diligent readers" whose "favourite authors were such as you may find at the book-stalls around Fulton Market; they were slightly physiological in their nature."[67] Derived from the subscription models that supplied many early Americans' reading materials, the methods sailors used

---

FIGURE 1.2: U.S. Navy Book List. The navy sought to standardize the libraries aboard its ships; this list, from 1839, is a representative example of the kind of library found on naval vessels in the 1830s and 1840s. (*AB8.Un33N.839f; by permission of the Houghton Library, Harvard University)

U. S. STEAM SLOOP

NARRAGANSETT'S

CIRCULATING LIBRARY.

RULES AND REGULATIONS.

Only one volume can be taken at a time. Books may be kept out FOURTEEN days A fine of TWO cents a volume will be incurred for each day a book is detained more than fourteen days.

No book to be loaned by a subscriber to any other person whatever.

None but subscribers to the fund to have the privilege of the Library.

Any injury done a book while in the hands of a subscriber, or any volume lost by him, must be paid for by him at a fair appraisal.

This Library will be open for the delivery and return of books, on Tuesday and Friday afternoons of each week, from 1 to 4 o clock P. M.

The YEOMAN will act as Librarian and will be held responsible for the safe keeping of the books, and the enforcement of these rules

[ARGUS PRINT, NORFOLK, VA.]

to acquire their own stock of books also reflected their position as a class of laborers whose profession required collective efforts. Seamen's attention to the circulation and value of popular works of fiction helped them to set the evaluative criteria for their own writing.

THE "SCRIBBLING VEIN"

When sailors produced accounts of their experiences, they followed conventions of eighteenth- and nineteenth-century writing in prefacing their narratives with remarks that testified to their truthfulness, as well as to their reasons for producing and circulating such narratives—that is, only upon the urging of interested friends. Sailors took care in their prefaces to foreground the conditions of their work. In many cases, this advertisement of the coincidence of their intellectual and manual labor took the form of an apology for seamen's "style." Sidney J. Henshaw writes that he "makes no pretensions" concerning his literary style but wishes to present a word "in apology for defects" the reader may encounter. Henshaw wants his reader to remember that "in the first place, the book was written on board ship; and any one, who has been at sea, must know full well that, 'A ship is a thing that one can never be quiet in.' " But Henshaw hopes that the "indiscriminate popularity" sea narratives hold with the reading public will make any stylistic deficiencies moot.[68]

More significantly, Henshaw stresses that his narrative was written amid the confusion of the decks, "without the privacy of a room, or a retreat of any kind."[69] Unlike those who have the luxury to write at leisure or in "retreat," sailors staged their literary production at the scene of their work. This lack of leisure becomes a mark of pride in sea writing and affirms the conjunction of work and contemplation in seamen's narratives. Most sea narratives, in fact, were adapted from journals kept while at sail or were re-creations of journals or logs lost at sea. The author of *Life in a Man-of-War* wished his readers to know the "many disadvantages one in my capacity had necessarily to labor under" when trying to write: "the interruptions I was subject to, and the noise and outcry that assailed me on every side, whilst indulging in my 'scribbling vein.' "[70] Charles Barnard, too, had "little leisure" for "literary pursuits," since he had spent his life "exposed to those vicissitudes which chequer" his narrative. But if his account is "inferior to many similar produc-

---

FIGURE 1.3: Catalog, U.S. Steam Sloop *Narragansett*'s Circulation Library, Norfolk, VA, 1860. This sixteen-page catalog lists 392 books in the order in which they were obtained; the novels of Cooper, Scott, and Marryat were early acquisitions. (Courtesy, American Antiquarian Society)

tions in elegance of diction," Barnard reasons, "it is vastly their superior in the veracity of its contents."[71]

Sailors' descriptions of the scene of their literary production likewise stressed truthfulness, as well as specifying the conditions of labor from which their work emerged. In many cases, mariner narratives anticipate reviewers' criticism. A remarkable preface from the narrative of Jacob Hazen, for example, displays his class consciousness, as well as a punning sense of seamen's status in the literary world. Hazen writes, speaking of himself in the third person,

> As a mechanic, and one of the toiling million who earn their bread by the sweat of the brow, he is conscious that [the narrative] must necessarily be defective—if not in subject matter, at least in thought, style, and composition; for it is scarcely to be supposed that literary perfection should emanate from the work-bench, or that the common *shoemaker* or *sailor*—whichever you will—should write with the propriety and grace of an Irving. Hence, it will become him to keep a bright lookout ahead for "breakers" in the "reviews;" and should critical assailants *pen* him too closely, he will, doubtless, be compelled to meet them *mechanically*, or, in other words, withdraw from his desultory rambles in the flowery fields of literature, and betake himself once more to delving in the gloomy corners of his humble shop. However, the pungent arrows of criticism will not afflict him very mortally, as he is far from being a professional book maker, and seldom moves in that sphere of life where they would be likely to reach him.[72]

In his elaborate sarcasm and anticipation of negative reviewers, Hazen shows his awareness of publication conventions, as well as his impudent refusal to be bound by their terms. His work might place him in the orbit of the sphere of "professional book mak[ing]," but Hazen disavows circulation in such a sphere. By meeting such attention *"mechanically"*—an amateur in bookmaking, but not in craft—Hazen is able to present his generic prefatory apology in his own terms.

The narrative convention of apologizing in a preface for poor or humble literary effort has been much remarked upon and documented most pertinently by Ann Fabian in *The Unvarnished Truth*, her account of nineteenth-century American paupers' narratives.[73] Such apologia, commonly given by those for whom literary production was not a practiced professional act, stressed that the principal merit a narrative could offer was truth. Sailor writing took up this characteristic of the narrative genre, and truth-averring prefaces, which glossed or justified sailors' use of nautical terms, became conventions of the genre of sea writing. Barnard offered his nautical account "to the judgment of his fellow citizens, dressed in the simple language of a seaman's journal"; he hoped "it may be received with that indulgence which it claims as a narrative of sterling truth."[74] Nathaniel Taylor similarly saluted the launch of his narrative: "Going forth to the world, it claims but one merit—fidelity to truth—and welcomes the reader to the iron realities of a sailor's home and a sailor's heart."[75] Another seaman author, Hawser Martingale, confessed that his narrative "may not contain much which is extraordinary or exciting; but the pictures it furnishes of 'life at sea,' the illustrations it gives of the character of the sailor, the temptations by which he is surrounded, and the moral as well as physical dangers which beset him on every side, have at least the merit—I had almost said the *novelty*—of truth."[76] The value placed on "truth" in Martingale's narrative is directly tied to the accessibility of the picture of maritime life it presents. Furthermore, Martingale's emphasis on the slippage between truth and "*novelty*" makes a sharp-witted point about the escalating claims to truthfulness made by sea narratives. It also demonstrates his awareness of the conventions of the literary marketplace, in which claims to truth were a standard aspect of narrative writing, yet so widespread as to be diluted of their meaning. Novelty should be a special selling point of sailor writing, since landspeople would have little access to its pictures of maritime life.

In displaying technical rigor as well as an awareness of contemporary literary conventions, sea narratives define what might be called an aesthetic of mechanical precision. In some ways, this aesthetic of mechanical precision is akin to what Neil Harris has described, in his work on P. T. Barnum, as an "operational aesthetic," or an "approach to experience that equated beauty with information and technique." Harris locates a pleasure in "observing process" in nineteenth-century how-to manuals, and sailor narratives invite similar conclusions.[77] Still, many sailors worried that the abundance of information in their writing might put off nonspecialized readers. Barbary captive Archibald Robbins, for example, prepares his journal with an aim "to be correct—to give a faithful and accurate detail of *facts*," although he recognizes that in doing so he had "observed a minuteness which many may think unnecessary." To those who would question this excessive "minuteness," though, Robbins offers an argument that appeals to his readers' aesthetic understanding: "As the variance of a few shades changes the complexion and general appearance of a piece of painting, so a few minute, and apparently unimportant particulars, affect, essentially, the general characteristics" of a work.[78] Even though Robbins here flatters the receptive eye of the general consumer of his text, most narratives justify their "minuteness" in terms of maritime reckoning. The technical specificity of the narratives is not meant to be prohibitive to a nonspecialist reader, though; the verisimilitude such specificity permits becomes essential to the account, rather than merely a relation of "curious" or "interesting" particulars.

The potential transparency of maritime literature for a nonnautical reading public was a topic of some interest to critics. When the narratives of sailors received critical attention, notices tended to be positive and saluted the seaman's ability to provide interesting pictures of unfamiliar modes of life. Representative of such reviews are the approving notices for Martingale's *Jack in the Forecastle* (1860), which stress the narrative's combination of literary and mechanical art: "The author of this book is not only well acquainted with the ropes of a ship, but is an adept of no ordinary skill in the art and mystery of pen-craft," wrote the *New York Tribune*, while the *New York Observer* agreed that the volume was "a capital book for those who are fond of sea life and truth. . . . It shows the real character of the sailor, the dangers, moral as well as physical, that beset him, and is well fitted to awaken interest in his behalf."[79] In particular the *North American Review*, one of the more august journals of the nineteenth century, reviewed sea writing—both American and European —years before it bothered to review American fiction. Sea narratives, in the judgment of the editors of the *North American*, owed their success to certain generic and textual prerequisites. Taking an interest in the materiality of the sea text, the reviewers applauded displays of nautical specificity—as Hazen may have noticed in his promise to meet reviewers "*mechanically*."

Strikingly, the content of a text under scrutiny often was only as important to the editors as the quality of the material text itself and the conditions of its textual production. When the *North American* reviewed sea writing—in the form of travel writing, Barbary captivity narratives, and naval memoirs—the magazine paid attention to the process of bookmaking. Indeed, the textual appearance and production of sea and travel narratives generally attracted far more attention than the material conditions of other genres of writing, which is perhaps a response to the promises of veracity and novel views made by such narratives. It is as if sea writing were valuable insofar as it physically embodied some piece of reality itself in its bookmaking. The *North American*'s notice of James Riley's Barbary narrative, in one instance, opens with an approving physical description of the elaborately titled volume, and this "external recommendation" is the point of the appeal of Riley's book: the "portentous title page is not the only external recommendation of the volume before us. It is ornamented with a portrait of the author, furnished with rare plates, illustrations of divers scenes, descriptions, and adventures, and supplied with an *original* map of the countries into which he was led by the stars of ill omen, that presided over his destiny. Attracted by these claims on our notice, as well as the novelty of the subject, we took up the book with eagerness."[80] The "claims" to which this passage refers are not Riley's own accounts of his suffering; significantly, the "claims" on a reader's interest are made by the edition itself, with its images and its emphatically "*original*" map. And while obscure "stars of ill omen" might have led Riley to North Africa, it is Riley's "good faith and sailor-like frankness" that imprints the "hand of truth" on the volume.[81] Certainly, truth-value would be an appropriate consideration for any travel or exploration account, but it is important to recognize that the quality of "sailor-like frankness" derives as much of its value from the sailor's minute concern with documenting place as from the explicitness (and often coarseness) of a sailor's vocabulary. That vocabulary is designated here as a positive mode of expression—a rare judgment, and one that argues for the value of the laboring sailor.

The *North American Review* similarly highlights the textuality of David Porter's account of his Pacific maneuvers during the War of 1812. Porter's *Journal of a Cruise made to the Pacific Ocean* (1815) is offered to the world "not as the premeditated labour of a regular voyage of discovery, but as the plain journal of a sailor, composed for his own satisfaction."[82] As a result, the magazine notes places where further editing is called for and finds the narrative's plates only "tolerably executed from drawings by Captain Porter." Porter was a captain (and a war hero), not an ordinary seaman. It is important to note, though, that even as the *North American* reviews the narratives of captains such as Porter, Riley, and Amasa Delano, it locates the value of the texts in their appearance as "plain" journals of sailors. Even as the review praises Porter's narrative skill and naval accomplishments, it concludes that if Porter were to put his journal "into the hands of some one versed in the mystery of book making, to correct these little faults, and strike out the useless parts of it, the work may form a very respectable addition to our books of travels."[83] In other words, for the *North American Review* Porter's naval and narrative talents are divorced from the mystifying aspects of the book trade, which confer respectability on the volume. An attention to "the mystery of book making" in the context of what seaman Nathaniel Ames called sailors' "mystery" would become a later preoccupation of James Fenimore Cooper's, as well as of Herman Melville's, as discussed in Chapters 3 and 4.

Yet while technical accuracy and material appeal are qualities prized by the *North American*, there are times when the magazine wonders if an overreliance on the terms of the sea trade could alienate the average reader. Accordingly, Amasa Delano's *Narrative of Voyages and Travels in the Northern and Southern Hemispheres* is reviewed in light of what it offers to Delano's fellow seamen, whether in terms of its observation of tides or currents or in terms of the instructive value it holds for young sailors. Recognizing that the flourishing American maritime trade helps to create a market for entertaining (and useful) texts like Delano's, the *North American Review* notes,

> In this country, where commercial enterprise is carried to a very great extent, the officers of our most valuable ships must often be young men, and not always fully experienced in the voyages they undertake—many of them too, from the nature of their early education, and their active duties, but little inclined to search for information in the voluminous and scientifick works. . . . A book of less pretension, written by one engaged in the same occupation with themselves, of the same country, possibly an acquaintance, and in the practical style, and homely, inartificial manner, which we should expect from a man bred upon the sea, stating those facts, which he had found by his own experience to be the most useful, would be much more likely to draw their attention.[84]

Always attuned to the conditions of book production and distribution, the magazine describes sea writing's practical and intellectual value in terms of its investment in nautical accuracy, the appearance of geographical exactitude, and the ambiguous quality of "sailor-like frankness." The benefit derived from Delano's text will not be the young sailor's alone, however. The "commercial enterprise" of the young nation is implicated in the sailor's education, and accordingly, any volume that can contribute in an accessible way to the advancement of a greenhand sailor is worthy of national critical attention. Such commerce is "carried to a very great extent," or in other words, it proceeds broadly and successfully; it is also "carried," though, by mariners, whose ships are the vehicles for the portage of most of the nation's commercial goods. In calling for more accessible books written by seamen, the *North American* suggests that what is good for the reading sailor is good for American industry. This same logic unites the efforts of maritime reformers with the rhetorical maneuvers of sailors themselves and in turn defines the literary culture in which seamen participated and to which they contributed.

Intensive and collective readers by definition, nineteenth-century American sailors produced narratives that were in turn read extensively by a broader community of readers. And thus when a member of the *"literati of the galley"* ventured a playful defense of maritime life, his real concern was how the figure of the laboring sailor appeared in the world of print as both a subject for fiction and a producer of literary texts. The question of how the narratives produced by sailors would represent their working and thinking lives was first raised by the American sailors who were held as slaves by the Barbary States of

North Africa. The accounts they wrote of their captivity, the first incarnation of the genre of sailor writing in America and the subject of the chapter that follows, were framed as strategically useful to sailors themselves. This rhetorical position helped secure for sailors a place not just in global trade but in the Atlantic world of letters as well.

2 BARBARY CAPTIVITY AND INTRA-ATLANTIC PRINT CULTURE

For most nineteenth-century readers of American sea narratives, actual experience of maritime life was hardly a prerequisite for appreciating the textual matter at hand. Sailor authors recognized that their reading audience was primarily composed of landspeople and framed their narratives accordingly. Richard Henry Dana's preface to *Two Years before the Mast* is representative of maritime writing's address to nonspecialists, as it encourages the domestic reading community to assimilate technical nautical language and customs through comparative reading practices. "There may be in some parts a good deal that is unintelligible to the general reader," Dana concedes, "but I have found from my own experience, and from what I have heard from others, that plain matters of fact in relation to customs and habits of life new to us, and descriptions of life under new aspects, act upon the inexperienced through imagination, so that we are hardly aware of our want of technical knowledge."[1] In prefaces like Dana's, sailors justified the value of their technical knowledge to land-based readers.

The rhetorical confidence of writers such as Dana—whose presumption of a domestic audience for his work proved well founded—had no purchase, however, in the one distinct class of American sea writing that made no such universalizing gestures toward its readership: Barbary captivity narratives, written by American sailors of the federal era. Whereas Dana's narrative and those of his contemporaries offered "descriptions of life under new aspects" to a "general reader," the Barbary captives, an earlier generation of sailor authors, stressed the serviceableness of their narratives to an audience of fellow mariners. Perhaps a consequence of this has been the fact that Barbary narratives form a body of writing little known to readers and critics of the sea genre. When they have been noticed, it has been within the context of the genre of captivity or slave narratives. The value of sailors as national subjects was a problem for a young nation with neither the hardware for a naval defense against piracy nor the financial reserves to ransom its captive nationals. As such, captive seamen consistently located the value of their writings not just in the affective appeals of the texts to nationalism or humanism but chiefly in their utility to fellow laboring mariners.

Federal-era Barbary narratives, unlike the more widely read sea writing of the antebellum period, were explicitly addressed to a reading community of fellow seamen. In a representative gesture, James Riley's narrative of Moroccan enslavement is prefaced by the author's belief that it will be "particularly instructive to my seafaring brethren."[2] Mariners would have had access to these narratives as part of the vibrant circulation of books in the Atlantic world, as Chapter 1 documents. Common sailors historically took great interest in a body of popular literature that prominently featured accounts of piracy, "true crime" registers such as the *Newgate Calendar* (an annual British archive of criminal activity), and later, the *Pirate's Own Book* (a piracy anthology), as well as fictional tales of corsairs. The subject matter of this body of popular narratives reflected the late-eighteenth-century perils of Barbary piracy and British impressment, threats that likewise traversed the indeterminate national boundaries of the Atlantic Ocean. By esteeming sailors as both reading and writing subjects, Barbary piracy narratives proposed a means for the physical and textual circulation of American sailors in an Atlantic world characterized, paradoxically, by terrific mobility and repressive confinement.

Narratives of sailors who were both authors of the stories of their own captivity and readers of their fellow sailors' captivities positioned themselves primarily for an audience of their own kind, but this did not mean that their audience was narrowly circumscribed. The intra-Atlantic circulation of the narratives among literate, actively reading sailors presumed a significant reading public. This presumption, in turn, esteemed sailors for their abilities both as readers and as workers. The invocation in Barbary narratives of the material conditions of maritime labor and navigation suggested that technical information could be a component of imaginative or literary work, too. Such a model validated the poetic value of the minutiae of maritime labor over more sensational aspects of sea life. This point is illustrated by William Ray's "Exercising Ship," a verse headnote in his Barbary narrative, in which Ray questions why the "*sweat*" of sailors goes unsung:

What then? must poets ne'er record a deed,
Nor sing of battles, but when thousands bleed?
Can naught but blood and carnage yield delight?
Or mangled carcasses regale the sight?

Which shews more God-like, men to save—or kill?
Their *sweat*, by exercise, or *blood* to spill?[3]

By stressing the salutary "deed[s]" that the "exercise" of maritime labor produced over the inert "mangled carcasses" of combat, sailors presented readers with an alternative narrative of their experience. This narrative championed their active and continuous work in transmitting their ships and themselves around the globe, rather than static accounts of their passing.

The two interrelated circulations in the Atlantic world—the exchanges of sailors' bodies and of sailors' literature between ships—allowed seamen to write their own bodily histories as well as to govern their exchange value. Sailors were historically international figures, both in their geographic mobility and in their social affiliation with men of many different nations and cultures.[4] In the face of piracy and captivity, sailors did more to resist these forces than simply pass around the histories of their trials. Significantly, sailors participated in and took rhetorical control over their own physical and imaginative circulation by means of instructive narratives that offered strategies for response to physical, cultural, and national threats.

THE PIRATICAL AND THE UNITED STATES

The vulnerability of American sailors to piracy at the hands of the North African Barbary States (encompassing present-day Algeria, Libya, Morocco, and Tunisia) occurred within a fixed set of historical circumstances. The Barbary pirates had intimidated the Atlantic world for centuries, taking slaves and demanding tribute. American sailors became at risk after the Revolutionary War, when the Continental navy lay in shambles and U.S. merchant ships were no longer able to count on the protection of the British navy. At the same time, American sailors continued to be victimized by British impressment during the Napoleonic Wars. The U.S. Department of the Navy was formed in 1798 explicitly to combat the pirates; that navy went on to confront the Barbary States in the Tripolitan War of 1805 and to fight the War of 1812, which ended the practice of impressment as well as other restrictive British shipping policies and blockades. American sailors were taken captive in North Africa primarily in three different stages, although these categories do have exceptions. First, Algerine rovers commandeered several American ships in 1785–86 and secured what would prove to be the longest-enslaved sailor captives. Tripolitan forces began a new surge of piracy in the second wave (1801–6), which culminated in the first war America fought after the Revolution. Finally, in a less temporally defined phase, many American sailors were shipwrecked or otherwise seized on African coasts between 1800 and 1820; these victims usually were held individually, unlike the more overtly political prisoners of the earlier stages, with whom the later seamen compared their lot. Between 1785 and 1820 more than 700 Americans were taken captive. Although some circumstances of the capture and liberation of American seamen in these periods differ, I examine the body of narratives produced by captive sailors as a unit. The implicit argument that animates this chapter is that sailors' Barbary narratives are an important part of the literary history of American sea writing, rather than an analogue to captivity or slave writing, as they have been generally read. The explicit argument is that the strong rhetorical similarity shared by Barbary captivity narratives establishes the generic terms taken up by later sailor writing of the antebellum period.

The Barbary pirates were distinct from other prominent historical pirates, namely the renegados, most of whom were European sailors who had deserted merchant or naval vessels or had otherwise broken ties with their place of origin, and who established independent piratical vessels primarily interested in booty.[5] The Barbary corsairs, in contrast, had the state support of their rulers, who negotiated ransoms and tribute and orchestrated the trade in Christian slaves.[6] By the eighteenth century, most of the European nations had established treaties or tribute arrangements with the North African "Piratical States"; beginning in 1646, for example, the British paid annual tribute to Algiers and soon were paying off Tunis and Tripoli as well. These purchased protections were not absolute, though, as some pirates refused to recognize the passes presented by tributary nations or else declared war so that the ships captured would be considered prizes (and thus legal targets) rather than loot.[7]

American merchant ships of the colonial period were relatively safe from the Barbary pirates, as they were part of the British Empire and therefore covered under the tribute policy. After the Revolutionary War, however, it became clear to American observers that the British consuls in North Africa were encouraging attacks on American ships, partially for retribution for Britain's recent losses and partially to present alternative (that is, non-British) targets to the corsairs. The United States had little recourse, for the few ships that had constituted the Continental navy had been destroyed or otherwise decommissioned by the end of the Revolution, and few American politicians —John Adams excepting—agitated for the formation of a navy. Although Thomas Jefferson was not an advocate for a strong navy in general, he did call for a decisive military response to the Barbary attacks.[8] In 1786, in the midst of debates about tribute payment for the release of the twenty-one captives in Algiers, Jefferson wrote to Adams that he "should prefer the obtaining of [peace] by war," explaining that "Justice" and "Honor" favored force over "buy[ing] peace."[9] Despite Jefferson's reasoning, the marshaling of a naval force was still years in the future. The tribute system, which had been adopted by many European states during their centuries of vulnerability to Barbary piracy, had early and anomalous success in the United States, for example, when the American brig *Betsey* was taken by a Moroccan raider in 1784. In response, Adams and Jefferson signed a settlement treaty with Morocco, the first treaty between America and a non-European nation. Although Jefferson wished that "the Algerines may be as easily dealt with," such a smooth resolution with Algiers was not to be.[10] The general conflict with Barbary began when the American vessels *Maria* and *Dauphin* were captured in quick succession by Algerine pirates in 1785; the crews of the two ships, which included later consul to the region James Leander Cathcart, would spend eleven years in slavery before they were ransomed for $1 million—one-sixth of the nation's budget—plus an annual tribute payment of $100,000. Such payments did not curb the threat, however, and in 1801 the Tripolitan pasha, Yusuf Qaramanli, finding the American government in default on its tribute payments, seized several ships.

The navy and the marines, which shortly before had been formed to combat the North African pirates, had somewhat more success than diplomacy and requests for tribute. In the midst of financial negotiations John Adams, while concluding that it would be "wisest for Us to negotiate and pay the necessary sum," nevertheless wondered if to "fight them" might be "a good occasion to begin a Navy."[11] The American response to piracy was finally militarized, spurred by the adaptation of the phrase "millions for defense, not one cent for tribute!"[12] The best-known (and most mythologized) moment of the conflict came after the American warship *Philadelphia* ran aground in Tripoli's harbor and was occupied by the enemy. Rather than see the frigate recommissioned and used against the American squadron that had been dispatched to the region, a daring party, led by Stephen Decatur, set fire to the *Philadelphia*. Those crewmen of the *Philadelphia* then languishing in slavery recalled with delight waking to "a most hideous yelling and screaming from one end of the town to the other, and a firing of cannon from the castle. On getting up and opening the window which faced the harbor, we saw the frigate Philadelphia in flames."[13] Although the "Turks appeared much disheartened at the loss of their frigate," the captives reported that "we could not suppress our emotions, nor disguise our joy at the intelligence."[14] After the payment of an additional compensatory sum, the hundreds of American sailors who remained in the prisons or bagnios were freed in an exchange of prisoners.

In general, conditions for American prisoners in North Africa were poor. Those sailors whose ships wrecked on coasts remote from North Africa's urban centers were forced on brutal marches across the desert, where urine, both human and camel, was frequently their only refreshment. Food rations were limited (sailors traded their stores when possible), and the Americans complained that their clothes were taken from them and their heads were shaved. The division of the slaves among the dey or pasha, the pirate ship captain, and the public slave market was usually determined by the captives' labor or ransom value.[15] In port cities, captives performed heavy labor on chain gangs, repairing walls and batteries; others were compelled to use their skills as blacksmiths or carpenters in service of their captors. The combination of punishing work and insufficient nutriment is detailed by one particularly unhappy Barbary captive, William Ray, who writes, "Sixteen of us were put to boring cannon; the labour was intense, and having neither bread nor any thing else to eat, until four o'clock in the afternoon, hunger and weariness were almost insupportable. Some of our men, by some clandestine means, were found intoxicated; for which they were inhumanly beaten, and confined in shackles."[16] Other manual work to which Ray's shipmates were assigned included raising a buried wreck from the beach. Robert Adams, a shipwreck victim, was employed in "building walls, cutting down shrubs to make fences, and working in the corn lands or in the plantations of tobacco" during his captivity.[17]

The labor sailors were forced to perform while held in slavery was not commensurate, in their accounts, with the nautical labor their writings esteem and describe in such detail. Even if the skills employed or exertion required might be similar, sailors register their labor in captivity as an unfree form of punishment, rather than the kind of technical work that their narratives seek to advertise, explain, and elevate for a nonnautical public. William Ray does, however, make comparisons between U.S. naval service and his enslavement. Ray provides parallels between the sufferings sailors endure at the hands of both their Christian officers and their Muslim captors, equating the use of flogging by the U.S. Navy with the use of the bastinado (a form of torture involving whipping of the feet by a cudgel of the same name) by the pasha's men.[18] But Ray's complaints are not with the work itself, targeting instead its supervision. In Ray's account, the failure of American ship captains to practice revolutionary ideals of liberty and justice is akin to the nation's broader failure to protect its maritime citizens from seizure and captivity. He intends his narrative to "prove that petty despotism is not confined alone to Barbary's execrated and piratical shores; but that base and oppressive treatment may be experienced from officers of the American, as well as the British and other navies."[19] Many other sailors who did not join Ray in comparing American leaders to despots nevertheless wondered why their redemption or emancipation from captivity was not more of a priority for the young nation. "Why are we left the victims of arbitrary power and barbarous despotism, in a strange land far distant from all our connections, miserable exiles from the country for which we have fought, forgotten by our contemporaries who formerly used to animate us in all our expedition with tales of liberty?" captive James Cathcart asked.[20]

The success of the navy in restoring autonomy to American ships in the Atlantic has often been cited as a crucial moment for the nation, when the United States could independently protect the integrity of its military and mercantile subjects. Yet mariners nevertheless remarked frequently (and with resignation) upon the tenuous nature of political and economic claims to sovereignty in the Atlantic world. The experience of sailor John Foss serves as one example; after his release from seven years of Algerian captivity, Foss tried to return to Philadelphia:

> I embarked in the quality of a passenger, on board . . . [a] poleacre . . . bound to Philadelphia. We sailed on the 4th, and on the 11th, was taken by a Spanish privateer and carried into Barcelona, was cleared on the 12th and sailed again, and on the 20th was captured by a French privateer, and carried into Almeria, treated politely and cleared on the 22d, and sailed. On the 29th, the wind having been contrary for several days, we run into Malaga, where we waited for a fair wind until the 21st of May. We then sailed, and on the 22d was boarded by his Britannic Majesty's ship Petterel, treated very well and permitted to proceed on our voyage.
>
> On the 23d, at 6 A.M. was boarded by two Spanish privateers.[21]

Foss's ship would encounter Spanish and British privateers two more times before arriving in Philadelphia, and his matter-of-fact recitation of this tiring sequence of encounters with ships of prey of several nations attests to the instability of maritime routine in the Atlantic at the turn of the nineteenth century.

The exchange of pirated national subjects from ship to ship was echoed, on a different scale, by the exchange of reading materials among sailors. Given the historical context presented above, sailor interest in stories of seafaring life takes on a special significance. In the face of the instability of their physical position within the Atlantic world, sailors did not become mere consumers of tales of piracy and captivity; more significantly, they produced narratives of their movement within such systems. Sailors, who were always inter- and transnational figures, responded to their shifting geographical and geopolitical positions by participating in the production and circulation of literature and true-crime texts that narrativized the circumstances in which they themselves lived.

Seamen saw their texts as valuable not only for their narrative particulars but also for their utility to fellow laboring mariners. To use a representative example, Judah Paddock claimed to write his narrative "in hopes it may be of some benefit to sea-faring men exposed to the like calamity,"[22] and he closed his tale of shipwreck and bondage with the following assertion: "However uninteresting the foregoing narrative, or parts of it, may appear to some, I do verily believe, if one of the same import and contents had fallen into my hands previously to our shipwreck, it probably, by guarding me against those rapid currents, which I then knew nothing of, might have been the means of preventing that dreadful catastrophe, and our no less dreadful captivity."[23] The production and reception of such narratives afloat and ashore, in the form of the multidimensional exchange between body, nation, and text, granted sailors some way of participating in and responding to their own transnational labor and literary histories. Frequently written during captivity, sailor narratives emphasized the material conditions of maritime life and work. In turn, the narrative asserted that the value of sailors as laboring Americans was commensurate with their value as members of a literate community.

Participation in this reading community was neither passive nor divorced from calls to action. For instance, William Ray, captured by Tripolitans while a crew member on the *Philadelphia* in 1801, prefaced his *Horrors of Slavery* with a poetic "Exordium" that pointedly challenges his readers and their experience of his text:

> If in the following, then, you find
> Things not so pleasing to your mind,
> And think them false, why, disbelieve them;
> Errors of weakness? then forgive them;
> And let our suff'rings and abuses
> For sev'ral *facts* make some excuses;
> And when you're captur'd by a Turk,
> Sit down, and write a better work.[24]

Ray's barbed closing couplet argues that his literary achievement is made possible and persuasive by his attention to the material conditions of his captivity. This understanding of sailors as a class of workers who actively participated in their own self-definition and circulation—in text and in body—has implications for recent studies of the Atlantic world as well as for the study of later antebellum sea writing. In recognizing that their value had both commercial aspects (as laborers, either for a captain or for a slave-owning dey) as well as imaginative aspects (as representative romantic figures on international display), seamen produced texts that dramatized their curious position and invited their readers to engage with the narratives on those very terms. The potentially liberatory effects of the sailors' narratives can be seen in the brisk transmission of the bodily sailor and his imaginative text throughout the late-eighteenth- and early-nineteenth-century Atlantic world. At the vanguard of the new nation's dissemination of its products and interests abroad, American sailors of the federal period simultaneously participated in the expansion of American print culture and helped define the nascent American literature.

AFRICAN SLAVERS, AFRICAN SLAVES

Barbary captivity narratives, which number over a dozen, have been neglected by the many scholars who have drawn on the Indian captivity narratives of early American colonists in order to tell stories about individual and national self-definition. Unlike the experience of Native American captivity, which occurred relatively locally and was recorded over a span of 200 years, Barbary captivity was a more temporally limited and geographically distant phenomenon that affected only sailors rather than continental residents.[25] Barbary narratives have likewise received limited attention in scholarship on the genre of American sea writing, which seldom dates its critical interest earlier than James Fenimore Cooper's novels. Recent critical attention to this Barbary version of the captivity narrative genre has been focused on the ways in which the narratives articulated the young nation's definitions of nationalism, liberty, and sovereignty in a turbulent maritime world; this scholarship has explored the effects of these texts on a domestic audience concerned either with the plight of "Christian" slaves in "Mahommetan" hands or with the ways in which Barbary slavery spoke to American enslavement of Africans.[26] Such critical attention that has been addressed to the Barbary captivity narratives (in contrast to the fictional and dramatic representations of Barbary captivity by such domestic writers as Royall Tyler and Susanna Rowson, who have received notice for *The Algerine Captive* and *Slaves in Algiers*, respectively) has focused on either the nationalistic and Christian rhetoric of the narratives or their interest in ethnography.[27]

Contemporary observers themselves were interested in how Barbary captivity rhymed with chattel slavery in America.[28] In *A Short Account of Algiers*, for example, Philadelphian Mathew Carey expresses concern for the treatment of the enslaved Americans who faced branding if they attempted escape—while reminding his readers that "we are not entitled to charge the Algerines with any exclusive degree of barbarity." Remarking variously upon the British slave trade, local newspaper advertisements for fugitive slaves, and the influx of slaves brought to Philadelphia by way of the French West Indies, Carey situates slavery in a transatlantic context. He asks, "Before therefore we reprobate the ferocity of the Algerines, we should enquire whether it is not possible to find, in some other regions of the globe, a systematic brutality still more disgraceful?"[29] By inviting readers to make an analogy between slave economies in Algiers and those throughout the Atlantic world, Carey attempts to narrativize the Barbary crisis in terms of its relevance to other American conflicts with transatlantic implications, such as that with Britain. Carey was not alone in exploiting this relationship, and captive and other American writers invoke either American or Algerine slavery to suit their literary and political ends.[30]

Carey's contemporaries in the domestic literary sphere also adapted the comparison of Barbary slavery to American chattel slavery in their writing. The two best-known fictional examples of the captivity genre, Rowson's drama *Slaves in Algiers* and Tyler's novel *The Algerine Captive*, promotes abolition in addition to their support for independence for the American colonials. Rowson's play, in which captive Christian Americans teach their Muslim captors about the freedom that the characters find inherent in American hearts and minds, is the best-known example of several Barbary-inspired Orientalist dramas. In these plays, according to Benilde Montgomery's astute reading, "the ideals of Revolutionary liberalism, which remained still unrealized in America—particularly as they concerned the fate of African Americans—are in these plays ironically realized abroad among the Muslim captors."[31] The experience of his own slavery is equally transformative for the protagonist of Royall Tyler's novel, Updike Underhill, who is scarcely twenty-four hours into his Algerine captivity before he is forced to reevaluate his worldview. If he could once again "taste the freedom" of America, Underhill promises, he would dedicate his life to "preaching against this detestable commerce." He continues, "I will fly to our fellow citizens in the southern states; I will on my knees conjure them, in the name of humanity, to abolish a traffic which causes it to bleed in every pore. If they are deaf to the pleadings of nature, I will conjure them for the sake of consistency to cease to deprive their fellow creatures of freedom, which their writers, their orators, representatives, senators, and even their constitutions of government, have declared to be the unalienable birth-right of man."[32] For Tyler as well as for Rowson, the trope of Barbary captivity was most useful for the way it allowed both writers to articulate a "Revolutionary liberalism" seemingly independent of the more horrific realities of institutionalized slavery. In the case of *The Algerine Captive*, Underhill's lesson, according to Cathy Davidson, is that "in a republic, one's tolerance of injustice in its most extreme form, slavery, is synonymous with one's complicity."[33]

Such literary works did serve the growing antislavery movement in America, though. And many former Barbary slaves themselves noted the hypocrisy of white Americans who enslaved Africans yet who called for an end to the enslavement of white Americans in Africa. The anonymous author of *Humanity in Algiers* remarks upon this inconsistency:

> Unconscious of our own crimes, or unwilling the world should know them, we frequently condemn in others the very practices we applaud in ourselves; and, wishing to pass for patterns of uprightness, or blinded by interest, pass sentence upon the conduct of others, less culpable than ourselves. . . . "A vile, piratical set of unprincipled robbers," is the softest name we can give [the Algerines]; forgetful of our own former depredations on the coasts of Africa, and the cruel manner in which we at present treat the offspring of those whom we brought from thence. When the Algerines yoke our citizens to the plough, or compel them to labour at the oar, they only retaliate on us for similar barbarities.[34]

These fictional and dramatic texts express sentiments found in the narratives of captive sailors. When Judah Paddock and his fellow captives are closely examined by Arabs in a public square, they feel like slaves in market. "It brought fresh to my mind the situation I had seen the poor Africans in, in the West Indies, and also in some of our southern states, yarded up for sale, and the like observations made on them as on us—for instance, That is a stout fellow, this is a sickly looking creature, not worth much, he will soon die, and so on," Paddock remembers.[35]

Furthermore, James Riley's narrative of his enslavement in Morocco ends with his declaration of devotion to the cause of abolition at home as well as his discovery of fellow-feeling for African slaves: "Adversity has taught me some noble lessons: I have now learned to look with compassion on my enslaved and oppressed fellow-creatures," who are "kept at hard labour and smarting under the savage lash of inhuman mercenary drivers."[36] Riley's narrative, like those of his fellow mariners, finds him in the striking position of being able to lament his own captivity in the context of his country's enslavement of the countrymen of his captors. Earlier in his narrative, indeed, he urges his fellow captive Clark to find a similar comparative understanding when the two Americans are mocked and tormented by a "negro" slave belonging to their master. Clark "could scarcely contain his wrath: 'it was bad enough, (he said) to be reduced to slavery by the savage Arabs; to be stripped and skinned alive and mangled, without being obliged to bear the scoffs and derisions of a d——d negro slave.' " Riley counsels Clark, " 'Let the negro laugh if he can take any pleasure in it; I am willing he should do so, even at my expense: he is a poor slave himself, naked and destitute, far from his family and friends, and is only trying to gain the favour of his masters and mistresses, by making sport of us, whom he considers as much inferior to him as he is to them.' "[37]

The relativism of Riley's feelings of "compassion" for African slaves ran counter to the generic expectations of the captivity narrative, broadly speaking. British narratives by former captives of the European renegados or African pirates of the Barbary Coast had their origins in the earliest English sea ventures to the Mediterranean. Similarly, in American critical history, the captivity narrative genre has usually been associated with Indian captivity, which originated with the earliest colonial settlement of North America. Narratives of Indian captivity, in fact, were newly republished and read during the Barbary crises. In neither of these traditional genres of captivity do the victims commiserate with or particularly humanize their masters, and unlike Riley, those victims rarely find "oppressed fellow-creatures." In fact, part of the appeal of the Indian and European versions of the captivity narrative was the format's standard positioning of a white, Christian captive subject against the threat of a usually darker-skinned, presumed "savage" or "heathenish" people, whether Native American, Arabic, or African. The juxtaposition called attention to national differences and presented the white victims as dependent on Christian providence for their protection.[38] Yet while the Barbary narratives mentioned above positioned their texts as abolitionist, in part because they saw the captives' status as analogous to that of African slaves in America, the comparison is critically imprecise. For one, the two systems of slavery were fundamentally different in organization and outcome. American chattel slavery was predicated not just on the labor it could extract from its victims but on their profound subjugation in a system designed to obliterate cultural, social, religious, and political identities. A self-perpetuating cycle, American chattel slavery presumed no end.

Barbary slavery, in contrast, had a different understanding of the uses of the corporeal slave. While hard labor and gruesome tortures such as the bastinado were a fact of Barbary captivity, the ultimate use of the Barbary slave was for ransom, redemption, or other economic exchange. Barbary captives served as a marker or commodity in this exchange and had corresponding value within the system; conversely, in a familiar observation, chattel slaves were not valued so highly as property because owners at least esteemed and protected their property. More freely circulating—potentially—than the chattel slave, the Barbary captive was not a particularly racialized target. Indeed, throughout the centuries of North African piracy, targets hailed from such ethnically diverse regions as the Levant, Russia, South America, and Northern Europe. While Islamic masters did use their Christian captives as galley slaves (hard labor from which Muslims were exempt) and did encourage them to convert (or in the Europeans' terms, to "turn Turk," a reference to the region's long occupation by the Ottoman Empire), cultural or racial differences between captor and captive were not the impetus for Barbary piracy.[39]

In one respect, though, Barbary captivity was similar to American chattel slavery: both sets of victims wrote narratives of their enslavement. Yet the material conditions under which such narratives were written and circulated reveal significant differences. For one, literacy was rare and often criminalized for chattel slaves in nineteenth-century America, and thus a slave's attainment of literacy was an important aspect of his or her narrative. Barbary captives, by contrast, had no legal or social fetters on their attainment of literacy, and their narratives often follow forms familiar to their fellow sailors, such as a log or journal format. Furthermore, even as slave narratives found publication (often through the help of abolitionists) and readership, the dangers of the system forced many writers to censor names, places, and events from their records, relying instead on paternalistic avowals of authenticity for their verifying apparatus. The truth-value of Barbary narratives, by contrast, was predicated on their rigorous rendition of the details and conditions of the writers' captivities. Sailors listed longitude and latitude measurements, drew maps, traced routes, and offered explicit suggestions to others who might find themselves in similar predicaments (see figs. 2.1 and 2.2). Indeed, John Foss advertises that his narrative's meticulous details will aid seamen: "Should, at any future period, from causes not seen, more Americans be doomed to wear the galling chain, (God grant that period may never arrive) a knowledge of the habits, manners, and customs of the place, may not be unserviceable."[40] The value of Barbary narratives was therefore invested in their appeal for a reading public of fellow sailors, for whom the texts would be useful on many levels.

The example of the only nonwhite American sailor to produce a narrative of his Barbary captivity, Robert Adams, brings many of these issues into relief. Adams's experience was in many ways typical of that of American sailors of the federal era. He had spent time on a British man-of-war early in his career. Later, while embarked upon an American trading voyage that made stops at Gibraltar and along the northwestern coast of Africa, his ship ran aground, and Adams and his fellow seamen were taken captive by Saharan Arabs. The fact that his experience of captivity formed the basis of a narrative was likewise

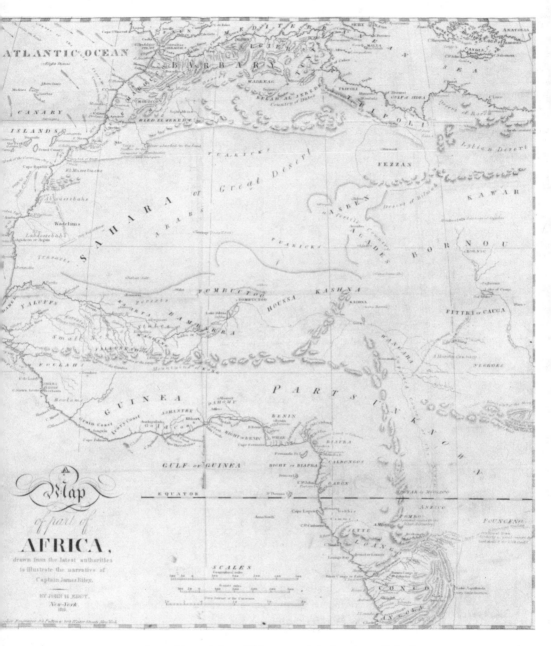

FIGURE 2.1: Map of Northwest Africa. This map, original to James Riley's
An Authentic Narrative of the Loss of the American Brig Commerce, shows the
route of his overland journey. The variable currents that caused his shipwreck
are indicated on the coastline near the Canary Islands. (The Library Company of Philadelphia)

THE ARABIC ALPHABET.

Value	Names	Initials	Centrals	Finals.
A	Alif			
B	Be			
T	Te			
TZ	Thze			
G	Gzim			
H	Ijha			
CH	Cha			
D	Dal			
DZ	Dhzal			
R	Re			
Z	Ze			
S	Sin			
SJ	Sjin			
S	Sad			
D	Dad			
T	Ta			
D	Da			
Y	Ain			
G	Ghain			
PH	Phe			
K	Kaf			
C	Kef			
L	Lam			
M	Mim			
N	Nun			
W	Wau			
H	Ghe			
J	Je			
La	Lamalif			

ENGLISH AND ARABIC VOCABULARY.

OF PERSONAL PRONOUNS.

Singular.			Plural.
I	anna	us	hanna
of me	anny	of us	ánná
to me	Lea	to us.	Lena
Thou	Enta	You	entume
of thee	ank	of you	ankum
to thee	Lik	to you	Likum
He	whoa	They	Hume
of him	anno	of them	anhume
to him	Leh	to them	Lihume

FEMININE GENDER.

She	Hea	they	hune
of her	anha	of them	anhune
to her	liha	to them	lihune

PRONOUNS POSSESSIVE.

Mine	emtay or dealy	Ours	emtáäna or dealna
thine	emtak or dealik	yours	entaakum or dealku
his	emtao or dealoo	theirs	entaahum dealhum

OF PRONOUNS DEMONSTRATIVE.

This	hadda	These	hadder
of this	anhadda	of these	anhaddi
to this	elhadda	to these	liixaddi
That	haddik	Those	hadduck
of that	anhiddik	of those	anhadduck
to that	lihaddik	to those	lihadduck

OF PRONOUNS RELATIVE.

Which	amaho, or ascoon, or min,	may be used
which of them	amaho fy him, or ashcunfy hum, or minfy hum,	alike.

OF PRONOUNS NUMERICAL.

Every	Kul
all	kulshy
many	shilla, or bizef, or yeser
every one	kul wahud
none	makine or makansky
nobody	hatta wahud
whosoever	kine min kan.

FIGURE 2.2: Arabic Alphabet and English and Arabic Vocabulary. The consular benefactor who facilitated James Riley's release from captivity furnished him with this vocabulary. (From Riley, *An Authentic Narrative of the Loss of the American Brig Commerce*, 554; The Library Company of Philadelphia)

representative of American maritime experience. And yet the material text of the narrative of Robert Adams's captivity signals the exceptional circumstances of his position in the Atlantic world of the late eighteenth and early nineteenth centuries. Adams is the only former captive sailor who is described as nonwhite; he is also the only former captive sailor whose narrative is related by third-person editors rather than written in the first person.

According to the voluminous authenticating text provided by his narrative's British editors, Robert Adams's "mother was a Mulatto, which circumstances his features and complexion seemed to confirm."[41] The text first published as *The Narrative of Robert Adams, an American Sailor, who was wrecked on the Western coast of Africa, in the year 1810; was detained three years in slavery by the Arabs of the Great Desert, and resided several months in the city of Tombuctoo* (1817) is overwhelmed by its editorial apparatus. This apparatus bears a remarkable resemblance to the prefatory and authenticating materials found in African American narratives of chattel slavery. And significantly, Adams's narrative is the only American-penned Barbary captivity narrative (of dozens) that is disbelieved by critical reviewers. The *North American Review*, for example, dismisses Adams's story as "a fiction, and a gross attempt to impose on the credulity of the publick."[42] Authenticity—in the sense of technical accuracy about the mechanics of the life of sail—was a driving impulse of the sea genre, and yet the rare circumstance of a racially identified sailor of color exposes a limitation of this model of authenticity. Barbary captivity narratives defined racial difference in a manner useful to abolitionists in America and Britain, who marshaled the experience of the American Barbary captives as a way of condemning slavery at home. Yet this imprecise comparison becomes unstable in the face of Robert Adams's narrative. The example of this particular "American Sailor" fits neatly into neither the body of Barbary writing invoked by abolitionists nor the genre of sailor writing spurred by the captivity crisis. In either case, models of authenticity are ill suited to the reception of Adams's narrative.

In this context, questions about the authenticity of Robert Adams's narrative take on special meaning. The text of the first American edition presents Adams's story related not in the first person but in the voice of an unnamed editor. The scant 53 pages of Adams's account are squeezed between 28 pages of introductory remarks and 115 pages of supplementary materials and concluding observations. Adams's narrative thus occupies only one-quarter of the volume. It is important to note that the editor was a representative of the African Trading Company, a British colonial venture that sponsored the publication of the volume and whose elite members verified its accuracy. Their interest in Adams is sparked by his knowledge of the semimythical city of Timbuctoo; in authenticating his description of the city, the African Company justified and promoted its own colonial venture.

The skeptical reviews Adams's text received seemed derived in large part from the authenticating apparatus of the material text. Noting that Adams's story was first presented to the British public, the *North American Review* summarizes the conditions of its publication in a "splendid quarto form"; it was "read before Lord Bathurst, Sir Joseph Banks, and several other gentlemen, [and] approved by them."[43] The "examination" Adams was given, which met with the approval of titled gentlemen, was rewarded with a fine edition whose value lay more in its endorsement by authenticating luminaries than in any intrinsic qualities. Yet the *North American* doubts this value precisely because of the these authenticating conditions. "The narrative first appeared . . . in a splendid quarto form," the magazine notes in a disparaging article in the following issue, "or rather it occupied a small corner in a book of this description; by much the greater part being composed of introductory details, copious explanatory notes by various hands and on various subjects, elaborate concluding remarks in defense of the story and the notes, together with two learned and well written appendices, which have no connexion with any other part of the book."[44]

By contrast, the *North American Review*'s notice of the Barbary narrative of James Riley—the captive who had discovered "fellow feeling" with black slaves in America—opens with an approving physical description of the volume. The review observes, "Th[e] portentous title page is not the only external recommendation of the volume before us. It is ornamented with a portrait of the author, furnished with rare plates, illustrations of divers scenes, descriptions, and adventures, and supplied with an *original* map of the countries into which he was led by the stars of ill omen, that presided over his destiny. Attracted by these claims on our notice, as well as the novelty of the subject, we took up the book with eagerness."[45] And what the magazine calls this "external recommendation" is the point of the appeal of Riley's book. This extends from his portrait (a feature absent in Adams's narrative) to his own first-person narrative voice (again, absent in Adams's narrative). The "claims" made by the material text of Adams's narrative are quite different, according to the *North American*. The supplementary materials in Adams's volume, the periodical suspects, "serve to give effect and interest, and what [is] of equal importance to the editor and booksellers, to swell the book into a comely size."[46] Here, the reviewer recognizes the interference of the editorial apparatus with any claims to narrative authenticity; this forestalls any acceptance of the "authenticity" of Adams's narrative in the terms that later sea writing will take up and refine.

Such claims to truth or authenticity helped promote the cause of captive seamen, for the situation of the American captives and the young nation's international standing was a topic of interest to a domestic audience. Frequent newspaper reports of the progress of negotiations or the military response to North African piracy were supplemented by letters from captive sailors themselves while the conflict persisted. The diplomatic letters of Richard O'Brien, the captain of the early captured ship *Maria*, were published in newspapers and in other periodicals such as the *Worcester Magazine*; in them he details the "indifference" of the British consul to the Americans' plight as well as his happiness, despite captivity, at being "relieved from a dependence"—on England—"so humiliating to Americans."[47] The *Columbian Magazine*'s foreign affairs column "Intelligence" kept the public apprised of the latest in ransom negotiations, and in fraught years such as 1787 the same magazine positioned articles such as "The Modern Customs in Barbary" directly opposite "Mr. Jefferson's Opinion upon the Establishment of an American Naval Force."[48] The letters of long-term-captive-turned-diplomat James Leander Cathcart were published widely; many of them were addressed to high-ranking American politicians such as the secretary of state, and they detailed both the conditions of the captives and the diplomatic maneuvering on their behalf.

The doctor aboard the captured *Philadelphia*, Jonathan Cowdery, also sent correspondence home that was extensively published in U.S. newspapers. In one letter, Cowdery reports that five American sailors have died and five "turned Turks"; he laments the condition of the captives set to repairing fortifications, who "complain much of hunger, cold, hard labor, and the lash of the whip."[49] For Cowdery, "the lively interest" with which readers greeted "the few extracts" of his captivity journal "that ha[d] occasionally appeared in the newspaper" was an inducement for him to plan a longer volume for a receptive public.[50] Indeed, the conditions of the publication of many of the Barbary narratives follow the model described by Cowdery. The poems written in captivity by William Ray, for instance, were printed in newspapers, and New England periodicals advertised his intention to publish a volume, inviting subscribers. The advertisement included a specimen of Ray's poetry that described the prisons or bagnios of Barbary and concluded, "Here thy brave tars, America, are found, / Lock'd in foul prisons, & in fetters bound."[51] Whether by a more general periodical readership or by a smaller circle of friends and relations, tales of captivity were eagerly digested. The familiar prefatory rhetorical insistence that an author sought print only upon the urgings of friends might have sounded a bit less conventional when uttered by a Barbary survivor, for whom the preliminary test audiences would have already spoken. The Barbary crises thus came to life in American periodical reading often in the words of the captive sailors themselves, whose writings positioned them as both initiates and advocates.

Although sailors wielded little to no overt political power, they had, in Simon Newman's observation, "witnessed and experienced revolutionary transformations" to a greater degree than most American workers.[52] In the absence of sailors' direct political influence, their printed appeals to American interest—in the financial sense—became an important element of the response to the seizures, as ransom by public subscription became one strategy for the captives' release.[53] The rhetoric of subscription and its concomitant promise of community dedicated to a common goal or project is widespread in Barbary narratives, some of which were offered to the public as a commodity for subscription. Subscription in fact redeemed many early colonial captives of Native Americans, and the failure of redemption by subscription distressed sailor (and later diplomat in North Africa) James Leander Cathcart. Cathcart made use of subscription as metaphor and practice during his time in the bagnio as he awaited redemption. For though Cathcart acknowledged that "the treasury of the period was very poor," for example, he was "so sanguine as to believe that the sum would be loaned immediately to the government by individuals, or that our fellow citizens would have raised it by subscription, but . . . I lived more than ten years after this in captivity."[54] An offer some years later to redeem the American captives by private British subscription was resisted by Cathcart, who recognized the implication of public endorsement and responsibility in turn such a move would have required. "You may aver that the proposed subscription will be effected by private donations, and has no concern with national funds or affairs," he writes, "but I am of the opinion that all subscriptions are more or less public, and must of course in such a nation as Great Britain, come under the inspection of those whose duty it is to oppose any such measures being carried into effect by the humane."[55] The import of successful subscription, and also of its failure, similarly occupies Philadelphia publisher and activist Mathew Carey, who in his *Short Account of Algiers* reminds readers of the committees appointed "to collect money, for [seamen's] relief, if not for their ransom." Yet a "most unaccountable torpor has taken place of benevolence and charity on this trying occasion," leaving a "business so extremely interesting, and undertaken with so much ardour," neglected by the public.[56] While Carey's exhortation was designed to appeal to a public whose support for a navy would be required, his rhetoric underscores the necessity in general for a community's collective action for the good of its citizens.

The process of subscription was vital to the operation of many Early American projects, from book publishing to insurance to education; its practice emphasized how the success of any community venture must be underwritten by the confidence of a collective group. Subscription was not too dissimilar from maritime labor in its collective agreement to fulfill a specific term of service or provision. That is, the term of service of a sailor was not open-ended, as it would be for many professions, but instead engaged in terms of the narrow conditions of a cruise. In a world in which seamen furnished themselves with books by means of a system that presumed their collective involvement and collective good, then, it is vital to recognize how the results of sailor subscription could be empowering. Working within this system, mariners appealed to the will of their fellows and received benefits in turn. Their assertion of solidarity was especially important in a moment when America's international power was seen as fragmentary. Subscription found a register between the systems of charity and taxation and proposed not that individual good brought public benefit but that the general good would ultimately reward the individual. The liberatory aspects of collectivity are crucial to an understanding of how federal-era sailors participated in a literary culture that allowed them to comment on the injustices of Barbary captivity and British impressment in writings that they prepared for and shared with fellow sailors.

Reading and writing becomes a communal enterprise for Cathcart, for example, during his years of slavery. Writing causes Cathcart to undergo the bastinado, something he endures only twice in his captivity: "once for writing and the last time for speaking to some of the Americans who belonged to the upper apartments."[57] His exercise of literacy is as dangerous as his communion with fellow captives in this instance, which echoes the situation of African slaves in American slavery, likewise forbidden to read and discouraged from exploring and solidifying bonds in kind. But Cathcart perseveres; while in the bagnio, he explains, "I employed myself in reading such books as I could borrow from the other slaves and writing, or teaching some of my companions practical navigation; this procured me the title of false priest, the moshabbe, and many other names of a similar nature."[58] Significantly, he is derided as a "false priest" by both his captors and the Catholic Spaniards who share his slave status. By trusting more in the powers of literacy than in any higher power to hasten his release or redemption, Cathcart elevates literacy from a practical tool to a strategy for resistance. Those who imperfectly exercise literacy are in fact scorned by the captive sailors, as they dismiss the American consul Thomas Lamb as someone who might have been "adequate to the task he had undertaken"—that is, to effect the release of the Americans

—but who instead is "extremely illiterate and as vulgar as can well be imagined, which did not create the most favorable opinion of the government which he said had sent him, nor were the impressions which he left behind him at all favorable to himself or his fellow citizens in captivity."[59] The exercise of literacy therefore is more than amusement or diversion but, in fact, a way to learn and practice codes for survival and social success.

MARINERS' SKETCHES

The strategic dispersal of such narratives at sea is indicated by the repeated cautions to sailors and captains in the prefaces to the narratives: the authors knew their audiences. The explicit address of the literate common sailor in these federal-era sea narratives is arresting. Captive Judah Paddock wishes his *Narrative of the Shipwreck of the Ship Oswego* to "be of some benefit to mankind generally, and more especially to sea-faring men exposed to the like awful calamities";[60] Charles Cochelet also positions his captivity narrative for the naval authorities and captains who should "in future receive instructions to avoid a shore [Africa], which has already proved fatal to so many human beings."[61] In his second edition of his journal of Algerine captivity, John Foss promises that he has "been more particular in the geographical description of the several places, in this edition than [he] was in the last, particularly of Algiers and Oran."[62] The revised preface to the third edition of James Riley's widely read *Authentic Narrative* offers factual corrections and a supplementary captivity narrative (of Judah Paddock's earlier ordeal), all of which revised testimony is given in the hope that "mariners, particularly, being thus apprised, will guard against the constant currents which have caused such frequent and dreadful disasters as death, slavery, and other almost incredible sufferings."[63] When describing how his ship ran aground before ultimately wrecking, Riley details his position for the reader of his narrative, explaining, "I mention this incident to warn the navigator of the danger he is in when his vessel is acted upon by these currents, where no calculation can be depended upon" (see fig. 2.1).[64]

Riley's narrative, especially, went to great lengths to offer aid to the mariner. "My observations on the currents that have heretofore proved fatal to a vast number of vessels and their crews on the Western Coast of Africa, are made with a view to promote the further investigation of this subject, as well as to caution the unwary mariner against their too often disastrous effects," Riley wrote in his preface. He also included a highly technical appendix, with explicit instructions to captains, which he glossed as "Observations on the winds, currents, &c. in some parts of the Atlantic Ocean, developing the causes of so many shipwrecks on the Western Coast of Africa:—a mode pointed out for visiting the famous city of Tombuctoo, on the river Niger, together with some original and official letters, &c. &c." In this appendix, Riley further explained, "I am particular in advising those ship-masters who are bound that way, by all means to make the Island of Madeira: it takes them but little out of their route, and from thence they will be sure of making Teneriffe or Palma, in steering the regular courses, when by due precaution against indraughts southward of those islands, they avoid the dangers of this terrible coast, and the dreadful sufferings or deaths which await all that are so unfortunate as to be wrecked on them."[65] The strong language of instruction or caution emphasizes the kind of cultural work these narratives did for sailors, work that was both practical and conceptual: practical in its instructive utility, conceptual in its positioning of sailors as figures of international sympathy.

Likewise, British impressment was equated with Barbary captivity in the minds and writings of many sailors, and its dangers inspired sailors to suggest mechanisms for response to their fellow tars. James M'Lean was no sooner released from African captivity than he was pressed onto an English man-of-war whose commander insisted that his American papers were forged and that he was a native Scotsman. His narrative, *Seventeen Years' History, of the Life and Sufferings of James M'Lean, an Impressed American Citizen & Seaman*, concludes with an address to his American "friends" in the form of an appendix that contains "the author's advice to those of his countrymen who should happen to be forced on board of any of the ships of his Britannic majesty." M'Lean's cautions, "Now is your time to avoid trouble."[66] The possibility that a newly redeemed or released Barbary slave would be impressed before he had a chance to return to America was a special danger in which seamen saw little irony. The unlucky impressment target Robert Adams deserts his ship, at which point he is taken captive by Saharan Arabs; later, when a patron redeems him from Barbary slavery, his panic at the thought of transport by a British ship causes his patron to reason that Adams "had once been on board a British Man of War, either on service, or detained as a prisoner." Fearing to sail again, Adams is calmed only by a promise that if, upon his sea travel home, he should "by any accident, be impressed, [then] his discharge, either by purchase or substitute, should be immediately effected."[67] The threat of finding oneself on a British ship was even a way to maintain shipboard discipline, as Judah Paddock threatened truculent sailors that they would "be put on board the first British ship of war that we should fall in with."[68] Joshua Davis, a victim of a press gang, sadly presented the case of the unheard-from "captive" victims of impressment; he addresses his readers, "My friends, doubtless you are ever anxious to know the fate of your fathers, husbands, brothers, uncles, cousins, or *sweethearts*, when they have left you in order to get a living on the briny ocean, which is now ruled by the ships of his Britanick Majesty —I can tell you in a few minutes. Many of them are on board those hellish floating torments, and wish to let you know where they are."[69]

These earnest appeals to the reading community of sailors accomplish several ends. First, they position sailors as figures of national, sympathetic importance in a time when mariners were typed as profane or degenerate, on the margins of "civil" society. The technical details of life and labor at sea were likewise valorized by this convention. By invoking a brotherhood of literate sailors, the narratives furthermore suggested that sailors had more power and autonomy over their own circulation in the Atlantic world than their potential for seizure might otherwise indicate. Indeed, a sense of autonomy or security would be particularly important for American sailors, as the uncertainty of the new nation's international status was a chief cause of its victimization by the Barbary States in the first place. Finally, the volatility of a maritime world populated variously by deserters, press gangs, pirates, renegados, and castaways is anchored somewhat by the positioning of the common literate sailor as the central figure of appeal for the maritime world's literature. For this figure, the "separation of mental and manual labor was never complete," according to Rediker, and it is in this conjunction of intellectual and physical labor that sea narratives find their truth and power.[70]

Barbary sailor narratives foregrounded their own materiality: the record-keeping practices of nautical life found their expression in the format of the narrative, which borrows the conventions of the log, the journal, and the ship's account. Judah Paddock's distress upon wrecking on the African coast is soothed by his and his crew's reiteration of shipboard habits before venturing into the desert. "When nearly ready for a start," he records, "my mate wrote up the log book and I finished my journal. . . . All things were now prepared, and we on the point of moving, when one of the sailors said, 'let us depart under flying colours;' the others joined him, and we were detained till they had erected a pole on the hill, and hoisted a very handsome ensign."[71] The familiar maritime tasks of keeping the log and maintaining symbolic display reassure Paddock and his men and allow them a way to claim the space of their displacement through ritual practice.

Retaining nautical discipline had practical advantages as well. William Ray recalls that when the weekly food allowance of the captive sailors of the *Philadelphia* was reduced by the Tripolitans, there was "much dissatisfaction and murmuring among the men, respecting the division of their late rations." Ray devises a solution that borrows from shipboard regulations: "I classed the men into messes of eight, and made them choose their messmates; then numbered the messes, as on board the ship. The meat was then cut up by two of the petty officers, and divided into as many heaps as there were messes." Later, when bread shortages find the captives much debilitated, the seamen stage a prison hunger strike.[72] "For several days we had been without bread or money, . . . and the men were unanimously determined not to labour any more unless one or the other was allowed us," Ray reports, and the tactic is successful.[73]

Like most travel and adventure narratives, the Barbary captivity texts aver their own truthfulness. Only sailors, in fact, could presumably be able to accept without question some of the geographical claims of the narratives regarding the location of the sites of their enslavement. The editor who relates Robert Adams's story points out that as a sailor, Adams "had the habit of noticing the course he was steering at sea; and therefore found no difficulty in doing so, when traversing the Deserts of Africa, which looked like the sea in a calm."[74] James Riley similarly cites his "long experience on the ocean," which taught him how "to ascertain the latitude by the apparent height of the polar star above the horizon."[75] For those who might have questioned how scrupulously a sailor could keep records while imprisoned and performing slave labor, John Foss mentions his customary journal-keeping while at sea and finds comfort in the practice while in what he calls his "severe captivity." He explains, "I wrote in the night, while in the *Bagnio* or prison, after our daily labour was over, the principal events of the day, merely to amuse and relieve my mind from the dismal reflections which naturally occurred."[76] The storytelling habits encouraged by nautical life find poetical expression in Foss's poem "The Algerine Slaves," in which the American captives find comfort in "tales of humour dress'd in sailor stile, / [which] The lonesome hours of gloomy night beguile."[77]

The enslaved sailors are directed and comforted by habits formed by maritime labor practices, and narrating such practices further helps to stabilize the dislocation of self- and national identity while at sea. As Linda Colley has noted of British captivity narratives, "Identities appear in strongest relief when problematic or under stress in some way, and this was usually the case in situations of captivity. Captivity narratives . . . offer access to people suddenly reduced to a state of liminality, taken away from their normal position in life, stripped of customary marks of status and identity, and removed in many cases from the reinforcement of their own kind. So positioned, men and women could be led to re-examine issues of national, religious and racial belonging, who and what they were, and how far this mattered."[78] In the face of such dislocations, sailors turned to a community of fellow laborers before the mast. Yet the seamen's strategies were not merely self-preservative. In addition, they established new strictures of authority independent of the powers that patrolled the Atlantic world. As described in the sailors' narratives, these alternative powers were vested in the laws of latitude and longitude and took as their subjects the fellow seamen who comprised the ideal reading public for the texts.

3 NAVAL MEMOIRS AND THE
LITERARY MARKETPLACE

In the midst of growing national interest in the condition of sailors, the early sea novels of James Fenimore Cooper—the first volumes of maritime fiction to be produced by an American author—were published. Barbary captivity and British impressment had awakened political and domestic sympathies for American seamen in the period between the Revolution and the War of 1812. Their cause was aided by the seamen's own writings: in the form of captivity narratives and anti-impressment tracts and in newspaper piecework and letters printed in literary magazines, American sailors documented their experience of international insecurity. Among those taking special notice of seamen's lives were reformers, and charitable societies for seamen appeared in great profusion, as discussed in Chapter 1. The actions of seamen's societies were part of a broader wave of reform movements in the United States in the 1820s–40s that preached temperance, religion, charity, chastity, and literacy. Other, more secular movements, especially those that concentrated on the working conditions of wage laborers, likewise included sailors in their efforts. The burgeoning sea trade and its galvanizing effect on the American economy made its own case for the value of sailors to the nation, especially in the aftermath of the largely maritime War of 1812. As seamen became objects of domestic sympathy, they became objects of literary interest as well. Their own memoirs found an audience with nonspecialist readers, even as fictional representations of maritime life (mostly by nonsailors) tried to replicate the authentic voice of the American mariner.

The maritime world might have appeared an especially inviting landscape for both literary exploration and national definition in the first half of the nineteenth century, particularly as nationalist periodicals of the early antebellum era issued the call for a distinctly American literature. If the nation's military and economic prosperity increasingly found their greatest expressions at sea, then America's literary productions could reflect that promise. The nineteenth-century Atlantic, as Thomas Philbrick argues in his 1961 study of Cooper's maritime fiction, "seemed to be as much America's peculiar domain as it had been England's in the previous century"; it thus became "inevitable that this wide and varied marine activity should find expression in the literature of a people seeking to create a national identity."[1] In the 1820s and 1830s, popular interest in maritime life was gratified by naval literature. Yet this interest in American naval experience did not last into the 1840s, when the generic demands of sea writing have been seen as shifting from historical romance to realism. More to the point, sea narratives of the 1840s and onward tended to reflect the primacy of the voice of the common laboring sailor rather than the naval officer. The story that critics (following Philbrick) have crafted to explain this transition in sea writing is a version of the received narrative of American literary progression told more broadly: the romanticism of early-nineteenth-century writing is thought to yield to an increasing realism by midcentury.[2] The many sea novels written in the antebellum period by Cooper—who had been a naval officer of short tenure—have been key to this literary historical account, as the subject matter and formal approach of his novels are thought to reflect this very shift from romance to realism. Cooper's writing has been seen as emblematic of a nautical realism that has strong affinities with later strains of American realism.

The model offered by Cooper's early fiction, however, misses the point of nautical realism as taken up and expressed in the scores of factual first-person narratives written by working seamen. Sailors themselves remark how the "ridiculous language" used by Cooper in rendering sailor speech in his novels "did discredit to our mystery," as one mariner, Cooper's critic Nathaniel Ames, put it.[3] Their criticism of Cooper's inability to represent the codes and terms of nautical labor exemplifies his fraught role as the public face of American sea writing. By the 1840s, sea writing displayed increasing technical specificity, but to what end? In Cooper's fiction, the details of sailors' lives and labor convey a certain kind of nautical realism to nonspecialist readers, a realism that simultaneously and paradoxically mythologizes maritime work. But the narratives of actual working sailors, as I argue throughout this book, feature such technical specificity in order to invite landspeople to inhabit the working lives of seamen imaginatively. Maritime labor is not romanticized or mystified in their accounts but is instead concretized in its material practices as the key to broader speculation. This chapter studies Cooper as an object of critique against which sailor writing can be measured in its own capacity for nautical realism. In the interest in genealogy and hierarchy taken by Cooper in his nautical fictions, which I discuss below, he misapprehends—to his own ideological end—sailors' belief in the value of empirical and imaginative knowledge offered by labor and labor alone, rather than rank or status. Any reading of nautical writing from the Revolution through the Civil War that traces too faithfully Cooper's own literary arc must necessarily misread this point, too.

It is my aim in this chapter, therefore, to understand Cooper's sea fiction within the context of the maritime writing that persistently offers a critique, both explicitly and implicitly, of the model of nautical knowledge inaugurated by Cooper's fictions. In turn, attending the tale of Cooper's creation of and engagement with the formal elements of American sea writing reorients the literary history of sea writing by dramatizing the influence of first-person maritime narratives on the structures of nineteenth-century American fiction. Cooper is the focus of extended discussion in what follows because his sea novels, even as they earned critical praise from literary critics, were the subject of pointed critique from actual working sailors. In this chapter I am less interested in offering a sustained reading of Cooper's own sea novels, however, even though Cooper's maritime fiction (unlike his Leatherstocking tales) is far from canonical today and is indeed little known. Instead, my attention to Cooper is designed to show how sailors' writings explicitly responded to the codes and terms of the sea fictions that were circulating in the literary marketplace.

Cooper's extensive sea writing includes eleven novels, an American naval history, a commentary on a prominent case of mutiny, and an edited narrative of the life of a former shipmate.[4] My focus in this chapter, though, is primarily on three of his works: his two earliest sea novels (*The Pilot* and *The Red Rover*) and a later narrative of an impoverished sailor whose life story Cooper edits (*Ned Myers*). The two sea novels, both historical romances, are the works of Cooper's most cited by sailors in their own narratives and thus are useful to the genre of sailor writing both genealogically and intertextually. The edited narrative of the unfortunate Ned Myers, which Cooper published two decades after his first sea fictions, has been seen—when read at all—as the work of Cooper's most akin to sailor narratives, one that might be classed with the genre of pauper narratives that Ann Fabian has separately documented in *The Unvarnished Truth*. Yet as I argue in the second half of this chapter, the form of *Ned Myers* obeys only some of the generic conventions of maritime writing and betrays the standards of labor knowledge established in contemporary first-person sea narratives.

In the first half of this chapter I focus on Cooper's revised prefaces to *The Pilot* (considered the first American sea novel) and *The Red Rover*. The late prefaces, written for the G. P. Putnam reissues of Cooper's novels in 1849 and

1850, respectively, offer a way of understanding how the model of sea writing he established was taken up and refined by other seaman authors as well as by Cooper himself in his later career. Cooper's original nautical fictions and the narratives that succeeded them were influenced by the literary nationalism of periodicals such as the *North American Review*. His early writing on the U.S. Navy, in whose service a youthful Cooper had spent three years as an officer (although he saw no action), focused on eighteenth-century events through the lens of historical romance. Poised to capitalize on the 1840s mania for sea tales, the respective 1849 and 1850 Putnam reprints of *The Pilot* and *The Red Rover* tell a significant story about the literary development of nautical writing in the more than twenty years since Cooper's novels had first been published. In the early novels he established the sea as a legitimate, indeed inevitable, landscape for literary historical exploration. In doing so, Cooper radically expanded the boundaries of what could be considered the material of American literature. Yet when Cooper added new prefaces to *The Pilot* and *The Red Rover*—after two full decades of sea writing inspired by his example—he adjusted the terms of his intervention into American literature in response to the nautical verisimilitude displayed in the writings of working seamen.

In the second half of this chapter I turn to Cooper's editorial work in *Ned Myers*, the narrative of a debauched career sailor, and see it as emblematic of his misappropriation of the later forms of the sea narrative genre. Cooper's early maritime novels helped to establish and celebrate clear nautical hierarchies; whether officers or pirates, his sailors knew their rank. Yet as the emphasis in sea writing shifted from the naval to the merchant service, sea narratives concurrently began to devalue the importance of rank or status in favor of the rhetorical and imaginative elevation of the value of the common laboring sailor. Although Cooper's work on the narrative of Myers is designed to appeal to this growing interest in the lives and condition of workingmen, in *Ned Myers* Cooper nevertheless reaffirms hierarchies that had become stale in 1840s nautical writing. In doing so, he displays a fundamental yet provocative misreading of the evolution of a genre that he had earlier engendered.

BEFORE AND AFTER THE SEA NOVEL

The sea writing produced after the War of 1812 capitalized on popular interest in the lives of American sailors, who had played a large part in the war. Unlike Barbary captivity narratives, which had been rhetorically directed to a reading public of fellow sailors, naval writings of the late federal era explicitly sought the sympathies of land-based readers. After the end of the Barbary threat and the War of 1812, sailors found themselves the objects of charitable and economic regard domestically, and consequently they began to identify a wider pool of sympathetic readers. The anxiety and insecurity of Barbary narratives, so desperate to prove that sailors had any value as symbolic figures, gave way to a new maritime confidence. This confidence was military and economic, certainly, but it also produced a recognition of sailors as proper subjects for writing and as writing subjects themselves. Magazines like the *North American Review*, one of the more respected critical reviews of the period, advanced the cause of seamen by reporting on their writing, in the form of Barbary narratives, sea travel accounts, and naval memoirs. The potential transparency of maritime literature for a nonnautical reading public was a topic of some interest to the *North American Review*, which had invested critical energy in reviewing sea writing—both American and European—years before it took up American fiction. Sea narratives, in the judgment of the editors of the *North American*, owed their success to certain generic and textual prerequisites. Taking an interest in the materiality of the sea text, the *Review* applauded displays of nautical specificity.

Into this atmosphere Cooper launched the first American sea novels; those of British writers Tobias Smollett and Walter Scott already enjoyed wide appeal among sailors and domestic readers alike.[5] When he began publishing nautical romances in the 1820s, Cooper was the solitary voice of the American mariner—in fiction; when his last sea tales appeared in the late 1840s, they shared shelf space with the explosive number of seafaring narratives and novels that had been produced in the previous decade, largely by sailors themselves. Whereas literary and popular history have remembered Cooper more for his Leatherstocking tales, his sea novels found enormous readership (and special critical praise for their author) in the antebellum period.[6] His literary achievements are indebted in large part to his astute appropriation of the language of literary nationalism. Responding to the literary nationalist urgings of the leading literary journals of the day, Cooper extended the moment of American naval confidence that followed the War of 1812 in his sea writing. Thomas Philbrick has argued persuasively for Cooper's "maritime nationalism," which Philbrick traces to the influence of Democratic periodicals that "called for writers who would challenge the literary supremacy of England as effectively as American seamen had challenged her naval supremacy; . . . for writers who would exploit national materials, among them the maritime victories and heroes of their country."[7] In conjoining the value of indigenous American writing with the political or military gains of the republic, this "maritime nationalism" brought greater visibility to the historically undervalued figure of the common sailor.

With the appearance in 1822 of W. H. Gardiner's long essay on Cooper's second novel, *The Spy* (1821), the *North American Review* began a process of evaluating individual fictional works as part of its continuing efforts to analyze the fitness of America as a site for literary production. The terms set by Gardiner in his essay on *The Spy* are taken up by Cooper in his initial sea novels. According to Gardiner, the problems facing American writers included uninspiring subject material, as the country and its inhabitants were presumed to be "utterly destitute of all sorts of romantic association." The traditional New England virtues of "cold uniformity and sobriety of character" combined to produce citizens who were "a downright, plain-dealing, inflexible, matter-of-fact sort of people."[8] To this dearth of heroic or magnificent characters was added a dreary "familiarity of things": in the young nation there are "no 'gorgeous palaces and cloud capped towers;' no monuments of Gothic pride, mouldering in solitary grandeur; . . . no ravages of desolating conquests; no traces of the slow and wasteful hand of time. You look over the face of a fair country, and it tells you no tales of days that are gone by."[9] In the absence of marks of visible history, Gardiner finds in the freshness of the American homestead's "elegant modern edifice" and "smiling cornfield" an encouragement to retreat to the pre-"civilized" "howling wilderness" first described by William Bradford and reinvoked by subsequent generations. Presenting fiction writing as a form of American exploration and settlement, Gardiner promises to the "adventurous" writer a "wide, untrodden field, replete with new matter admirably adapted to the purposes of fiction."[10] His call for novel writing as an expansive practice confronts the new nation's histories of Indian fighting and revolution.[11] And these histories, for Gardiner, are apt subjects for fiction—especially historical romance, a genre popularized by Walter Scott's novels.[12]

Operating within this rhetoric of colonial possession, the *North American's* review of *The Pilot*, Cooper's third novel and first sea tale, tried to place American fictional production into a more familiar model of settlement or ownership of the landscape: "Our literature . . . is like our territory, the greater part as yet uncultivated and wild." Comparing the writer to the yeoman farmer, whose agricultural efforts "in the midst of the wilderness" turn him into a "peaceful conqueror, a champion," the *North American Review* positions the American author as a similarly transformative colonizing figure who "reclaims and makes fertile the intellectual waste."[13] For all its hearty interest in the kind of labor that can have terrestrial as well as poetic uses, though, the magazine at times recoils from too hearty a representation of labor itself. For example, the *North American* concludes its essay on *The Pilot* by noting, "This, like the preceding stories of the author, is thoroughly American; in one respect too much so; as, for one instance, where colonel

Howard is said to take a little time, 'to remove the perspiring effects of the unusual toil from his features;' a sort of writing, which is too much in use with us, and may be said, perhaps, to constitute a national characteristic of our literature, if there be such a thing."[14] At this moment the *North American*, in its distaste for the physical sweat of work, wants to pose its idealized yeoman writer far from the actual field of his or her efforts.

For Cooper, the "untrodden" field of historical romance was attractive precisely because that field could be vigorously worked. What Gardiner deplores as the "sad reality and utility" of American sensibility, Cooper embraces as a subject for fiction. He represents this "reality and utility" as a feature of landscape and architecture, human agency and historical causality. His embrace of such "matter-of-factness" is not always affectionate, though. Writing to the publishing house of Carey & Lea in 1831, Cooper is ambivalent about his choice to use American materials, noting that "Europe itself is a Romance, while all America is a matter of fact, humdrum, common sense region from Quoddy to Cape Florida." In the same letter, Cooper also defends his status as an American sailor and writer in the face of what he sees as the disadvantages of that state, despite popular opinion that held "no writer ever enjoyed so favorable an opportunity as I, because I am an American and a Sailor. As to the sailor part of the business," he continues, "it is grossly absurd, for what advantage has an American sailor over any other?" While claiming that he could "get £3000 for a nautical tale that shall celebrate English skill to-morrow," Cooper gallantly refuses to "prostitute" himself to the market for British naval tales. "Remember how much I forego," Cooper reminded Carey & Lea, "by abstaining from the use of such materials as fleets, victories, historical characters and all the etcet[e]ra of [British] annals."[15] Cooper, whose most enduring nineteenth-century appellation was "the American Scott," clings to his "Sailor" status despite the literary and cultural disadvantages he perceives in that role. Crucially, much of Cooper's grievance lies in the fact that America's maritime past cannot provide the glorious subject matter ready-made in the British Royal Navy's rich annals. Having access to a grand national tradition, Cooper implies, would make his literary labor much more lucrative. A similar investment in historical glory and the actions of the elite is present in much of Cooper's nautical writing and significantly absent in much of the writing of working sailors.

What is more, Cooper makes a show of dismissing the readily available generic tools at his disposal. The absence of the gothic mode suggested by Gardiner as an available mark on the landscape is no matter to Cooper, and even when the geographical setting of *The Pilot* provides an excuse for a picturesque ruin, he extravagantly discards its symbolic value. For example, the old English building that serves as the stage for much of the dramatic action in *The Pilot* is atmospheric—it has the perfectly gothic qualities of being "part house, part abbey, part castle, and all prison"—yet Cooper nevertheless stands resolute in the face of gothic possibility:

> There were divers portentous traditions, of cruel separations and blighted loves, which always linger, like cobwebs, around the walls of old houses, to be heard here also, and which, doubtless, in abler hands, might easily have been wrought up into scenes of high interest and delectable pathos. But our humbler efforts must be limited by an attempt to describe man as God has made him, vulgar and unseemly as he may appear to sublimated faculties, to the possessors of which enviable qualifications we desire to say, at once, that we are determined to eschew all things supernaturally refined. . . . Our business is solely to treat of man, and this fair scene on which he acts, and that not in his subtleties and metaphysical contradictions, but in his palpable nature, that all may understand our meaning as well as ourselves.[16]

Rejecting subtlety, "metaphysical contradictions," and "refine[ment]" in favor of the "vulgar and unseemly actions" of "man . . . in his palpable nature," Cooper makes an aesthetic argument for the value of conventional or familiar human actions.

In a literary environment that questioned whether America could provide sufficient material for fiction, then, Cooper highlights what he considered the vernacular materiality of his fictions. And this materiality—humble, yet fiercely nationalistic and ideological—proved his strongest currency with critics.[17] Yet although Cooper's depiction of nautical life was widely praised by contemporary reviewers, it was nevertheless a target for abuse at the hands of actual sailors. The most trenchant criticism came from a fellow former navy man and literary competitor, Nathaniel Ames. Ames was the author of a popular volume of nautical reminisces, *A Mariner's Sketches*, which in one instance records how Ames was reprimanded for bringing a copy of Scott's *Woodstock* to the masthead when he was supposed to be on lookout. Ames's tastes might have run to Scott, but they did not extend as far as Cooper's fiction, which is a source of much ridicule at the hands of Ames and his shipmates. What worries Ames is as much the undiscerning tastes of landed readers as Cooper's own literary offenses. If landsmen "generally have very mistaken notions concerning sailors, and most of those notions are absurd and ridiculous," then Ames locates the blame in Cooper's novels *The Pilot* and *The Red Rover*. Finding Cooper's "sea dialogues" to be "disgusting and absurd, from being stuffed with sea phrases," Ames continues, "Sailors do not (except when describing some nautical transaction) converse in technical terms, . . . nor do they swear so much, or at least not more than landsmen, though there is more energy and *pathos* in a sailor's oaths than in the stiff and labored imprecations of a mere '*terrae* filius.' "[18]

The integrity of sailors' language is paramount to Ames. When he reads a few passages of *The Pilot* aloud to his topmates, Ames finds that the prose "seemed to please them well enough, until I came to one of the *rope-yarn* dialogues." At this point, Ames records, his topmates became derisive: " 'Pshaw! heave the d——d thing overboard,' broke out from the lips of half a dozen men of war's men at once."[19] The seamen are chiefly offended that Cooper's strained prose misrepresents their eloquence. Recognizing that Cooper's popularity is seated as far from the actual nautical trade as possible—he cites "exquisites and boarding school girls" as representative readers—Ames underscores why Cooper's technical language might appeal to nonexperts. For such readers, there is romance in seamen's opaque language; for Ames, though, the mystery of what sailors actually do and how they express themselves is not a novelty.

Most critics, to be fair, did not have Ames's experience on the main, and indeed, few landspeople took issue with Cooper's representation of nautical art. As the *New-York Mirror*'s review of *The Pilot* breathlessly put it, "Cooper is, body and spirit, a sailor. . . . We hear the roar of the waves—the splash of the oars—the hoarse language of the seamen. We see the waters—the ships—the manning of the yards—the heaving of the lead—the very cordage of the vessels. Every movement—from that of the tracking of the frigate to the launching of the whaleboat, is visible to our eyes, and we actually take part in the proceedings and conversations of the crew."[20] Cooper's figuration as "sailor" is here more important than his profession as author, and the *Mirror* places perhaps a greater value on the evidence of manual labor than it does on the literary. The enactment of maritime labor, conjured for a readership presumably unable to recall such pictures from its own memories, is presumed to be perfectly transparent: the reader "actually take[s] part" in the work.

Other sailors who had seen action in the War of 1812 and wrote of their experience found the critical public similarly receptive to the terms of their maritime labor. In fact, seaman authors who prefaced their works with demurrals of literary accountability because of their profession found themselves urged to lean more heavily on their professional experience. William Leggett, for example, includes only a few poems about the sea in his sentimental verse collection, *Leisure Hours at Sea* (1825), despite his desire to inspire other adventurers to enter "the world of letters." Anticipating further effusions from Leggett's pen, the *North American Review* advises, "We hope he will talk less of things on shore, and more of those around him. The sea, with its

thousand brilliant perils and accompaniments, is rich in materials for poetry."[21] The sea has long served as a subject for poetical contemplation, certainly, although most poets, as landspeople, would not have direct access to
maritime experience. It is significant, then, that the author of *Leisure Hours at
Sea* is urged to employ his experience of ship labor as poetic capital. Four
years later Leggett did take up this suggestion and released a deceptively titled
series of sketches, *Tales and Sketches by a Country Schoolmaster*, which largely
revisited his experience at sea. Valuing marine labor as a material source for
literary production would pay huge dividends in the decades to come, for
both seaman authors and their increasing body of landed readers. Indeed, it
paid even for Leggett, who became the editor of the *New York Evening Post*
after he retired early from the navy: his follow-up volumes to *Leisure Hours at
Sea*, especially *Naval Stories* (1834), present an accomplished range of short
sketches of life at sea. In one instance, after noting that "to a true sailor there
are few circumstances more annoying than a perfect calm," Leggett describes
sailors as sails, which move sluggishly while the ship lies in a calm but "rouse"
and become "animated" in a breeze.[22] For Leggett, then, poetic expression
becomes an apt way to display the conditions of maritime labor. He conflates
the bodily sailor with the physical equipment of his trade and by extension
imagines the ship as a text to be read.

Nathaniel Ames's sketches of sea life attracted similar notice for the way in
which the sea narrative text and the body of the sailor could be metaphorically and metonymically combined. His follow-up to *Mariner's Sketches*, the
collection *Nautical Reminiscences*, appeared to one reviewer to be "dressed
somewhat in a tarry jacket," just as any working sailor would be. In his future
works, advises the reviewer in the *New England Magazine*, Ames should
eliminate "almost all topics but his description of nautical affairs."[23] In the
hands of the new generation of American sailors, metaphor was forged from
the very material of seamen's labor. The growing body of sea narratives was
the target of some playful commentary in the *American Quarterly Review*,
which remarked on the equation of maritime labor and literature: "Authorship and travelling are all the fashion. Sailors wash the tar from their hands and
write verses in their log-books; midshipmen indite their own adventures; and
naval commanders, not content with discovering countries and winning
battles, steer boldly into the ocean of literature."[24] Cooper's most direct prog-
eny, what he himself called the "tolerably numerous school of nautical romances" (5) that bobbed in the wake of *The Pilot* and *The Red Rover*, cite their
debt to Cooper while still criticizing the sometimes creaky mechanism of his
representation of maritime life. But if Cooper helped establish the imaginative conditions for the genre of sea writing, he also undercut them.

Cooper's Long View

The narratives of seamen such as Leggett and Ames owe a great deal to Cooper's nautical romances, despite their disapproval of the effects of such fictions. Yet what is the genealogy of Cooper's sea novels? On the basis of a frequently cited anecdote, Cooper is presumed to have written *The Pilot* as a corrective to the poor seamanship displayed in Walter Scott's *The Pirate*. Crucially, this genealogy for *The Pilot* and *The Red Rover*—that is, that both novels were explicitly designed to be more expertly nautical refutations of the lubberly prose of Scott—is not recorded until 1849, in a revised preface to the G. P. Putnam reprint of Cooper's first sea novel. The reissues retrospectively cite a paternity they never originally claimed.

The account of how he decided to write a sea novel, first narrated publicly by Cooper's late-nineteenth-century biographer Thomas Lounsbury, has been little altered or questioned when retold in the 100 years since the publication of Lounsbury's biography. This biography, the first on Cooper (who did not permit biographies while he was alive), describes Cooper in conversation with friends over the question of the authorship of *The Pirate*, widely thought to be Walter Scott. The prevailing opinion in this dialogue, however, was that he could not be the author, since *The Pirate* is a sea romance and Scott was no sailor. Yet it was for that very reason, Lounsbury writes, that Cooper was convinced of Scott's authorship: "To one like [Cooper] whose early life had been spent on top-gallant yards and in becketing royals, it was perfectly clear that 'The Pirate' was the work of a landsman and not of a sailor."[25] As a corrective to Scott's prose, Cooper supposedly formed a determination to write his own sea tale as a follow-up to his first two historical novels. But this enterprise had its own peril, according to Lounsbury: "Sailors, he was told, might understand and appreciate it, but no one else would. Minute detail, moreover, was necessary to render it intelligible to seamen, and to landsmen it would be both unintelligible and uninteresting on account of the technicalities which must inevitably be found in minute detail."[26] The result, *The Pilot*, nevertheless found enormous readership and amassed critical praise for the salty-tongued character Long Tom Coffin and for the novel's invigorating take on the possibilities for staging fiction in a maritime context. The very values cited by Lounsbury as impediments to broader readership among landspeople —minuteness, technical details—would in fact become sea writing's greatest strengths.

The genealogy that Lounsbury established for the first American sea novel has been unquestioningly reinscribed throughout the history of critical reception of Cooper's sea novels. Cooper's first three sea novels attracted wide attention for their depiction of seamen in the model of Byron's *The Corsair*, the central figure of which Philbrick describes as "not only the amorous captain of classical romance, but the noble outcast, the aloof and inscrutable superman, the passionate, guilt-ridden sufferer of Byron and his imitators."[27] Yet despite this oft-cited allegiance to models of European romanticism, Cooper does not invoke a desire to correct Scott as an impetus to or condition of his literary enterprise in the 1820s. Instead, in the preface to the first edition of *The Pilot*, he meditates on the fitness of America for historical romance, a topic suggested to him by critics in publications like the *North American Review*.

Cooper's preface to the first edition of *The Pilot* stresses his interest in recovering the nation's young history for literature; he laments the "obscurity" under which the heroes of the Revolutionary War lie buried. The "object" of this novel (whose central unnamed character, the shadowy pilot, is John Paul Jones) is to "excite some attention to this interesting portion of our history" (4). This aim is consistent with *The Spy*, which similarly featured a Revolutionary War hero, in that case George Washington. In both novels, the feeling of historicity is as important to Cooper as any strict historical accounting; as he puts it in the preface to *The Spy*, "We do not absolutely aver, that the whole of our tale is true; but we honestly believe that a good portion of it is; and we are very certain, that every passion recorded in the volumes before the reader, has and does exist."[28] He desires to bind his readers in an affective sympathy with the "passions" of their historical forebears. Cooper's opening remarks find him trying to define his readership.

The 1823 preface to *The Pilot* begins with Cooper's attempt to navigate between "the prerogatives of truth and fiction," the reconciliation of which is the job of the "Historian" as well as "the writer of Romances" (3). For any who might struggle to reconcile the "facts" of the one with the "fiction" of the other, Cooper suggests, the persevering reader will "find good poetical authority for every material incident in his veritable legend" (3). This formulation would seem to be the inverse of what is expected—that is, doubts about the probability of fictional episodes usually are resolved by the authority of material evidence. Cathy Davidson notes that Cooper presumes a similar inversion of the positions of history and romance in his review essay on Royall Tyler's *The Algerine Captive*; Davidson usefully summarizes Cooper's position as follows: "History is a fiction and the novelist is the true historian."[29] In the preface to *The Pilot*, though, Cooper identifies "poetical authority" as the confirmation of "material incident[s]" unfamiliar to the reader —presumed to be a landsperson—who must rely on literary or aesthetic judgment as the stamp of truth on the sea tale. This imagined reader would seem to be the most representative of Cooper's mass audience: alienated by the more technical language of maritime life but willing to credit the author's word. Cooper remarks the dependent situation of this reader at several points in *The Pilot*. In one instance, the officer Barnstable spots an obscure signal that his ship is safe and "rub[s] his hands together, with a sort of ecstasy, that probably will not be understood by the great majority of our readers" (268). In another example, the reader's eye is filtered through the more practiced eye of another officer, Griffith, as he scans the course of navigation: "The unpractised reader will be able to comprehend the case better by accompanying the understanding eye of Griffith as it glanced from point to point, following the whole horizon" (391). The presumption is that this reader will accept the view of marine life offered by Cooper—the reader's eye becomes "understanding" only so far as it shares the character's vantage point. Cooper's "unpractised reader" here would become Lounsbury's landsman, supposed to be bored and alienated by Cooper's technical details.

In the 1823 preface Cooper does specify two classes of skeptical readers, although their numbers are described as relatively much smaller than the sympathetic readers': the "Critics," who are distinguished mostly by their lack of nautical knowledge, and the "old seaman," whose critical eye is flattered but disregarded. This does not mean that Cooper frames his novel in terms of its presumably expert seamanship in the face of Scott's deficiencies—again, this is a move he makes only in 1849. When maritime terms are invoked with any specificity in the 1823 preface, they are used to dismiss potential critics rather than to signal the special virtues of his novel. Cooper deflects criticism by labeling his detractors as alienated novices: "As to the Critics, he has the advantage of including them all in that extensive class, which is known by the sweeping appellation of 'Lubbers.' If they have common discretion, they will beware of exposing their ignorance" (3). By dismissing critics with that most contemptuous of seamen's terms for a nonsailor, Cooper calls attention to their inexperience with the life of sail. But Cooper's real argument is with those "Critics" who will reject the shared vision of Cooper's authorial directive. The other potential reader explicitly invoked in the preface is the "old seaman," who might "happen to detect any trifling anachronisms in marine usages, or mechanical improvements." To this discerning and potentially resistant reader, Cooper claims that "it was not so much his intention to describe the customs of a particular age, as to paint those scenes which belong only to the ocean, and to exhibit, in his imperfect manner, a few traits of a people who, from the nature of things, can never be much known" (3). His assurance to the old tar both depicts and appeals to that figure's sense of marginalization, as a way to forestall criticism of any maritime errors. What is important to reiterate, though, is that in 1823 Cooper made no argument for his own seamanship or his ability to represent maritime life with strict accuracy. Nautical verisimilitude for Cooper was a rhetorical posture rather than a generic requirement.

In the preface, Cooper does refer to Tobias Smollett—and not, significantly, Scott—in defining his attempt to "paint those scenes which belong only to the ocean." Smollett's bawdy *Roderick Random* had created an enduring fictional image of sailors as licentious, drunken revelers, although his novel is only nominally concerned with the sea. In endeavoring to write a sea narrative, Cooper explains (referring to himself in the third person), "though he has navigated the same sea as Smollett, he has steered a different course; or, in other words, that he has considered what Smollett has painted as a picture which is finished, and which is not to be daubed over by every one who may choose to handle a pencil on marine subjects" (3). In other words, Cooper's new view of sailors will not be a corrective to the deficiencies of Smollett's "picture"; in focusing on competent and principled American naval officers, Cooper's picture is executed in a very different medium.

Nautical specificity and technical language are used by Cooper to drive the romantic plot, rather than the historical plot, of *The Pilot*. By referring to the romantic plot I mean both the romantic image of sea fraternalism Cooper evokes and the intimate relations between the officers and their American lovers, for *The Pilot* features a robust double (and almost triple) love plot, one hardly replicated in other sea writing. Cooper's employment of maritime language in the romantic plot is put to best use in the characterizations of *The Pilot*'s female actors. In the 1823 preface Cooper's reading audience is never specified by gender, even though his 1849 preface determines that *The Pilot* "could scarcely be a favorite with females. . . . His [the author's] aim was to illustrate vessels and the ocean, rather than to draw any pictures of sentiment and love" (7). The "pictures of sentiment and love" that do appear in *The Pilot* are in many ways conventional. The "females" (to use Cooper's awkward term of choice) of the novel include Katherine Plowden and Cecilia Howard, who are the sprightly yet modest intended brides of Barnstable and Griffith, the American officers who serve as the central characters of *The Pilot*. A third woman, the somewhat older Alice Dunscombe, is destined to be alone when she refuses to renounce England as a condition of pledging herself to her old flame, John Paul Jones, the pilot himself. The younger women, born in and sympathetic to the colonies, have been taken to England by their loyalist guardian, who keeps them virtual prisoners in the abbey that serves as the setting for much of the novel's action, rather than the sea.

Katherine and Cecilia display many standard virtues of filial respect mixed with romantic daring, yet to Katherine's portrait is added one arresting detail.

In order to aid her lover, Katherine devises a version of a nautical signal book, complete with silk flags of her own ingenious design. Shown her efforts, her admiring lover Barnstable exclaims, "What a log-book she would keep!" (68), and accepts the teasing of his fellow officers, who wonder whether he courted Katherine "with treatises on the art of navigation, and the science of signals" (82). Katherine's signal book invokes nautical flag communication and advances the plot, although sometimes at the expense of believability; her flags can spell out such phrases as "*When the Abbey clock strikes nine, come with care to the wicket, which opens, at the east side of the Paddock, on the road: until then, keep secret*" (311). The effective practice of nautical arts is here marshaled to support a romantic plot, rather than to describe the maneuvers of or communication with a ship. Katherine's talents are more than simply symbolic, as her flags do provide for crucial information to be transferred; but still, her employment of such skills—a flirtatious point of appeal for her lover—is more precious than practiced.

The figure of Long Tom Coffin, second only to Natty Bumppo as Cooper's most enduring fictional figure in the nineteenth century, would seem automatically to have more nautical authority than Katherine Plowden. His surname bespeaks his Nantucket origins, and the reader is repeatedly reminded that he spent much of his nautical life on a whaling ship and wields a harpoon to prove it. A lifetime sailor, Long Tom is even at one point linked to Neptune himself, god of the seas. Cooper is not alone in making the comparison: critics, contemporary and present-day, praise Coffin and his representation in the strongest possible terms.[30] Yet metaphor is more commonly the operative idiom of Coffin's salty speech. The cockswain is introduced in *The Pilot* as he unfolds his six-foot, six-inch frame from a whaleboat and prepares to go ashore with Barnstable and Griffin. In search of the mysterious pilot who is to lead them out of treacherous waters off the coast of England, the landing party is amused by the idea of the veteran seaman Coffin trying to walk "on terra firma" (17). Coffin is uncomfortable with their proximity to the rocks; his first utterance in the novel is less a response to the current situation, however, than an expression of his philosophy: "Give me a plenty of sea-room, and good canvass, where there is no 'casion for pilots at all, sir. For my part, I was born on board a chebacco-man. . . . I'm sure the sight of [land] always makes me feel oncomfortable, unless we have the wind dead off shore" (19). Tom's speech, factual and metaphorical all at once, is characteristic of the way Cooper employs nautical vocabulary and knowledge: the metaphorics of Tom's rhetoric would be accessible to the reader who might not be familiar with its technicalities.

Indeed, Cooper's characters often cannot express themselves outside this rhetoric, even when prompted by their fellows. When Tom Coffin improbably kills a whale while at anchor off the English coast (a scene widely and positively recited at length in reviews),[31] he laments having no access to the riches such a whale would bring in the Boston market, and by extension a comfortable retirement: "There's nothing left for poor Tom Coffin to do, but to veer and haul on his own rolling-tackle, that he may ride out the rest of the gale of life, without springing any of his old spars." When an officer chides him for becoming "sentimental," or shipwrecked "on the shoals of poetry," Tom responds, "Them rocks might wrack any vessel that struck them, . . . and as for poetry, I want none better than the good old song of Captain Kidd" (205). Coffin and his shipmates are so constrained by their idiom that even their search for alternate forms of literary expression—whether poetry or the legend of Captain Kidd—always refer back to the same narrow set of signification. Nevertheless, the newness of such language to many (if not most) readers might have been a point of appeal rather than a source of confusion or ridicule. When Richard Henry Dana Jr. defends his own use of technical language in the preface to the 1840 *Two Years before the Mast*, in fact, he cites Cooper's *Pilot* as his justification: "Thousands read the escape of the American frigate through the British Channel, . . . and follow the minute nautical manoeuvres with breathless interest, who do not know the name of a rope in the ship; and perhaps with none the less admiration and enthusiasm for their want of acquaintance with the professional detail."[32]

Dana employs Cooper's *Pilot* to justify his own use of specialized nautical vocabulary. *Two Years before the Mast* inspired a great number of sea narratives similarly attuned to the specificity of maritime labor "before the mast" by the common sailor. Critics were keen to praise Dana's technical sea language as well as his ability to make the "work" of sea life stand in for the "work" of artistic composition. After all, a review argued, Dana "went out to work, not to speculate or describe."[33] The *North American Review*'s favorable notice pointed out that "hard labor is necessary to effect any thing considerable in literature; and probably few works ever cost more, if we may reckon the toils, sacrifices, and temptations of a common sailor, as part of his preparation for a memorable narrative of sea life." The narrative would find favor, the review successfully predicted, with any reader "curious to know what the sea really is; what the life of a mariner is in the merchant service; and the daily history of all that is going on in the little craft, or stately ship, which is holding its solitary course for months together, in search of commodities for landsmen."[34] The "commodities" that circulate with the help of sailor labor can be thought to include sailor narratives, which have a decided value for "landsmen."

Dana himself disavows any romantic notions of sea labor: "The romantic interest which many take in the sea, and in those who live upon it, may be of use in exciting their attention to this subject, though . . . the sailor has no romance in his every-day life to sustain him, but that it is very much the same plain, matter-of-fact drudgery and hardship, which would be experienced on shore."[35] The standard of literary value set by *Two Years before the Mast*—that is, the degree to which a sea narrative could represent the experience of maritime "work"—was in part a logical response to an increasingly urbanized population that appreciated increasingly realistic literature. While the publication and popularity of James Fenimore Cooper's sea novels in the 1820s had signaled the moment when the instruments of sea navigation and labor became expressive media in sea novels and narratives, it was not until Dana's narrative that such tools could be employed on behalf of the speculative project of representing maritime experience. In other words, while sea narratives and their raw accounts of shipboard life might be thought to end the "dreaming" for "those who know nothing of the sea, and those who know everything," the reality, according to the *North American Review*, is that "it would be juster to say, that we have surrendered our false fancies, and with full compensation, so much more animating and productive is the truth, as here [in *Two Years before the Mast*] set forth, than our former guesses."[36] The achievement of antebellum sea writing lies in its author's ability to make the "truth" of sea labor a productive compensation for any loss of the reader's romantic notions of life at sea.

The Issue of the Reprint

After a decade of maritime narratives that took their cue from Dana's example, thirteen of Cooper's early novels were reissued in handsome new editions by G. P. Putnam between 1849 and 1851. The Cooper series, inspired by Putnam's success with a revised "author's edition" of the works of Washington Irving, was designed to present a uniform edition of a well-known author's work. Besides Cooper and Irving, Putnam published the works of Catherine Maria Sedgwick in similar fashion.[37] The thirteen Cooper novels reissued by Putnam included all five Leatherstocking novels; the project, incomplete, was abandoned after Cooper's death in 1851. *The Pilot* and *The Red Rover* volumes featured new prefaces written by Cooper; his third sea novel, *The Water-Witch* (1830), did not have a new preface for the Putnam edition.[38] The three rereleased sea novels, *The Pilot*, *The Red Rover*, and *The Water-Witch*, were able to build on the resurgent popularity of a genre that few denied Cooper invented. The brief notice in the *United States Democratic Review* of the Putnam edition of *The Pilot*, for example, remarks on this particular impetus: "The 'Pilot,' on its first appearance, met with universal favor, and became the model for a large class of sea stories, a taste for which was awakened in the public mind by the grace and vividness with which Mr. Cooper introduced his seamen to the reading public." The review also notes that the debt to Walter Scott is cited for the first time in this edition: "In the present preface he informs us, that the admirable story was the result of an impulse derived from conversations with a friend, whose unqualified praise of Scott's Pirate, roused in the author the desire to produce a story founded on accurate seamanship."[39] Only at this late point in his career and his life, when the expectations of the genre of sea writing were well established, does Cooper adapt and internalize this critical praise for his ability to make sea labor materially present for the reader. Although *The Pilot* is dedicated to a naval officer, William Branford Shubrick, with whom Cooper had served (and who became his nautical proofreader), its first preface had invoked the novel's maritime context defensively, rather than claiming it for authorial design. Recall that the 1823 original preface had apologized to the "old seaman" reader for any inaccuracies. The late-1840s occasion of a "present preface" to his decades-earlier sea fiction allows Cooper to respond, obliquely but deliberately, to the body of popular sea narratives that had appeared in the previous decade.

When Cooper explains in his 1849 preface to the Putnam reissue of *The Pilot* why he decided to write a sea novel, his description of his literary inspiration and writerly aims both credits and undermines Walter Scott, the influence so avidly courted by Cooper in his early novel writing. Cooper describes an early 1820s conversation with a friend, "a man of polished tastes and extensive reading," about the authorship of the sea novel *The Pirate* (Scott's novels were published anonymously). The debate at hand concerns Scott's claims to authorship, Cooper reports, which was doubted "on account of the peculiar and minute information that the romances were then very generally thought to display. The Pirate was cited as a very marked instance of this universal knowledge, and it was wondered where a man of Scott's habits and associations could have become so familiar with the sea" (5). Cooper charitably points out that *The Pirate* did not advertise itself as a nautical work, yet he objects to the public's embrace of its "seamanship" as a proof of its value. The very fact that he deliberates this point—that is, whether a man of Scott's "habits and associations" would have detailed knowledge of nautical practice—with a well-read member of the social elite suggests that the technical details of maritime writing would hold value even for those far removed from the docks. Furthermore, the conversation reveals Cooper's investment in the judgment of nonnautical elites. "The result of this conversation," Cooper concludes, "was a determination to produce a work which, if it had no other merit, might present truer pictures of the ocean and ships than any that are found in the Pirate. To this unpremeditated decision, purely an impulse, is not only the Pilot due, but a tolerably numerous school of nautical romances that have succeeded it" (5).

The impetus Cooper here describes for his own foray into sea novels is doubly reactive. He announces his intention for *The Pilot* to be a corrective to Scott's own inauthentic seamanship, for one. But Cooper also claims that his inspiration came from a desire to refute in particular those readers who praised Scott's maritime sensibility. This "provocation" is telling and under-scores the drive in sea writing to represent accurately the quality of the lives of seamen to an uncomprehending or disinterested public. In other words, Cooper is less scandalized by Scott's own factual errors than by the public's easy acceptance of them. And whereas in his 1823 preface Cooper had in-voked a readership of sailors only to apologize for any errors of seamanship, in the 1849 preface he makes this audience of sailors the primary one: after "an old messmate" reads the draft with approval, Cooper has the "most gratifying assurance that the work would be more likely to find favor with nautical men, than with any other class of readers" (7). The "favor" Cooper here seeks from reading sailors is likewise telling, for by the 1840s his literary reputation had taken some blows and suffered from the publicity of other personal scandals. (These include Cooper's protracted involvement with libel lawsuits as a result of his description of Oliver Hazard Perry in the Battle of Lake Erie in his *History of the Navy* and of his defense of the mutineers in the *Somers* case.)[40] The revisionism of Cooper's prefatory changes is ideological, not merely the product of a literary disagreement with Scott. Whereas the rhetoric of the earlier preface had been employed in the service of romance, the late preface rhetorically appeals to a readership composed substantially of sailors. Coo-per's late embrace of the value of the reading sailor is notable, especially since seamen, again, were not identified by Cooper as part of his target audience of the first edition of *The Pilot*.

Cooper's second sea novel, *The Red Rover*, was also reissued by Putnam, and its revised preface of 1850 repositions the novel even more provocatively than the preface to the 1828 first edition. (Herman Melville's well-known review of the reissued *Red Rover* is discussed in Chapter 4.) By the time of the 1850 *Red Rover*, sea novels and narratives constituted a bustling trade in the literary world and presented landed readers with scenes of nautical life in every imaginable variety, from romance to realism, from ethnographic en-counter to individual reflection, and from salacious to reformist impulses. Yet Cooper's 1850 preface to *The Red Rover* does not mention the explosive growth of sea writing in the decade previous, just as his 1849 preface to the

Putnam reissue of *The Pilot* sought to place that novel in a historical trajectory that likewise did not acknowledge the recent past. In both cases Cooper cites far distant literary and nautical models; in *The Red Rover*'s 1850 preface he refers again to the previous century's nominally sea-themed novels by Tobias Smollett, as he had in the first edition of *The Pilot*. The new preface opens with a claim that Smollett's success with nautical tales "required a new course should be steered in order to enable the succeeding adventurer in this branch of literature to meet with any favour." Cooper continues, "This difficulty was fully felt when this book was originally written, and probably has as much force to-day as it had then, though nearly a quarter of a century has intervened."[41] The criticism that Cooper levies at sea writers of "to-day"—that is, their works have done little to set "a new course" away from Smollett's influence—is curious, considering that comparatively few writers of sea narratives, if any, cite Smollett as an influence. The other major European sea novelist, Walter Scott, whom Cooper invokes in his 1849 revised preface to *The Pilot*, is likewise not a trenchant literary model for most sea writers. Cooper himself is far more commonly singled out, but it does not seem as if modesty governed his embrace of Scott and Smollett.

The field of historical romance that had been claimed by Scott and recommended to Cooper by early essays on his literary career in the *North American Review* remained difficult terrain for the writer, who even in his 1850 *Red Rover* preface confessed, "The history of this country has very little to aid the writer of fiction, whether the scene be laid on the land or on the water." The distinction between "land" and "water" that Cooper makes here is significant, since, as he continues, "it would be very difficult to turn to a single nautical occurrence on this part of the continent, in the hope of conferring on a work of the imagination any portion of that peculiar charm which is derived from facts clouded a little by time" (429). Rather than valuing the nautical setting for the credit it confers on laboring seamen, as most sea writers do, Cooper is still, at the relatively late date of 1850, averring that American maritime history is thin: "a circumstance," Cooper says, "that is doubtless owing to the staid character of the people, and especially to that portion of them which is most addicted to navigation" (429). To most observers, the sea writing of the previous decade could be characterized as anything other than "staid."

By inscribing, at the relatively late date of 1849–50, an authorial genesis that emerged from the tradition of historical romance, Cooper seems deliberately to avoid placing his novels alongside the volumes of sea writing that had proved so popular in the previous decade. These sea narratives, which owe very little to the traditions of historical romance, were nevertheless often generous in recognizing Cooper as their structural and inspirational model. And even though the revised prefaces never find Cooper himself inscribing this genealogy in print, he did so readily in a long 1843 letter to Rufus Griswold that detailed the course and motivations of his literary career. On his plan for *The Pilot*, Cooper wrote,

> Pilot came next. This book was on a plan so novel, that the critics, if there are any in this country, did not know how to receive it. For several weeks its fate was doubtful. Its American reputation certainly came from the East, though the North American "damned it with faint praise" as it had previously done the Spy. In Europe its success was quick and decided. It has been said there is no original literature in America. I confess an inability to find the model for all the sea tales, that now so much abound, if it be not the Pilot. This book was written in consequence of a conversation with the late Charles Wilkes of New York, touching the Pirate. The universality of the *knowledge* of the author of Waverly was much extolled on account of this book. To me it proved that he had undertaken a subject he did not understand, and Mr. Wilkes was told that a book should be written that a seaman could understand, at least, might feel some sympathy with.[42]

Cooper seems to be posing an epistemological question—what does "*knowledge*" consist of in sea writing?—in petty literary and commercial terms. To Griswold, Cooper claims an originality of generic form that he is reluctant to cite in his revised prefaces, which invoke historical romance. Authorial modesty, to be sure, would prevent Cooper from claiming to have rectified the problem of having "no original literature in America," but modesty does not necessarily explain why he goes to such pains to rehabilitate his novels as romances in the vein of Smollett or Scott. It is curious that Cooper publicly rejected his justly earned title to the antiromantic nautical specificity of the contemporary narratives.

But nautical specificity has its dangers. Cooper's insistence in *The Red Rover*'s original preface on technical accuracy had created a problem: some readers believed that there had to be an actual historical antecedent for the heroic pirate Red Rover.[43] In an attempt to reconcile his call for textual factuality in the face of his literary fancy, Cooper added a revised preface to the 1834 Standard Novels London edition of *The Red Rover*. The new preface promised corrections that, while technical, were still more literary than nautical: faults of "style, orthography, and taste" had been corrected (427) in the edition. Further, Cooper sought to distance his literary invention from the demands of his readers, who had been trained by Cooper's earlier prefatory remarks to look for historical or nautical verification of the events of his novel. In an admission that echoes some of the 1820s *North American Review* manifestos on the subject of America's fitness for literary production, Cooper writes, "America is a country nearly without traditions, the few there are being commonly too familiar to be worked up in fiction. The object of the book is to paint sea scenes and to describe nautical usages and nautical charac-ter, and not at all to embody any real events" (427). Confronted with readers who found the piratical Red Rover a less heroic subject than John Paul Jones, the eponymous focus of *The Pilot*, Cooper here stresses that the mood evoked by his sea writing is more significant than its historical particularities. He retreats from the demands of historical fiction, describing his goal instead as a desire to give readers a sense of maritime life. At the same time, Cooper does not go so far in this 1834 preface as to claim that "nautical usages and nautical character" constitute any part of American "traditions." The coming decades would give Cooper ample reason to continue to revise his authorial claims, however. Seaman authors, newly empowered and visible as national figures of interest thanks in part to charitable reform and labor movements of the 1820s and 1830s, did not feel the burden of having to evoke historical scenes as a condition of their textual output. Instead, in later narratives sailors valued their own labor experience as an apt subject for literary effort.

When given the opportunity to describe the role of his own novels in serving as formative texts for the great volume of American sea writing that followed him, however, Cooper ignores such factual narratives in his atten-tion to the novels of Scott and Smollett. His revised prefaces thus strategically misrepresent the genre of sea writing, which by the 1840s overwhelmingly found its expression in first-person factual narratives by working sailors, rather than in novels by professional authors. By identifying a genealogy for sea writing that largely excluded sailors themselves, Cooper reaffirms the interests in rank and hierarchy—on the level of cultural authority—with which his oeuvre at large might be said to concern itself. This preoccupation with classification marks his editorial experiment with the narrative of the common sailor Ned Myers.

BEFORE AND AFTER THE MAST

A profligate, alcoholic, and disabled lifetime seaman, Ned Myers was among a class of laborers who registered in the annals of nineteenth-century American history as either objects of charitable sympathy or harlequins or otherwise comic figures. The aging sailor, unlike the robust Jack Tar of familiar fiction, hardly animated the popular imagination. Like many sailors of his generation who had come of age during the War of 1812 and who continued in the merchant service throughout the subsequent boom decades of the American maritime economy, Myers found himself in retirement without pension or prospects. He had spent his life in and out of the naval and merchant services and in and out of trouble with the law. Myers deserted ships he did not fancy, earned and then imbibed fortunes, and established few human connections, despite attempts at moral reform. In many ways, his career exemplified the vicissitudes of early-nineteenth-century maritime life.

Some sailors in Myers's position tried to support themselves by writing and circulating narratives of their youthful maritime adventures. After naval seaman Joseph Hoxse lost his arm in battle with the French, for example, he produced a narrative that he peddled himself: "Having got this work up in a handsome style, and at a great expense, I have concluded to make a tour through the principal towns in this and the adjoining states, and to call personally upon every individual who may wish to purchase one of the books." He reasons that the proof of his absent arm—his "receipt"—would make it a "hard task for any person to counterfeit [his] experience."[44] Elisha Dexter found himself in similar straits after his whaleship sank; his narrative concludes, "I now am penniless . . . I have lost it all; and with gray hairs, and a shattered constitution, I am now compelled to commence life upon the land, anew. And now, being no longer able to follow the seas, I am trying to turn even my bitter misfortunes to some account, by the sale of this 'NARRA-TIVE.' "[45] Another destitute sailor, Reuben Delano, wrote a narrative that he dedicated to the "superintendent of the state lunatic hospital . . . as a slight testimonial of gratitude for his kindness and attention while under his care." Delano ended up in the Massachusetts Asylum for the Insane in Worcester because of his drunkenness and indigence; he hopes his narrative "might prove as a beacon light, to enable some young men to steer clear of the shoals and quick-sands that came so near my total destruction."[46]

The forms of literary circulation practiced by Hoxse and Delano were enabled in the first half of the nineteenth century by growing charitable interest in seamen and particularly by an increasingly democratic literary marketplace.[47] Ned Myers himself could read better than he could write. His maritime career, however, included one passage with a future literary giant: as a boy, in 1806–7, Myers had shared a transatlantic voyage with seventeen-year-old James Fenimore Cooper. Nearly four decades after their voyage the debilitated sailor contacted the now-famous writer, and Cooper subsequently offered himself as amanuensis for a reform narrative of Myers's adventures with war, impressment, tyranny, and riotous port life. The resulting work, *Ned Myers; or, A Life before the Mast*, is known to literary history as the product of

Cooper's authorship, not Myers's. Even so, *Ned Myers* earns scarce mention in the genealogy of Cooper's own literary output. Part of this oversight, notable even within the context of the relatively limited attention paid to Cooper's sea novels as opposed to his frontier tales, may have to do with the hybrid form of *Ned Myers*. The narrative is described as the "biography" of a common sailor, yet it is told in the first-person singular and "edited" by Cooper.

The unusual form of *Ned Myers* helps to illustrate both the status of sailors in the antebellum literary marketplace and the pressures on Cooper's later career as a writer of maritime fiction. Neither strictly first-person account nor biography, neither wholly Cooper's own imaginative work nor his editorial production, *Ned Myers* is peculiar within both the body of first-person narratives written by working seamen and the measure of Cooper's novels. As an unsentimental portrayal of the trials endemic to a life at sea, *Ned Myers* would seem to embrace the 1840s model of the sea narrative genre. Yet its recognizable subject matter is at odds with the anomalous form of the narrative itself. It was highly unusual for a sailor's narrative to appear under the imprint of another's authorship, for one. American sea writing set its own value in terms of the authentic portrayal of maritime life offered by its authors, however rudely delivered. Of the scores of antebellum sea narratives in American maritime archives, for instance, I have found only two others besides *Ned Myers* that advertised an amanuensis. One such narrative was dictated by a blind sailor; the other is that of former Barbary captive Robert Adams, a mulatto sailor whose narrative (discussed in Chapter 2) bears the editorial apparatus of slave narratives. Neither of these, it should be noted, cite their amanuenses on their title pages but instead credit the sailors themselves.[48] Yet the title pages of the 1843 first American edition of *Ned Myers* by Lea & Blanchard (as well as the 1844 first British edition by Richard Bentley) credit Cooper as the editor of the volume, but do not list an author; Myers's own name appears only in the title. If, as contemporary and present-day critics maintain, *Ned Myers* represents Cooper's most "authentic" portrayal of maritime life, then the narrative's form and production call into question the terms of authenticity stipulated by the broader genre of sea writing and Cooper's place within it.

The voice of Myers, in the narrative's conclusion, stresses that "this is literally my own story, logged by my old shipmate."[49] The use of a nautical metaphor in summoning the figure of the logbook is provocative: for many of his reviewers, Cooper's sense of maritime "reality" was widely seen as the best recommendation of his work. Stressing the admirable prosaic (that is, not poetic) quality of Cooper's writing, one contemporary reviewer remarked of his portrayal of the sea, "He is not her poet, but her secretary and copyist."[50] It is this sense of Cooper as "secretary" to or "copyist" for maritime experience that is of interest to this book. Whereas in the 1820s Cooper felt compelled to ally his sea writing with the cultural value of historical romance, by the 1840s he tried to refashion his writerly genesis in the technical nautical terms authorized by scribbling sailors and an appreciative public.

There is a deep inconsistency, though, between Cooper's proficient use of realistic techniques in the nautical scenes of *Ned Myers* and his misapprehension—and therefore misuse—of a tacit but fundamental aspect of the sea narrative genre. By this I refer to the sailor's own belief in the value of his story, however humble, which customarily lends a sense of confidence and authenticity to even the most injured sailor's history. Cooper errs in misplacing his narrative's authority, yoking it to his own editorial pen rather than to the voice of his subject. Ned Myers the sailor proves to be a subaltern in his own narrative. *Ned Myers* attempts to claim a freshness or immediacy of narrative tone, as the narrative is presented in the first person, yet Cooper's editorial voice intrudes awkwardly at points. For one, the narrative distinguishes between the "old shipmate" that Cooper had been and the "gentleman" he had become. By associating himself in print with the semiliterate Myers, his "old shipmate," Cooper attempts to reenlist in nautical life and labor. Yet Cooper's absorption of Ned Myers's "own story" betrays his misreading of the formal elements of the sea narrative genre and its definition of authenticity. At the same time, it suggests Cooper's broader devotion to social and economic hierarchies, which are further enforced within *Ned Myers* itself.

Cooper's Realities

Ned Myers has been described as anomalous within Cooper's body of work because of its clarity, directness, and unsentimental voice—what one contemporary review called Cooper's "unusual perspicuity."[51] Yet this very quality marks the narrative as prosaic within the broader body of sea narrative writing, such as Dana's *Two Years before the Mast*, as well as the host of imitators that had emerged in the years following its 1840 publication. The subtitle to Myers's narrative—*A Life before the Mast*—appropriates Dana's language, just as many narratives did in stressing that their subjects sailed "before the mast" as common sailors, rather than as officers.[52]

Cooper's correspondence in the 1840s makes clear his desire to remain relevant to the burgeoning sea narrative genre. In several letters to Richard Henry Dana Sr., famous literary father of the author of *Two Years before the Mast*, Cooper is eager to report the times young Dana's authorship is called into question. After first reading *Two Years*, Cooper writes to the senior Dana, "I do not know whether your son will be inclined to take it as a compliment or not, it was first introduced to me by a question from Jos. R. Ingersoll, who wished to know whether Dana were not a nom de guerre *I* had taken to write a sea narrative. He did not suppose the book fiction, but *truth* barbacued a little."[53] Several years later, when young Dana had not published anything new other than the nautical manual *The Seaman's Friend*, Cooper takes up the theme anew with the father: "What has become of your chap? . . . I do not know whether the compliment is to me, or to himself, but many persons asked me if I had not written his book, when it first appeared."[54] Cooper is at pains to clarify that the misrecognition of authorship does not invalidate the stamp of truth assigned to Dana's nonfictional narrative. He does this not so much to praise Dana, however, as to esteem his own "fiction" for having the taste of "*truth* barbacued a little." More palatable, presumably, to a reader, Cooper's "*truth*" is the product of a literary transformation. The larger degree of transformation registers in two ways: first, in Cooper's own late-career espousal of the intellectual utility of maritime truths and, second, in the larger literary historical interest in the materiality of literary texts. Still, if Cooper thought that *Ned Myers* would capitalize on the popularity of Dana's narrative, he was mistaken, as the book failed to meet his expectations. Although a commercial disappointment, *Ned Myers* offers an illuminating glimpse not only of life before the mast but of the professionalization of sailor authorship in America.

The economic and technological conditions that facilitated America's nautical successes, Cooper understood, also included what he called "the restlessness of moral excitement." This inducement to a life at sea was propagated in part by a literary culture of adventurous enterprise. "This cause is more active in America," Cooper argued, "where the laboring classes read more, and hear more of adventure than any where else."[55] Laboring men— who "read more" adventure literature in America—were inspired by their reading in turn to help swell the ranks of working seamen and to continue America's maritime prosperity. Yet in the case of *Ned Myers*, Cooper, decades removed from the authenticating experience of actual nautical labor, felt the need to generate the writing subject of the narrative from a fusion of the seemingly at-odds figures of the "gentleman" author and the "old shipmate" Cooper himself had once been. The lack of harmony between these roles, as will be seen, was detrimental to the successful publication and marketing of *Ned Myers*.

When, in fact, Cooper revisited his early sea novels such as *The Pilot* in the late 1840s, he likewise cited the value of representing the "truth" of maritime life versus the "false fancies" readers might have entertained. And since Dana's narrative had been saluted as much for its antiflogging reform tendencies as for its portrait of maritime reality, Cooper was eager to reestablish himself within the genealogy of popular sea writing. In the wake of the reform movements of the 1820s–40s, Cooper is therefore able to reevaluate one key function of the success of *The Pilot*. "Sea-tales came into vogue"—among landsmen—as a result of its healthy sales, Cooper notes in his new preface to his first sea novel, "and as every practical part of knowledge has its uses, something has been gained by letting the landsman into the secrets of the seaman's manner of life. Perhaps, in some small degree, an interest has been awakened in behalf of a very numerous, and what has hitherto been a sort of proscribed class of men, that may directly tend to a melioration of their condition" (7). The kind of "interest" described by Cooper here refers to the rash of "Peace Societies, Temperance and Moral Reform societies" that included sailors as objects of their charitable attentions. It is interesting to note that unlike the great majority of seaman authors who invoked reform, Cooper was not uniformly against the practice of flogging, an issue of terrific concern for sailors; many men, he opined, "would be greatly benefited by a little judicious flogging" (8, 7).

While it is nevertheless fair for Cooper to credit *The Pilot* for the "awakened" interest in seamen, it is also fair to point out that Cooper did not express particular concern for the conditions of seamen in his early sea fiction. The officers of *The Pilot* are able to move successfully from ship to shore, from the longboat to the parlor, yet the one common sailor characterized in the novel, the towering Long Tom Coffin, cannot exist independently of his ship and goes down with it. Out of touch, perhaps, with the concerns of the common seaman (an accusation made by Dana and others), Cooper's call for landsmen to become involved in sailors' lives was the kind of impulse that other mariners, such as Nathaniel Ames, rejected: reformers, wrote Ames in his popular memoir *Mariner's Sketches*, "have volunteered a feeble crusade against the vices and sins of seamen and have accordingly stuffed ships full of tracts which have entirely defeated their own object."[56] What Cooper calls the "secrets of the seaman's manner of life" could almost constitute the rhetorical equivalent of the city mysteries genre, which had similarly flourished in the 1840s (and had similarly drawn both excited readership and the attentions of reformers). Cooper's newly expressed interest in the "melioration of [sailors'] condition" speaks powerfully to the social changes that had both inspired and responded to the generic changes in literary production and helps underscore *Ned Myers*'s own attention to reform.

Falling Astern

Cooper's editorial preface to *Ned Myers* advertised the narrative primarily as a reform manual that possesses "interest and instruction for the general reader." This reader presumably would learn frugality and sobriety from Ned's own mistakes on this score. Even for those readers who might find "amusement" in Myers's "perils and voyages," Cooper hoped that "the experience and moral change of Myers may have a salutary influence" (1). Ned Myers struck Cooper as an exemplary figure for charitable interest. Indeed, he helped to procure employment for Ned and for his family members (including a stepdaughter who served as the Coopers' maid). Furthermore, Cooper personally agitated on behalf of Myers for a naval pension for injuries sustained in the War of 1812, describing Ned to Secretary of the Navy George Bancroft as "a man who is deserving of some rewards for his sufferings and conduct in the last war."[57]

Yet within the narrative itself, Myers expresses a fatalism about his economic and societal position. Even while acknowledging that he has wasted his wages and the goodwill of charity-minded friends, Myers does not sustain any interest in advancement, whether spiritual, social, or economic. He knows his place—his role as a common sailor—and rarely seems to chafe at the restrictions of maritime hierarchy. In fact, Ned seeks clearly defined class systems, disdaining one group of relatively poor ship's owners because "they were too near my own level to create respect" (146). He prefers the naval to the merchant service, because in the former a sailor is "pretty certain of having gentlemen over him, and that is a great deal" (212). Further, Myers is all too willing to take demotions—he repeatedly sails before the mast even after earning mate's berths—and never negotiates for more favorable conditions. Desertion, usually, is Ned's mode of protest. Any chance for advancement, or "preferment," to use Ned's term, is suspect: early in his sailing career, Ned is offered a promotion to a master's mate's berth but reports, "I felt too much afraid of myself to accept it. I entered the navy, then, for the first time as a common Jack" (52). The reasons for his fear are mysterious, as this moment predates his long struggles with alcohol. This unexplained sense of fear prevents Myers from ever taking comfort in his one living family member, a sister, whose efforts to meet Ned are brusquely rebuffed—he "was afraid to venture on that," Ned says (108).

As he reaches the sailor's middle age of thirty, Ned's unspecified fear turns to apathy—"I had felt a singular indifference whether I went to sea as an officer, or as a foremast Jack," he explains (172). Part of this indifference can be attributed to Ned's inability to master mathematical navigation and "the lunars." He turns down an offer to work toward a captaincy because "I was honestly diffident about my knowledge of navigation. I never had a clear understanding of the lunars, though I worked hard to master them" (203). Yet despite Ned's tough luck with math, he takes pleasure in reading the Bible's narratives: "The history of Jonah and the whale, I read at least twenty times. I cannot remember that the morality, or thought, or devotion of a single passage struck me on these occasions. In word, I read this sacred book for amusement, and not for light" (206). Easily influenced, when Ned reads Tom Paine, he finds "practical evidence of the bad effects of his miserable system. I soon got stern-way on me in morals . . . . I began to think that the things of this world were to be enjoyed" (241). Even though the end of his narrative finds Ned embracing sobriety and Christianity—influenced by a Bible he is given with "prayers for seamen bound up with it" (271)—he died of alcoholism several years after his narrative was published. "I am sorry to say our friend Ned Myers has fallen astern," wrote Cooper during Ned's final debauch, and Myers passed without preferment.[58]

Myers's embrace of Cooper as the public face of his life story therefore registers as wholly consistent with Ned's ostensible comfort with clear, established hierarchies and with his own relatively modest place within them. Myers is very happy to have Cooper serve as the "gentleman" who authorizes his narrative. Yet for Cooper, the value of *Ned Myers* lies not in his own hierarchical remove from Ned but, rather, in his presumed shared experience with his "old ship-mate." This is a paradox that the narrative itself struggles mightily to reconcile, especially because Cooper himself profited from his lofty position within established hierarchies. How can Cooper stand both as an authentic former sailor before the mast and as a gentleman-editor enjoying literary status? If the narrative is designed, in part, to serve the interests of reform, then Myers's habitual self-deprecation would be inconsistent with the production of the narrative. That is, if Myers considered himself too unworthy even to meet with his only sister or to accept a promotion, it seems unlikely that he would offer up his own life as a model for charitable attention to seamen's issues. Within this context, Cooper's role as Myers's "superior" is telling. Ned rekindles their acquaintance after nearly thirty-five years, writing Cooper a letter in which he asks if the famous author is the young man whom he knew in 1809 ("I had taken it into my head this was the very person who had been with us in the *Sterling*," Ned reports [276]). Myers addressed this letter to "Mr. Fenimore Cooper," and sent it to the town that bears the writer's widely known family name. Known to all as "the author of many naval tales, and of the Naval History," Cooper nevertheless replied familiarly: "I am your old shipmate, Ned" (277).

This sense of intimacy does not penetrate the narrative to a great extent, however. In his career as a sailor, Ned had been indifferent to any personal claims for agency or self-definition, and the production of his narrative is no exception. Unlike slave narratives, many of which also feature amanuenses, *Ned Myers* lacks the full editorial apparatus testifying to the narrative's authenticity and truth-value: no one vouches for Ned's story other than his editor. That is, Cooper's voice is presumed to have its own authority, both within the field of sea writing and in the broader literary marketplace, in endorsing Ned's story. And Cooper's authority is, ultimately, the point. The preface to *Ned Myers* displays a provocatively elastic use of the terms "editor," "writer," and "author." This elasticity is revealing: in which role is Cooper best cast in Ned Myers's narrative? If Cooper's fittest role, according to his critics, is to serve as "copyist" for maritime experience, then Cooper's position as amanuensis for Ned Myers's account of his life at sea should be transparent. Such, however, is not the case.[59] Cooper's eagerness to associate his own writing—as well as his own position as sailor-author—with that of Richard Henry Dana Jr., for example, makes for some confusion in analyzing Cooper's influence over Myers's own *Life before the Mast*. This difficulty occurs in part because literary historians have often overlooked *Ned Myers* in discussions of Cooper's body of work; some reprints of Cooper's complete works have even omitted it completely. Thomas Philbrick's *James Fenimore Cooper and the Development of American Sea Fiction* devotes fewer than three pages to *Ned Myers* and mentions it mostly to praise the freshness and authenticity of its narrative voice when compared with what Philbrick finds to be the "hackwork" of other seaman authors. Finding the style of the narrative to be a "minor triumph" and exceptional within Cooper's body of work, Philbrick argues that Cooper succeeds in "preserving the idioms and intonation of the seaman and imposing, at the same time, the order and control which are so conspicuously lacking in the narratives of other literary tars."[60] The authenticity that Philbrick values, in this case, depends more on Cooper's editorial skill than on Myers's unadulterated voice.

Cooper himself contributed in some fashion to the narrative's subsequent critical neglect and bibliographic confusion, however inadvertently. In a letter to Richard Bentley, his usual London publisher, Cooper explains that his newest book will be "*a real biography*, intended to represent the experience, wrecks, battles, escapes, and career of a seaman who has been in all sorts of vessels, from a man of war to a smuggler of opium in China"; Ned himself has been visiting him, he continues, and "I have been at work on him with great zeal."[61] Here Cooper conflates the physical Ned with the text his narrative will produce. His preposition is telling: he has been working *on* Myers, not *with* him, and this suggests that Cooper views the old salt as a ready-made work-in-progress, a text for the taking. But the printed work is not, strictly speaking, a biography, as it is told in the first person. In claiming the category of biography rather than that of narrative, Cooper may be attempting to elevate the status of both Myers's life and life story. As Fabian has persuasively argued in *The Unvarnished Truth*, the personal narrative genre in the antebellum period was embraced by destitute and forgotten men on the margins of society. "Biographies," on the other hand, more typically served to place the life of an individual (usually an elite) within a specific (usually richly evoked) historical or cultural context, and this broader perspective tended to be beyond the interests of the narrative form.

The preface to *Ned Myers*, however, does not feature the word "biography," despite Cooper's promises to Bentley. In it, Cooper initially refers to himself as "the editor," but he is an editor who is also a writer, as he explains: "The reader will feel a natural desire to understand how far the editor can vouch for the truth of that which he has here written" (1). From this point in the preface onward, Cooper calls himself "the writer" of the narrative, who was "determined to produce the following work" upon hearing Ned's story (2). This slippage between editor and writer—with Cooper inhabiting both roles—creates some confusion for the reader. This confusion was reflected in the few reviews of *Ned Myers* that appeared in periodicals. *Graham's*, for example, was initially skeptical of the claim that Cooper served only as editor to the volume; its review begins, "The words '*edited* by J. Fenimore Cooper,' in the title-page of this volume, have, no doubt, a suspicious appearance." Given the examples of works such as *Robinson Crusoe* and *Arthur Gordon Pym*, the review continues, "the reader will naturally be induced to suspect Mr. Cooper, who professes to *edit* '*Ned Myers*,' of having, in fact, composed it himself."[62] While *Graham's* ultimately endorses the volume, not all were so forgiving; another review finds *Ned Myers* to be "scarcely worth the attention bestowed upon it by its distinguished *editor*."[63]

Such perplexity only increases in the narrative's footnotes. In one instance, a note to a given regimental number reads that "the writer" had in fact left a blank for this regiment (6 n. 1), yet the next footnote is credited to the "Editor" (8 n. 2). The presumption that the former footnote might refer to Ned ("the writer") and the latter to Cooper ("the Editor") turns out not to be true, as in the course of single paragraphs Cooper refers to himself variously as editor and writer. He only intrudes upon the text to point out Ned's errors—"The names of Ned are taken a good deal at random, and, doubtless, are often misspelled" (16 n. 3), reads one note—although many of these errors are of the sort that, presumably, someone in the position of editor would be able to correct. Cooper appears to want to call attention to such minor errata, rather than silently correcting them, as a perverse way to authenticate this narrative of a common sailor.

Strange, though, are the terms under which Cooper does correct Ned's own account. The value of Myers's narrative lies in part in Ned's extensive travels throughout the broader world, from Canton to Quebec, yet Cooper, referring to himself here in the third person, reveals that "in a few instances he has interposed his own greater knowledge of the world, between Ned's more limited experience and the narrative; but this has been done cautiously, and only in cases in which there can be little doubt that the narrator has been deceived by appearances, or misled by ignorance" (2–3). Cooper would have "greater knowledge of the world" than Myers in some senses, certainly, but not in the view of the world that matters here—the view offered by Ned's narrative of global voyaging. The "limited experience" Cooper here attributes to Myers likewise could not refer to any aspects of his life that would confer value on a travel or sea narrative; Ned's experiences are, in this regard, prodigious. Further, stamping Ned as an occasionally "deceived" or "misled" narrator of his own experience undercuts many of the expectations of the narrative genre: that is, whereas readers or critics might disbelieve an account, the text itself should endorse its own veracity, from preface to endnote. Cooper's qualifications seriously undercut his observation that in Ned he finds "a man every way entitled to speak for himself; the want of the habit of communicating his thoughts to the public, alone excepted" (3). It is Cooper, after all, who suggests publishing the narrative, or as Ned puts it, Cooper is "disposed to put into proper form the facts which I can give him" (5). The result, Myers is made to proclaim, is "literally my own story, logged by my old shipmate" (278).

Logbook Truths

The figure of the log is instructive. Shipboard experience is most commonly recorded in the form of the logbook, which in practice is the record of a nautical voyage, complete with distance, longitude and latitude readings, seamen's muster, and occasionally, events of note. Even though most logbooks contain almost no narrative detail, the logbook is often invoked figuratively in sea narratives as a stand-in for truth, or as an objective register of experience. In the mouths of Cooper's sailors, the logbook is primarily referred to as a standard of historical fact. In *The Pilot*, for example, Tom Coffin's boast of having killed more than 100 whales is met with skepticism, to which Tom rejoins, "It's no bragging, sir, to speak a log-book truth!" (202). Tom Coffin here alludes to the fact that a ship's official log is often replicated and amplified by a sailor's narrative or journal, as both record the circularity of a successful voyage. Indeed, logbooks are the model for many sea narratives, which adopt either the logbook's diary-entry form, or at least its insistence on a meticulous chronological progression. Logs likewise display the precision of navigational measurements and reflect the discipline of record-keeping practices aboard ship. They presume a linear narrative structure and make date, time, and location a vital narrative preoccupation of sea fiction. The metaphor is elastic for Cooper; he makes the reach of the log-book far more expansive in his fiction than it would customarily be in practice. Ever alert to a useful nautical metaphor to describe mortality, Cooper observes in *The Pilot*, for example, that human intervention "can do but little to clear the log-account of a man whose watch is up for this world" (249). He recognizes the poetic value of the rigor of a log's documentation in the face of the inscrutability of a sea that permits no records.

More significantly, in his 1828 preface to the first edition of *The Red Rover*, Cooper avows that "the true Augustan age of literature can never exist until works shall be as accurate, in their typography, as a 'log-book,' and as sententious, in their matter, as a 'watch-bill' " (425). In elevating the logbook and the watch bill (the schedule of sailors' labor) to serve as the standards of literary excellence, Cooper underscores several points. First, he stresses that technical accuracy and informational brevity will be goals of his literary efforts. This is a bold choice, given the skepticism magazines like the *North American Review* held in the early years of the nation's literary production for America's "matter-of-fact sort of people," presumably inadequate to literary attention.[64] Second, Cooper asserts the value of both the American mariner and his writings, since they will stand as a model for classic ("Augustan") literary achievement. But the final and most important point that Cooper makes in this passage from *Red Rover* concerns bookmaking. The "typography" of the logbook is what is most valued here, as well as the admirably pithy—or well-edited—watch bill. This sentence concludes a paragraph in the preface to *Red Rover* in which Cooper apologizes for inaccuracies any "keen-eyed critic of the ocean" might spot, such as "a rope rove through the wrong leading-block, or a term spelt in such a manner as to destroy its true sound" (425). And although he hopes such critics will impute such errors simply to "ignorance on the part of a brother," Cooper's real target for blame is the bookmaker. He continues, "It must be remembered that there is an undue proportion of landsmen employed in the mechanical as well as the more spiritual part of bookmaking, a fact which, in itself, accounts for the numberless imperfections that still embarrass the respective departments of the occupation" (425). The "landsmen" of the book trade bear responsibility for a sea novel's failures, which could be textual (in the form of inaccurate typography), or what Cooper calls "spiritual," which seems to indicate a failure of editorial or industrial support. Even as Cooper positions the publisher or printer as an antagonist to the seaman author, he provides the possibility that the "undue proportion of landsmen" in the trade might someday be evened out. Sailors, he implies, should enter the trade in order to ensure the kind of literary accuracy that could have "mechanical" as well as "spiritual" dimensions.

For all Cooper's insistence on the logbook truth of his edition of *Ned Myers*, however, such truth-value proved of little interest to readers. In a letter Cooper wrote to his wife two months after the narrative's publication, he complained, "I am afraid 'Ned' has not done much after all. No one I meet, appears to know any thing of it, and, you know, these people wait to be told what to do, say, or think by the newspapers. The last have maintained a dead silence. Nothing but murders appear to move the public mind now, and even murders begin to be stale."[65] A public dining on critical opinion and hungry for fresher and more startling tales of truth chose to pass on Cooper's latest fare. The truth-value of a narrative helps sell its story, in every sense. While his old friend, navy man William Bradford Shubrick, praises the volume as a "pleasant . . . compagnon de voyage," Shubrick does express concern that the narrative's value as a tale of truth might not be made evident in the literary marketplace: "It is to be regretted I think that the book is advertised in some of the papers as 'a novel.' There are many persons who would read it as a statement of facts who would not read it as a novel."[66] Cooper, in this case, cannot even enjoy the kind of readership that might prefer fiction, for as he frets to Shubrick, "I am inclined to think you are mistaken as to the circulation of Ned Myers. It may have gone off pretty well at Baltimore, but I see no signs of any movement in New York, nor do I hear any thing from Philadelphia. Baltimore is only a secondary market for a book, the place yielding very little to authors I believe; less than any town of its size in America, I think I have been told. I can not even see an advertisement in a New York paper. In long lists of other works, Ned is not even named."[67] The attention to the marketing and reception of the work that Cooper displays above is consistent with his method of promoting his works to publishers. A tireless agitator for American copyright law, Cooper tended to be very precise in his demands of publishers. Here, provocatively, *Ned Myers*'s progress as a text is discussed as a hopeful mimic of the real Ned Myers's own maritime circulation.

Ned Myers was first published in November 1843 in America by Lea & Blanchard of Philadelphia and in Britain by Richard Bentley of London; both were Cooper's usual publishers. The quality of these simultaneous editions varied widely, however. The American edition was cheaply printed, in wrappers, and its front cover lists the price at 37½ cents; it featured ads for volumes ranging from *The Complete Cook*—a domestic treatise, oddly, not the narratives of the famous explorer—to the novels of Smollett, Fielding, and Cooper himself. The quality of this edition was consistent with many of Lea & Blanchard's productions of the time.[68] None of the advertised books cost more than 50 cents, with the exception of a handsome bound set of Cooper's *History of the Navy*.[69] The British edition, on the other hand, was bound in two volumes, the spine of which read, "Edited by F. Cooper, Esq., Author of 'The Pilot,' 'The Spy,' etc."; it did not include advertisements, nor was the price listed. This wide discrepancy in the print quality of various editions of *Ned Myers* reflects Cooper's own sense of the unusual status of this particular volume.

For the finer quality of the British edition was not, ultimately, predictive of the narrative's success. Cooper was anxious to see *Ned Myers* in a cheaper edition, as he wrote to Bentley: "I anticipate an extensive sale for this book, which has been read in sheets here, by two or three good judges, who think it *must* take. . . . I think you ought to get this book out in a popular form, though you know your own market."[70] When Bentley revealed that he intended a run of only 750 copies, Cooper became concerned by what seemed to him an "extraordinarily small edition" and pushed further for "a cheap edition to make returns of such a book," which Cooper told Bentley would become "a standard book of its class."[71] Cooper's distress increased when Bentley replied that the attention given to *Ned Myers* had been unfavorable, especially in comparison with Dana's *Two Years before the Mast*; this, according to Bentley, obviated any advantage in issuing a cheap edition. Agitated, Cooper attempted one last sally, writing to Bentley nearly six months after the book was published, "Do you not mean to publish a cheap edition of Ned Myers? Or have you done it? That is the form in which to circulate such a work."[72] Bentley reported that since no copies of *Ned Myers* had been sold in the preceding three months, he was "persuaded that a cheap edition would not succeed."[73]

Cooper's further justification to Bentley that the demands of veracity would not permit him to embroider Myers's narrative into a length of two volumes is arresting: "I was writing truth, and did not feel justified in spinning out the facts, and as to any comments of my own they would have impaired the identity of the whole affair. I was forced to stop, when Ned had no more to say."[74] Caught between the literary market's interest in tales strictly of truth and his own instinct for "spinning out the facts," Cooper finds that he must repress his drive to expand a narrative he hints is incomplete. To have intruded too much would have "impaired the identity" of the work, he writes. But what, finally, is the identity of *Ned Myers*? One that requires cheap publication, apparently, in order to meet an authenticating "standard" of its peculiar class. In writing to Bentley that he has "anticipated that [*Ned Myers*] will become a standard book of its class," Cooper reveals how strategic his embrace of the form of the first-person sea narrative has been. But this strategy does not earn Editor Cooper the esteem or sales of a narrative like Dana's.

Myers's own reluctance to esteem his life story is not typical of the genre of sea writing, in which sailors might acknowledge the comparatively debased status of seamen in the broader culture but would almost never debase their own value. That is, Dana's reform-minded sea narrative had insisted on the value of the individual laboring sailor, whereas Ned Myers could not bring himself to accept a promotion. The text of *Ned Myers* registers both the changes and distortions of the genre of the maritime narrative between the 1820s and 1840s and Cooper's own struggles in the face of these changes. His unease with the form is a reminder that the impetus to introduce Ned's narrative to a reading public did not, crucially, come from the laboring sailor himself. Sea narrative writing may not have been of the highest class, but it had its standards.

Part II MARITIME EPISTEMOLOGY

AND CRISIS

4 THE SEA EYE

In the first half of this book my aim has been to detail the participation of antebellum American sailors in literary print culture: how they achieved literacy, how they acquired and shared books while at sea, and what forms their own forays into authorship took. By the 1840s, sea writing was a well-established genre, and its practitioners drew on several important antecedents. Captivity in North Africa motivated the first collection of sailor writing. The nautical fictions of James Fenimore Cooper subsequently built on the interest in America's maritime standing and history that emerged after the War of 1812, when sailors were relatively safer from piracy and impressment. The narrative model provided by Dana's *Two Years before the Mast*, in turn, became the touchstone for the literary productions of dozens of common seamen. In discussing the literary culture of American sailors, I have been interested in how their working lives coexisted with—indeed, mutually drove—their imaginative lives. In the first three chapters, my attention to the intellectual lives of seamen has been focused on their reading practices and on the formal and rhetorical means through which their writings presented nautical experience to their audience. I now turn to the theoretical work that sailor narratives perform. The three chapters that follow explore the system of maritime knowledge of seamen's narratives in its visual aspects, its textual incarnation, and its moments of failure.

In the second half of this book I propose that sailors developed a materialist epistemology by which the practices of mechanical labor become the empirical basis for both applied and imaginative knowledge.[1] Their narratives insist on a recognition of the physical work that enables moments of reflection and speculation. Sailors were not unconscious mechanics; they accumulated knowledge through physical and mental work, yielding a generalized form of nautical expertise. In turn, this expertise allowed them to "read" the sea as a text, a form of vision I call the "sea eye," a term derived from sailors' vernacular. The sea eye extends beyond the mechanics and the peculiarities of shipboard labor to encompass the intellectual and cultural sphere of writing.

For seamen, the notion of work had a meaning different from that of contemporary writers who also contemplated labor and literature together. Cindy Weinstein and Nicholas K. Bromell have written the most compelling explorations of the scene of writing as work in antebellum America. As Bromell states the question, "What happens when we read a literary work (as product) *through* literary work (as activity)?" For Weinstein, too, the moments when authors call attention to their own literary labor expose the effort behind an art that should appear effortless.[2] Acknowledging the difficulty of representing work in textual form, both Bromell and Weinstein invoke Ralph Waldo Emerson's well-known directive, "But do your work, and I shall know you. Do your work, and you shall reinforce yourself."[3] Emerson's formulation reflects a contemporary interest in the potential union of manual and mental labor, visible in social experiments such as Brook Farm. Yet the mental laborers represented by Emerson and the other prominent literary figures discussed by Bromell and Weinstein were not, in fact, manual laborers. For all their conception of their literary exertions as work—and despite the broader cultural interest in developing notions of professionalization—Emerson and his contemporaries began from a position as literary laborers. That is, their interest in manual work emerged from their experience of intellectual work, and the analyses of Bromell and Weinstein proceed along an analogous trajectory. What I am interested in exploring is the inverse case: what happens when the scene of manual work is primary and intellectual work materializes from the experience of physical labor? The subsequent chapters are mindful of the general antebellum interest in the symbiotic relationship of mental and bodily work, but to sailors, the kind of work imagined by the contemporary discourse could only be metaphorical. The view that seamen took of the matter is the subject of what follows, and this view, while retaining speculative aspects, is based on material experience.

The sea is an irregular environment for labor, and the nineteenth-century ship that took the ocean as a work space had no analogue in the factory, the shop, or the farm. Maritime work was precarious. As dangerous as factory work could be in the late eighteenth and nineteenth centuries, maritime work was exceptionally deadly, as accidents, storms, disease, and drowning claimed many sailors. Most sailors were wage laborers, but they could not readily walk off the job site or be replaced. Although their work was divided into shifts, called watches, sailors were subject to the erratic and inexorable demands of weather. The ship's captain was an absolute boss, against whom there was little recourse; action against a tyrannical captain could be judged mutinous and punishable by death. Well into the middle of the nineteenth century, until a successful reform effort driven by sailors themselves, captains had the authority to administer corporal punishment in the form of flogging. Such was the brutality of this practice that sailors routinely compared flogging victims to chattel slaves and captains to slavemasters. Labor reformers who focused on the mills at Lowell, for example, did not have to contend with the licensed whipping of factory workers.

Yet for enduring such hardships sailors were not especially well compensated. The merchant service and related trades paid seamen a monthly wage based on rank and experience. Their pay was often withheld until the end of a voyage; many seamen thereafter squandered their accumulated wages while carousing ashore between voyages. In lieu of banks some sailors deposited their savings with port landlords, many of whom proved untrustworthy or exploitative and were coined "landsharks." The more speculative whaling industry was a general exception to the system of wage labor, as it held on to a payment system essentially feudal in nature. Whalemen were promised a set fraction of a voyage's profits, called a lay; an unsuccessful voyage could therefore financially capsize ordinary seamen as well as ship owners and investors.

In its codes and its structure, maritime work was necessarily collective; by virtue of sailors' geographical isolation, time off duty was spent communally as well. Leisure at sea, like labor, was dictated (and often abbreviated) by the environment. Mariners at rest spent time mending clothing, overhauling gear damaged by use or weather, writing letters home, reading, and telling stories or yarns. Their attention to and concern for order, neatness, and utility speaks to the paradoxical domesticity of life at sea.[4] The economic system of maritime labor—anomalous in its setting, schedule, and demands—reflected its natural environment to a degree unmatched by other forms of nineteenth-century work. Seamen's desire for control and management of their space of both work and leisure became especially important, if especially fraught, given the ocean's hostility to the imposition of human will. Marcus Rediker, in his work on the collectivity of eighteenth-century Anglo-Atlantic maritime labor, explains how sailors responded to this circumstance: "Their outlook, fundamentally shaped by the nature and the setting of their work, was based upon an essentially materialistic view of nature, a desire to make an omnipotent nature seem orderly and comprehensible, and a need to entrust to each other their prospects for survival."[5] In Rediker's formulation, sailors' materialism is grounded in their observation of a causal relationship between their environment and their work, and this observation, for Rediker, tended to ignore the extent to which historical patterns or economic realities dictated the conditions of their labor.

Yet sailors, as I argue, had an awareness of the broader material conditions that structured their labor—that is, not just the conditions of the natural or physical world, but of the economic and hierarchical realities of labor as well. The labor of sailors followed a strict set of codes and forms, as dramatized in their writing, and when these practices were not enacted to the letter, the results could be ruinous. For one, the floating industry of the ship required every hand to operate in synchronicity for survival; there were no superfluous workers among the crew. Furthermore, the presence of a system, a transparent set of rules for conduct, was presumed to help prevent seamen from becoming overwhelmed by the natural environment and its frequently fatal indifference to the presence of humans.

In the necessary simultaneity of their management of domestic space and work space, then, sailors developed a view of the world—what Rediker calls their "outlook"—that strove to accumulate information and experience while keeping tight control on the potential for such knowledge to proliferate without limit. Sailors sought to allow their labor to facilitate experience and understanding rather than restrict it; at the same time, they recognized that autonomous intellectual activity disengaged from the physical experience of labor could be both physically and economically hazardous. For at sea, the alienated labor of shipboard industry was, compared with the hazards of shipwreck or other forms of loss, the lesser of two evils. The very conditions of labor that might seem otherwise to render sailors subalterns became the very means through which they could manage their intellectual and working lives. In their desire to make labor and thought coextensive, antebellum sailors are unlike more familiar figures such as the late-century seamen in Joseph Conrad's *Heart of Darkness* or *The Nigger of the "Narcissus."* In his trip up the Congo River in *Heart of Darkness*, for example, Marlow avoids being seduced by the perceived wildness of the shore by maintaining his focus on "rivets," or the physical integrity of his ship. Rather than succumb to the madness around him, Marlow says, he "had to mess about with white-lead and strips of woolen blanket helping to put bandages on those leaky steam-pipes. . . . I had to watch the steering, and circumvent those snags." He concludes, "There was surface-truth enough in these things to save a wiser man."[6] Marlow believes that his focus on the practice of his job can "save" him from the dangers of unregulated thought. But nineteenth-century sailors did not imagine their practical knowledge to be wholly divorced from figurative understanding, and as I argue, their narratives stipulate an experiential vision of the world that encompasses both labor and speculation.

Sailors were not automatons, and at the scene of their work they found opportunity for reflection. Their narratives stress the interpenetration of these two spheres of labor, manual and intellectual, and propose strategies for the difficult work of managing both tasks at sea. Mariner William Ray, for example, explains what happens when sailors cannot maintain a balance. He describes the problem in terms of seamen's carousing while in port between cruises: "Their minds, actions and passions being so long under restraint, like water, obstructed by a mound, when yet loose overflows its channels, they lose themselves in the torrent of dissipation and lasciviousness, and are caught like fishes when the pond is drained; and like them, impatient to return to their congenial and favorite element, they plunge again into the vortex of the ocean, and entangle themselves with perplexities, from which they are unable to extricate the mind, until the tedious routine of another cruise."[7] The sailor needs to be able to regulate both his working self and his thinking self, for each depends on the other. Labor knowledge and practice, in Ray's formulation, can cure the "perplexities" that can afflict the sailor caught in the "vortex of the ocean." The solvent for the corrosive effects of unbounded thought, then, becomes "another cruise."

Strikingly, maritime experience is routinely figured in sea writing as a form of reading or book knowledge, which requires—and produces a special capacity for vision. The narratives produced by sailors after the 1830s, subsequent to Cooper's early novels as well as the earlier Barbary narratives, demonstrate a shared interest in identifying the experiential eye acquired by able seamen. William Leggett's *Naval Stories*, for example, features a young midshipman "full of blood and blue veins" who has an "inexperienced eye"; to this novice—who thinks he "see[s] all there is to be seen"—a visible calm means a "dull and lazy night."[8] Only the "practiced and keen eye" of a weathered old seaman, Vangs, who unlike the well-placed midshipman is a common sailor, can discern a coming gale. He presents his experiential knowledge of the future storm to the young officer as a text: "I read [the storm] in a book I have studied through many a long cruise."[9] What he reads in the sea's book, in fact, is not just the "dirty" weather illegible to his younger shipmate but his own imminent death at the hands of that very storm. Vangs's "book" is the accumulated record of his life at sea, and reading is presented as a metaphor for sailor experience. Vangs's sea eye is represented here not merely as the experienced, reactive organ of a master sailor but as a proscriptive tool that can create the text it reads. This text is not necessarily available to the young officer, however, who must receive it as a third party, removed from the text and the sea eye that scripts it. Similarly, in Cooper's *The Pilot*, the common seaman Tom Coffin has "studied" the weather; he avers to his captain, "It is hard to learn the true signes of the weather, Captain Barnstable, and none get to know them well, but such as study little else." Long Tom further observes, "A man is soon expart" in knowing how "to knot a reef-point or pass a gasket, but it takes the time of his nat'ral life to larn to know the weather."[10] The visionary knowledge that a long term of maritime service grants cannot be easily picked up by an officer, no matter how well schooled. Long Tom becomes naturalized to the sea in a way that still retains his knowledge as a form of reading practice.

George Little's narrative of his life at sea likewise presents nautical knowledge, or "reckoning," as both experiential and textual, and the veteran's job is to point out to the greenhand what in his own relative inexperience he cannot read. Little records a conversation with an "old salt" whose long tenure at sea he details; the salt tells him, "I'll miss my reck'ning, if we don't have some play with these shooting-irons tomorrow." When Little questions this logic, the veteran replies, "I never knew such a day and night of calm as this, in all my going to sea, that was not followed by a brush or a storm of some kind."[11] In Dana's *Two Years before the Mast* an analogous moment finds the tyro Dana chastised by a more experienced hand, who tells him, "You think, 'cause you been to college, you know better than anybody. You know better than them 'as seen it with their own eyes. You wait till you've been to sea as long as I have, and you'll know."[12] And in yet another example, William Henry Gillman invokes the "lessons" contained in the "boundless" ocean's "volumes" in a letter written at sea to his sister: "Happy is he, who can look out on these infinities with a mind strengthened by the lessons of their wonderful volumes."[13] Their narratives present the vision of sailors as the result of an aggregation of experience rather than as a passive exposure to God's book of nature. Their knowledge is composite, learned collectively and supplemented by the random bits of wisdom picked up in social and literary exchange among different crews and ports.

Yet if experiential knowledge is imagined as reading a book, then the practice of reading or crafting a book is in turn figured as akin to sailing. The practice of writing aboard ship, whether in keeping the ship's log or in more literary creation, is presented in sea narratives as an exemplary model for seeing or documenting the world. In other words, rather than presenting fantastic images of distant lands, sea writing brings the ship and its practices ashore in a way that legitimizes its form of expression. Furthermore, many mariners' narratives even depict books as ships, or ships as books, making each a vehicle for sailor experience. The naval memoir *Life in a Man-of-War* embodies this metaphor most fully, understanding narrative production as a form of ship's governance and recognizing little difference between a trim ship and a well-printed text. The anonymous author provides the most notable example of this process when he uses the preface to his narrative as a way to talk about prefaces. In doing so, he demonstrates a playfully acute sense of both contemporary textual production and sailors' involvement in book making. His fellow seamen know what literary publication demands and are intimate with the geographies of both the sailing ship and the print public sphere. The narrator explains, in an arresting passage,

> I had made up my mind whilst on our homeward-bound passage to slip the moorings of the present little *Craft* and let her glide before the public without anything in the shape of the prefatory remark; but as soon as I mentioned the circumstance to some of the *literati of the galley*, they condemned loudly and emphatically my determination. "What," cried one old weatherworn customer, "print your book without a preface, that ain't ship-shape no how; I thought you have more *savey* than all that; damme, man, now-a-days a book without a preface is like a topmast without a *fid*, its whole dependence gone, small as it is."—"Aye," chimed in a second, "or like a purser's jacket, without naval buttons; nothing to set off the quality of the article."—"Or like," remarked a third, "a sailor's jack-knife without a *laniard*, a most essential thing wanting."—"Or like a gun without a *touch-hole*," cried a fourth, "well enough to look at, but *that* little thing required to give it force and effect."
>
> They would have assailed me with fifty other nautical similes, to prove that my work wouldn't be worth a single cent without the appendage they were so anxious for; and to save myself from their incessant solicitations, I promised I would try my hand at something of the kind; and so, readers, I have made a beginning.[14]

This passage exemplifies the work of American sea writing, as I have been arguing. For one, the narrator purports to write his narrative during his actual naval cruise, and what is more, he contemplates how it will appear in print long before he even returns to shore. His fellow sailors—whom he describes later in the book as the "Literary Tars" for their avidity in selecting books from the ship's library—are involved at every stage of the production of the narrative, from its composition to its publication. These mariners, "*the literati of the galley*," know what a preface's place is in the narrative: it confers a flourish, a descriptive touch that is nevertheless crucial for more than its ceremonial position. The preface, the narrator's shipmates argue, offers the reader access to the narrative. The men conflate book making with seaworthiness, and to them the comparison is not idle: they are active laborers and readers alike. Most significantly, the simile-wielding sailors are mindful of the demands of contemporary publication. "Now-a-days," prefaces are textual requirements; anyone with "*savey*" would know how to "print [his] book."

Sailors integrate labor with reflection through the figure of an experiential eye. They apply their experiential vision in the narratives in part by their close attention to the technical requirements of labor, which is closely related to their interest in the material details of book making and textual production. What I call the sea eye, taking my cue from sailor writing, reflects both their specialized labor knowledge and their absorption of broader antebellum culture through their consumption and production of literary texts. Incorporating both the sailor's specialized labor knowledge and his special vantage point in an environment inaccessible to most people, the sea eye identifies the laboring body of the sailor as a vital component of imaginative vision. In their writings, sailors portray their experiential knowledge as an eye that can "read" maritime conditions invisible to the novice or the landsperson. More broadly, the sea eye synthesizes labor and cognitive practice, primarily in the form of sailors' literary production.

While the sea eye encompasses seamen's actual views at sea, I do not intend the term to describe optics alone; in addition, the sea eye synthesizes the presumably incommensurate experiences of labor and reflection. In the section that follows, I describe how sailors invoke the figure of the eye in providing a perspective both before and atop the mast. Melville's *Moby-Dick*, which I discuss later in this chapter, provides a theory of how the broader genre of sailor writing combines the spheres of physical and intellectual activity. Melville's debts to—and borrowings from—dozens of contemporary maritime narratives have been frequently noted in critical history.[15] But I propose that we consider *Moby-Dick* as a commonplace book, an accretion of fragments of sailor experience, which in turn identifies all sea narratives as commonplace books testifying to sailors' collective labor and literary knowledge. In this formulation, the "Etymology" and "Extracts" sections with which *Moby-Dick* begins provide the key to understanding how book knowledge and labor practice can produce a materialist vision. As the assimilation of fragmentary knowledge drawn from the totality of a sailor's maritime experience, the sea eye functions analogously as the epistemological apparatus that grows out of the material practices it organizes. By this I mean that the sea eye is an industry that helps process the broader forces that produce maritime literature.

THE VIEW FROM THE MASTHEAD

The perspective provided by the sea eye has practical as well as imaginative applications and reflects the paradox of space at sea. While the ocean appears boundless and vast, the experience of shipboard life is characterized by confinement and tight regulation. A conceptual oscillation between the broad and the narrow is evident in the records of maritime life. Shipping out to see the world, a young sailor soon discovers that there is nothing to view while on a long cruise: no interruptions to the horizon, no landmarks. In describing their first voyages, most seamen stress the emptiness of an environment they had presumed to be full of interest. This is rendered comic in *Moby-Dick*: Peleg instructs the restless Ishmael to look out to sea at the "unlimited, but exceedingly monotonous" prospect, without "the slightest variety," and mocks him, "Can't ye see the world where you stand?"[16] But for most sailors the experience is unsettling. "It is certainly a great event in the life of every man when land for the first time fades from his vision and he experiences the feelings of a wanderer upon the trackless ocean," Nathaniel Taylor wrote of his whaling voyage; "Oh, what a throng of deep thoughts and feelings moves the heart and imagination at such a time—thoughts which find no voice, for they are unutterable."[17] William Whitecar feels a similar sense of dislocation after losing sight of shore for the first time:

> With the consequent hurry and excitement attendant on tacking ship, little leisure was left to us for reflection; but as the sun sank low in the horizon, and the blue hills of the land of my birth, and love, and veneration—the home of me and mine—were gradually becoming more and more indistinct—as I looked around me on the expanse of water, extending on every side, I felt alone; and then, and not until then, did I feel the momentous character of what I had undertaken; . . . I leaned my head on the bulwarks, and felt as if I knew what desolation and heartsickness were for the first time. This state of affairs could not last long, so I rallied and attempted to look brave and careless.[18]

The tyro's response to this "trackless" vastness is to turn his eye inward in order to focus on the behavioral codes and internal workings of the ship: its rigging, its routines, its special language, all of which are rendered in maritime writing in exquisite detail. Only after his comfortable mastery of the mechanics of sail is the novice able to manage his fears and to see more than blankness in the sea around him.

Once the sailor is out of sight of land and out of contact with the domestic and sentimental comforts of what Whitecar calls "the home of me and mine," his physical and mental energies are initially consumed by the immediate demands of the ship. At this stage, most find that their working and thinking selves are subject to a temporary separation and that their vision of life at sea (especially for those new to the trade) is confined to the mechanics of maritime labor. Yet a signal moment, recurring in many sea narratives, illustrates the instant when the sailor's vision encompasses the potential simultaneity of manual and intellectual labor. This comes when a sailor is on lookout duty in the ship's masthead—the highest point of the ship—alone and with scant foot- or handhold. When aloft, he is supposed to be keeping a sharp eye for whales, for rocks, for other ships, or for land, as the case may be. Yet instead of focusing solely on the task at hand, the sailor often finds that this vantage point provides him with an opportunity to exercise his vision in a way different from the one mandated by his job. "What scene can be more sublimely beautiful than the sea when gazed upon from the mast-head of a ship," the narrator of *Jack in the Forecastle* wonders; "What a time this is for study, for contemplation, for enjoyment!" This moment of pleasure and rumination could only be possible, however, if the sea were calm and if "the energies which call THE SAILOR into life would no longer be necessary."[19] *Jack in the Forecastle* suggests the difficulty of reconciling the demands of work with the pleasures of "study" and "contemplation."

Some mariners used their time aloft for the concrete enjoyments of literary exploration. In fact, the pleasures of reading while on duty were common enough that sailors could use reading as an excuse when caught napping in the masthead. Nathaniel Ames's turn in his *Mariner's Sketches* finds him on a " 'lookout' in the main top mast cross trees from twelve till four." When Ames dozes, he is confronted by an officer who accuses him of falling asleep. " 'No, sir, I was reading,' " Ames counters, and at this the officer demands to see the book. "I produced from my bosom a volume of 'Woodstock,' that had just arrived on the coast," Ames writes; he is reprimanded, " 'Next time you have a look-out, don't you take a book aloft with you.' "[20] Even though in this instance Ames was in fact not reading while neglecting his lookout duty, it is notable that he carries a book with him in any case. Ames is not the only one to take books into the tops; J. Sidney Henshaw's nautical memoir recalls the punishment suffered by the ship's ample library in the face of the notorious storms at Cape Horn: "A far worse fate seemed to attend the books in [sailors'] hands when coming around the Cape. Many were taken by the winds from the tops, . . . and floated into the dirty scuppers, and more of them were torn or dropped overboard."[21] As attractive as the masthead might be to the literary-minded sailor, it presents clear disciplinary and environmental hazards to one spending time in study.

Such hazards extend to the production of literary texts, too. The winds that disrupt Henshaw's reading affect William Nevens's ability to produce his narrative. Although Nevens endeavored to keep journals during his forty-year career at sea, they were lost in various storms and wrecks. "I now feel the loss of those journals, which the deep, ever insatiate, and ever yawning to

devour, has deprived me of," he laments at the commencement of his narrative.[22] Such losses are not only caused by weather; Richard Henry Dana's
journal disappeared along with the sea chest in which it was stored when
Dana returned to the Boston docks. Thus when the author of *Life in a Man-
of-War* offers his "humble attempt at bookmaking" to the critics, he wishes to
remind them of the difficulty a sailor has "with regard to bringing his ideas to
a *focus*; and how much the vociferous turmoil and noisy outcry, that assail him
at all turns, from the 'high and giddy mast' to the confines of the hold below,
help to bring his mind to anything like a contemplative mood."[23]

The experience of standing in the masthead represents the sailor's struggle
to regulate both his working and thinking selves while at sea. The elevation
and the solitariness of the sailor's position, combined with what Herman
Melville describes in *Moby-Dick*'s "Mast-Head" chapter as the "drowsy"
winds and the "languor" of a ship's movement, can impart a "sublime un-
eventfulness" to the lookout's time aloft. In turn, this relaxation of climactic
and shipboard responsibility—and the rare time alone—encourages the sailor
to keep "sorry guard" by engaging in inward reflection. But the problem in
thinking too much and working not enough is not just disciplinary: when
Ishmael takes his own turn in the masthead in *Moby-Dick*, he finds himself
physically imperiled by the lure of disembodied thought. The danger of a
vision produced by the "lean brow and hollow eye" of the contemplative
masthead stander extends, further, to the material concerns of the ship.
"Whales must be seen before they can be killed," Ishmael points out, and by
failing to engage in the lookout duties to which he was assigned, a "sunken-
eyed Platonist will tow you ten wakes round the world, and never make you
one pint of sperm the richer" (158–59). In *Moby-Dick*, a sailor's metaphorical
reading profile can indicate his philosophical predisposition as well as his
seaworthiness; in his reference to a whaleman as an intellectual "Platonist,"
Ishmael alerts captains to the sailor who ships "with the Phaedon instead of
Bowditch in his head" (158). Most sailors, of course, would be familiar with
Nathaniel Bowditch's standard sea manual *Practical Navigator*. Yet the *Phaedon*
is a curious textual counterpart for the speculative mariner; Plato's treatise on
immortality (and idealism) would seem to be incompatible with a job whose
mortal dangers (and empiricism) were real and present for the laboring sailor.

Melville's depiction of Ishmael's proclivity for reflection while standing a
masthead watch has been compared, in criticism of *Moby-Dick*, to Washington Irving's "The Voyage," the opening sketch in *The Sketch-Book* (1819–
20).[24] The view that Irving's Geoffrey Crayon sees from the masthead is far
different, however, from the one seen by Ishmael and other common sailors
before the mast. Predictably for a gentleman sea passenger, alienated from the

labor that propels the ship over the waters, Crayon finds that "all is vacancy" on his Atlantic passage, a view that real sailors soon revise. The emptiness of this "vast space of waters" to Crayon is so complete as to seem a "blank page in existence."[25] Yet there are moments when Crayon finds matter enough for contemplation:

> I said that at sea all is vacancy; I should correct the impression. To one given to daydreaming and fond of losing himself in reveries, a sea voyage is full of subjects for meditation; but then they are the wonders of the deep and of the air, and rather tend to abstract the mind from worldly themes. I delighted to loll over the quarter railing, or climb to the maintop, of a calm day, and muse for hours together on the tranquil bosom of a summer's sea; to gaze upon the piles of golden clouds just peering above the horizon, fancy them some fairy realms, and people them with a creation of my own; to watch the gentle undulating billows, rolling their silver volumes, as if to die away on those happy shores.[26]

Crayon's experience of life at sea is dreamy and enchanted; the sea is "tranquil," the waves are "gently undulating," and all natural forces take on the generous, unthreatening air of "daydreaming." That his reveries are unimpeded by "worldly themes" should not be surprising. Were he a laboring seaman, Crayon would be compelled by duty to ascend the masthead, yet as a passenger who climbs to the height of the maintop only by choice, he is under no responsibility to look out for anything but his own interior thoughts. Nor is his reverie interrupted by duty. The "subjects for meditation" that a sea voyage can suggest for an idle passenger, therefore, are necessarily passive or pictorial.

Tracing Melville's genealogy through Irving has been useful to the many scholars who have noted metaphysical concerns in *Moby-Dick*, yet Ishmael's physical danger—the very threat countermanded by the proper performance of his job—contains little of the abstract. In its attention to the conjunction of work and contemplation, *Moby-Dick* invokes the many sailor narratives of the 1830s and 1840s that feature similarly fraught scenes of masthead standing. In a typical scene, from J. Ross Browne's *Etchings of a Whaling Cruise*, the narrator describes the masthead as a "little world of peace and seclusion, where I could think over past times without interruption. . . . It was here I could cast a retrospective glance at my past life." When distracted by thought, however, Browne too becomes physically endangered: "Whenever I became so wrapped up in these visionary dreams as to forget that I was not placed at the mast-head for that special purpose, the loud, harsh voice of the captain would arouse me, with a friendly hint to 'keep a sharp lookout for whales, or he'd wake me up with a rope's end.' "[27]

The relationship between a young sailor's achievement of nautical skills and his ability to contemplate the broader world is made explicit in the popular *Jack in the Forecastle*; author Hawser Martingale relates, "I devoted the hours which I could spare from my appropriate duties to the acquisition of a knowledge of seamanship, and developing its mysteries. I was fond of going aloft when the vessel was rolling or pitching in a strong breeze. I loved to mount upon the top-gallant yard. . . . I also loved to gaze from this elevated position upon the broad ocean, . . . [where] I indulged in daydreams of the most pleasing description." But the "mysteries" of seamanship that Martingale ponders while aloft pose a danger for him as they do for Ishmael, although this time at the hands of a superior officer: "A check was suddenly put to my vagabond thoughts and flowery visions, and I was violently dragged back to the realities of life by a strong hand, which, seizing me roughly by the collar, jerked me to my feet!"[28] The mariners in these works cannot long indulge the quiet conditions that engender Crayon's sea vision of "fairy realms."

Ishmael's masthead reverie in *Moby-Dick*, in which disembodied communion with the universe is interrupted by the threat of bodily death, has commonly been read as a rejection of Emersonian transcendental vision as principally outlined in *Nature*. Understood in the context of the masthead stands of the other sea narratives of the period, however, Ishmael's vision in fact offers a perceptive rereading of an essential condition that enables transcendent thought: a sturdy material base. Emerson's "transparent" eyeball, after all, relies for its tripod on the "bare ground," the "fields and woods" of the physical landscape. Rather than "becom[ing] nothing" when seeking an "original relation to the universe," as Emerson's formulation in *Nature* would hold, a sailor seeks to align the practice of contemplation with his labor experience.[29] What Melville seems to be particularly revising in *Moby-Dick* is the idea of the transparency of Emerson's eyeball, its reception of universal light as well as its immaterial nature. In "The Mast-Head" Ishmael cautions the dreamer: "Over Descartian vortices you hover. And perhaps, at mid-day, in the fairest weather, with one half-throttled shriek you drop through that transparent air into the summer sea, no more to rise for ever" (159).[30] The very transparency that allows for successfully looking out from the masthead —the fulfillment of the sailor's job—becomes a danger for the sailor who wholly forsakes his physical task in favor of incorporeal vision. The pastoral conditions of "summer," "mid-day," and fair weather in Melville's warning refer to what Leo Marx has called, in discussing the scene, the "horrifying idea of a fall from the heights of pastoral reverie into the undersea vortex of material reality."[31] Marx's (and Melville's) "vortex" here calls to mind William Ray's "vortex of the ocean," in which sailors "entangle themselves with perplexities," as quoted above. And yet Marx's strict dichotomy overstates the case: material reality can support reverie, Melville suggests, but only when the "transparency" that enables the sailor's exercise of his sea eye allows him to "see all," to use Emerson's terms, but does not erase his corporeal self, as when Emerson "become[s] nothing" in his moment of transcendental vision in *Nature*.[32] For Emerson, the transparency of the eye allows it both to see without interference from the corporeal self and to be adapted by others for whom the disembodied eyeball would pose no barrier. The sea eye in maritime narratives, however, provides a model of vision that does not erase the embodied eye. The sea eye provides a vision that is predicated on the sailor's experience of maritime work.

How the eye can perceive, describe, and even possess the landscape has been an enduring topic in American literary history. The form of the discovery narrative, what Wayne Franklin has called "an adventure of the eye alone," allows the discoverer, "through perception alone," to perceive transcendent meaning in a landscape. Other critics have discussed how the Emersonian "eye" as the "I" can, in Richard Poirier's terms, take "visionary possession of America." In Myra Jehlen's articulation, the "I/eye" becomes "not only the worker but the work" that "incarnates" a vision of the physical fact of America.[33] This eye has a generative power to combine discrete elements into a coherent vision, one that has both a material and an imaginative meaning. The importance of an eye that can combine visionary power with material experience (or physical knowledge of a landscape) can be seen, to use one example, in Emerson's own discussion of local perspectival differences. "Certain mechanical changes, a small alteration in our local position, apprizes us of a dualism. We are strangely affected by seeing the shore from a moving ship. . . . The least change in our point of view gives the whole world a pictorial air," he writes in *Nature*. Part of this "dualism" lies in the reader's recognition that "mechanical" change allows for aesthetic change, by which the world can seem "pictorial," neatly arranged and framed by mechanical and artistic energy. This "dualism" is not only locational but vocational, as Emerson describes how the "sensual man" works differently from the "poet," who is invested with the ability to change perspective, to "unfi[x] the land and the sea": "The sensual man conforms thoughts to things; the poet conforms things to his thoughts. The one esteems nature as rooted and fast; the other, as fluid, and impresses his being thereon. To him, the refractory world is ductile and flexible."[34] In Emerson's romantic conception, this "sensual man" has tactile experience of nature but is unable to take visionary possession of it.

Emerson's rejection of the possibility for imaginative engagement by "sensual" or embodied men is related to Rediker's description of seamen's view of nature as materialistic. Both argue that the immediate empirical world alone determines the thoughts of workingmen and, by extension, imply that the sea in particular would be richly evocative of broader meaning only to those who bear no laboring relationship to it. But in their narratives, sailors tell a different story. They find meaningful space for reflection and strive to reconcile the requirements of their job with their intellectual exploration. The resolution of these competing demands, proposed again and again in sailor narratives, comes when a seaman cultivates a vision of the world that makes labor knowledge—in other words, the experience and understanding produced by his commerce with nautical custom—the foundation of any broader contemplation. In this manner antebellum sailor narratives are attuned to what Jonathan Crary has described as a "sweeping transformation in the way in which an observer was figured in a wide range of social practices and domains of knowledge" in the nineteenth century.[35] The account of subjective vision offered by Crary stresses "the inseparability of two models usually presented as distinct and irreconcilable: a physiological observer who will be described in increasing detail by the empirical sciences in the nineteenth century, *and* an observer posited by various 'romanticisms' and early modernisms as the active, autonomous producer of his or her own visual experience."[36] Sea narratives recognize that the universal subjectivity presumed by Emersonian transcendentalism is not passive but inseparable, as Crary suggests, from the physical contours of the "bare ground" that supports it. Sailors were both "physiological observer[s]" and "active, autonomous producer[s]" of their perspectival experience. The narratives they wrote—the product of their coextensive manual and intellectual labor—were, in turn, deeply invested both in the specificity of maritime work and, significantly, in the material form of the narrative texts themselves.

ETYMOLOGIES

When Emily Dickinson wrote, "There is no frigate like a book / To take us lands away," she invoked the potential of literature to afford otherwise distant perspectives.[37] Indeed, many have similarly envisioned literature as capable of literal and metaphorical transportation of readers. Dickinson's simile assumes that travel itself has its limitations, though—no frigate is as good as a book for the kind of intellectual tourism she invokes. For seaman authors of the nineteenth century, however, the relationship between ship and book is more elastic, and meaningfully democratized. The sea eye could produce not only legible seas but also books whose own legibility derives from an acknowledgment of the diversity of the labor practices that created them.

"A Thought on Book-Binding," Melville's impudent review of the Putnam reissue of Cooper's *Red Rover* (discussed in Chapter 3), takes this notion literally. Like the shipmates of the author of *Life in a Man-of-War*, Melville concentrates on the physical text rather than the content of the volume. In doing so, Melville demonstrates an awareness of sailors' own attention to the textuality of their narrative writing and reading and provides a commentary on the state of maritime publishing. The review is worth quoting at length:

> The sight of the far-famed Red Rover, sailing under the sober-hued muslin wherewith Mr. Putnam equips his lighter sort of craft, begets in us a fastidious feeling touching the propriety of such a binding for such a book. Not that we ostentatiously pretend to any elevated degree of artistic taste in this matter—our remarks are but limited to our egotistical fancies. Egotistically, then, we would have preferred for the "Red Rover" a flaming suit of flame-colored morocco, as evanescently thin and gauze-like as possible, so that the binding might happily correspond with the sanguinary, fugitive title of the book. Still better, perhaps, were it bound in jet black, with a red streak round the borders (pirate fashion); or, upon third thoughts, omit the streak, and substitute a square of blood-colored bunting on the back, imprinted with the title, so that the flag of the "Red Rover" might be congenially flung to the popular breeze, after the buccaneer fashion of Morgan, Black Beard, and other free and easy, dare-devil, accomplished gentlemen of the seas.
>
> While, throwing out these cursory suggestions, we gladly acknowledge that the tasteful publisher has attached to the volume a very felicitous touch of the sea superstitions of pirates, in the mysterious cyphers in bookbinders' relievo stamped upon the covers, we joyfully recognise a poetical signification and pictorial shadowing forth of the horse-shoe, which, in all honest and God-fearing piratical vessels, is invariably found nailed to the mast. By force of contrast this clever device reminds us of the sad lack of invention in most of our book-binders.[38]

Melville's opening description of *The Red Rover* as a representative of the "lighter sort of craft" printed by Putnam is not necessarily an insult to Cooper; as a novel, *The Red Rover* would occupy a position historically disparaged as "light." The description of the novel's binding—a "sober-hued muslin"— clues the fact that Melville really targets here "Mr. Putnam" and his use of a generic binding for the edition. Melville's declaration later in the review that books' "bindings should indicate and distinguish their various characters"[39] is contextualized by Jeffrey Groves as part of "the growing realization on the part of mid-nineteenth-century publishers that they could achieve such a qualitative statement through the appearance of their books."[40] What I find more interesting about this passage, however, is how it identifies Cooper's Red Rover—ship, captain, and novel—as embodied in its various forms. Further, the "artistic taste" that Melville disavows but clearly (and "ego-tistically") invokes might speak to the writer's recognition that sea writing accomplishes the embodiment of the figure of the sailor for a land-based reading audience. Sea knowledge can be said to exist as a relationship, the product and result of an interpretive community characterized by the aesthetic relations of readers with the text and not simply a fixed set of terms or events.

Focusing solely on the physical artifact of the reprint is not just a puckish gesture on Melville's part. In panning the novel by refusing to focus on its literary content, Melville directs attention to its position in a larger world of print. As he notes, "That we have said thus much concerning the mere outside of the book whose title prefaces this notice, is sufficient evidence of the fact, that at the present day we deem any elaborate criticism of Cooper's Red Rover quite unnecessary, and uncalled for." His review concludes, "Long ago, and far inland, we read it in our uncritical days, and enjoyed it as much as thousands of the rising generation will, when supplied with such an entertaining volume in such agreeable type."[41] The circumstance of the "present day" seems impor-tant to Melville. In part this could be because Cooper's reputation—and the popularity of *The Red Rover* itself—had been well enough established to preclude any late attacks on the novel. Yet the "present day" Melville cites has as its counterpoint the "uncritical days" in which Melville and the large pool of readers included in his royal "we" first read *The Red Rover*. Several things make that long-ago period "uncritical," including the presumed youth of Cooper's readership (the "rising generation" for whom the reissue is designed is likewise marked as young). The crucial fact that Melville read the volume "far inland," or before his career as a common sailor, also speaks to his uncritical eye; without nautical experience or a developed sea eye, the young "inland" reader would not question the novel scenes presented by *The Red Rover*—featuring the "gentlemen of the seas." Still, the larger point Melville seems to be making here is that Cooper's sea novels were first printed and first read in an age that offered no literary counterpoints: the novelty of their maritime scenes was sufficient recommendation. In the "present day" of Melville's *Literary World* review, sea narratives had proliferated and achieved aesthetic regard to such extent that comparative criticism could be possible and potentially offered by sailors themselves. The terms invoked by Melville reflect the interest, both playful and serious, that sailors took in the material details of the production and consumption of literature.

By paying no attention to the content of Cooper's *Red Rover* in his review and focusing solely on the material text, Melville diagnoses a problem faced by sailor authors: How would readers perceive their narratives? Would they be alienated or confused by the specialized terms of the trade? Would the broader view of the world offered by sailors be legible or even appealing to a land-based public? To address these potential problems, most sailor narratives began with a preface that sought to assure "the general reader" that the sailor's "technical knowledge" would not be "unintelligible."[42] Yet rather than making an attempt to translate unfamiliar terms or references for the comfort of the land-lubber reader, sailors insisted that their readers perform some work. Their narratives ask readers to enter an experiential relationship with the text and to integrate the various pictures of maritime life and labor offered by their writing. Sailors' prefaces argue that such an effort will reward land-based readers with a view of life at sea that approximates the kind of work done by seamen themselves in assimilating a broad range of likewise unfamiliar skills and situations. Readers would theoretically be dissuaded from taking too romantic a view of maritime life—the kind of idealized view offered by those who viewed the sea as a metaphor, say, rather than a sphere of labor—and would instead develop an appreciation for mariner labor based on readers' own efforts to conceive of the material demands of an exceptional environment.

The prefaces to most sea narratives gesture toward literary conventions in advancing this argument, as I discuss in Chapter 1, as they apologize for deficiencies of style and claim the merit of "sterling truth."[43] In this sense they prepare land-based readers for their reading experience by using recognizable literary codes and forms. Melville's own sea writing pays some attention to this convention: *Typee*, *Omoo*, *Mardi*, and *White Jacket* all open with a brief statement about the relevance of the author's own experience to the truthfulness of the narrative that follows (*Redburn* launches without apology). *Moby-Dick*, on the other hand, opens with two hard-to-categorize sections, "Etymology" and "Extracts," whose removal from the narrative text is such that they are routinely not recalled as part of the novel. By this I mean that popular culture remembers the opening line of the novel as the famous invitation, "Call me Ishmael." This effectively erases the book's actual first line ("The pale Usher—threadbare in coat, heart, body, and brain; I see him now") as well as the rest of the "Etymology" and "Extracts" sections from the narrative itself (xv).[44]

The etymology provided, of course, is for the word "whale," and it is followed by a collection of eighty quotations, "extracts" from the long literary history of references to whales, from the Bible to the popular sea narratives of Melville's day. These two opening sections bear no obvious relationship to the prefaces of sailors' narratives, and when critical attention has been paid to "Etymology" and "Extracts," it has seen the sections as adding heft and "ballast" to a mixed-form novel, as well as indicating the difficulty in classifying language or human experience.[45] Most relevantly, Cindy Weinstein reads "Extracts" as a "moving homage to authorial labor," evidence of Melville's authorization by a "community of writers."[46] Yet "Etymology" and "Extracts" are primarily the result, I argue, of a shrewd reading of the genre of sailor narratives. Just as Melville's review of *Red Rover* conflated the material conditions of sailors' labor with the materiality of the literary texts sailors produced and consumed, his composite introductions to *Moby-Dick* theorize the relationship between the sea narrative text and the view of maritime life and labor that sailors strove to provide to the reading public—and which they recounted for their own benefit as well. The example provided by "Etymology" and "Extracts" helps, in turn, the process of assimilating *Moby-Dick*'s seemingly disparate halves, the action-driven plot featuring Ahab and the long treatises on the science of whaling. The sea eye prescribed by sailor writing and revisited time and again in *Moby-Dick* is ultimately able both to integrate the novel's parts and to read its repeated references to books by means of an experiential epistemology.

"Etymology," which opens the book, provides four etymologies of the word "whale," all of which follow different logics: the Hackluyt passage considers the whale through the logic of determinant linguistics; Webster's dictionary addresses the bodily quality of the whale; Richardson's dictionary focuses on the action of the whale; and the iterations of the word in thirteen different languages provide a logic of comparative linguistics (xv–xvi). These etymologies, which are inconsistent yet not in outright contradiction, hint that the process of seeking unity or consistency in *Moby-Dick*—or in anything—may be misguided, despite the book's interest in taxonomy. Yet while definitional or derivational etymologies would presumably be free from subjectivity, such is not the case in "Etymology." The paragraph that opens the section establishes a provenance for the etymologies: they are "supplied by a late consumptive usher to a grammar school" (xv). This "pale Usher" spends his time "dusting his old lexicons and grammars, with a queer handkerchief, mockingly embellished with all the gay flags of all the known nations of the world." His pleasure in the task of dusting the books—not likely a healthy job for one with consumption—is based on its association with death, as the act reminds the ghostly usher of "his mortality." The handkerchief with which he performs this task mocks him in its representation of internationalism and of comprehensive global knowledge ("the known nations"). For this "thread-bare" usher, confined to a lowly grammar school, the scope of the known world is confined to material texts rather than travel or experience. The poverty of the picture of scholarship and knowledge represented by the usher casts the etymological knowledge that follows his introduction in a dim light.

The historical references in published literature to whaling that follow in "Extracts" are similarly furnished by a fictional character: the lowly usher of "Etymology" is matched in "Extracts" by a "Sub-Sub Librarian." The fact that there are embodied characters preserving this information calls attention not only to the textual quotations themselves but also to the conditions of the labor of their assembly. The sub-sub librarian of "Extracts" is a "painstaking burrower and grub-worm" who furnishes the quotations from a hetero-geneous range of books, sacred and profane, fictional and nonfictional (xvii).[47] The narrator stresses the "random" and "higgledy-piggledy" quality of these statements; as encyclopedic as the whaling information provided later in the narrative might be, the extracts do not aim for comprehensiveness. Rather, they afford "a glancing bird's eye view of what has been promis-cuously said, thought, fancied, and sung of Leviathan" (xvii). The promise of a "bird's eye view" evokes the language of the city-mysteries popular in Melville's day; such urban exposés promised readers a view of the city that revealed its secrets and vices yet kept the reader safely elevated and thus isolated from the teeming streets and tenements below. Yet within the con-text of sea narrative writing, a "bird's eye view" takes on a different cast. In this case, the elevation of perspective reflects the masthead stands of working sailors and the attractions and dangers of reflection they find while engaged in maritime labor.

But neither the pale usher nor the sub-sub librarian has any firsthand experience with whales or whaling. The sub-sub is told to "hie aloft to the royal-mast," but only metaphorically, and in their dusty, underworld exis-tence neither is represented as having any experience with the world outside their texts (xviii). Nor do they represent actual scholarship, for both serve more as functionaries than as producers. As collectors of knowledge, the usher and the librarian are "hopeless," yet the narrator finds space to senti-mentalize the sub-sub, "with whom one sometimes loves to sit" and drink (xviii). Faceless, unnamed drones like the usher and the librarian are rarely subjects of poetic apostrophe, but in this case the kind of labor that they perform invites sympathetic attention. Neither claims a sovereign role in the formation of knowledge, but in their collection of evidentiary materials, the usher and the librarian present a tool kit, as it were, for an active reader to use. The extracts compiled by the sub-sub librarian usually have been read as an appendage to the novel, but their foundational narrative function may be encoded in the narrator's bracketed salute to the "poor devil of a Sub-Sub, whose commentator I am" (xvii). In one sense, the authorial "I" comments on the person of the librarian himself. Another reading, however, offers a compelling way to rethink the extracts: the authorial "I" could be commenting on what the librarian actually produces from the archives. Rather than the extracts serving as footnotes to the novel, the novel itself might instead be understood as the footnotes to the extracts.[48]

This allows for an understanding of *Moby-Dick* as a repository of sailor writing, rather than its epitome.[49] The novel gathers a body of maritime knowledge whose circulation in and against the broader literary world has been as obscure as the labor of the seamen who produced it. In both "Etymology" and "Extracts," the reader is asked to assimilate a diverse archive of thought, including information drawn from philology, taxonomy, natural history, and literature. These sections might be thought of as modified commonplace books, just as all sea narratives could be versions of commonplace books, accretions of sailors' collective literary and labor knowledge. The maritime commonplace book, in turn, is the ultimate product of the sea eye. In the form of the commonplace book, which emerged in the Early Modern period, readers recorded significant or memorable passages from their reading. The collection of passages served both as a textual repository of memory and as a way to cope with an excess of information, in an age when printed material first became rapidly and widely available. In turn, commonplace books became registers of broader experience that, if they lacked unity on a point-by-point basis, nevertheless provided a comprehensive picture of a version of empiricism. In their juxtaposition of facts, impressions, and allusions, "Etymology" and "Extracts" are versions of commonplace books that reflect a body of knowledge and experience. Like commonplaces, they may be "higgledy-piggledy," but they are useful to keep close and to rehearse on occasion. Yet the traditionally direct relationship between reader and commonplace book is absent in *Moby-Dick*. The usher and librarian are isolated from the adventure and practice of whaling that follows in the narrative; they catalog at a remove from maritime experience.

The material conditions of the sea and of ships are inescapable, literally and figuratively, in *Moby-Dick*. The form of the novel is a perfect enactment of the process of acquisition, accretion, and collaboration that characterizes sailors' special relationship to labor and contemplation. The logic of empiricism present in sailor narratives is represented in Melville's work as an archival logic. *Moby-Dick* dramatizes questions present if underarticulated in maritime writing: What do sailors know? And how is that knowledge registered or measured? An arresting scene in *Moby-Dick* illustrates the commonplace proximity of hard facts and imaginative reflection in sea writing. In "A Bower in the Arsacides" Ishmael has the opportunity to view a whale's skeleton, which he measures. The statistical record of this experience finds its way onto a curious material text, however. As Ishmael explains, "the skeleton dimensions I shall now proceed to set down are copied verbatim from my right arm, where I had them tattooed; as in my wild wanderings at that period, there was no other secure way of preserving such valuable statistics." The statistical record of the scale of the whale's inner structure is incomplete, though: "As I was crowded for space, and wished the other parts of my body to remain blank for a poem I was then composing—at least, what untattooed parts might remain," Ishmael confesses, "I did not trouble myself with the odd inches" (451). Ishmael's conflation of poetry with scientific fact as matter for permanent record speaks less in this instance to a theoretical idea of writing on the body than it does to the embodied nature of the performance of sailors' writing.[50] On Ishmael's arm, poetry is reserved to replace the "odd inches" of skeleton dimensions, but poetry is still a space, not filled or rendered; it is a space that erases the specificity of inches. *Moby-Dick* raises the question of what record of the embodied sailor can be inscribed in that vacancy.

Ishmael's record keeping is one of many incidents in *Moby-Dick* in which textuality—whether the practice of writing or of reading books—is aligned with the science of whaling. The "Cetology" chapter, in which Ishmael catalogs whale sizes in terms of book sizes (large whales are folios, the smallest are duodecimos, and so forth), is perhaps the most visible of these. To guard against becoming "lost" in the ocean's "unshored, harborless immensities," Ishmael proposes as a defense to classify the whale, to give a "systematized exhibition of the whale in his broad genera" (134). Yet such a system must always be in "draught" form, like the narrative itself—for as Ishmael proclaims again and again, "Any human thing supposed to be complete, must for that very reason infallibly be faulty" (136, 145). It is significant that the narrative's classification systems are not simply incomplete; they are in draft form, which invites the reader's participation in the work in progress.[51] In this way Melville absorbs the sailor narrative's interest in work—not just the manual labor that propels the ship, but the intellectual labor that emerges from the sailor's investment in the materiality of texts.

In the extensively analyzed "Doubloon" chapter, Stubb, the *Pequod*'s most representative sailor and materialist, concretizes how sailors approach books.

Stubb observes how different members of the *Pequod* interpret the text and images on the Ecuadoran gold coin in vastly different ways; each provides "another rendering" of the "one text" that is the doubloon nailed to the mast (434). Stubb's own reading focuses on the zodiacal signs visible on the coin, and he invokes other sign systems and their guidebooks—ones familiar to sailors—in his analysis of how the symbols work: he mentions the common arithmetic text by Nathan Daboll, a Massachusetts almanac, and Nathaniel Bowditch's *Practical Navigator*, the sailor's bible. "Book! you lie there; the fact is, you books must know your places," Stubb intones; "You'll do to give us the bare words and facts, but we come in to supply the thoughts" (433). On one hand, in putting books in their places Stubb refers to the fact that the works he cites are themselves reference books, providing a manual for decoding the mathematical, navigational, astrological, or meteorological symbols useful to the seaman. On the other hand, Stubb's address to the figure of the book emphasizes the work that readers must necessarily do to "come in to supply the thoughts."[52] A similar point is made in "Cetology," when Ishmael points out that "of real knowledge there be little, yet of books there are a plenty" (135).

And this, ultimately, is the point of the empiricism of sea narratives: the sailor's work is a process of receiving information and transforming it, through the application of manual and intellectual labor, into knowledge—knowledge that has a material, and thus institutional, existence. In turn, as *Moby-Dick* makes evident, taxonomies or classifications are not just guidelines (like Stubb's manuals) but standing invitations to engage actively with the material text. Melville derives this formula from sailor narratives, the commonplaces of which saturate *Moby-Dick*. By its necessarily interactive nature, the epistemology of sea narrative writing is not absolute. In *Moby-Dick* the sea eye operates both in Ishmael's attempts to amass knowledge about the science and practice of whaling and in the reader's attempt to assimilate the narrative's wildly heterogeneous forms.

The two chapters that follow, the first on the Galapagos Islands and the final on death and burial at sea, explore a challenge to the model of knowledge proposed by sailor writing. As I discuss in the next chapter, Melville took up the issue of the eye anew in his later series of sketches of the Galapagos Islands, "The Encantadas," which were first published in *Putnam's Monthly Magazine* in 1854. Episodic and digressive, "The Encantadas" displays a similar drive to encyclopedism that characterizes the vaster *Moby-Dick* and similar urges toward narrative organization. Its publication in *Putnam's Monthly* is significant, for G. P. Putnam's magazine took up the challenge offered by earlier periodicals like the *North American Review* to present American literary and scientific thought. But whereas the *North American Review* advocated American topics while remaining skeptical about the fitness of American history and geography as a subject for literature, *Putnam's Monthly* believed that an American "eye" had transformative properties that could render any subject useful for American advancement. In "The Encantadas," as in *Moby-Dick*, the reader's eye is directed to engage with the text in an experiential fashion and thus is asked to synthesize a broad range of intertextual invocations of other sailors who have written on the Galapagos Islands. But the eye in this case has another function as well: Melville explores how the eye functions within the context of *Putnam's Monthly*, a publication explicitly committed to helping frame an active and distinctly American vision.

5 · THE GALAPAGOS AND THE EVOLUTION
OF THE MARITIME IMAGINATION

The Galapagos Islands, a volcanic cluster located in the Pacific Ocean approximately 500 miles west of Ecuador, scarcely registered on the map of American geographical knowledge prior to the publication of Charles Darwin's *Journal of Researches*, which was issued in America in 1846. Today more commonly known as *Voyage of the "Beagle,"* Darwin's *Journal* found wide readership; it had great appeal as a travel book and as an engrossing record of what would be to British and American readers exotic natural and geological history. Darwin's text appealed to and was positioned for a nineteenth-century audience hungry for travel and sea narratives. Even the editions that were titled some variation of *Journal of Researches* emphasized the exploration aspects of the text, as the spines on reprints of 1845 and 1860 bear the titles *Naturalist's Voyage* or *Naturalist's Voyage Round the World*.[1] This was not a prohibitively technical text, although Darwin would later use the data collected in the *Journal* to craft his theory of evolution in *The Origin of Species*. For the reader who was not a student of science, the maps and woodcuts of various flora and fauna included in many early editions provided an accessible glimpse of the Galapagos.

Herman Melville bought a copy of Darwin's *Journal* in its first American edition and read it as early as 1847.[2] He himself had traveled to the Galapagos archipelago on the whaler *Acushnet* in 1841, and his sketches of his own travels appeared in *Putnam's Monthly Magazine* in 1854 as "The Encantadas, or Enchanted Isles." The title reflects the name Spanish explorers gave the islands, finding their location difficult to fix. Darwin and Melville were not alone in recording the peculiar qualities of these Pacific islands. The narratives of sailors such as James Colnett, William Dampier, Amasa Delano, and David Porter—all of which Melville credits as source material in "The Encantadas" —also provided tantalizing glimpses of the region. The 1815 *Journal* of the

War of 1812 hero David Porter, for instance, retained enough general interest that it was summarized as the lead article in *Harper's* as late as 1859; one of the accompanying illustrations showed sailors catching tortoises in the Galapagos.[3] A common watering and outfitting spot for whalers, naval vessels, and merchant ships alike, the Galapagos Islands are also a convenient landmark in the history of sailor writing. The islands offered mundane and weird qualities for ships' crews as well as for sea literature more generally. Freshwater and meat abounded, yet the meat came from outlandish giant tortoises, esteemed by sailors for their ability to live belowdecks without sustenance for years.[4] The Galapagos offered a rare haven in the wide Pacific, yet unpredictable tides and atmospheric conditions made the islands tough to navigate and sometimes hard to see. The volcanic character of the islands combined with their lack of vegetation made them largely inhospitable; the behavior of those few who did set up residence was so bizarre that it produced anecdotes repeated in multiple sailor narratives. The islands had an imaginative hold over the writers and readers of eighteenth- and nineteenth-century seafaring narratives long before Charles Darwin's theory of evolution had immortalized the Galapagos as the Eden of modern biology.

Thus while the land-based reading public learned about the Galapagos Islands principally through Darwin's *Journal of Researches*, sailors knew about the archipelago through the writings of other mariners decades earlier. The references that nineteenth-century sailors make to the Galapagos in their narratives are highly intertextual and display a common body of knowledge gleaned from maritime accounts. They marvel at the tortoises, whose meat is sweet and plentiful, and at the volcanic character of the islands. James Colnett describes the land as "barren and rocky; in some parts it has the appearance of being covered with cinders; and in others with a kind of iron clinker, in flakes of several feet in circumference, and from one to three inches thick: in passing over them, they sound like plates of iron."[5] Amasa Delano—best known as the historical source of Melville's "Benito Cereno"—confirms, "When we walked over this clinker the tread of our feet would cause a remarkable sound, as if walking on bell metal."[6] Their wonder at the islands' topography is not the only shared sailor response, however. In a sign of their collective experience, visiting sailors inscribe their own names in the rocks by the shore, so that when spotting "many names that were familiar," as one sailor wrote, "they recalled to mind many pleasing recollections of the past."[7] Most narratives also note a particular gravesite dating from the days of Porter, or the War of 1812; as the narrative of Reuben Delano (no relation to Amasa) records, "On Porter's island, one of the group, may be seen the grave of an American

Midshipman, who sailed with Capt Porter in the Essex, during the last war, and who was killed in a duel with a brother officer."[8]

Another frequently noted feature of the Galapagos is a post station on an otherwise uninhabited island in the archipelago. According to William Nevens, "It consists of a box made water tight, with a close cover, into which every captain that enters the harbor, puts in an open letter telling his 'where from, where bound, what luck,' and all about When we came into the harbor there were many letters in the 'post office' and we knew by reading them where all 'the whalers' were bound."[9] These letters are never personal but are instead addressed to the broader Pacific fleet of whalers and sealers. Their contents are both informational and cautionary, as when one letter read by Reuben Delano reports that an English vessel had lost a man two days previous who "fell dead with a terrapin on his back, from the excessive heat of the sun."[10] Nevens, like Delano, mentions having read Porter's narrative, as do several others. Porter and the earlier British whaling surveyor James Colnett are the principal reference points for most sailor accounts, for as Amasa Delano mentions, "The best general account of the Gallipagos Islands, that I have seen, is that of captain Colnett, which is tolerably correct information, though we found some things different from his statement."[11]

Melville cites or alludes to many of the above accounts in his own Galapagos writing. Hardly a traditional sea narrative despite its frequent invocation of the writings of other sailors, "The Encantadas" is even less a travel narrative or a history. It consists of ten loosely related sketches that progressively describe the islands' geographical features, plant and animal life, and use and nominal settlement by humans. In its lack of a linear plot, "The Encantadas" resembles the technical or cetological chapters in *Moby-Dick*, and in it, Melville elaborates on some of the theories about the epistemology of sea writing that he first addressed in the better-known novel. This chapter begins with a recognition of the lure the Galapagos Islands held for sailors and for sailor writing and treats Melville's "The Encantadas" as a case study of the broader applications of the sailor's experiential eye. By publishing his Galapagos sketches in *Putnam's Monthly Magazine*, a periodical that explicitly sought to provide to Americans a new type of literary and scientific vision, Melville tests how the sea eye might function in the sphere of American literary periodicals. The allusive and elusive structure of "The Encantadas" is particularly appropriate to the context of its publication in *Putnam's*, since like the majority of the pieces the magazine published, and in the model of the sea narratives of its day, "The Encantadas" was designed to elicit a certain kind of response from its readers.

"The Encantadas" begins with a descriptive paragraph whose address to the reader functions not as an evocation but as a command: "Take five-and-twenty heaps of cinders dumped here and there in an outside city lot; imagine some of them magnified into mountains, and the vacant lot the sea; and you will have a fit idea of the general aspect of the Encantadas, or Enchanted Isles."[12] Melville's hortatory "Take" here signifies more than a passive appeal to "consider": rather, "Take" functions as the scientific "given," on the basis of which the reader is ordered actively to imagine a transmutation. Instead of inviting a direct comparison—asking the reader to contemplate islands that appear as if they were heaps of cinders magnified and relocated—Melville's double metaphor in fact solicits a process of conversion by which imaginary heaps of cinders are posited as the a priori basis for envisioning actual mountains. In turn, these mountains themselves are metaphorically constituted as larger heaps of cinders. The authorial command to negotiate actively with the sketch's visual terms rhetorically compels the reader to enter an experiential relationship with the text, a call to action that asks that the reader seize imaginative control over the islands' character and formation. The resultant "fit idea" of the Galapagos is an individualized response to the textual matter, one the reader tailors to "fit" his or her own vision of the given material.

An otherwise simple figure, the "heaps of cinders" become for Melville a complex representation of how a reader can be impelled to respond to a set of geographic or scientific conditions whose material reality is not actually at hand. For the reader who might never visit the Pacific islands, the Galapagos could still be a productive site for imaginative labor. Melville's writing suggests that the islands' material reality must somehow be replaced, and not simply represented, by the text. In his Galapagos sketches Melville tests expectations of textual form and visual dynamics, interests that he adapts from sailor narratives and had explored earlier in *Moby-Dick*. His rhetorical experiments are further pitched in terms of a broader nineteenth-century reevaluation of the practice and methodology of scientific expression. "The Encantadas" was first published in *Putnam's Monthly Magazine of American Literature, Science, and Art*, a periodical whose mission statement promised a new form of American vision, directed through the lenses of art and science. The magazine called this "taking the reader . . . by the eye."[13] *Putnam's Monthly's* explicitly defined relationship to its writers and readers underwrites the seemingly paradoxical thought experiment Melville describes when he proposes that imagination have a textual and material referent.

Melville's and *Putnam's Monthly's* joint interest in the relationship between fact and imagination finds its most graphic embodiment in the form of the population charts included in "The Encantadas" (which take their visual inspiration from Charles Darwin's Galapagos charts in his *Journal of Researches*) and in the magazine's report on the American census. In what follows I argue that the statistical tables provide Melville and *Putnam's* with a way of imagining facts, an interpretive process that Melville derives from his reading of sailor narratives and of Darwin, and which he uses to address *Putnam's Monthly*'s own ideological investment in an imaginative project based on representing empirical reality as concretely as possible.

"HIS DREAMS ARE MATERIAL"

Editorial statements in *Putnam's Monthly* directly exhort the magazine's audience to articulate a vision of its content based on a reader's experience of America. The boldness of its editorial advice is arresting: the opening statement of the magazine's first number compares its mission to that of Columbus:

> Why do we propose another twelve-month voyage in pea-green covers, toward obscurity and the chaos of failures?
>
> These are fair and friendly questions, while we stand chatting at the portal. With the obstinacy of Columbus,—if you please—we incredulously hear you, and still believe in the West. No alchemist, after long centuries of labor, ever discovered the philosopher's stone, nor found that any thing but genius and thrift would turn plaster and paper into gold. . . .
>
> So our Magazine is a foregone conclusion. Columbus believed in his Cathay of the West—and discovered it.[14]

The analogy is provocative: for *Putnam's* and Columbus, imaginative energies can make a proposed venture into a "foregone conclusion," one perceived by the seemingly presupposed "American eye." Here, "plaster and paper" are materials that cannot literally be transformed into gold, but that does not make their materiality irrelevant. The value that the would-be alchemist finds in "plaster and paper" lies in their potential capacity for transformation through intellectual practice, as certain alchemical conversions can, in fact, be made using those materials: "genius" (and "thrift") can sculpt plaster into architecture; paper, into literature. For Columbus, the process is analogous— he "believed" in something, and his imaginative labor turned raw material into intellectual and geographical fact, thus "discover[ing] it." The importance of Columbus's discovery for *Putnam's*, despite his geographic and ethnographic error, lies not in the intrinsic truth of its physical existence (that is, that the continent he visited was not Asia but a different landmass) but in his power to impose his own meaning on a geographical truth. His ability to do so forms the model for the monthly's attempt to adapt geographical perspective to an empirical understanding of the world.

The magazine's comparison of its mission to that of the old-world figure of Columbus, however, evokes a method of creatively altering fact, without providing an actual methodology for the transformation. Without a coherent methodology, this "old-world" model of discovery could be compromised by an inability to adapt the powers of its "American" vision of destiny to the circumstances of a local reality. Melville also invokes Columbus in his story "Benito Cereno," which was serialized in *Putnam's Monthly* in 1855. In "Benito Cereno," the American captain Amasa Delano (who in his wrongheadedness is a kind of Columbus figure in the story) demonstrates the failure of American vision in his grotesque misperception of the situation aboard the Spanish slave ship he encounters.[15] Melville's invocation of Columbus is meant to display the dangers of a too-quick or undertheorized transformation of the representative figure of the explorer. Christopher Columbus is positioned as the figurehead on the Spanish ship in "Benito Cereno"; after the slaves revolt, the figurehead is replaced by the cannibalized skeleton of the murdered Spanish shipowner and slaveholder, under which is chalked the warning "Follow your leader." Melville here seems to be reevaluating the invocation of Columbus in the magazine's opening editorial directives, in which the Columbian quality of "obstinacy" is refigured as a positive attribute. Instead, his writing works to dislodge empiricism from such forms of ideological and imaginative proscription.

In extrapolating the figurative meaning of Columbus to its dramatically violent termination, Melville casts a critical eye on the magazine's comparison of itself to Columbus. Yet what he criticizes is not so much the person of Columbus himself but, rather, how that figure is appropriated without the kind of rigorous intellectual apparatus that would allow for his transformation into a model of visionary instruction. The invitation in *Putnam's Monthly* for the reader to enlist in the "twelve-month voyage" of the magazine's "discovery" is an example of the imperial eye identified by Mary Louise Pratt; that eye records "visual descriptions [that] presuppose—naturalize—a transformative project" embodied in the colonist.[16] And for Pratt as well as for Melville, this eye produces scientific and narrative accounts. Pratt calls such narratives "Linnaean" travel accounts, which organize their narrative "by the cumulative, observational enterprise of documenting geography, flora, and fauna. The encounter with nature, and its conversion into natural history, forms the narrative scaffolding."[17] The "narrative scaffolding" of *Moby-Dick* takes a similar taxonomic form.

The imaginative taxonomy posited by Pratt would have appealed to

George Palmer Putnam, the activist publisher of *Putnam's Monthly*. He was the author of several volumes of "tabular histories," among them *The World's Progress* and *American Facts*, which presented readers with elastically comparative statistical tables of world events and literary history (see figs. 5.1 and 5.2).[18] His "Literary Chronology," for example, aligns the careers of those working in fields Putnam identifies as "Imagination," "Fact," and "Speculative and Scientific." One axis stages a comparison in those respective fields between "Wm. Leggett, 1802–1840, Poems, Miscellan., Polit."; "A. S. Mackenzie,—1849, Travels in Spain, &c."; and "Jas. Madison, 1751–1836, Politics" (the Leggett in question is the sailor-turned-newspaper-editor whose naval memoirs are mentioned in earlier chapters). Finding that "elaborate and ponderous works" of history are too often "repulsive to the general reader," Putnam hoped his "Tabular Views of General History" would authorize a reader to compose "the full pictures of these events" as well as to "classify them correctly."[19] The publisher has confidence in the ability of his readers both to generate intellectual products from the raw materials that constitute his tables and graphs and to synthesize their discrete elements into "full pictures," whose composition owes as much to "fact," to use the terms that head his "Literary Chronology," as to "imagination" and the "speculative." As in the case of *Moby-Dick*'s "Doubloon" chapter, the individual reader synthesizes the facts with his or her thoughts. Indeed, Putnam's popular tabular and statistical volumes—*The World's Progress* alone went through twenty editions in his lifetime—introduced a provocative nationalistic structure through which to organize a view of the world.[20]

Putnam's ability to systematize knowledge of the world as well as his belief in the importance of licensing individual agents likewise found expression in his magazine. *Putnam's Monthly* offered American authors a place to display their work in a periodical unlike its contemporaries, which tended to favor reprints of British serials. In a solicitation letter sent to more than seventy writers, Putnam proposed that the magazine would be "as essentially an organ of American thought as possible."[21] The magazine's content advertised its own authority, since it explicitly promised to provide to Americans a viewpoint presented by Americans, each representing a different national experience. Even though at Putnam's directive most of the pieces run by the magazine were anonymous—with the notable exception of Melville's "The Encantadas," which appeared under a pseudonym—the magazine's explicit editorial support of individual American worth and of a proscriptive authorial power allowed for a provocative relationship between reader and text.[22] Like the magazine itself, this authority consisted of a design for the greater collective interest that still allowed for the possibility that the individual could have his or her own

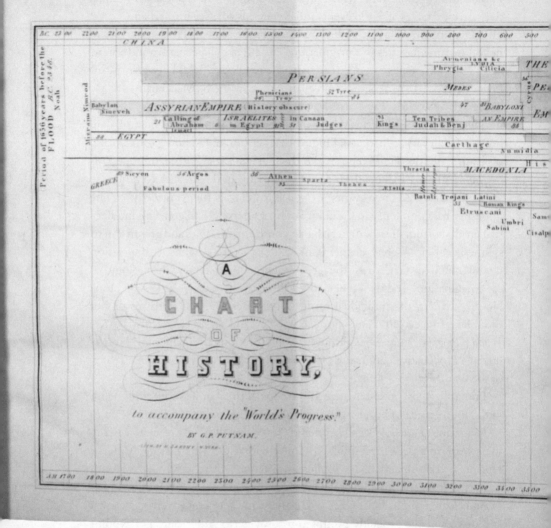

FIGURE 5.1: "A Chart of History.". This chart is an example of the kind of "Tabular Views of General History" that Putnam promoted in *The World's Progress* and *American Facts*. (From Putnam, *World's Progress*, ii; courtesy, American Antiquarian Society)

100 0AB 100 200 300 400 500 600 700 800 900 1000 1100 1200 1300 1400 1500 1600 1700 1800

Moguls · India · Tartar Tribes · Hindoos · N. Tartars · China India. East Empire Tartary

HIANS · PERSIANS · THE · SELJUKIAN · EMPIRE OF THE · Asiatic

CHRISTIANS · EASTERN · EMPIRE · TURKS · Genghis Khan · TARTARS · EMPIRE · Persia · Turkey

THE · Crusaders · Mamelukes

Independent Arabs · Fatimites · Arabia

EMPIRE · OF THE · Egypt · Nubia · French possession · Algiers

Goths · Saracens · Castile · SARACENS · Moors · Morocco · Spain · Portugal

ROMAN · EASTERN or GREEK EMPIRE · SPAIN · TURKS · European Turkey · Greece · Ital. Duchies · Austr. Emp.

Venice · Kings of Italy · Republic of Venice · Republic of Genoa · Modena · Tuscany · Sardinia · Tuscany · Capedom

LOMBARDS · Dominion of the Pope · Savoy & Piedmont · Sardinia · Naples · Switzerland · Holland · Belgium

Sicily · Naples · subject to Spain

Bretagne Alsace Earls of Flanders · HOLLAND · France

EMPIRE · WESTERN EMPIRE · FRANKS · Welch · Normans · ENGLAND · FRANCE · Great Britain

Saxon Heptarchy · Scots · Prussia · Austria · German States · Sweden

Irish · Huns, Suevi Goths Vandals Saxons &c · Franks · GERMAN EMPIRE · HUNGARY · Austria · PRUSSIA

GOTHS · BOHEMIA · NORWAY · Denmark

VANDALS · Sarmatians Scythians · Dukes of Russia · DENMARK · RUSSIA · Russia

HUNS · POLAND · Moguls · Brit. America

French · English · United States

New England · New York Dutch · Pennsylvania · U.S.

INDIAN TRIBES · Louisiana · Virginia · Florida · California · Mexico · Mexico · New Granada &c · Peru-Bolivia

Jews Free · Peru · SPANIARDS · La Plata · Peru · Chili · Brazil · Portuguese · Brasil

New Holland, New Zealand &c · Brit Empire

ASIA · AFRICA · EUROPE · AMERICA

4900 5000 5100 5200 5300 5400 5500 5600 4700 4800 4900 5000 5100 5200 5300 5400 5500 5600 5700 5800

IMAGINATION.	FACT.	SPECULATIVE AND SCIENTIFIC.
1600	1600 Ferishta, Hist. of India. Abulgazi, 1605—1663, Hist. of Tartars. T. Haji Khalifeh, d. 1675, History.	P. 1600 Nured. Shirazi, Metaph. Moham. Hossain, 'Borhani Kata,' Dictionary.
1700	P. 1700 Gholam Hussein, Annals of Hindostan.	1700 Gholam Ali, Grammar.

UNITED STATES OF NORTH AMERICA.

IMAGINATION.	FACT.	SPECULATIVE AND SCIENTIFIC.
1600	1600 Wm. Hubbard, 1704, Hist. of Massachusetts.	1600 Thomas Hooker, d. 1627, Sermons, &c. John Cotton, d. 1652, Theol. Cotton Mather, 1662-1728, Sermons, 'Magnalia,'&c.
1700 John Adams, 1705—1740, Poems. Benj. Church, 1739—1776, Poems. Wm. Livingston, 1723—1790, Poems. John Trumbull, 1750-1831, 'McFingal,' &c. Joel Barlow, 1755—1812, 'The Columbiad.' John Blair Linn, 1777—1804, Poems.	1700 Inc. Mather, 1723, 'History of War with Indians.' Thos. Prince, d. 1757, Hist. of New England. Cadwallader Colden, 1688-1776, History of the Five Nations of Indians. John Bartram, d. 1777, Botany, Travels. Thos. Hutchinson, d. 1780, Hist. of Massachusetts. David Rittenhouse, d. 1796, Astronomy. Jeremy Belknap, 1798, History of N. Hampshire, Amer. Biog. &c. Geo. R. Minot, 1802, 'Hist. of Massachusetts Bay.' Isaac Backus, 1806, Church History of N. England.	1700 Benj. Colman, d. 1747, Theology. Jona. Edwards, d. 1757, Theology. Samuel Davies, d. 1761, Sermons. John Clayton, d. 1773, Botany. Jos. Bellamy, d. 1790, Theology. Benjamin Franklin, 1706—1790, Natural Philosophy, Politics, &c. Jas. Otis, d. 1783, Politics. John Hancock, 1793, Politics. John Witherspoon, d. 1794, Theology, Politics. Patrick Henry, d. 1796, Politics. Samuel Adams, 1803, Politics. Samuel Hopkins, 1721—1803, Theology. Fisher Ames, d. 1808, Politics.
1800 Chas. B. Brown, d. 1810, Novels. Robt. Treat Paine, 1773—1811, 'Invention of Letters,' 'The Ruling Passion,' and other Poems.	1800 Jas. Sullivan, d. 1809, Hist. of Maine. David Ramsay, d. 1812, 'Life of Washington,' 'American Revolution,' 'Universal History.'	1800 Thos. Paine, 1737—1809, Politics, 'Age of Reason,' 'Rights of Man,' &c. Jos. S. Buckminster, d. 1812, Theology. Alex. Hamilton, 1757—1804, Politics.

IMAGINATION.	FACT.	SPECULATIVE AND SCIENTIFIC.
1800 Paul Allen, 1775—1826, 'Noah,' (a poem,) [Hist. of Am. Revol.]	1800 Alexander Wilson, d. 1813, 'American Ornithology.' Hugh Williamson, d. 1818, Hist. of N. Carolina. Benj. S. Barton, d. 1815, Botany.	1800
		Gouverneur Morris, 1752—1816, Politics. Timothy Dwight, 1752—1817, 'Theology Explained and Defended.' Levi Frisbie, 1784—1822, Moral Philosophy. Wm. Pinckney, 1764-1822, Law, Politics.
	Wm. Bartram, d. 1823, Botany, Travels. Jedediah Morse, d. 1826, Geog., Statistics, &c.	Jno. Marshall, 1755—1835, Law. W. E. Channing, 1780—1842, Sermons, Criticism.
J. G. C. Brainard, d. 1826, Poems.		
	Nathl. H. Carter, 1788—1830, 'Letters from Europe.' Edmund D. Griffin, 1804—1830, Travels in Europe, Lectures on Literature, &c. John D. Godman, d. 1830, Anatomy, Natural Hist., &c. John Marshall, 1755—1835, Life of Washington, &c. Jno. Armstrong, 1758-1843, 'War of 1812.' Abiel Holmes, 1763—1837, Annals of America. Timothy Flint, 1780—1840, Hist. of Mississ. Valley. A. S. Mackenzie, —1849, Travels in Spain, &c.	Thomas Jefferson, 1743—1826, Politics, Philos. John Adams, 1735—1826, Politics. John M. Mason, D. D., 1770—1829, Divinity, Sermons, &c. John H. Hobart, D. D., 1776-1830, Sermons, &c. Jos. Story, 1779—1845, Law. Henry Wheaton, 1782—1848. ——— Edw. Livingston, 1764—1836, Criminal Code, &c. David Hosack, 1769—1835, Medicine. Jas. Madison, 1751—1836, Politics.
Wm. Wirt, 1772—1834, 'British Spy.'		
Robt. C. Sands, d. 1832, Poems. J. Q. Adams, 1767—1847, Poems. Washington Allston, 1779—1843, Painter, Poet, and Novelist. Timothy Flint, 1780—1840 Novels. Jas. A. Hillhouse, 1789—1841, Poems. Wm. Leggett, 1802—1840, Poems, Miscellan., Polit. R. H. Wilde, 1789—1840, Poems, Researches on Tasso, &c.		Alex. H. Everett, 1790—1847, Essays. R. Harlan, 1796—1843, Natural History. James Kent, 1763—1847, Comment. on Am. Law. Hugh S. Legaré, 1797—1843, Miscellanies. Jas. Marsh, 1794-1842, Metaphysics. Albert Gallatin, 1761-1849, Ethnology, Philology. J. C. Calhoun, 1782—1850, Politics, Speeches.
E. A. Poe, 1811-1849, Poems, Tales.		

FIGURE 5.2: "Literary Chronology—United States of North America." Putnam organized his tabular literary history under the categories of "Imagination," "Fact," and "Speculative and Scientific." (From Putnam, *World's Progress*, 646–47; courtesy, American Antiquarian Society)

local relationship to matter, whether textual or geographic. Putnam's compendium *American Facts* presented its statistical resources as a response to the (presumably foreign) skeptics who would exclaim that they have had "quite enough" of Americans' "facts and their fictions," finding that "facts are dry things—who will read them? . . . Figures make but very dull music."[23] In *Putnam's Monthly*, "facts" were supplemented by fictions from literary standouts, but the periodical made very little distinction between the strains of music produced by each, so long as the resources specified in the magazine's introduction were cataloged as American.

Putnam's Monthly Magazine first appeared in January 1853 and lasted just twenty-eight issues in that incarnation, although its cultural impact was significant; designed as the voice of American authorship, *Putnam's Monthly* featured the leading writers of the day.[24] Its introductory editorial statement advertised that unlike the popular *Harper's Magazine*—which was composed almost entirely of reprinted materials—this magazine of "American Literature, Science, and Art," at least, would present original periodical materials from a nationalistic perspective, noting that "local reality is a point of the utmost importance." After all, the introduction to this first number maintains, a magazine "must be founded upon fact."[25] What results is the deliberate conflation of natural facts with national resources evident in this introduction, which emphasizes the magazine's celebration of America's native bounty: "It is because we are confident that neither Greece nor Guinea can offer the American reader a richer variety of instruction and amusement in every kind, than the country whose pulses throb with his, and whose every interest is his own, that this Magazine presents itself to-day. The genius of the old world is affluent; we owe much to it, and we hope to owe more. But we have no less faith in the opulence of our own resources."[26]

But the magazine's mission was not solely to furnish a previously neglected local viewpoint. *Putnam's* stressed that the trained and knowledgeable American eye could perceive other views, whether geographical or philosophical, from a fresh and powerful new perspective originating from a "local reality." This eye never loses sight of how "fact" can be transformed or generated, like Columbus's Cathay, by the powers of imagination. The "Introductory" to the first number of *Putnam's* posits an explicitly shared American vision. This eye has receptive powers as well as interpretive powers that render "intelligible" what it sees, transforming "life" from mere image to text and meaning. In one sense, the magazine's embrace of an American perspective demonstrated that a native literature could be profitable and of high quality.[27] In another sense, the magazine's commitment to American texts called for an individual's vision to be based on an experiential knowledge that could be collective. The shared "Americanness" of author and reader, like a shared understanding of cinders dumped in a city lot (to use Melville's opening image from "The Encantadas"), provides a method whereby the magazine's reader could acquire his or her own empirical view of another place in the world.

In their editorial statements, *Putnam's Monthly* editors G. W. Curtis, Parke Godwin, and Frederick Briggs proposed that material reality be understood as a product of intellectual and imaginative ambition—and that the reciprocal relationship could be true, as well. In its series "Our Young Authors," *Putnam's* defined Herman Melville by his relationship to material fact: "From forms, and forms alone does Melville take his text. . . . Matter is his god. His dreams are material."[28] This analysis would at first seem to argue that Melville is totally reliant on "forms," devoted to concrete models, in the creation of his text. But the article's subsequent judgment, that his "dreams are material," creates an ambiguity in the cause-and-effect relationship of "matter" to imagination—whether Melville is empirical or romantic. That is, are his dreams material because they are tangible, or are his dreams material because they provide him with subject matter for literary labor? The dilemma revises a Wordsworthian concept of the imagination and gestures to Ishmael's turn in the *Pequod*'s masthead, as discussed in the previous chapter: matter becomes important to the romantic only when it evokes reflection. For Melville and other sailor authors, the matter that propels contemplation is assured of its materiality only after imaginative labor has been performed on it. And in this instance such matter consists of the status of intellectual labor itself in its tools and devices, its material conditions. This factual base can be graphically rendered in the text, in the form of the Darwin- and Putnam-inspired statistical tables in Melville's sketches as well as the tables in other *Putnam's Monthly* articles, as I discuss below. *Putnam's* seems to set up Melville's worship of the "god" in "matter" as a kind of pagan practice in which perceived reality operates by a fantastic logic. But Melville does not fetishize matter: rather, he conjures knowledge from it by arguing in empirical terms that perceive reality itself as a product of fantasy—that is, of intellectual labor. Melville's abandonment of naturalistic imagery in favor of a transformation of familiar terms and genres (the "cinders" of the opening "Encantadas" passage; the form of the magazine fiction piece) into something new (the Galapagos Islands; his sketches of indeterminate structure) would consequently be a process that solves the dualism *Putnam's* identifies between "material" and "dreams." Melville's placement in *Putnam's*—a periodical that actively recruited his work—therefore helps to revise and clarify the magazine's proposal to understand its "local reality" using imagination.[29] In Melville's case, this imagination was empirical rather than imperial.

"The Encantadas" suggests that a reader's initial impression of the Galapagos must be determined by the experience of understanding how one's own vision can embody an image of the Galapagos that is based on, but not limited to, familiar American industrial-age referents such as the vacant lot or the pile of cinders. How, precisely, do Melville and *Putnam's Monthly* interpret the empirical evidence of their local conditions? Crucial to their respective intellectual projects is the positing of a literal as well as an imaginative space in which an American reader could engage in similar experiential and epistemological questioning. For the purposes of the maritime writing at hand, the most methodologically compelling model of this interpretive work is suggested by George Putnam's own tabular histories; such tables serve as analogues for the population charts of the Galapagos island of Albemarle (rendered in "The Encantadas") and of the United States (featured in the *Putnam's* article "The National Inventory"). Moreover, Melville's table in "The Encantadas" alludes to and revises an Albemarle population chart produced by British naturalist Charles Darwin, whose own earlier Galapagos expedition provided Melville with a way to think about how scientific fact is organized imaginatively. These charts thus not only present, or represent, empirical data but also provide the interpretive key with which a reader can formulate a vision of the Encantadas that is situated in the realms of the scientific and the imaginative.

Putnam's, then, seeks to divert American eyes from the familiar landscape of periodical literature's recognized order. Yet the vision of the Galapagos that Melville presents to America in "The Encantadas" is not wholly original; he borrows heavily from previous explorers' narratives, such as those of the historical sailor Delano, as well as Porter's and Colnett's narratives. The eye that most memorably perceived the Galapagos was the scientific gaze of Darwin, and in "The Encantadas" Melville incorporates Darwin's own experience of the view provided by and seen from the Galapagos. In an emphatically national magazine, Melville's appropriation of Darwin acknowledges the transatlantic conditions of intellectual innovation. How can a reader organize all the information into a "fit idea" of the Galapagos? Like the sea eye, the vision proposed by Melville in *Putnam's* has two components, material and imaginative. In the first sense, the writings of Melville and Darwin, as well as in other articles in *Putnam's*, provide graphic charts in the body of the text itself. In the second sense, "The Encantadas" invites a reader to visualize and respond to a range of authorial commands and accounting practices with what may be called a proprioceptive sea eye, one that extends its vision outward only upon anchoring itself in relation to its local referents. In "The Encantadas," Melville argues that the "original" eye proposed by *Putnam's*—

much like *Moby-Dick*'s commonplaces of sailor writing—synthesizes a composite view, drawing from an admixture of sources and perceptions.

CHARTING THE ENCANTADAS

The organization of the natural observations in Darwin's *Journal* is deliberate and cosmogonic, describing the features of the land, then the vegetative life, and next the animal life. Similarly, Melville's sketches first map the islands conceptually and then progressively populate them. Darwin's usefulness to Melville as a model for organizing and interpreting evidence is most apparent in "The Encantadas" in the form of a chart describing the population of Albemarle, one of the islands in the Galapagos group especially fruitful for Darwin's work. Melville's chart in "The Encantadas" invokes a population table found in Darwin's *Journal of Researches*, a table that likewise describes island populations, in this case that of the Leguminosae plant family (see figs. 5.3 and 5.4). The two population charts can be seen as provocative examples of how factual knowledge was disseminated and understood in the nineteenth century, a time when the uses and organization of empirical evidence were under debate. Although Melville's table could seem wholly parodic of Darwin and of the terms of factual discourse and systematic knowledge, I find that the intellectual drive of Melville's table is in fact similarly directed toward questions of epistemology. The difference between the two charts is that while Darwin presumes the narrative of his factual information to be inherent in its graphic representation, Melville requires the reader first to recognize the artifice of such structures of understanding and then to participate actively in their formation. The result is a democratization of the terms of intellectual inquiry.

In her work on the history of the modern fact from the sixteenth through the nineteenth centuries, Mary Poovey has made a compelling case that statistical accounting, generally thought to be objective and unprejudiced in part because of its reliance on the "truth" and inviolability of numerical evidence, should instead be seen as highly subjective and interpretative. According to Poovey, the nineteenth century signaled a shift in knowledge production after which the work of statistics was thought best turned over to "professionals" who were presumed free from a moralizing or political drive that otherwise would bias systematic knowledge. In this context numbers would be seen as noninterpretive and "different in kind" from the analytical account of their meaning.[30] Even though Darwin himself harvested the evidence he wrote up, Poovey's distinction between numbers and narrative is relevant here, since the appearance of numerical evidence in Darwin's *Journal*

Name of Island.	Total No. of Species.	No of Species found in other parts of the world.	No. of Species confined to the Galapagos Archipelago.	No. confined to the one island.	No. of Species confined to the Galapagos Archipelago, but found on more than the one island.
James Island	71	33	38	30	8
Albemarle Island	46	18	26	22	4
Chatham Island	32	16	16	12	4
Charles Island	68	39*	29	21	8

* Or 29, if the probably imported plants be subtracted.

FIGURE 5.3: Darwin's Chart of Galapagos Populations. This chart shows the incidence of the Leguminosae plant family on various islands in the Galapagos. (From Darwin, *Journal of Researches*, 2:169; The Library Company of Philadelphia)

of Researches advertises a marked confidence in the unimpeachability of the subsequent narrative account. Indeed, Darwin's belief in the immanence of his own conclusions when they are derived from numerical tables is strong. The appearance of the Galapagos chart in his text (fig. 5.3), for example, denotes a transition from the speculative uncertainty that preceded it, when Darwin had warned that "too much confidence . . . must not be placed in the proportional results" of his survey, which he claims "have as yet been only approximately worked out." After the point at which the table is displayed in the body of the text, though, the cautious tone of the narrative disappears, as Darwin declaratively calls attention to "truly wonderful fact[s]" that are rendered still more "striking" by further "illustration."[31] The graphic table concretizes a speculative account into fact, in an instance of numerical evidence asserting its own "truth" in its own terms. In other words, Darwin's chart, and his subsequent description of the chart in the language of the chart, presumes its own narrative, one undifferentiated from the terms of its organizational structure.

Melville, on the other hand, has long been considered skeptical of and even hostile to the kind of scientific accounts and structures used by Darwin.[32] Yet Melville's fictive exploration of the discourses of factual understanding and the organizing principles of the imagination would do more than mock the possibility of scientific explanations of the world. Darwin's example became further useful to Melville in a later instance. In his long poem *Clarel* (1876), Melville cites the moment in *Journal of Researches* when Darwin invokes a line of Shelley: "The wilderness has a mysterious tongue, / Which teaches awful doubt."[33] For Melville, the reference is provocative:

> If now you desire the population of Albemarle, I will give you, in round numbers, the statistics, according to the most reliable estimates made upon the spot:
>
> | | |
> |---|---|
> | Men, ... | none. |
> | Ant-eaters, ... | unknown. |
> | Man-haters, ... , . | unknown. |
> | Lizards, ... | 500,000. |
> | Snakes, ... | 500,000. |
> | Spiders, ... | 10,000,000. |
> | Salamanders, ... | unknown. |
> | Devils, ... ; . . | do. |
> | Making a clean total of . . . . . | 11,000,000. |
>
> exclusive of an incomputable host of fiends, ant-eaters, man-haters, and salamanders.

FIGURE 5.4: Melville's Chart of Albemarle Populations. Here, in "round numbers," Melville details the population of the largest island on the Galapagos. (From Melville, "Encantadas," 318; The Library Company of Philadelphia)

> Darwin quotes
> From Shelley, that forever floats
> Over all desert places known,
> Mysterious doubt—an awful one.
> He quotes, adopts it. Is it true?
> Let instinct vouch; let poetry
> Science and instinct here agree,
> For truth requires strong retinue.[34]

Darwin's ability to quote and adopt "Mysterious doubt" raises questions for Melville, who remains committed to seeing "truth" as the synthesis of "poetry / Science and instinct." Darwin himself could not find intellectual recourse in poetry at the end of his life; in his late-written autobiography, he confesses that he can no longer "endure to read a line of poetry," although it had formerly given him "great delight." Nevertheless he finds that his "mind seems to have become a kind of machine for grinding general laws out of large collections of facts."[35]

"The Encantadas" finds Melville making a case for seeing scientific organization as a subjective organizing structure that has a narrative. In other words, his arresting "scientific categories"—those lizards, salamanders, and devils—compel the reader to craft his or her own narrative, rather than definitively declaring the terms by which the chart must be read. This narrative begins with a requirement that the reader subjectively interpret the facts contained therein—that is, arrive at his or her own image of a devil or a man-hater. What Poovey calls the "conjectural" nature of numerical categories of fact, as opposed to their presumed position as "divorced from theory," is made deliciously visible in the form of Melville's chart, in its playful genera and the absurd claims of what he calls its "statistics."[36] Making meaning of this chart by stabilizing imaginative categorization enables the reader to participate in the process of a cosmogonic "creation" of the Galapagos. In this world, there are things taxonomically accountable, such as the reptiles that make up virtually all of the nonplant life of the volcanic islands, and things unaccountable, like mythical and semimythical creatures such as "man-haters" and "salamanders"; but even the unaccountable help populate islands through their inclusion in the table. And the fictive creatures of Melville's cosmogony seem somehow less fanciful in light of Darwin's conclusion to his discussion of his own Galapagos population chart, when he points out that in "reviewing the facts here given, one is astonished at the amount of creative force, if such an expression may be used, displayed on these small, barren, and rocky islands."[37] The idea of this "creative force" is important enough for Darwin to have called the reader's attention to his perhaps presumptive use of the phrase. The fitness of the Galapagos Islands as a site for creative energies does have different implications for the two writers, of course: for while Darwin presumes no distance between the facts represented in his population chart and the narrative of what those facts say, Melville embeds in the form of his chart a recognition that the "statistics" themselves are subject to interpretive labor, as the sly categories and irresponsible numbers indicate. In many ways Melville's table exemplifies the crisis in representing knowledge of the world that Poovey identifies and that could include Darwin's method of science. But any view of this crisis in separating facts from their interpretation must account for how Darwin, who tends to credit the immanence of the narrative of his statistics, can nevertheless find room for speculation. This force can also be available in the form of creativity: Melville makes it a practical requirement for understanding the process of systematic knowledge.

Returning to the matter of the opening passage of "The Encantadas" ("Take five-and-twenty heaps of cinders"), then, we see how material evidence is assembled, read, and transformed. Introducing the Encantadas by demanding intellectual labor is quite different from beginning with a description of the islands. Instead of simply evoking a comparison using known quantities so that the reader might have a reference point, Melville's directive instead forces the reader to contemplate a transformation, rendering literal and visible the mechanics of analogy. The sooty and graceless terrain prescribed here is defined by its likeness to urban aspects with which an American reader, who is presumably not a traveler to the Galapagos, might be familiar: dross, slag, the piles of trash that accumulate on an abandoned lot. The "enchantment" that characterizes the Encantadas is a complicated alchemical process, the somewhat magical transformation of crude material—the cinder, the vacant lot—into a new composition, one of increased value.

In commanding the reader to perform the transformative exercise for himself or herself, Melville suggests that the islands are created anew by each reader of his text. Oddments, suggestions, excerpts, and discarded fragments are the composite materials of these imagined islands, much as the sketches that make up "The Encantadas" are composites of literary quotations, allusions, and the narratives of other sailors and explorers, as well as their maps and discoveries. Yet its randomness is not indicative of contingency or sloppiness. Instead, "The Encantadas" shows how even scientific accounting practices, like sailor narratives, can be seen as variegated accretions, the assembly of known and newly discovered bits of information into a coherent, readable vision of the world. The Encantadas are "discovered" to the reader in terms of another, analogous referent (cinder heaps), and the imaginative process of that discovery forces one to see the islands as part of a science that fuses hard fact with narrative fancy.

This is how Melville receives the view of the Encantadas offered by Darwin's chart and, in turn, by his reading of other sailors' narratives: he puts a name to the numbered populations specified in Darwin's journal, showing his intimacy with the facts as they are native to his concept of the world. In other words, Melville requires that experiential understanding be a product of imaginative labor. Darwin's confidence in the ability of factual knowledge unsupplemented by experience to help him find his way in the world can be seen in an observation he makes elsewhere in his journal. While visiting Maldonado in South America, Darwin writes of an evening spent with local hosts, who exhibited "unbounded astonishment" at the sight of his compass. Darwin explains, "In every house I was asked to show the compass, and by its aid, together with a map, to point out the direction of various places. It excited the liveliest admiration that I, a perfect stranger, should know the road (for direction and road are synonymous in this open country) to places where I had never been."[38] Navigational tools allow Darwin to acquire the knowledge of a resident and the power to penetrate into regions, whether geographical or social, to which he would not automatically have access; indeed, he is able to visit a young woman under quarantine who requests to see the compass. His knowledge of the topography, studied from the maps made by others familiar with the region, allows him introduction to the region's inhabitants. Only with the aid of mechanical tools such as the compass does the "map" of this road become legible and navigable to the foreigner. The Uruguayans, although entranced by Darwin's tools, cannot use them, and yet such ignorance does not deny them access to the road.

It is precisely this twofold alienation—Darwin from local intimacy, the Uruguayans from their latitudinally defined place in the world—that Melville seeks to address in his suggestion that a place cannot exist until one can document it both textually and imaginatively. Melville's participatory vision helps to resolve Darwin's imperial fiction of geographic mastery. It is striking here how categories of knowledge can be computed and compared: a "compass" (a tool of measurement) plus a "map" (a two-dimensional graphic rendering of landscape) equals "direction" (a relative theoretical concept), which in turn equals "road" (a tangible product of collective human labor). Similarly, a simple taxonomy of population figures, when properly read, can impart a knowledge of place. Melville's huge, round population numbers give the impression that his observations are less meticulous than those of Darwin, whose own numbers are listed with precision rather than estimation. In recording figures that are either large and imprecise or else uncomputed, Melville calls attention to the disputable nature of the numerical unit itself. No unchallenged term, the number becomes a random unit to be stipulated by individual readers. Put another way, the number of "man-haters" on Albemarle may be "unknown," but it is not unknowable.

Detailed accounts of populations of Pacific islands are certainly an important part of nineteenth-century travel narratives, a genre to which Darwin's and Melville's works both owe a debt. Darwin's description of the Fuegians of South America, for example, is a product of this tradition. Still, questioning the terms of taxonomy may have had a special urgency for Melville in antebellum America. *Putnam's Monthly* can be seen to authorize Melville's reading of Darwin's chart in its own displays of graphs, particularly the U.S. population chart that accompanies "The National Inventory," its story on the 1850 census, which appears in *Putnam's* two months before the first installment of "The Encantadas." The table purports to show how rapidly the American population is growing (see fig. 5.5). "A column of figures is said to be, and undoubtedly is, dry,—as dry as an old logarithm," the article states, "and yet, there are circumstances in which one may get from it a deal of succulent nutriment."[39] And indeed, "The National Inventory" offers its figures for consumption. The article claims that America's size, resources, and relative lack of natural obstacles make it the ideal place for the "seat of a homogenous civilization," even though the chart's separation of racial and political categories into "classes" implies a heterogeneity. "Politicians may rant about the dangers of disunion," the article points out, "but we think that nature has wisely provided against any possible failures on that score."[40] The "disunion" threatened, of course, would occur as civil war. It is noticeable that the "classes" identified here are based on racialized rather than geographical population distinctions. The chart in *Putnam's* harmonizes disunited racial and political categories in a curious way: the two summary categories at the bottom half of the chart—"total free" and "total colored"—are both composite categories, but composites of different terms. The "total free" population includes "whites" and "free coloreds" (two different racial categories), while the "total colored" category includes "free coloreds" and "slaves" (two different political categories). The implication is that various combinations of political and racial groupings can achieve a material and imaginative union, even a homogeneity. George Palmer Putnam's tabular history in *The World's Progress* similarly invites synthesis precisely by throwing distinctions into relief (see fig. 5.1). What is striking here is that the numbers do not add up, either in Putnam's or in the magazine's graphs: the bottom line is not the sum of its elements. Melville's piece, as well, places different categories of subjects into a comparative chart, again without balancing the columns—his "clean total" is compromised by the "unknown" quantities whose place is held in the table. Melville's indeterminate "man-haters" keep company with "devils," a group that could include any number of political, social, or mythological entities. The union of these collections of ant-eaters and slaves, salamanders and total free people, into imaginative and taxonomic arrangements is possible given America's "territorial eminence," as *Putnam's* calls it. This fantasy relies on a vision of American geography based as much in imperial imagination as in physical fact. The article justifies this expansive use of American material information by announcing: "Figures . . . are not always as fleshless as skeletons. They have a very present life in them, and may carry with them a fascination beyond figures of speech. It is a simple work, perhaps, the putting them together, but once rightly arranged, they hold the most significant meanings."[41] *Putnam's* authorizes the reader who can "rightly arrange" imaginative material and thus enact the transformation from what is "simple" to what is "significant." The magazine does not register any crisis of epistemology. Instead, *Putnam's* calls for the democratization of scientific knowledge— for a method that requires an engaged, imaginative use of material evidence rather than what Poovey describes as the professional distancing of knowledge production from its interpretation in the nineteenth century.

CLASSES.	1800.	1810.	1820.	1830.	1840.	1850.
Whites,	4,304,489	5,862,004	7,861,987	10,537,378	14,195,695	19,553,068
Free Colored,	108,395	186,446	233,524	319,599	386,303	434,495
Slaves,	893,041	1,191,364	1,538,038	2,009,043	2,487,455	3,204,313
Total free,	4,412,884	6,048,450	8,195,461	10,856,977	14,581,998	19,987,563
Total colored,	1,001,436	1,377,810	1,771,562	2,328,642	2,873,758	3,638,808

FIGURE 5.5: "The National Inventory": 1850 Census. This table presents data culled from the 1850 census. (From "The National Inventory," *Putnam's Monthly Magazine*, January 1854, 19; The Library Company of Philadelphia)

For Melville, though, scientific knowledge is never undemocratic. While not scientifically trained, Melville approaches the Galapagos self-consciously with a mariner's understanding of navigation and space. Like Darwin, he provides his readers with technical, factual information, albeit playfully rendered at times. What his text accomplishes, however, is quite different; Melville makes intellectual and imaginative demands of his reader while continually maintaining that this knowledge be based in meticulous empirical experience. Even experiential knowledge will not always lead to mastery, he hints at times. This is why, for example, Darwin's account of the islands, along with the writings of other explorers, becomes what Melville calls in "The Encantadas" "barren, bootless allusion" (346). References to other texts are only helpful when a reader can assemble the references into a kind of visionary chart, with its rigidity of form but fluidity of imaginative potential. Dry quantifying unaccompanied by imaginative accounting cannot present a coherent map of nature, especially since the nature being observed—that is, an "encantada" or enchanted one, famously bedeviled by strange tides and weather phenomena—can offer no stable boundaries, no fixed landmarks, no discernible depths. There can be no technical fixity in such regions, and that very indeterminacy allows for the writer's own autonomy in describing the world.

A PRESCRIPTION TO SEE

The evidence provided by charts notwithstanding, an image of the islands must incorporate more than the matter displayed in such tables. How, then, to see the Encantadas? The best way, the reader is told, is from the prospect of Rock Rodondo, a towering vertical outcropping. The world that the reader has been compelled to create may be accessed only after the completion of certain prerequisites:

If you seek to ascend Rock Rodondo, take the following prescription. Go three voyages round the world as a main-royal-man of the tallest frigate that floats; then serve a year or two apprenticeship to the guides who conduct strangers up the Peak of Teneriffe; and as many more respectively to a rope-dancer, an Indian juggler, and a chamois. That done, come and be rewarded by the view from our tower. How we get there, we alone know If we sought to tell others, what the wiser were they? Suffice it, that here at the summit you and I stand. (317)

This prescriptive voice can provide only a certain kind of advice: it can tell the reader how to acquire the knowledge that will allow him or her to scale the prospect of Rock Rodondo, but it will not provide the instructional mechanics outright. The summit and the view it affords can only be accessed by one who has mastered several exotic varieties of climbing skill, not simply one. The hyperbolic, satirical tone of this directive has contributed to the widespread critical perception of Melville as a writer who pokes fun at scientific methods. Yet while Melville's tone here is absurdist and expansive, his objective is meticulous and quite serious. In one respect, the list of prerequisites reinforces the difficulty of the physical challenge; the level of skill required to scale the rock cannot be understood by one who, like the "strangers" conducted up Tenerife, finds himself or herself at the top through the efforts of others. The Tenerife guide might be compared to the authorial voice here: both can tell an individual how to get to the top of the rock and what can be seen from there, but that individual will not know how to get there himself or herself. The list of elaborate training exercises therefore stipulates that the reader cannot be the passive recipient of the knowledge of the author/climber: although cinder heaps are transformed into volcanic islands through imaginative labor, physical and metaphysical heights must be scaled with hard-won skill. Once at the top, the climber discovers a fraternity —those who "alone know" how to summit, those for whom seeking "to tell others" how to climb would be a futile exercise. This would seem a rather strange exclusiveness following a "prescription" for how to scale Rock Rodondo, but it underscores the importance of active labor over received knowledge.

The voice of command continues: "Look edgeways, as it were, past [the islands], to the south. You see nothing; but permit me to point out the direction, if not the place, of several interesting objects in the vast sea, which . . . we behold unscrolling itself towards the Antarctic Pole" (318). This curious relationship among what can be seen, what can be suggested, and what remains blank is best considered in light of the subtitle for this Sketch

Fourth, "A Pisgah View from the Rock." In the Bible, Moses is afforded a glimpse of the promised land (which he does not reach before he dies) from the top of Pisgah, a mountain in Jordan. A "Pisgah view," in Melville's allusive usage, grants a broad prospect of a landscape that one may never actually set foot in or on. This view is contingent on the guidance, or the instruction, of one who has more knowledge, whether god or expert climber. Although the disciple may try to read the text of the sea as it "unscroll[s]," the literacy of the disciple is inferior to that of the guide. Still, he or she is not a passive observer, for the information then related by the guide or the teacher must be digested before the observer can undertake to acquire his or her own vision, a vision never free of the lingering images from that first Pisgah view. The reader/observer will incorporate the view as received knowledge, much as a map is studied, before incarnating a new proprioceptive vision, using the previous referents as foundation. *Putnam's* calls this process "taking the reader . . . by the eye."[42]

The commitment of *Putnam's Monthly* to science as well as to art and literature allowed it to see the eye's cosmogonic power more broadly, in a way that can accommodate both rootedness and fluidity. The first words that appeared in the magazine's premier issue were visionary and exhorted the reader to see:

> Astronomers assert that the nebulous mist with which the ether is charged is perpetually taking form—that the regions of space are but a celestial dairy, in which the milky way is for ever churned into stars. . . . It will not, therefore, surprise the public to see a new Magazine. The reader, like the astronomer cognizant of infinite star-dust, knows very well that in the rapid life of this country there is a constant scintillation of talent, which needs only a nucleus to be combined into beams of light and heat.
>
> Taking the reader, therefore, by the hand, or rather by the eye, here at the portal, we invite a moment's conversation before he passes within.[43]

The "nucleus" that would anchor the constellation of native talent was, of course, the magazine, but this was not the only way *Putnam's Monthly* aimed to direct the vision of its audience. In addition, the passage suggests, the reader can be a passive receptor of these "beams of light and heat," as well as becoming proficient in the formative process of the nucleus. The relationship between vision and the material is evident in the magazine's conflation of taking one by the eye and taking one by the hand. The reader's eye is recruited into an active, generative process, much like that of the climber at the summit of Rock Rodondo. It can receive data and transform the meaning of the data into more than its aggregate parts. That this process is expressed, in part, by the device of a metaphor that envisions space as a "celestial dairy" is particularly appropriate and important: for like a dairy that churns milk into butter, this visionary process transforms existing materials into other usable qualities that are still in part constituted by their original organic matter. By asserting that these imaginative products are "perpetually taking form," *Putnam's* acknowledges that this process is never static or complete but always generating matter, printed and physical.

In an article titled "Islands of the Pacific," which appeared in *Putnam's* in 1856 (two years after "The Encantadas"), the magazine detailed the "discovery" and exploration of various Pacific islands. At the end of the article, *Putnam's* reminded readers of Melville's skill in his Galapagos sketches in "playing with fact and imagination." Melville's conjunction of these two qualities seems appropriate to its landscape, the piece concludes, for "slight is the difference between good fiction and well-told fact, especially when either lies in the atmosphere of the great western ocean."[44] The distance of the Pacific from the seat of America's leading literary periodicals invests the western ocean with fantastic qualities. Its distance from the Atlantic seaboard of North America, however, registers in a different way in many sea narratives, when sailors are faced with the trauma of death at sea. The final chapter takes up this crisis in discussing Pacific island gravesites and burial at sea.

6 FROM PREFACE TO POSTSCRIPT:
DEATH AND BURIAL AT SEA

The dead did not have far to travel in eighteenth- and early-nineteenth-century America. Most cemeteries evoked the living populations of the towns in which they were located: clusters of relatives bordering neighbors and various town figures. The rural cemetery movement, which began in the 1830s as American cities expanded, promoted lush, beautifully landscaped cemeteries that served as America's first public parks as well as places of resort, not just for the relatives of the deceased but for tourists and the public. Burial grounds became a place for meditation as well as a site for grief and remembrance of the bereaved; before the eighteenth century, writes Philippe Ariès, "the pious or melancholy visit to the tomb of a dear one was an unknown act."[1] The word "cemetery," meaning "sleeping place," came into more common use with the new burial modes and suggested that death was a temporary rest rather than a permanent finality.[2] Cemeteries provided a space for meditation and consolation and offered the illusion that the dead were still home, still part of a community, still lovingly visited and tended. Allowing the living to experience a geographical intimacy with death, nineteenth-century cemeteries replaced the absent body with the tangible presence (and the promise of continuity) of a memorial.

For the long-voyaging sailor of the nineteenth century, however, the comfort of such object reminders of death, in the form of a static landscape or memorial to which a mourner could return, was generally inaccessible. The bodies of departed seamen (those who did not drown) were usually wrapped in their hammocks, weighted, and dumped into the ocean. The alternative, for some, was an impermanent grave on an unfamiliar shore half a world from their families. For sailors, death was a special "subject for contemplation"; yet unlike mourners on land, sailors lacked an object to contemplate.[3] Seamen's narrative response to death at sea took two primary forms, depending on whether a dead man's body was submerged in keeping with nautical custom or, in certain rare cases, interred on a distant island.

This chapter addresses how seamen accounted for dead bodies, whether present or absent. As I have maintained throughout this book, the material practices of work aboard ship were fundamental to sailors' intellectual and literary projects. Yet death at sea, for reasons I enumerate below, disables the experiential model of knowledge proposed by sea narratives. In the first half of this chapter I examine how certain American sailors were memorialized on Pacific islands. Such men had fortunately avoided the physical annihilation of sea burial yet were preserved at terrific remove from those who would mourn them. Survivors debated what kind of textual record, whether doggerel rhymes transcribed from gravesites or a more permanent form of geographical inscription, could best remember their fallen shipmates. Seamen worried that their labor would be forgotten in the invisibility of their passing. As an article in a sailors' journal put the matter, "The benefit of their [sailors'] exertions is daily felt in the security given to commerce, and the lives of their fellow men; but nothing remains to mark the scene of their suffering and their triumph, but a few frail, perishing memorials, which the hand of friendship has erected."[4] Yet not every sailor could enjoy a fixed resting place. In the second half of this chapter I thus consider the theoretical problem that death posed both for the sailor and for the sea narrative genre, and I address how burial at sea was conceptualized within nineteenth-century thought. If labor and contemplation were conjoined, as sea narratives stipulated, then the obliteration of a sailor's working body would be a threat to understanding. Recognizing this, Herman Melville and Edgar Allan Poe used their sea fictions to diagnose what they saw as a flaw in the materialist epistemology of nonfictional maritime writing, which could not accommodate death. Into the void in nautical custom left by death, Melville and Poe insert the collective practices that become conditions of possibility only for fiction.

AMERICAN GRAVES, PACIFIC PLOTS

Joseph Clark spent fifteen years as a sailor when the maritime economy was thriving. The highlight of his career was the five years he served as a seaman and a marine corporal with Charles Wilkes's United States Exploring Expedition (1838–42), the mammoth federally sponsored voyage to the Pacific and Antarctic regions. The Exploring Expedition's scientific achievements and global reach were widely celebrated in American popular culture. Before Wilkes sailed, he had invited, variously, Washington Irving, James Fenimore Cooper, and Nathaniel Hawthorne to act as mission historian. When all three declined, Wilkes himself wrote the narrative of the expedition. The result, a splendid edition of five leather-bound volumes (including a separate atlas and scores of engravings, sketches, and plates), cost $25 and was considered by one reviewer to be "the handsomest book published in this country."[5] Still, this narrative was beyond the means of the mass of readers, as Wilkes's seaman Joseph Clark recognized. When he produced his own narrative of sailing life, Clark offered a criticism of the elitism of Wilkes's history: "The Journal of the Exploring Expedition, published by the government, being a very expensive work, places its very important and interesting matter beyond the means of the working classes."[6] He trusts that his own narrative of the Wilkes expedition, priced for the laboring class, will amplify the official record.

Clark's attention to the class formation of Wilkes's reading audiences helps shape his own narrative, which is keenly concerned with how maritime life is presented to the domestic public. Clark recognized that the sailor's site of labor was necessarily isolated from the "ennobling" influences of sentimental culture, and these circumstances, he writes, make it "inevitable that [seamen] should assume a kind of *distinctness*, should become a class, yet not a *caste*, to which the tendency of the past age has been so much inclined."[7] The careful distinction Clark makes between consigning sailors to a lower rank of humanity and recognizing that they achieve a special social grade is emblematic of his narrative's broader interest in the codes and metaphors of collective maritime experience. Clark is further critical of the antebellum reform efforts that targeted sailors' spiritual condition at the expense of their working conditions, asking pointedly, "Of what avail is it that we go to the sailor shivering on the beach, escaped from the wreck, with religious books? A dry jacket, or food, would be much more acceptable."[8] Clark is quick to point out the vanity of paying attention to the spiritual condition of sailors at the expense of their physical comfort. The results of this problem, though, are often invisible, as the ship captain and seamen's advocate R. B. Forbes writes, because elderly sailors become "a small class, hard to find." Their deaths are unnoticed: "Like the old ships," Forbes writes sharply, "they sleep beneath the waves on which they have spent their lives, with this difference—that the underwriters have paid for the ships, and their memory rests in the ledger of the owner, while the sailor is forgotten; no granite or marble has been wasted in commemorating his resting-place."[9] Forbes confirms Clark's fear that the material needs of sailors are obscured in popular and reform discourse.

An issue that concerned both the spiritual and physical needs of seamen, and one of pervasive interest to American sea writing, was the question of how best to memorialize dead sailors. Indeed, one of the most striking points of comparison between Clark's personal history of the Wilkes expedition and the official account of the voyage is found in their respective focuses on death and burial. Both narratives are attentive to the modes and practices of the burial or memorialization of the dead, and both devote a good deal of energy to describing such practices; but the thrust of their interest differs. For Charles Wilkes, this attention takes the form of an extended description of the formal (and secret) burial of two murdered expedition members, one of whom was Wilkes's nephew, as well as a discussion of a memorial to Captain James Cook, the British circumnavigator who was killed in the Sandwich Islands, or Hawaii. As part of the mission of the expedition, too, Wilkes relates the habits and customs of burial among the various Pacific Island peoples he encounters. Joseph Clark, on the other hand, is far more concerned with the island gravesites of common seamen that he encounters on leave from the ship. He registers the difference between Protestant and Catholic graves and transcribes the memorial verses found on their rough tombstones. He does pause over the death of Wilkes's nephew; but whereas Wilkes uses his state-sponsored authority to name an island after the fallen midshipman, Clark's response is to write a memorial verse in his honor, which forms a different kind of record of the young man's passage.

This discrepancy is unsurprising: after all, the Exploring Expedition was partially anthropological in nature, and Wilkes would understandably be charged with documenting both the customs of the island natives he encountered and the posthumous treatment of famous men such as Cook. Clark, on the other hand, presumably would be more concerned with the memorials to sailors like himself, who had been unlucky enough to die far from home. The difference between Wilkes's position and that of the "masses" whom Clarks represents, and for whom he writes, becomes manifest. Yet there is a compelling question to be explored in the difference between the two narrative responses to death and burial in the Pacific, one that extends beyond hierarchical explanations: namely, how does the sailor's materialist epistemology function in the face of death? Wilkes's memorialization of his nephew's death, for which he rewrites the map of Pacific island names, differs from Clark's narrative reinscription of the occasional rhymes composed in memory of common seamen. Wilkes's acts are presumed to transcend secular distinctions such as class, while Clark's memorials embrace the experiences that structure maritime life and labor.

In the first half of this chapter I examine the narrative treatment of remote burial spaces available to the nineteenth-century American sailor. Death was an epistemological emergency to sailors, whose knowledge system was predicated on material practices. In sea burial, a sailor's body was erased from terrestrial memory, leaving no physical trace in the form of preserved corpse or monument. As such, it disallowed sailors from understanding death in terms of the material practices of funereal observance. Whereas the second half of this chapter deals with absent corpses, I focus in the following sections on what happens to the few, relatively fortunate sailors whose death occurs close enough to land to justify a burial place. As these earthly plots are frequently found on remote Pacific islands, far from families who might gather near them to mourn, they raise questions about the narrative treatment of the kind of territory claimed by the dead. In particular, I am interested in the doggerel verses—composed by common seamen and often memorializing ship labor—customarily left behind to adorn sailors' rude graves.

Wilkes and Clark were hardly the only sailors to write about the burial of their shipmates. The great majority of narratives written by American seamen in the nineteenth century include a description of the customary practice of sea burial, in which a sailor's body is weighted and committed to the deep, necessarily without coffin or monument. The ceremony makes a special impression on most seamen, and the degree to which the mariner C. S. Stewart is affected by the experience is representative: "A funeral is a melancholy and impressive service any where," he writes, "but particularly so at sea."[10] The reason for this, as other sailors such as Francis Warriner note, is the fact that "no marble monuments mark the place of their repose." Warriner concludes that it is "a melancholy thought, that when a man dies, his memory perishes with him."[11] For most sailors, death at sea represented a putative erasure from terrestrial and human memory. In what follows I discuss a variety of Pacific sea narratives, including Wilkes's and Clark's, as well as David Porter's *Voyage in the South Seas*, Dana's *Two Years before the Mast*, and Melville's "The Encantadas," in order to consider how the rare terrestrial grave for a sailor lost in the Pacific establishes an American historical, political, and poetic record in maritime literary geography.

Poets of the Forecastle

Sea writing's general concern with the methods of remembering absent seamen took on a special urgency when death struck in the Pacific Ocean, remote from the northeastern ports of origin of most American long-voyaging ships. Sailors interred on Pacific islands were hardly honored with the "marble monuments" of Warriner's imagination, and few, if any, would be visited by the family members and loved ones for whom burial grounds are usually designed, especially in the contemporaneous age of rural cemeteries. The occasional rhymes that sailors invented to commemorate their fallen messmates took special note of their displacement from a national home; many use the terms "foreign" and "native" to underscore this difference. The verse that

William Price's messmates composed for his grave off the coast of Peru, for example, laments the sailor's distance from home as a permanent condition:

> A mother's eye will look,—but look in vain,—
> For her lov'd son returning from the main;
> He left his home to tempt the fickle wave,
> And now reposes in a foreign grave.[12]

Another sailor, Walter Colton, demarcates the difference between land and sea burial in his narrative of naval life, addressing his reader directly: "You will be buried beneath the green tree, where love and grief may go to plant their flowers and cherish your virtues; but the poor sailor is hearsed in the dark depths of the ocean, there to drift about in its under-currents."[13] Given the dismay this "drift" induces in sailor narratives, it is understandable that mariners carefully document the gravesites they encounter on their cruises. This record keeping often takes the form of descriptions of the places of rest and full transcription of any words etched at the burial spot.

Colton himself has the opportunity later in his voyage to perform such documentation, while on the Pacific coast of Peru. Of his visit to a Protestant cemetery, which was rare in the Catholic colonies of Spanish South America, Colton reports,

> Here rest many sailors far away from their native shores. A humble slab, erected by their messmates, gives you their names and that of the ship to which they were attached; and sometimes a nautical epitaph, like the following:
>
> > "Here lies the rigging, spars, and hull
> > Of sailing-master David Mull."
>
> This to a landsman seems trifling with our poor mortality; not so to the sailor. His technicalities have with him a meaning and a force which, in his judgment, more than sanction their use on the most grave and melancholy occasions.[14]

Colton's defense of the value of a sailor's "technicalities" is striking. The term refers to the material practices of sea life and labor and performs the metaphorical function of imagining the sailor's body as a ship. Since a sailor's affiliation with a particular ship is his most important form of identification, next to his name, the figure is apt. And the epitaph's wit and playfulness, which Colton is at pains to preserve and communicate in the face of those who might find the comparison "trifling," are characteristic of sailors' epitaphs.

Joseph Clark, while with Wilkes's Exploring Expedition, also visited a non-Catholic burial ground on the island of San Lorenzo, off Callao. Clark recorded five different epitaphs, four for American sailors and the following for a British naval victim:

> Sacred to the memory of William Edwards, late of the Royal Marines, on board H.B.M. ship Harrin, who departed this life at Callao, November 29th, 1839.
>
> > I'm here at rest from busy scenes;
> > I once belonged to the Royal Marines;
> > I'm now confined within these borders,
> > Remaining here for further orders.[15]

This epitaph, like the one that caught Colton's attention, envisions a sailor's future state in the language and imagery of sea life and labor. His identity is defined by his work: only in death is this sailor excused from the "orders" given amid the "busy scenes" on a ship deck. Shortly after returning to sea after his visit to the seamen's graveyard, in fact, Clark witnesses how ocean burial serves as only a momentary interruption to the work aboard ship. When a shipmate dies of a "brain infection," all hands are called to bury the dead. After "the plunge" of the body into the sea, "silence pervaded the ship for a little space of time, and then all was again bustle and confusion."[16] The epitaphs for the American soldiers on San Lorenzo that Clark transcribes are similarly attuned to the common sailor's lack of respite from work. Even in death, Thomas Hendrick, a sixteen-year-old American sailor on the U.S. Navy ship *North Carolina*, is still following orders: "Death's mandate all has superseded,— / The latest order Tom obeyed."[17] The hierarchy of their maritime world is absolute, a power that sailors can only challenge in their gravesite doggerel. These rhymes, after all, are composed by the dead man's messmates (those who work the same shift), not by his superior officers.

The subversive spark of wit visible in these funerary rhymes is characteristic of the writings of working sailors. The maritime trade was a notoriously dangerous profession—Warriner speaks for many in writing that "death is rendered the most familiar of spectacles to seamen"—and humor is used throughout the body of American sea writing as a way to neutralize the capriciousness of ocean life as well as of the commands of sailors' superiors.[18] The drolleries found in sea narratives are lost, however, on land. The memorials found in the Seaman's Bethel in New Bedford (memorably referenced in Herman Melville's *Moby-Dick*) contain none of the light linguistic touch of the remote grave notices. A typical example from New Bedford reads:

This cenotaph was erected by the
officers & crew of Ship
Awashonks of Falmouth
to the memory of
PETER C. CROPSY,
of State Island N. York,
who fell overboard and was drowned
July 9, 1847,
Aged 18 years & 9 months.[19]

The function memorials serve in the chapels of the northeastern United States differs from their purpose on distant (and generally inaccessible) Pacific islands.

The cenotaphs found in mariners' chapels from New Bedford to New London, from Nantucket to Salem, are designed to reinter dead sailors in the memory of their home communities. Such memorials create an imaginative space of burial that circumnavigates the global distance between the sailors' material corpses and the community that would honor them in absentia. This becomes necessary as a result of what one narrative notably calls the "*vacancy*" created by death at sea.[20] The notion is from Dana's *Two Years before the Mast*, and Dana's aching sense of loss and his physical awareness of absence make it hard for him to understand the vacancy of understanding left in death's wake.

Musings on death in *Two Years before the Mast* and other sea narratives therefore become meditations on the utility of and the limitations inherent in establishing a geography of burial spaces. Dana's sense of the metaphysical implications of loss is balanced by his experience of the hard work that results from the loss of a crew member. Poetry, whether crudely practiced or invoked as an aesthetic standard for understanding, is an important key to Dana's experience. This becomes especially clear when Dana has another opportunity to confront the evidence of death. While his ship travels the California coastline, Dana spies a small, uninhabited island distinguished only by a cross, indicating the grave of a sailor. The isolation of the gravesite strikes Dana as significant: "Had it been a common burying-place, it would have been nothing," he remarks. The rural cemetery movement that had emerged in Dana's time made burial spaces into welcoming communal spaces that offered a comforting security from any association with death as decay or dissolution. But on this unnamed Pacific island, the uncommonness of the solitary grave seems appropriate to Dana: "The single body corresponded well with the solitary character of everything around. It was the only thing in California from which I could ever extract anything like poetry."[21] The point-to-point correlation between death and the object—if there is a cross, then a man must have died, his existence therefore confirmed and recorded—"corresponded" to Dana's understanding of what the site, or sight, of death should signify. And the presence of this object frees Dana to make metaphorical comparisons, even "extract . . . poetry." The poetry that Dana can extract from this grave is very unlike the radical unsettlement and vacancy that accompany burial at sea, for which poetry and art are insufficient. Occasional rhymes, after all, are composed for burial on land, not at sea.

In fact, for most sailors the evidence of death on the spots of land touched on a Pacific voyage could be reassuring to the point of celebration. The end of "The Encantadas" narrates how a "rude finger-post, pointing inland" directs a sailor to the grave of a dead officer from the legendary American warship *Essex*. Melville continues,

> It is known that burial in the ocean is a pure necessity of sea-faring life, and that it is only done when land is far astern, and not clearly visible from the bow. Hence, to vessels cruising in the vicinity of the Enchanted Isles, they afford a convenient Potter's Field. The interment over, some good-natured forecastle poet and artist seizes his paintbrush, and inscribes a doggerel epitaph. When, after a long lapse of time, other good-natured seamen chance to come across the spot, they usually make a table of the mound, and quaff a friendly can to the poor soul's repose.[22]

Just as the parks that emerged in the rural cemetery movement in the antebellum period created opportunities for the living to congregate in socially reassuring circumstances, this landed grave is so cheering that it inspires celebratory drinking; the sailor passing by can pay his respects while feeling soothed by the permanence of the grave's memorialization of a brother tar. In fact, the "poetry" that Dana reads in the lonely cross in California is artistically relevant to Melville's sailor as well, who finds the following occasional rhyme at the gravesite:

> Oh, Brother Jack, as you pass by,
> As you are now, so once was I.
> Just so game, and just so gay,
> But now, alack, they've stopped my pay.
> No more I peep out of my blinkers,
> Here I be—tucked in with clinkers![23]

Death's significance in this rhyme is, in some ways, literal: a dead mariner cannot see anymore—the "blinkers" that are the sailor's eyes no longer define the limits of his sight, like a horse's blinders—nor can he draw his wages. The gravesite, the object reminder of death, encourages the sailor to limit his contemplation of death to its material interruptions of service, rather than its more dislocating historical and intellectual consequences. Other sailors anticipated the lack of sentimentality evinced by this epitaph; Dana's conclusion to the first edition of *Two Years before the Mast*, for example, warns against romanticizing the nautical life. The sailor "learns that it is but work and hardship, after all. . . . And if in our books, and anniversary speeches, we would leave out much that is said about 'blue water,' 'blue jackets,' 'open hearts,' 'seeing God's hand on the deep,' and so forth," Dana concludes, "the sailor would benefit."[24] Making metaphor is not a valued labor in this conception, unless it be sportive.

Melville's concluding bit of doggerel forms the final words of "The Encantadas," as the rhyme serves as the epitaph for Melville's sketches (or the clincher, for which the word "clinker" is a variant).[25] The "good-natured seamen" who pause by this "Potter's Field" and the lack of solemnity with which they consecrate this particular grave represent Melville's satire of nineteenth-century sentimental death conventions, whether consolation poems or landscaped rural cemeteries. The dead sailor is tucked in with "clinkers," as the volcanic rocks of the Galapagos are called throughout the sketches. But "clinkers," in an instance of sharp punning, refers also to the awkward poetics of Melville's rhymes. This sailor's final ignominy is that he is put to rest—body, memorial, and short story—with a false note. And what makes Melville's memorialization of a "tucked in" crewman an especially discordant note on which to end "The Encantadas" is the fact that terrestrial burial, of course, would be a rare circumstance for sailors.

This sketch in "The Encantadas" is, in fact, substantively derived from David Porter's journal of his exploits in the War of 1812. In redefining the space for death provided by Captain Porter's narrative, Melville's adoptions and revisions underscore the distance (both spatially and imaginatively) between the Pacific graves of Atlantic-originating American sailors and their aesthetic and historical status. Whereas Porter's sober record of the Pacific plots of his fallen sailors attempts to fix them in a recognizable social and political sphere, Melville recognizes how burial on "foreign" shores is a rupture in the social and political fabric of survivors' maritime lives. At the same time, however, such graves suggest the necessity for an overdetermined American artifact, such as a gravesite or a flag, to designate imaginative terrain. Porter's *Voyage in the South Seas* details the cunning attacks of the USS *Essex* captain perpetrated on the British whaling fleet in the Pacific, particularly in the Galapagos Islands, during the War of 1812. Porter, too, includes several occasional rhymes found at sailors' plots on the islands and reproduces the inscriptions placed on the gravestones of his own dead men.

Even though he tends to focus on the more solemn memorials, Porter does include one waggish example: when a drunk seaman falls from the mainsail top to his death, the memorial penned by his messmates notes that in his inebriated state,

> Without a sigh,
> He bid this world adieu;
> Without one pang,
> His fleeting spirit flew.[26]

But Porter finds other uses for gravesites on the Galapagos and, in turn, takes advantage of one island grave for national military ends. This incident occurs after one of Porter's most promising young officers dies in a duel on James Island in the Galapagos. The victim receives the following inscription on his tomb:

> Sacred to the memory
> OF LIEUT. JOHN S. COWAN,
> Of the U.S. Frigate Essex,
> Who died here anno 1813.
> Aged 21 years.
> His loss is ever to be regretted
> By his country;
> And mourned by his friends
> And brother officers.[27]

(No such inscription is recorded, nor is the burial described, of a quarter-gunner who had committed suicide by arsenic two months before.) While the "friends" and "brother officers" of this young lieutenant would have the opportunity to mourn his loss, his "country"—remote both spatially and temporally—presumably could not. What is notable about Porter's textual account of this remote Pacific burial plot, though, is how it creates a space for the private and public memorialization, indeed validation, of the individual American's presence in the international world. As a result, the containment of a Pacific-buried sailor within the body of the sea narrative text provides for his imaginative reinterment in the American national sphere.

But there is a problem with this logic in Cowan's case. Porter's triumphs in the War of 1812 came about through harassment and seizure of British whaling ships; Porter relied on constant subterfuge for his successes, including disguising his ship and its national origin. Cowan's death, unrelated to the war, is exploited by Porter as a way to confuse the British. At the foot of Cowan's grave, Porter erects a mail station (a common feature on the Galapagos Islands); "with a design of misleading the enemy," he writes, "I left in a bottle suspended at the finger-post, the following note." In the note, Porter claims falsely that forty-three crew members had been killed by "scurvy and ship-fever," leaving the *Essex* in much-reduced circumstances.[28] Cowan's grave, presumably, would serve as confirmation of Porter's account. This plot obscures more than Cowan's means of death; it transforms his place of rest from a little-seen memorial spot to a territorial pawn in a larger international conflict. Porter's manipulation violates the hoped-for sanctity and relative permanence of the remote burial spots.

The Geography of Memory

Who or what, then, is sovereign over these sailors? Or to ask the question another way, what kind of place do dead sailors have in the broader geography of the maritime world? Charles Wilkes's response to the death of two of his expedition members offers one answer; Joseph Clark's narrative concern with the condition of seamen provides another.

Charles Wilkes's official narrative of the United States Exploring Expedition takes respectful note of the burial customs of the Pacific islanders visited on the voyage, such as when the mission's artist documented the tomb of a native chief in New Zealand (see fig. 6.1). Still, two memorials to the deaths of Anglo-American naval officers occupy much of Wilkes's descriptive energy in reports on death. The first, and one commemorating an incident best known to popular memory, is found on the Sandwich Islands. Captain James Cook was killed on a beach by Hawaiians who had previously received him peaceably; on the stump of the tree under which he fell, a later British ship carved a sedate and respectful monument to "the renowned circumnavigator, / who discovered these islands" (see fig. 6.2). This, to Wilkes, would have been a fit memorial, but as he notes with some distaste, subsequent ships have embroidered the epitaph. The emendations carved below the original epitaph, and Wilkes's response to them, are described in the narrative:

> THIS SHEET OF COPPER AND CAP PUT ON BY SPARROWHAWK,
> SEPTEMBER 13TH, 1839,
> IN ORDER TO PRESERVE THIS MONUMENT TO
> THE MEMORY OF COOK.

> I could have wished that the first inscription [the epitaph itself], related solely to Cook, was the only one; the other, it seems to me, was not worthy of being associated with any thing connected with so great a name; and good taste and proper feeling I think would have shrunk from inscribing it as well as the following on another part, "*Give this a coat of tar.*"[29]

FIGURE 6.1: Tomb of a New Zealand Chief. Among the hundreds of illustrations in Wilkes's narrative are images of the burial grounds of the various peoples the expedition encountered, such as this one of a native New Zealander's gravesite. (From Wilkes, *Narrative of the United States Exploring Expedition*, 2:387; courtesy, American Antiquarian Society)

Despite the rough and provisional nature of this monument to Cook, Wilkes insists on its permanence in the geography of memory. That is, he rejects any inscription that testifies to the need to preserve the physical memorial (the copper sheeting and the coat of tar would protect it from the elements), for Wilkes seems uncomfortable with the idea that memorials have a short material tenure. More importantly, Wilkes knows that the memorial will find a wide audience not in terms of visitors to the spot but in terms of the circulation of the text of the inscription in sea writing. Any suggestion written on the memorial itself that its commemoration is not timeless but subject to environmental ravages would disturb Wilkes's idea that there is an immutable maritime geography of burial spaces.

The most harrowing event of the Exploring Expedition, however, occurs when two members, Lieutenant Joseph A. Underwood and Midshipman Wilkes Henry (Captain Wilkes's nephew), are betrayed and killed by natives of Malolo, an island in the Feegee (Fiji) group. Wilkes's grief is marked by his deep distress at the idea that their fallen bodies would be subjected to the

CAPTAIN COOK'S MONUMENT.

The following is the inscription on it:

NEAR THIS SPOT

FELL

CAPTAIN JAMES COOK, R. N.,

THE

RENOWNED CIRCUMNAVIGATOR,

WHO

DISCOVERED THESE ISLANDS,

A. D. 1778.

HIS MAJESTY'S SHIP

IMOGENE,

OCTOBER 17TH, 1837.

THIS SHEET OF COPPER AND CAP PUT ON BY SPARROWHAWK,

SEPTEMBER 13TH, 1839,

IN ORDER TO PRESERVE THIS MONUMENT TO THE MEMORY OF COOK.

FIGURE 6.2: Cook Memorial. Wilkes transcribed the inscription found on the rough memorial to Captain Cook. (From Wilkes, *Narrative of the United States Exploring Expedition*, 4:93; courtesy, American Antiquarian Society)

"shambles of these odious cannibals." A rescue party retrieves the corpses of Underwood and Henry, but Wilkes worries that burying the bodies within sight or reach of the Malolo natives would be a dangerous temptation; "Even the grave might not be held sacred from their hellish appetites," he writes, in a tone unusual for Wilkes. He continues, "I thought of committing them to the open sea; but one of the secluded sand-islands we had passed the day before occurred to me as a place far enough removed from these condor-eyed savages to permit them to be entombed in the earth, without risk of exhumation."[30] Ten miles from Malolo, Wilkes locates a suitable deserted island, and Underwood and Henry are buried with due ceremony. Wilkes's fears of grave violation prevent the expedition from installing a marker on the island. "I felt as if to refrain from marking the spot where they were laid, deprived us of one of the consolations that alleviate the loss of a relative and friend," he confesses, but he feels a great deal of relief when it occurs to him "to fix a more enduring mark on that place, by naming the island after my nephew, 'Henry,' and the pretty cluster of which it forms one, 'Underwood Group.' "[31]

Wilkes's "more enduring mark" is registered on a global plan, as Henry and Underwood take a kind of territorial possession over their gravesite through an imperial act of naming. This treatment is exceptional, made possible by the national sponsorship of Wilkes's mission as well as the elevated status of the victims in shipboard hierarchy. And this is not the only memorial to Henry and Underwood. An officers' meeting after the killings produces the following resolution: "Resolved, That as a mark of affection and respect for our lost associates, we cause a monument, designed among ourselves, to be erected to their memory, in the cemetery at Mount Auburn" (see fig. 6.3).[32] Notably, Wilkes calls for this memorial to be located in one of the best-known rural cemeteries of the antebellum period, thus guaranteeing that a broader public will have the opportunity for reflection and recreation offered by the monument.

Other sailor graves are not so singular. If their resting places are ever noticed by a broader American public, such notice takes a form similar to the following tidbit, which was published in the *Sailor's Magazine, and Seamen's Friend* (a religious magazine for sailors as well as for those with their charitable interests at heart). Having spotted an unknown Pacific island, a correspondent files the following report: "It is very low and dangerous, and is I expect the last resting place of the crews of some of the ships that have been lost in years gone by. . . . [There] were several little hummocks, each with a tall upright stone upon it, undoubtedly the graves of the poor fellows who had escaped from the wreck of their vessel and died on this dreary spot, where perhaps, they had spent months in vainly looking for a passing sailor to relieve

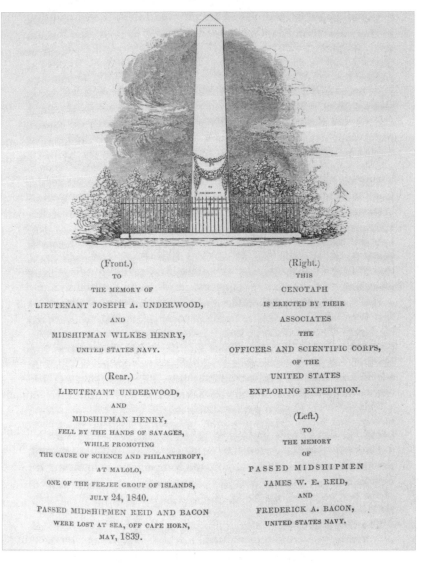

(Front.)
TO
THE MEMORY OF
LIEUTENANT JOSEPH A. UNDERWOOD,
AND
MIDSHIPMAN WILKES HENRY,
UNITED STATES NAVY.

(Rear.)
LIEUTENANT UNDERWOOD,
AND
MIDSHIPMAN HENRY,
FELL BY THE HANDS OF SAVAGES,
WHILE PROMOTING
THE CAUSE OF SCIENCE AND PHILANTHROPY,
AT MALOLO,
ONE OF THE FEEJEE GROUP OF ISLANDS,
JULY 24, 1840.
PASSED MIDSHIPMEN REID AND BACON
WERE LOST AT SEA, OFF CAPE HORN,
MAY, 1839.

(Right.)
THIS
CENOTAPH
IS ERECTED BY THEIR
ASSOCIATES
THE
OFFICERS AND SCIENTIFIC CORPS,
OF THE
UNITED STATES
EXPLORING EXPEDITION.

(Left.)
TO
THE MEMORY
OF
PASSED MIDSHIPMEN
JAMES W. E. REID,
AND
FREDERICK A. BACON,
UNITED STATES NAVY.

FIGURE 6.3: Mount Auburn Monument. This cenotaph honors Lieutenant Joseph A. Underwood and Midshipman Wilkes Henry and mentions the deaths at sea of Passed Midshipmen Reid and Bacon as well. (From Wilkes, *Narrative of the United States Exploring Expedition*, 3:311; courtesy, American Antiquarian Society)

them from their weary prison."[33] The epitaphs of these men are unread, and their names are recorded on no nautical charts. How does their loss measure in national memory, if at all? Anonymous burial on foreign shores seems to offer its own kind of residency in the territory of nautical writing, which forms the only textual monument to the life and loss of such sailors.

Dana's postscript to his narrative takes up these issues. When Dana returns to a newly bustling California after the Civil War, as he documents in "Twenty-Four Years After" (an endnote that replaced the "Concluding Chapter" in all editions of *Two Years before the Mast* published after 1869), Dana finds the coast radically altered by settlement. His recollections of his past experience are "sad, and only sad," especially since he can find scant physical evidence of his former residence on the coast: "All, all were gone! not a vestige to mark where one hide-house stood. . . . I alone was left of all, and how strangely was I here! What changes to me! Where were they all? Why should I care for them,—poor Kanakas and sailors, the refuse of civilization, the outlaws and beach-combers of the Pacific! Time and death seemed to transfigure them. Doubtless nearly all were dead; but how had they died, and where?"[34] Of all the questions Dana poses here in his survivor's lament, the most provocative question must be "Why should I care for them?" The "them" in question, the Kanakas—a common term used by sailors for Hawaiian or other Pacific islanders—and the other "refuse of civilization" exist as outsiders whose own narratives are appropriated for the truths they reveal. Without their remains and without any evidence of how they died and, crucially for burial memorialization, where they died, Dana struggles to remember why he should care for them at all. Much as conventional mourners do, Dana returns to the site of his history, yet rather than finding comfort and companionship in the marks of the past, he feels lost without the vestiges of the physical remains. His former companions have been "tranfigure[d]" by death, and the absence of their material confirmation transforms their status in his memory.

Yet memory, for workingmen such as Joseph Clark, has a material component. The substitution of a text for a body resonates with Louis Marin's notion that the function of cenotaphs is "to ground a representation." Marin argues that "a monument, a vain tomb, is a representation-sign; in other words, it is the image that restores absent objects to us as memory and idea."[35] Yet cenotaphs—as well as reformatory spiritual efforts—do not adequately represent what Clark calls the "peculiarities" of sailor life, which sailors strive to represent in their narratives. What is radical, ultimately, in the class consciousness of seamen such as Clark is its rejection of the use-value of the disembodied honorariums offered to sailors. Cenotaphs and reform-inspired spiritual concern do not fit with what Clark calls the "peculiarities" of sailor life. He explains, "There are peculiarities among all the varied classes and conditions of society, and this diversity constitutes the necessity of an adaptation of reformatory labors to these peculiarities. In this view of the subject, no one, it is presumed, will question the propriety of the issue of books which will be particularly interesting to the sailor as such, or those that will canvass such topics as are interesting and important, not only to seamen but landsmen."[36] In this call for "reformatory labors" to be devoted to seamen only in their own terms, Clark anticipates a response to the kind of thinking that produces Dana's empty lament for the lost "refuse of civilization," invisible in a prospering California. In a similar fashion, Marin's idea that monuments help "ground" or secure a notion of absence can be discerned, in somewhat altered form, in the class awareness of sailors. As Clark observes, "No one, it is presumed, will question the propriety of the issue of books which will be particularly interesting to the sailor as such, or those that will canvass such topics as are interesting and important, not only to seamen but landsmen."[37] And for Clark, this response takes the form of writing. Books of interest and importance to seamen, Clark suggests, will provide the best account of how sailors live and die.

SURVIVING BURIAL AT SEA

Relatively few sailors had the luxury of a terrestrial grave, even one thousands of miles from home. How, then, did the majority of sailors and sailor narratives account for the total erasure of a shipmate's material self? Typical of the way the problem of death at sea is described in maritime narratives is the response of Hawser Martingale to his captain's death in his memoir *Jack in the Forecastle*. Martingale, a common sailor, is concerned with finding correlatives to the concrete, familiar aspects of terrestrial burial that are necessarily unavailable at sea. He discovers how death powerfully dislocates the sailor's sense of community, society, and history:

> Far away from the friends of his youth, with no heart-stricken relatives to gather around the coffin, and form a mournful procession to the grave, and hallow the burial spot with the tears of affection, the mortal remains of our worthy commander were launched into the deep. They were committed, not to the silent tomb, but to that vast burial place, that "God's Acre" of almost illimitable extent, where deep caves, and recesses invisible to mortal eye, have served for ages as the last resting-place of myriads of human beings, cut off untimely, without warning not of preparation, from the hopes and disappointments, the joys and sorrows,

of this world; where, without headstone or monument, inscription or epitaph, to mark the place, with only the rushing winds to mourn their departure, and the murmuring waves to chant their requiem.[38]

At first, Martingale evokes by negation the standard sentimental and pastoral tropes of death in nineteenth-century American fiction: the "heart-stricken" loved ones, the tears that consecrate the burial. And Martingale repeats other conventions of literary observations of death, such as how his commander has been "cut off untimely" from the world. Participation in such familiar tropes helps to prevent death's meaning from breaking rank with the careful procsession of public death commemoration, even as it notes their absence. Yet while he borrows the rhetoric of land burial, Martingale emphasizes the degree to which death alienates seamen from the domestic and the ritualistic practices of home and community. The ocean's grave severs these local relationships. Indeed, Martingale's recognition that the "vast burial place" of the ocean is the antithesis of the local landed cemetery is what makes death for him and for other sailors "illimitable" and unimaginable. Faced with the ocean's "vast" space, he is quick to acknowledge its range and power, what the narratives of other sailors have called the "unfathomable resting-place" of the "dark depths of the ocean sea grave."[39]

Yet Martingale imagines physical attributes in the undersea landscape through which this illimitable quality can be invoked. What is especially striking is how Martingale, in his horror at the lack of a terrestrial resting spot for his captain, seeks to limit the ocean's plot even as he purports to show its "almost illimitable extent." Rather than accepting the literal boundlessness of the sea's landscape and the likelihood that a body would drift without check, he creates for his dead captain tidy, confined resting places, "deep caves" and "recesses" that enclose the corpse. What these caves might be thought to contain is the horror of the idea of death unmoored and endlessly proliferating. Roland Barthes, in discussing Jules Verne's nautical fiction, similarly recognizes what might be called a desire for domesticity in the sailor's impulse toward enclosure: "An inclination for ships always means the joy of perfectly enclosing oneself, of having at hand the greatest number of objects, and having at one's disposal an absolutely finite space. . . . A ship is a habitat before being a means of transport. . . . The vastness of their circumnavigation further increases the bliss of their closure, the perfection of their inner humanity."[40] The same logic applies to the sailor's desire for such an "absolutely finite space" in death, too, which Martingale expresses as a wish for "caves" and "recesses." In his descent to a subaqueous grave, the sailor can presumably be enclosed only in the metaphorical confinement of Davy Jones's locker—safe, in the memory of his shipmates, from the threat of infinite physical and metaphysical drift.

What makes a cemetery a place of comfort to mourners on land is its existence in material reality: a terrestrial grave is not a metaphor, and the practice of visiting a burial ground is an established ritual. Yet aboard ship, metaphors and practices are necessarily linked. That is, seamen's desire for the "closure" represented by Barthes's "absolutely finite space" is derived from the material conditions of maritime labor, in which stowage, confinement, and restraint—of men and of things—are fundamental practices. When death at sea can only exist as a metaphor (represented by the figures of a locker, a cave, or a grotto), rather than as a material practice that they can perform, sailors discover a breach in their understanding of the poetics and practices of maritime life.

In this sense, Martingale's difficulty in formulating a conceptual response to death, given the absence of a secure grave plot, is typical of the broader body of maritime narratives in antebellum America: the majority of the popular narratives produced by working seamen in the period similarly express bafflement and a sense of dislocation in the wake of sea burial. Charles Newhall, for one, quotes Byron's "Childe Harold's Pilgrimage" in order to express the futility of memorializing death at sea:

> Roll on, thou dark and deep blue ocean—roll!
> Ten thousand fleets sweep over thee in vain;
> Man marks the earth with ruin—his control
> Stops with the shore; upon the watery plain
> The wrecks are all thy deeds, nor doth remain
> A shadow of man's ravage, save his own,
> When, for a moment, like a drop of rain,
> He sinks into thy depths with bubbling groan,
> Without a grave, unknell'd, uncoffin'd, and unknown![41]

William Leggett likewise turns to familiar poetry in expressing his distress at what happens to the "uncoffin'd" among sailors, quoting William Dimond's "A Mariner's Dream" from the popular anthology *Home Book of Verse*:

> No tomb shall e'er plead to remembrance for thee,
> Or redeem form or frame from the merciless surge;
> But the white foam of waves shall thy winding sheet be.
> And winds, in the midnight of winter, thy dirge![42]

Another mariner, Samuel Leech, remembers the burial of his shipmate Black Tom as a similar eradication: "A plunge, a sudden opening in the water, followed by an equally sudden return of the departed waves, and Black Tom was gone forever from his shipmates!" Like his fellow seaman authors, Leech discovers that there is little pause in nautical routine in the event of death, as he immediately continues, "In a few moments the yards were braced round, and our frigate was cutting her way again through the wide ocean waste."[43]

The sense of helplessness in these sailors' accounts can be explained, in part, within the context of sea writing's emphasis on a materialist epistemology. As I have been arguing throughout this book, sailors predicate their engagement with and in literary culture on the mechanical practices of sea labor, which are enumerated in their narratives. Thus if metaphysical understanding can be derived from nautical experience, as sea narratives suggest, then the failure of death at sea literally to account for itself would be understandably disorienting. Furthermore, burial at sea does not allow even for the formation of the kind of imaginative knowledge proposed by romanticism; the burial space of the sea is defined, in Robert Pogue Harrison's meditation on what he calls the "dominion of the dead," by its "irresponsibility, its hostility to memory, its impatience with ruins, its passion for erasure." In the body's absence, Harrison writes, mourners "were at a catastrophic loss, their grief could not find its proper object; hence the work of mourning, by which the dead are made to die, was destined to fail."[44] The sailor's act of contemplation reflects this deep fidelity to the importance of material understanding as the basis for reflection.

Dana's *Two Years before the Mast* is exceptionally attuned to how a lack of physical evidence poses a crisis for understanding. When a shipmate falls and drowns, Dana considers the event's significance:

> Death is at all times solemn, but never so much so as at sea. A man dies on shore; his body remains with his friends, . . . but when a man falls overboard at sea and is lost, there is a suddenness to the event, and a difficulty in realizing it, which give to it an air of awful mystery. A man dies on shore—you follow his body to the grave, and a stone marks the spot. You are often prepared for the event. There is always something which helps you to realize it when it happens, and to recall it when it has passed. A man is shot down by your side in battle, and the mangled body remains an *object*, and a *real evidence*; but at sea, the man is near you—at your side—you hear his voice, and in an instant he is gone, and nothing but a *vacancy* shows his loss. Then, too, at sea—to use a homely but expressive phrase—you *miss* a man so much.[45]

What makes death at sea so traumatic for Dana here is not simply its suddenness or its arbitrariness. Without an identifiable corpse or the "*real evidence*" of the effect of death on a body, Dana cannot provide an account of it. Even the customary lessons of death and the usual practices of remembrance become impossible without the "*object*"; indeed, the event of death is actually hard "to recall . . . when it has passed." Dana's empiricist language—his emphasis on the words "*object*" and "*real evidence*," followed by his stress on the idea of "*vacancy*"—demonstrates how in the seaman's conception, the body, even a "mangled" one, is essential to arresting the flight of understanding that comes with death. Dana's emphases also suggest that the true horror of death's "*vacancy*" lies in its resistance to empirical understanding. The words "realize" or "real," which Dana uses several times in this passage, help him to describe how he would ideally conceive of death. What is important for Dana is not how death is realized by being understood but how death is realized by being made *real* by an individual; similarly, Harrison, in *The Dominion of the Dead*, finds that "the corpse, or remains thereof, possesses a certain kind of charisma, and . . . in many cases the event of death remains unfinished or unrealized until the person and remains have been reunified."[46] Thus the absence of any "*real evidence*" of the sailor's body makes this process—making death real—fraught with difficulty for the shipmates left behind.

Sailors' faithful attention to objects therefore becomes a conceptual tool for translating into materialist terms the absence caused by death: that is, the objects, labor practices, and shipboard exchanges that comprise the true targets of death's effect. If artifacts represent culture to the degree that they can be made to represent a history of human work, then the inability of the body of the dead sailor to do work, both literally and imaginatively, presents a double obliteration of value and cultural presence. Since death is not experienced by a corpse but by the social and interpretive system that the corpse leaves behind, then an absent body challenges sailors' dependence on materiality in the formulation of understanding. The theoretical crisis that death provokes is not solved in the larger body of sea narratives, and only in fiction, as I discuss below, can death find a place in maritime writing.

Recent critical studies on the place of burial in American cultural and political life in the eighteenth and nineteenth centuries have paid particular attention to sentimental representations of death in material culture. Matthew Dennis, one of the only critics to address dead sailors (specifically, naval prisoners of war), stresses the ways in which "the remains of common soldiers and sailors—both identified and unidentifiable—would continue to cultivate memory, nationalism, patriotism, . . . even though such bones received fewer 'rites' than those of elite soldiers and statesmen."[47] And yet this social system of memorialization does not allow the majority of dead sailors, merchant seamen who were visible in neither the public nor the private spheres of

American political and cultural life, to continue to serve a role as citizens, or even as the figures Russ Castronovo identifies as "necro citizens."[48] Sailors were invisible in death and scarcely more present in life, and their transitory status resists categorization within the material cultures of death in America.

The cemetery and the ship, as historical and emblematic spaces, take on concurrent and special meaning as the prime definitional sites for Michel Foucault's notion of heterotopia. Foucault defines the heterotopia as a social space that exists "outside of all places" but that can be located in reality, such as the world captured in a mirror's reflection. A cemetery can be seen as a heterotopia in how existing social arrangements are faithfully reproduced in the ordered lanes of the graveyard, and yet it is not a real social space, merely a lifeless representation of a society. In a similar fashion, the sailing ship is illustrative for Foucault:

> If we think, after all, that the boat is a floating piece of space, a place without a place, that exists by itself, that is closed in on itself and at the same time is given over to the infinity of the sea . . . , you will understand why the boat has not only been for our civilization . . . the great instrument of economic development . . . , but has been simultaneously the greatest reserve of the imagination. The ship is the heterotopia *par excellence*. In civilizations without boats, dreams dry up, espionage takes the place of adventure, and the police take the place of pirates.[49]

Foucault's model of the heterotopia is useful for the interests of this chapter because it helps demonstrate how the limitations of containment within a restricted space are overcome through extrapolation by the imagination as well as through physical release. The comparison between the terrestrial operations of "espionage" and the "police" (both functioning as coercive and secret systems) and the seagoing drive of "adventure" and "pirates" (presumably more open or daring) is meant to show how the freedom to cast about in the "reserve of the imagination" is especially available and potent for the sailor. This may account for why, upon acknowledging that the promise of boundless adventure first drives him to the sea, the sailor spends the first portion of his voyage, and of his narrative, seeking to limit the expanding ring of the natural landscape of the sea through the stabilizing practices of shipboard labor. Only when he recognizes how physical enclosure secures him from the environmental terrors of his position may the sailor explore beyond the reach of that physical containment to the metaphysical possibilities of his surrounding space. Death at sea is especially disorienting and disorderly for sailors precisely for its removal of these ordered, imaginative spaces; the heterotopia of the sailor's narrative can invoke them rhetorically, even while describing the vertigo of their absence.

Yet this account does not specify how the "reserve of the imagination" is exploited in the service of the "economic development" for which, Foucault claims, the ship is "the great instrument." If, as I have been arguing, mariners stipulate the simultaneity of labor and contemplation, then their interest in the material aspects of life at sea should be evaluated in terms of their relationship to capital. Yet as discussed in Chapter 4, sailors were wage laborers governed by forces very different from those that affected other workers. Cesare Casarino's *Modernity at Sea* takes up Foucault's concept of the heterotopia in order to provide a compelling response to the generic and theoretical problems presented by sea narratives' reliance on materialism. Noting that "the preeminent exigency of the modernist sea narrative was to secure the heterotopia of the ship in textual form," Casarino in fact sees the genre as the conduit for modernism: "If the world of the sea, whose practices and centrality to political economy was largely inherited from an older mode of production, suddenly became an indispensable element in the emergence and consolidation of a new mode of production and of its imperialist enterprises, the nineteenth-century sea narrative was an archaic form of representation that suddenly began to perform according to new narrative structures and to fulfill new cultural imperatives, and that, hence, played a direct role in the emergent cultures of modernity."[50] Casarino's understanding of the sea novel · as the textual manifestation of the heterotopia amplifies a long critical history that has recognized that shipboard life is wholly isolated from the landed community while still reinforcing its organization and hierarchy. Casarino pays attention to how sea fiction values the laboring body of the sailor, and in this respect his analysis of the genre can fruitfully suggest methods for determining the exchange value of sea writing itself.

Yet the nonfictional accounts produced by sailors at or near the space of their labor do not factor into Casarino's readings. His focus solely on Herman Melville, Joseph Conrad, and Edgar Allan Poe invites the question of how his theory of the sea novel speaks to noncanonical sailor narratives. For the problems of value and exchange presented in the wider body of sea writing frequently manifest themselves in ways very different from those in *White Jacket*, *Moby-Dick*, or *The Nigger of the "Narcissus."* That is, those novels work as exemplars of the genre in spite of their extra-generic response to certain problems of maritime life that are visible in the narratives, such as why sailors yearn for the rituals of shore life when confronted by death. No other maritime event spurs a similar desire to overturn the peculiar rites of sea life. How, then, do sea narratives answer for the failure of their materialist epistemology when applied to death? To put it another way, what kind of work is performed by dead sailors? The ship may in some ways be a heterotopia like the cemetery and like the sea narrative, but there is no place for death in this conceptual apparatus, which ultimately is insufficient to account for death's obliteration of material understanding.

The problem of how to contain the idea of death finds a literal solution in two sea novels of the period: Poe introduces a coffinlike box into the maritime world of *The Narrative of Arthur Gordon Pym*, and the form of the coffin is put to similarly dramatic use by Melville in *Moby-Dick*. The narrative solutions to the problem of representing death that these two fictional narratives propose, however, cannot be replicated in actual sea life or labor, a fact that Melville and Poe understood. The balance of this chapter examines how *Arthur Gordon Pym* and *Moby-Dick* respond to the conceptual limitations of the sea narrative genre. My claim is not that Poe and Melville are reinventing or improving the form; instead, my interest in *Pym* and *Moby-Dick* is derived from both novels' canny diagnosis of a formal problem with the genre. In this sense, my discussion of death and burial in Melville and Poe emerges from my reading of sea writing, rather than from existing critical discourse on their fictions. Both authors explore a fault in the epistemology of the genre of sea writing, which cannot furnish a methodology for interpreting death.. Melville and Poe, I argue, are second-degree responders to the debates of a period that saw the rise of rural cemeteries and new burial practices. They responded in *Moby-Dick* and *The Narrative of Arthur Gordon Pym* to the way that sailors themselves understood the question of death, not primarily to the question itself.

A Space for Death

Arthur Gordon Pym and *Moby-Dick* were published in 1838 and 1851, respectively, years that roughly bookend the period in which nautical literature and trade in America saw their greatest and most robust success, and yet the representation of the rituals of sea burial in these books is hardly consistent with that of most of the genre. The novels' portrayal of exceptions to the usual practices of sea burial help, in turn, to critique how death is represented in the larger body of antebellum nautical writing. As incisive readers of contemporary sea writing, Poe and Melville remark the absence in narrative sea tales of a way to describe or delimit the idea of death and its lost remains. Their solutions cannot take material form in real maritime life—there are no actual coffin burials at sea—and therefore the coffins used by Arthur Gordon Pym and by Queequeg and, later, by Ishmael account less for mortality than for a breach in textual representation. The questions Poe and Melville raise about bodily enclosure find their best expression in the textual enclosure of their novels, both of which feature prefaces and endnotes that struggle to account for how the narrative itself is preserved.

The literary artifice of introducing coffins to maritime life, the oddity of which is remarked upon even within the fabric of the fictions, becomes more than an ironic form of compensation. Recognizing that a coffin is a container that proves inadequate to its task of containing death's proliferation, in all its forms, Poe and Melville challenge sea narratives' reliance on vulgar materiality as both an epistemological strategy and a textual practice. Their extra-generic solution to the problem of death at sea serves, perhaps paradoxically, to elevate the status of the sea narrative text itself, in its own material form, as the apt container for contemplative understanding. In other words, Poe's and Melville's exposure of the limits of the methodology of the sea narrative genre nevertheless makes a case for the genre's possibilities. For while the figure of the coffin must be symbolically and materially unattainable in factual sea narratives, in these rare (yet canonical) fictional examples in sea literature, it can serve as the container for physical and spiritual salvation. In what follows, I discuss how Pym's buried locker and Queequeg's coffin become placeholders for the absent narratives of dead sailors. And they are more than placeholders: both for Pym and for Queequeg, coffins become spaces for writing and reading that ultimately illustrate the failure of the kind of understanding of maritime life and labor provided by texts alone. The anomalous materials that bracket each novel further emphasize the distance between the material text and what it struggles to represent.

Both Poe's and Melville's novels find the occupants of the coffins alive at the end of the voyage. This incongruity is perhaps not so strange in light of the fact that the genre of the novel allows for the rhetorical latitude that enables the peculiar circumstance of burial and containment in the first place. Poe's Arthur Gordon Pym, to begin, is preserved from a mutiny and massacre while prematurely buried in the hold of his ship. Yet even as Poe intimates the safety of confinement, his novel's refusal to obey narrative conventions of resolution suggests the dangers of promises of containment. Poe's employment of the formal conventions of the sea genre is deliberate and defiant: *Pym*'s obfuscatory bracketing materials create narrative assurances of enclosure or definition that prove dangerously unstable. Suspended between its preface and endnote, Poe's narrative resonates differently than the standard sea text, but in this variation may be found strategies for understanding the view of the phenomenal world offered by sea narratives more generally. The physicality of the sea text itself is key to this strategic understanding. The sea narrative presents a way for death's consequences and memorialization to be contained within the space of the narrative's body. Ultimately, the sailor's desire for bodily enclosure can only be realized in this textual form.

The Narrative of Arthur Gordon Pym describes a young man's adventures as a stowaway on a whaling ship; he survives mutiny, shipwreck, and cannibalism. Late in the narrative, as Pym sails southward toward the pole, having escaped murderous islanders, the narrative abruptly ends, offering no explanation for Pym's later return to America or his subsequent, seemingly unrelated death. The sea adventure or polar narrative would not have been an obvious choice for Poe for his only novel, despite the genre's popular appeal in the first half of the nineteenth century. Most sea stories describe journeys made consciously toward broader vistas and expanded social and geographical horizons; most of Poe's fiction, however, is concerned with interior narratives, confinement, and a concurrent terror of the unknown. What many sailors writing in the sea narrative tradition discover, though, is that despite the promise of a wider world, the sea paradoxically becomes a place of enclosure, as sailors spend the vast portion of their time in cramped quarters. Poe's insertion of his usual concern with claustrophobic spaces into a maritime setting, therefore, shrewdly exposes a discrepancy in sea narratives' ambitions to expansive opportunity.

The kind of burial that first endangers Pym is premature burial in the bowels of the ship on which he has stowed away. Pym's entombment in the hold of the whaleship *Grampus* is not the only instance of premature burial in Poe's works, and it is not even the only instance in his writing of that sensational event at sea. The crude ending of the bugaboo story "Premature Burial" finds the narrator, who dreamed that he had been buried alive, awaking to the narrow wooden confines of a sailor's sleeping berth. The spatial limitation is well noted by Poe, for the irony in many narratives is that the young man who goes to sea to flee social confinement finds himself sharing far more intimate space on the ship than he would ashore.

Just as the restraints of life on land chafe for many of the young men in the contemporary narratives after which Poe models his novel, Arthur Gordon Pym, too, is drawn to the sea, even though an early, drunken sailing adventure with his friend Augustus ends poorly. The dangers of maritime life exposed in Pym's first nautical experience only sharpen his interest, and he and his friend conspire to smuggle him aboard Augustus's father's outgoing ship. Their plot requires that Pym be hidden in the hold of the ship in a coffinlike "ironbound box . . . full six feet long, but very narrow."[51] Even as Pym is, as his friend terms it, "buried" in the box, the box itself is interred in the crowded hold and sealed off from the decks above by a trapdoor. Initially quite comfortable, Pym embraces what Barthes's domesticated sailor knows as the "joy" of "absolutely finite space."[52] In many ways, Pym even prefers this confinement to occupation of a seaman's berth, which, for Pym as well as for the young man of Poe's story "Premature Burial," proves to be a nightmare in waking; neither green sailor is a product of his narrative's genre.

Pym's lack of access to the vocabulary of the sea genre is reflected in his chosen reading material while in the box: the narrative of the terrestrial Lewis and Clark expedition. Pym's fears upon waking after three unconscious days are of "suffocation, and premature interment" (1030), dangers not faced by Lewis and Clark. But neither are these the customary fears of the sailor—drowning and accidents are more real threats. Pym's inability to recognize such conventions causes him to misrepresent shipboard confinement as premature burial. It is further important to note that Pym has no direct experience of reading sea texts himself: he, like Milton's Eve, chooses to learn of the sea from the stories of his friend Augustus. His initial perusal of the record of the Lewis and Clark expedition therefore exposes his distance from the generic interests of his proposed sea adventure.

The more important scene of reading that takes place during Pym's "entombment," however, comes when he finally receives a message from Augustus, who sends his dog into the hold with a note around its neck. The delivery comes when Pym is at his most frantic about the length of time he has spent without word from above, a panic heightened by his discovery that his light supply has dwindled to a few bits of phosphorus. Fortunately for Pym, those specks are enough to enable him to see the page Augustus has sent. As Pym narrates, "A clear light suffused itself immediately throughout the whole surface; and, had there been any writing upon it, I should not have experienced the least difficulty, I am sure, in reading it. Not a syllable was there, however—nothing but a dreary and unsatisfactory blank" (1033). Pym here is "sure" that he would have been able to recognize and understand the written text, had there been any to perceive. The "dreary and unsatisfactory blank" Pym finds here anticipates the narrative void that ends his text. But if the narrative's own legibility can be obscure, it might be because the reader, like Pym, does not know how to look at things in the right light: for after Pym tears up the "blank" page in anger, "the thought suggest[s] itself that [he] had examined only one side of the paper" (1034). The delay in Pym's—and consequently the reader's—awareness that the page has two sides, the other of which might contain text, provides a commentary on both reading and writing practice. The reader's confusion, for example, troubles the confidence of the record promised by the narrative form.

Poe here seems to challenge one of the fundamental presumptions of sea literature: that sailors can participate in a culture of reading and writing while at sea. If the wooden box in which Pym is interred functions as a scale model of the domestic arrangement of the sailing ship, then Pym's poor reading choice (of Lewis and Clark's journals) and poor reading ability (in his failure to decipher Augustus's note) might therefore stand in for Poe's more general skepticism about sailor writing. By staging a scene of reading in a coffin, Poe argues for the structural limitations of producing and preserving literary expression while in the paradoxical confines of a ship on the broad ocean. In this light, his subject material in *Pym* becomes an interrogation of the expectations of the sea genre.

Poe recognizes that sea writing has at its heart a deep interest in documenting mechanical practices, a project that also inspires the polar explorations that he mines for their popular and imaginative potential. Like the professional sailors who write many of the contemporary sea tales, Poe includes such information as topographical diagrams and latitude and longitude measurements. Critical history, though, has generally viewed Poe's technical information as sloppy or plagiarized, if not deliberately calculated to deceive or parody. Part of this impression of inauthenticity stems from the fact that unlike most of the authors of the contemporary sea narratives, Poe himself was no sailor. He had a strong interest in polar exploration, however, which took several forms and which was sustained by the wave of American expeditions to the South Seas and polar regions, as has been well-documented by Lisa Gitelman. Poe was famously captivated with Jeremiah Reynolds's accounts of his own South Seas travels (Poe is even reported to have cried out Reynolds's name on his deathbed) and closely followed his agitation for an American South Sea exploration expedition. Further, Poe was intrigued by the outlandish theories advanced by John Cleves Symmes, who claimed that the earth was hollow, with entrance points at either pole. In addition, the publication of *Pym* itself was delayed to coincide with the launch of Charles Wilkes's mammoth federally sponsored expedition to the Antarctic region.[53]

Yet little or no critical attention has been given to why the form of the sea narrative might have appealed to Poe independent of its contemporary popularity, what it would have offered to him stylistically, or what insights Poe's novel bears for the study of sea narratives. One reason for this critical oversight has been *Pym*'s unresolved and mystifying ending, in which Pym and his companions are driven south in boiling milky seas toward a cataract from which rises an immense figure—at which point the narrative precipitously terminates. This literal textual whiteout is unlike the conventional sea narrative ending, which presumes that a sailor completes a round-trip voyage. Sea stories are circular and not simply because they begin and end at home: the great majority begin with a preface that attests to the text's veracity and importance, and many conclude with a synthesizing endnote. What makes

The Narrative of Arthur Gordon Pym peculiar is that the narrative breaks off as if it ends with Pym's death in the South Sea, yet Pym survives and returns home, only to die in other, unnarrated circumstances, as we are told by the note's unidentified author. The promise of resolution that the form of the endnote should offer is betrayed: the reader knows neither what happened to Pym in either instance nor who or what the unidentified narrative voice in the endnote embodies. It becomes what Edgar A. Dryden calls, in discussing the epilogue to *Moby-Dick*, an "imperfect or mutilated supplement" to the narrative.[54]

Poe's invocation of the conventions of sea narratives helps him to articulate his concerns with death and the limits of textual representation, concerns that are manifest in his gothic and detective fiction. More importantly, Poe's exploitation of the genre exposes the flaws in the model of knowledge proposed by sea writing and calls attention to the epistemology of the sea narrative's compositional and material form. The fragmentation of *Pym's* textual body enacts a threat ever-present in sea narratives. In particular, Poe's treatment of death at sea—his most compelling revision of sea literature conventions—powerfully establishes how the text of the sea narrative itself becomes the artifact, the monument to the life of the sailor, which actual sea burial cannot deliver (in the lack of the "caves" and "lockers" described by Martingale). "In giving voice to the wound of mortality itself," Robert Pogue Harrison suggests, "literature houses or gives a home to even the most desolate kinds of grief. . . . Works of literature, then, are more than enduring tablets where an author's words survive his or her own demise."[55] The scene of perverse and anomalous shipboard burial in *The Narrative of Arthur Gordon Pym*, as well as the novel's baffling preface and endnote, challenge the empiricist faith of a writer like Dana or, by extension, the assumptions of Martingale. Poe identifies the value of the truth of the sea narrative as a monument while still making a claim for that monument's muteness.

Surviving the Self

Much as Pym is saved by his coffinlike box, the epilogue to *Moby-Dick* describes Ishmael, sole survivor of the wreck of the whaleship *Pequod*, floating to rescue on a sealed and empty coffin originally intended for Ishmael's bosom friend and shipmate, Queequeg. This coffin has a late but important provenance in the novel. Constructed in advance of the production of any actual corpse, it joins a list of material objects whose meaning is overdetermined in the novel: whale, harpoon, doubloon, and ivory leg. Imagining the coffin as a life buoy, however, accomplishes more than a provocative reassignment of an object's meaning and use, for the coffin reveals how physical containment at sea is wholly necessary for conceptual as well as bodily survival. That an untenanted coffin exists at all on the *Pequod* is due to a whim of Queequeg's. The Polynesian harpooneer originally requests the coffin to be built when he is seized by illness and prepares for death; he "shudder[s] at the thought of being buried in his hammock, according to the usual sea-custom" and requests a coffin modeled on the Nantucket burial "coffin-canoes," which have no keel. Although Ishmael points out that without a keel the coffin-canoe would offer "uncertain steering, and much lee-way adown the dim ages," it would at least protect Queequeg's corpse from "death-devouring sharks" as he drifts through time.[56]

However, only after the coffin ceases to be a space for death—after Queequeg remembers an errand on land and decides to live—does the coffin become a significant container for the narrative. Queequeg transforms it into a sea chest or locker and meticulously inscribes it with replicas of his own tattoos, which, the reader is told, narrate "a complete theory of the heavens and the earth, and a mystical treatise on the art of attaining truth" (480). This "theory" would be lost if Queequeg's body were to be committed to the sea without enclosure; the recognition inspires his desire to record his fleshly secrets on a more permanent and inscribable monument, yet one that is no longer designated as a space for the dead. But the accessibility of the text of the coffin to the *Pequod*'s living audience does not make Queequeg's riddling flesh, "a wondrous work in one volume," more legible; in fact, his "mysteries not even himself could read" (481). The puzzle of Queequeg's tattoos is not clarified when they are transposed to the surface of the coffin. Nor is the coffin a stable object in its own right, for its original use is abandoned when it is subsequently made into a sea chest and, finally, into the official life buoy for the *Pequod*. The instability of the coffin's object function in *Moby-Dick* is compellingly described by Bill Brown: "[When] Queequeg reproduces the hieroglyphic tattoos of his body, he might be said to inscribe himself within the physical object, but the object, like the man, remains a riddle. And the vast cetological and phrenological knowledge that Melville incorporates into the text never eventuates in explanatory power. . . . Melville prefigures the modernist epistemological shift *away* from objects as a source of secure meaning that is nonetheless an aesthetic shift *toward* objects as the source of phenomenological fascination."[57] Brown, like Casarino, finds in Melville's novel the workings of the engine of modernism and likewise shares his sense of Melville's revision of old orders of meaning and circulation. To think that Brown's insight would imply that Queequeg's coffin could stand in for the once-stable object whose meaning has become fraught, however, would be to misapprehend Melville's formal understanding of the sea genre. Never a present object in the first place in maritime writing or life, the coffin instead serves a deictic function for Melville in identifying the conceptual limitations of sea writing's reliance on such very objects.

The text of the coffin, as a record of Queequeg's cosmogonic tattoos, might be profitably considered in light of the last will and testament of his bosom friend Ishmael. This he composes after the *Pequod*'s first, perilous whale hunt—or he revises rather than composes, for the hazards of "nautical life" have made it necessary to produce three previous drafts of his will. For Ishmael, the very process of drafting a will serves as a resurrection, after which he claims "a supplementary clean gain of so many months or weeks as the case might be." Conflating corpse and text, Ishmael continues, "I survived myself; my death and burial were locked up in my chest" (228). Ishmael's sea chest, here·functioning as a coffin for the burial of his old self, is analogous to Davy Jones's locker of seamen's mythology. His sea locker preserves narratives of both his life and his death, and to him the solace of this containment constitutes a second (or fourth) chance at life outside the box.

The coffin is the literal grave marker for the *Pequod*, evidence, rare in a shipwreck, of how its whalers lived and how they died. The ironic reversal of its usual function for Ishmael, who floats on the empty coffin after the *Pequod*'s destruction, does not diminish its signification because, in a double reversal, the coffin retains its original function as a grave marker for the living to read, remember, and understand. And still the most vital meaning of the coffin is explicitly engraved on its face: Queequeg's theory of the meaning of the world can be seen, perhaps, as an alternate record of the voyage, one that influences Ishmael's retrospective narration in its presentation of the "devilish tantalization" (to Ahab in particular) embodied by Queequeg's inscribed flesh. Dryden finds this record to be inadequate, lacking the "quiet dignity and formal purity of an epitaph or monument."[58] Yet the "devilish tantalization" that Ahab identifies in Queequeg's bodily text must have a material component: as Casarino argues, "Both meaning and value need first to be posited as real entities if they are then to be dialectically reconceptualized and revealed as empty and nonexistent—and such a revelation leads [Ahab] to angst and *horror vacui*."[59] This is the "*vacancy*" that so tears at Richard Henry Dana, who cannot find a box to define the limits of that vacancy; instead, it proliferates in the broader body of sea writing.

The coffin, analogous to the tombstone as a symbolic marker of the lifeless organic form, raises a question vital to sailors' contemplation of death at sea: what "theory," what "truth," can grave markings tell? When death is memorialized using tangible relics, does it cease to become a potential space for theoretical or imaginative exploration, and is it thus instead managed and neutralized? The failure of any of *Moby-Dick*'s characters (including Quee-queg) to read the hieroglyphics of his tattoos after they have been transferred to the body of the coffin helps to emphasize the unavailability of legible representations of death at sea. Ultimately, the fact that Queequeg does not use his own coffin becomes the very reason that relic of death does not itself become subsumed under the "shroud of the sea" when the *Pequod* disinte-grates and sinks. It provides a space for containment that, crucially, does not contain a corpse.

Book Ends

The narrative of *Moby-Dick* can be told because it ends structurally with Ishmael left alone on a coffin to tell the tale. Pym, as discussed above, began his voyage in a coffin that proves his protector; his survival of later calamities and his finally obscure death are possible only because of the reemergence of his buried body. And although the coffin scenes in *Arthur Gordon Pym* and *Moby-Dick* are placed at opposite ends of their respective texts, they both signal how a coffin can paradoxically deliver both a live survivor and the narrative itself. Scenes of writing and reading frame the appearance of the coffins in both texts, just as each novel is bracketed by prefatory remarks (the preface in *Pym* and the "Extracts" in *Moby-Dick*) and by endnotes (the note that ends *Pym* and the epilogue to *Moby-Dick*). The affinities between the respective endnotes are evident, as each accounts for the fate of the novel's narrator and offers some closing thoughts on nature's permanence and its illegibility to humans.

In this manner *The Narrative of Arthur Gordon Pym* narrates what most sea texts allude to but do not deliver in any material form: the dissolution of narrative that is the ultimate consequence of death at sea. This loss of narra-tive, neither author nor text materially remaining, is the theoretical compo-nent of the lack of a record of burial ("without headstone or monument, inscription or epitaph, to mark the place") so often lamented in sea narra-tives.[60] Most sea narratives seek to recuperate that missing or fragmented body in their closure, their return home. *Pym*'s bracketing materials prepare the reader for the fact that the lost sailor's story, as well as his body, might be irrevocably lost at sea, unable to be assimilated into any memorial text. Therefore, given the context of "true" sea stories, *Pym*'s narrative unre-liability is not so much indicative of sloppiness or generic mockery than it is a strategy for shielding the reader from the narrative annihilation of sea death.

For the status of the body of Pym as the author or subject of his own narrative is as under question as the conditions of the narrative's textual production. The preface makes claims for its narrator's ultimate survival that prove false; the reader learns in the endnote that Pym survives his sea adventure and completes his narrative but dies before the text can find its way to print in completion, since the final chapters are "lost." The confusing structure of *The Narrative of Arthur Gordon Pym* underscores the complexity of the relationship of author to text, and of text to artifact, as the conditions of the narrative's and the narrator's survival are tenuous at best. The ambiguities written into *Pym*'s textual production begin in the novel's preface, in which "A. G. Pym" accounts for the different forms his story has taken in print. "Pym" worries that his account, drawn as it is from memory rather than a journal, would not have the "*appearance* of that truth it would really possess," lacking the "minute" details of the factual account. Further, Pym explains that the opening chapters of the text have already appeared in print, presented "as fiction," in the *Southern Literary Messenger*, there attributed to "Mr. Poe" (1007–8; emphasis in original). Poe's own elaborate efforts to present the novel as nonfiction include an endnote supposedly penned by an unnamed third writer, who refers both to the sudden death of "Pym" ("The circumstances connected with the late sudden and distressing death of Mr. Pym are already well known to the public" [1180]) and to the inability of "Mr. Poe" to recognize certain facts about the narrative ("The facts in question have, beyond doubt, escaped the attention of Mr. Poe" [1181]). This underscores how perceived truths, such as Pym's interest in the "*appearance* of truth" cited above, become a way of accounting for the narrative's authorial and textual existence. That is, the existence of the material sea narrative seems to promise the survival of the sailor, but this is a promise betrayed by Poe's ability to cast doubt on the veracity of the text as well as on Pym's survival "alone to tell" the reader.

The novel's bewildering end, which comes as Pym and his companions encounter a "shrouded human figure" with skin "the perfect whiteness of snow," suggests that *Pym* is a linear narrative that ends with the narrator's death (1179). But the text survives, under circumstances made only more obscure by the endnote. This note is penned by a third narrative voice, neither Poe nor Pym. It begins, "The circumstances connected with the late sudden and distressing death of Mr. Pym are already well known to the public through the medium of the daily press. It is feared that the few remaining chapters which were to have completed his narrative, and which were retained by him, while the above were in type, for the purpose of revision, have been irrecoverably lost through the accident by which he perished himself" (1180). The note alludes to texts that the novel's reader will never see, one of which is the "daily press" report of Pym's bodily death. The mention of the medium of the press places his corporeal death squarely back into the realms of both the popular adventurous narrative and the period's frequent newspaper mentions of shipwrecks.

But the greater loss is the destruction of the manuscript, or the story of how Pym survived the shrouded white figure. In the end, *Pym*'s prefatory and closing materials are forced to do the work of a coffin—that is, to contain the limits of understanding and of writing itself. The reader is shielded from the trauma of the novel's textual disintegration, as the "loss" of the narrative is literally inexpressible. This is not to say that Poe's novel sanitizes the demise of the physical body. The terror of the unknowability of death in the majority of sea narratives is focused on the body's disappearance under the waves, where it might disintegrate or be devoured. The preservation of a corpse preserves the idea of its material value, yet without access to the memorializing effects of terrestrial burial, the body becomes so much trash. In one of his more shocking revisions of the conventions of standard sea narratives, Poe imagines a standard sea burial that contains nothing of the "indescribable" or "inconceivable"; indeed, it is all too graphically described. Augustus, Pym's original companion, dies mid-adventure, and when his companions dispose of the body just twelve hours later, they discover that it is "so far decayed that, as Peters attempted to lift it, an entire leg came off in his grasp. As the mass of putrefaction slipped over the vessel's side into the water, the glare of the phosphoric light with which it was surrounded plainly discovered to us seven or eight large sharks, the clashing of whose horrible teeth, as their prey was torn to pieces among them, might have been heard at the distance of a mile" (1107). Augustus's accelerated decomposition dramatizes the otherwise unseen effects of burial at sea upon a corpse: grotesque ingestion at the hands of the "death-devouring sharks" so feared by Queequeg. This actualization of all the imagined horrors of interment stands in sharp contrast to the occult nature of conventional sea burial in other narratives, in which the fragmentation of death can be arrested only within the neat space of the narrative.

The reader of *The Narrative of Arthur Gordon Pym* is denied access to the material facts of Pym's bodily death yet helps to set the terms of his textual death. The distance between actual and symbolic death in these sea narratives can be oceanic: the symbolic resurrections of Pym and Ishmael are vital to the characters' life of writing, whereas in most sailor narratives, death at sea is not symbolic of anything. The kind of grave marker that sailors search for in vain is one that must be imaginatively created within the limits of writing. The text can be an appropriate receptacle for death only when its prefatory and concluding apparatus can brace the narrative against the drift of the dead body at sea.

AFTERWORD

*Dana and Melville created a world, not by
the discovery, but by the interpretation of it.*
—W. CLARK RUSSELL

*We study the sailor, the man of his hands,
man of all work; all eye, all finger, muscle,
skill, & endurance[;] a tailor, a carpenter,
cooper, stevedore, & clerk & astronomer
besides. He is a great saver, and a great
quiddle by the necessity of his situation.*
—RALPH WALDO EMERSON

In February 1892, several months after Herman Melville died, a long essay titled "A Claim for American Literature" appeared in the *North American Review*. Written by W. Clark Russell, a British writer of nautical fiction and an advocate for seamen, "A Claim for American Literature" revisits the sea writing of Melville and Richard Henry Dana, whose contributions to their national literature Russell finds an unmatched literary achievement in a time "when men thought most things known." Significantly, he views Melville's and Dana's artistic efforts as a kind of exhumation of the class of seamen: "Two American sailors, men of letters and of genius, seizing the pen for a handspike, prized open the sealed lid under which the merchant-seaman lay caverned."[1] In Russell's figure, Melville and Dana rescue seamen from the recesses of obscurity through literary attention to the particulars of maritime life. Yet the consequences of a less symbolic burial inform Russell's reading as well: Melville's recent death (Dana had died ten years earlier) seems to have summoned this image of excavation for Russell. Melville, as is known, had been largely forgotten in literary circles by the time of his death, and Russell laments his late irrelevance for more than the sake of his literary reputation. If

Melville's works and name are lost, Russell argues, then "to all intents and purposes the American sailor is a dead man, and the American merchant service to all intents and purposes a dead industry."[2]

Does sailor writing have an afterlife? I pose this question independently of the historical conditions (commercial, technological, and sociological) of the second half of the nineteenth century that gradually rendered masted sailing ships obsolete for labor and commerce. Nor am I referring here to the resurgence in the last decade of the publication of narrative tales of adventure in inhospitable natural environments, with their self-consuming attention to their own technologies and paraphernalia.[3] Rather, what Russell's perceptive reading of the state of sea literature recognizes is that its "industry," in the sense of both its mechanical practices and its liveliness, was contingent on its translation into an intellectual sphere. The epigraph from Russell[4]—which proposes that Dana and Melville, unlike Columbus, incarnated a view of the world through interpretation rather than through discovery—insists that the work of creation done by Dana's and Melville's writings lies in their methodological rigor, a claim this book has been making for sailors' epistemology. But whereas Russell evaluates the work of interpretation in American literature within the context of the death of one of its architects, I have sought to emphasize the renascent possibilities for the genre within the literary and critical landscape of nineteenth-century America, considering how sailors' literary culture produces not only a body of texts but an epistemology that strives to encompass the simultaneity of manual and mental labor but does not always succeed. Dana and Melville were not the only maritime intellectuals, Russell's encomium notwithstanding; my aim has been to animate study of their shipmates in letters.

The second epigraph, from an entry Emerson makes in his journals while sailing from Boston to Malta in 1833, describes what Emerson, a passenger, sees as the sailor's interdisciplinary working role, as he is simultaneously "a tailor, a carpenter, cooper, stevedore, & clerk & astronomer besides."[5] In an image that would be familiar to his contemporaries, many of whom viewed manual labors as unreflective collections of body parts, Emerson envisions the sailor as "the man of his hands, man of all work; all eye, all finger, muscle, skill, & endurance." Yet Emerson also intuits the sailor as a "great saver, and a great quiddle by the necessity of his situation." The marvelous depiction of a sailor as a "quiddle"—a "fastidious person"—underscores the methodology of saving, of accumulating, which characterizes a sailor's labor in both its mechanical and literary dimensions.[6]

Consider the figure of Owen Chase, first mate on the Nantucket whaleship *Essex*. In 1820, while cruising in the equatorial Pacific, the *Essex* was rammed twice and destroyed in an attack by a sperm whale, an assault that

Chase described as an act of "premeditated violence" by a whale evincing "resentment and fury."[7] The surviving crew, divided into three small whale boats, drifted for three months. The fate of one boat was never discovered; the crew members of the other two boats survived on the flesh of fellow sailors, some of whom had died of natural causes and one of whom was shot for food. After his return to Nantucket, Chase published an account of the ordeal under the title *Narrative of the Most Extraordinary and Distressing Shipwreck of the Whale-ship Essex of Nantucket* (1821).[8] Owen Chase became a successful captain of many later voyages but never forgot his experience with cannibalism: Nantucket lore reports that the elderly Chase, described in a letter by his cousin as "insane," stashed food in his attic as a hedge against starvation.[9]

Chase's narrative of the disaster outlives his hoarding practices as a literary incarnation of such accumulation, which in turn enables other collections and circulations to take place. By this I refer to the resonance Chase's story has had in its multiple retellings in the nearly two centuries since his narrative was published.[10] Until the recent National Book Award–winning *In the Heart of the Sea* (2000), a cultural history of the *Essex*, those who knew the name Owen Chase would have encountered it primarily in *Moby-Dick*, in which the fate of the *Essex* is cited in an affidavit for the white whale's ostensible malevolence. Melville first read Chase's *Narrative* at sea, when a copy was passed to him by Chase's son, whom Melville met while a sailor on a gam in the Pacific in 1841 or 1842. Melville's notes in his copy of Chase's narrative document the current of conversation that circulated amid the Pacific whaling fleet; while he himself was on the whaler *Acushnet*, Melville remembers, he had heard from an unrelated ship that Chase had "recently rec[eive]d letters from home, informing him of the certain infidelity of his wife, the mother of several children, one of them be[in]g the lad of sixteen, whom I alluded to as gi[vin]g me a copy of his father's nar[ra]tive to read."[11] Such stories migrate and are collected in the course of their maritime transit.

Yet the image of the elderly Chase secreting food in his attic persists. Not simply the anxious repetition of trauma or a curiosity of senility, Chase's hoarding can be seen as the haunting continuation of a life spent packing whaleships with barrels of sperm oil. Filling his attic with food becomes the spectral invocation of one more venture, the sailor's epistemological fastidiousness extrapolated to the point of insanity. Chase shores up a life spent as Emerson's "great saver, and a great quiddle." In its discipline and its diligence as a method for understanding, nautical routine often outlives even "the necessity of [its] situation." Maritime habit dies hard; its inheritance is the literature produced and circulated by sailors.

NOTES

INTRODUCTION

1. Melville, *Moby-Dick*, 158–59.
2. In the epigraph, Morell adapts a line from "Tom Tough," a popular sea chantey by the prolific composer Charles Dibdin. In the original lyric, sailors "*love* and feel like other folks," not "feel and *think*" (emphases added); Morell's misquotation remembers his fellow seamen as thinkers. See Morell, *Narrative of Four Voyages*, 254.
3. As Cesare Casarino observes, sea labor is "altogether resistant to the increasingly parcelized and mechanic rhythms of an industrial environment such as the factory" (*Modernity at Sea*, 54). See also Rediker, *Between the Devil and the Deep Blue Sea*.
4. Emerson, *Nature*, in *Essays and Lectures*, 10.
5. Dana, *Two Years before the Mast*, 38–39.
6. Thomas Philbrick, the most comprehensive chronicler of American sea writing (although his focus is overwhelmingly on novels and other fictions), explains, "With the end of hostilities in 1815 the country entered what has aptly been called the golden age of American shipping, a period of thirty-five years during which American seamen came to challenge and even to displace the British hegemony of many of the most important areas of maritime activity." After the whaling industry collapsed following the discovery of petroleum (which was easier to mine and therefore cheaper fuel than whale oil) in 1859, after the completion of the transcontinental railroad, and after the rise of the steamship, the age of sail was reduced to more of a sporting interest. Philbrick further writes, "The year 1850 . . . is a convenient point at which to fix the start of the abrupt decline of American nautical activity and interest, a decline that reduced the United States from supremacy in many of the most important areas of commerce and shipping to near extinction as a maritime power in the years following the Civil War" (Philbrick, *James Fenimore Cooper and the Development of American Sea Fiction*, 2, 260).

7. *The Tempest* is one of the earliest New World narratives to deal with this theme; other examples include Richard Steere's *Monumental Memorial of Marine Mercy* (1684) and numerous sermons and broadsides, including *A True and Particular Narrative of the Late Tremendous Tornado*, which details a 1792 event "When several pleasure-boats were lost . . . and thirty Men, Women and Children, (*taking their* Pleasure *on that* Sacred Day) were unhappily *drowned* in Neptune's raging and tempestuous *Element*!!!!!!" (qtd. in Springer, *America and the Sea*, 52).

8. See Chapter 1 for a more detailed discussion of sailor literacy and working-men's libraries.

9. For more on the expansion of print in the early nineteenth century, see Baym, *Novels, Readers, and Reviewers*; Charvat, *Literary Publishing in America* and *Profession of Authorship in America*; Davidson, *Revolution and the Word*; Denning, *Mechanic Accents*; and Warner, *Letters of the Republic*.

10. The first figure is derived by Rediker, *Between the Devil and the Deep Blue Sea*, 158; the second, from research done by the Merchant Seamen's Bible Society, qtd. in Skallerup, *Books Afloat and Ashore*, 22–23.

11. Little, *Life on the Ocean*, 68.

12. The more prominent of these societies included the Seamen's Friend Society, the American Tract Society, and the Merchant Seamen's Bible Society; also see Chapter 1.

13. Edgar Allan Poe is an exception to this rule, but his *Narrative of Arthur Gordon Pym* exploits so shrewdly the codes of the sea and exploration narrative that it demands inclusion and is discussed in Chapter 6.

14. See Denning, *Mechanic Accents*, and also Streeby, *American Sensations*, and Fabian, *Unvarnished Truth*. Neither Denning, Streeby, nor Fabian discusses sea narratives.

15. Martingale [Sleeper], *Jack in the Forecastle*, 9–10. Martingale refers to the popular 1727 pamphlet narrative *The Hermit: Or the Unparalleled Sufferings and Surprising Adventures of Mr. Philip Quarll, an Englishman. Who was lately discovered by Mr. Dorrington a Bristol Merchant, upon an uninhabited Island in the South-Sea; where he has lived above Fifty Years without any human assistance, still continues to reside, and will not come away* and to Robert Paltock's *Life and Adventures of Peter Wilkins* (1751).

16. Forbes [Bennet], *Appeal to Merchants and Ship Owners*, 22.

17. Little, *Life on the Ocean*, 39.

18. Delano, *Wanderings and Adventures*, 63.

19. Whitecar, *Four Years in a Whaleship*, viii. Whitecar claims that "the entire matter comprised in my journal was written at sea, on a sailor's chest, amongst seamen, by night and by day, amid storm and calm, in localities situate between the latitudes 41° 30′ north and 45° south, and longitudes 71° west and 170° east—embracing a wide field for observation" (ix–x).

20. In this sense sea narratives are akin to William Andrews's notion of slave narratives as self-consciously generic, not merely documentary. See Andrews, *To Tell a Free Story*.

21. The overview of sea writing in this section has been aided by Philbrick, *James Fenimore Cooper and the Development of American Sea Fiction*; Springer, *America and the Sea*; Bender, *Sea-Brothers*; Foulke, *Sea Voyage Narrative*; and Peck, *Maritime Fiction*.

22. For more on British sea writing, see Klein, *Fictions of the Sea*; Foulke, *Sea Voyage Narrative*; and Leyland, *British Tar in Fact and Fiction*.

23. Familiar examples include William Bradford's description of the *Mayflower's* providential crossing and Increase Mather's chapter on sea deliverance in *Essay for the Recording of Illustrious Providences*. In an Early Modern era of public fascination with monstrous forms, sea monsters had special appeal, a trend mocked in later nineteenth-century broadsides such as Eugene Batchelder's "A Romance of the Sea Serpent; or, The Ichthyosaurus" (1849).

24. The original title of Defoe's narrative attests to its generic status: *The life and strange surprizing adventures of Robinson Crusoe, of York, mariner; who lived eight and twenty years, all alone in an un-inhabited island on the coast of America, near the mouth of the great river of Oroonoque; having been cast on shore by shipwreck, wherein all the men perished but himself : With an account how he was at last as strangely deliver'd by pyrates / Written by himself.*

25. David Kazanjian discusses several black sailors' accounts of the Middle Passage in *Colonizing Trick*. Vincent Carretta, in his *Equiano the African*, argues that Equiano was in fact born in South Carolina and could not have experienced the Middle Passage; his conclusion, therefore, is that *Interesting Narrative* is the first African American novel. Yet in my reading the "truth" of narrative writing lies not in its verifiable facts but in its ability to represent the codes and interests of the genre, which Equiano's narrative amply accomplishes.

26. On the subject of such narratives, see Kazanjian, *Colonizing Trick*; Bolster, *Black Jacks*; and Gates and Andrews, *Pioneers of the Black Atlantic*.

27. Cooper's first sea novels were *The Pilot: A Tale of the Sea* (1823) and *The Red Rover* (1828). Royall Tyler's *Algerine Captive* (1797) featured the sea but cannot be as cleanly characterized as a sea novel, since its intervals of ocean settings are more circumstantial than essential.

28. *Sailor's Magazine, and Naval Journal*, March 1829, 219 (emphases in original).

29. *Life Boat*, April 1860, 253.

30. Dana sailed before the mast—not as a gentleman or passenger—even though he was the Harvard-educated son of the well-known writer and founder of the *North American Review*, Richard Henry Dana Sr. He went to sea to cure a weakness of the eyes presumed to be brought about by too much reading, an activity that Dana and his fellow seamen nevertheless participate in to a great extent throughout the voyage.

31. Philbrick (and other critics following his example) has seen Dana's narrative as a turning point, after which sea narratives strove to represent the experience of the common sailor, rather than the officers whose narratives appeared in greater number in the 1830s, before Dana's 1840 narrative. While acknowledg-

ing that officers composed more narratives than common sailors prior to Dana, I do not find that the content and interests of the narratives differ to a marked extent. While officers certainly occupied a more privileged position than seamen before the mast, their narratives are equally concerned with issues of labor and reflection and engaged with literary culture at sea to no greater degree. See, after Philbrick, *James Fenimore Cooper and the Development of American Sea Fiction*, the unpublished dissertation by Egan, "Gentlemen-Sailors."

32. While Buntline is best remembered for *The Mysteries and Miseries of New York* and for his embrace of William "Buffalo Bill" Cody, his early fictional output is largely based on the sea. Examples include *The King of the Sea* (1847); *Cruisings, Afloat and Ashore* (1848); *The Last of the Buccaneers* (1856); and *Seawaif* (1859), among many others.

33. Springer, *America and the Sea*, ix.

34. Philbrick, *James Fenimore Cooper and the Development of American Sea Fiction*, viii. See also Foulke, *Sea Voyage Narrative*, and Peck, *Maritime Fiction*.

35. There are promising avenues for further study of maritime narratives revealed in the new global criticism, nevertheless. Some of the strongest work in this direction has been produced by Peter Linebaugh and Marcus Rediker in their Marxian analysis of eighteenth-century Anglo-Atlantic sailors; David Kazanjian, who extends the work of Linebaugh and Rediker (as well as that of Jeffrey Bolster) in theorizing how black sailors interacted with mercantilism; C. L. R. James in his meditations on labor, colonialism, and literature; Paul Gilje in his historical analysis of sailors and the concept of liberty; Linda Colley in her overview of the British sailor in crisis; and Paul Gilroy in his conception of the Black Atlantic. Their works invoke the world of maritime labor with exemplary specificity, using evidence derived from seamen's writings, yet most could do more to analyze the rhetorical achievements of sailors, who were remarkably attuned to the very theoretical and political questions raised by such scholars. See Linebaugh and Rediker, *Many-Headed Hydra*; Kazanjian, *Colonizing Trick*; Bolster, *Black Jacks*; James, *Mariners, Renegades, and Castaways*; Gilje, *Liberty on the Waterfront*; Colley, *Captives*; and Gilroy, *Black Atlantic*.

Also worthy of note is Casarino's *Modernity at Sea*, which reads the sea novel as the textual manifestation of Foucault's "heterotopia." Yet in focusing his readings only on the exceptional sea novels produced by Melville and Conrad (and, to a lesser degree, Poe), Casarino misses an opportunity to test his theory of the genre of the sea novel against the voluminous nonfictional narratives produced by laboring seamen at, or near, the scene of their work. Similarly, Margaret Cohen's work on sea fiction and modernity (forthcoming as of this writing) promises an important reading of transatlantic maritime fiction and modernity. Cohen is interested in sea novels' representations of work, what she calls "know-how," but the work and the writings of actual sailors are not addressed in an essay on the topic she published in 2003; see Cohen, "Traveling Genres." A recent collection of essays edited by Bernhard Klein and Gesa

MacKenthun, *Sea Changes: Historicizing the Ocean*, admirably attempts to move beyond metaphorical investigations of the meaning of the ocean; yet again, sailors' own writing little factors into this history.

36. In this vein my work is particularly indebted to Michael Denning's scholarship on working-class culture and popular fiction in *Mechanic Accents*; Ann Fabian's historical study of personal narratives in nineteenth-century America in *Unvarnished Truth*; Shelly Streeby's analysis of class, labor, and sensational fictions in *American Sensations*; Thomas Augst's meditation on clerks and literary culture in *Clerk's Tale*; Jonathan Arac's work on narrative forms in the antebellum period in *Emergence of American Literary Narrative*; and Cathy Davidson's foundational work on the rise of the novel in America in *Revolution and the Word*. Michael Gilmore, Nicholas Bromell, and Cindy Weinstein have helped me understand how the work of writing functions alongside literary representations of other, more embodied forms of labor in nineteenth-century literature, even though sailor narratives do not, as I argue, display what Bromell calls a "distinction between manual and mental labor, which in turn rested upon an assumed dichotomy of mind (and soul) and body" in the antebellum period (Bromell, *By the Sweat of the Brow*, 7). On this topic, see also Gilmore, *American Romanticism and the Marketplace*, and Weinstein, *Literature of Labor and the Labors of Literature*.

Furthermore, *The View from the Masthead* speaks to the long history of scholarship on visual possession, or what Myra Jehlen calls the product of the "eye/I," such as the work of Mary Louise Pratt, Richard Poirier, Wayne Franklin, and Jonathan Crary. Most directly, my work is attentive to the ample critical work on Herman Melville's fiction. Yet this book breaks with the work of those scholars who, in reading his novels alongside contemporary sea narratives, have mostly taken David Reynolds's cue in isolating—and elevating—Melville's work from its sources and analogues.

37. Forbes [Bennet], *Appeal to Merchants and Ship Owners*, 6.

CHAPTER 1

1. *Life in a Man-of-War*, xv.

2. The phrase *"cacoethes scribendi"* or "scribbler's itch," originating with Juvenal, would be familiar to an antebellum reading audience from Catherine Maria Sedgwick's 1830 short story of that name. Another sailor, Sidney J. Henshaw, likewise admitted to being infected by the dreadful *"cacoethes scribendi"* (Henshaw, *Around the World*, 1:x).

3. *Life in a Man-of-War*, v. The narrator takes this line from Thomas Moore's ballad "Boat Glee," from his comic opera *MP; or, The Blue-Stocking*. The original reads,

Nothing is lost on him, who sees
With an eye that Feeling gave;

For him there's a story in every breeze,
And a picture in every wave. (Moore, *Prose and Verse*, 259)

4. *Life in a Man-of-War*, 96.
5. Ibid. 97.
6. Dana, *Two Years before the Mast*, 282.
7. See Chapter 4 for a fuller elaboration of the structure of maritime labor.
8. Cathy Davidson adapts this terminology from the German scholar of *l'histoire du livre* Rolf Engelsing in order to describe reading practices of eighteenth- and nineteenth-century Americans. See Davidson, *Revolution and the Word*, 70–79.
9. Browne, *Etchings of a Whaling Cruise*, 110–11.
10. Dana, *Two Years before the Mast*, 282.
11. Browne, *Etchings of a Whaling Cruise*, 110–11.
12. Stewart, *Visit to the South Seas*, 1:28–29.
13. Log 143, 184–85.
14. *Life in a Man-of-War*, 107.
15. Forbes [Bennet], *Appeal to Merchants and Ship Owners*, 6.
16. Whitecar, *Four Years in a Whaleship*, 27–28.
17. Sullivan, *Scarcity of Seamen*, 8–9 (emphasis in original).
18. I elaborate on this notion in my essay "Atlantic Trade." See also Linebaugh and Rediker, *Many-Headed Hydra*, and Rediker, *Between the Devil and the Deep Blue Sea*.
19. Gilje, *Liberty on the Waterfront*.
20. See ibid. and Bennett, *Union Jacks*.
21. See Rediker, *Between the Devil and the Deep Blue Sea*, and Linebaugh and Rediker, *Many-Headed Hydra*.
22. Little, *Life on the Ocean*, 369.
23. See Dye, "Early American Merchant Seafarers," and Rediker, *Between the Devil and the Deep Blue Sea*, 307.
24. Skallerup, *Books Afloat and Ashore*. Some more recent but quite specialized critical work on sailors and their texts includes Simon Newman's fascinating look at seamen's tattoos in his article "Reading the Bodies of Early American Seafarers." Also see Hovde, "Sea Colportage," and Nunis, "Books in Their Sea Chests."
25. Skallerup, *Books Afloat and Ashore*, 12.
26. Chetwood et al., *Voyages and Adventures of Captain Robert Boyle*, 22.
27. "Literary Pursuits of Sailors," 484.
28. Little, *Life on the Ocean*, 128, 163.
29. Rediker, *Between the Devil and the Deep Blue Sea*, 164.
30. Ibid., 158.
31. Lockridge's quantitative *Literacy in Colonial New England* established the signature standard as a default method, and his statistics remain widely quoted, although recent scholars have taken issue with his numbers. Dissenters include

Margaret Spufford, who finds in *Contrasting Communities* that those who signed their wills with an *X* had been able to write signatures on other documents, and Cremin, "Reading, Writing, and Literacy." Davidson usefully summarizes this debate in *Revolution and the Word*, 56–63.

32. Hall makes this case most persuasively, in *Cultures of Print*, 57.

33. Ibid., 83 n. 12.

34. Davidson, *Revolution and the Word*, 27.

35. According to Lockridge's mark-signature calculations, New England became "a society of nearly universal male literacy . . . . The raw data show that as of 1660 only 60% of men signed their wills, whereas by 1710 the figure had risen to 70% and by 1760 it was up to 85%. Samples from Suffolk and Middlesex Counties, Massachusetts, indicate that male signatures on wills approached 90% by 1790" (Lockridge, *Literacy in Colonial New England*, 13). New England, of course, provided ships with the largest percentage of their crews, and sailors were predominantly urban. Ira Dye calls the late-eighteenth-century sailor a "creature of urban origins," pointing out that while only 5 percent of the general population lived in urban areas between 1796 and 1815, 49.5 percent of white sailors and 27.9 percent of black sailors came from cities (Dye, "Early American Merchant Seafarers," 339–40). Julie Hedgepeth Williams, acknowledging the difficulty of fixing literary statistics, nevertheless confirms that "colonial Americans spoke fondly and frequently of reading. Their talk about printed works and their efforts to obtain books, pamphlets, and periodicals illustrate the fact that they were, indeed, readers" (Williams, *Significance of the Printed Word in Early America*, 9). See also Casper, Chaison, and Groves, *Perspectives on American Book History*, and Amory and Hall, *History of the Book in America*.

36. Qtd. in Skallerup, *Books Afloat and Ashore*, 22–23.

37. On antebellum reform, see in particular Garvey, *Creating the Culture of Reform in Antebellum America*; Dorsey, *Reforming Men and Women*; Ginzberg, *Women and the Work of Benevolence*; and Glenn, *Campaigns against Corporal Punishment*.

38. Other reformers on behalf of sailors targeted unscrupulous landlords and agitated for rest or retirement homes for seamen. See Gilje, *Liberty on the Waterfront*, 195–227.

39. "Ship Libraries," *Sheet Anchor*, 15 August 1846, 124.

40. "Books for Seamen," *Sailor's Magazine*, March 1844, 231.

41. *Sailor's Magazine, and Seamen's Friend*, April 1863, 232.

42. "Libraries," *Eleventh Annual Report of the Board of Directors of the Boston Seaman's Friend Society*, 11.

43. *Third Annual Report of the American Seamen's Friend Society*, 6.

44. John Sherburne Sleeper, "The Cause of Seamen," *Sheet Anchor*, 7 January 1843, 5. Under the pseudonym "Hawser Martingale," Sleeper was also the author of two popular sea narratives.

45. "Life at Sea," *Sheet Anchor*, 20 September 1845, 140–41. Of the other periodi-

cals that targeted sailors, many had a charitable aim. These included *The Sea Bird: Devoted to the best interests of seamen and their families*; *The Sailor's Magazine, and Naval Journal*; and *The Life Boat*. Secular periodicals included *The Monthly Nautical Magazine, and Quarterly Review* and *U.S. Nautical Magazine and Naval Journal*. The definition of what made a book good was adaptable, though; as a workingman's advocate urged laborers,

> Read none but good books. And by this I do not mean that reading should be confined to Baxter's "Saint's Rest" or Bunyan's "Pilgrim's Progress," which —capital books as they are in their sphere—would not serve to fill one's mind with very accurate scientific facts. But I mean that, in whatever department you may wish to read, it is better to read the best authors than to wade through the dilutions of their works to be found in gaudily bound and badly printed "Gazetteers," and "Histories of the World," which profess to contain in one volume all that the ages have served to accumulate. (Haley, *Words for the Workers*, 87; emphasis in original)

46. Colton, *Deck and Port*, 19.
47. Sullivan, *Scarcity of Seamen*, 23.
48. Ames, *Mariner's Sketches*, 241.
49. Haley, *Words for the Workers*, 91.
50. According to Franklin, his library was constituted by "mostly young trades-men" and had the effect of making "the common Tradesmen & Farmers as intelligent as most Gentlemen from other Countries" (Franklin, *Autobiography*, in *Writings*, 80, 71).
51. *Boston Commercial Gazette*, 4 July 1821 (emphases in original).
52. "Seamen's Library," *Boston Commercial Gazette*, 6 August 1821. This letter, from First Lieutenant William Augustus Weaver, was also published in the *Washington Gazette*, the *Charleston City Gazette*, and the *New York Spectator*.
53. *Essex Register* (Salem, Mass.), 8 August 1821.
54. The following is a transcription of fig. 1.2:

> The following books will be furnished for the use of Vessels of War when on a cruise, and for the use of Navy Yards, until otherwise ordered.
> Navy Department June 10th 1839.

Nicholson's Mathematics.	Porter's Voyage, 2d Edtn, pub-
Euclid's Elements.	lished by Wiley, N.Y.
Bowditch's Navigation.	Ross, Parry's & Franklin's Voyages.
Maury's do.	Life & Voyages of Columbus.
Ramsay's Universal History.	Bancroft's History of the U. States.
Gibbon's History—Decline & Fall	Prescott's Ferdinand & Isabella.
of Rome.	Cooper's Naval History of the U.S.
Ferguson's History of Roman	do. Pilot.
Republic.	do. Red Rover.

Gillies' History of Greece.

do.   Water Witch.

Rollin's ancient History.

do.   Homeward Bound.

Lingard's History of England.

Encyclopedia Britannica.

Constitution of the U.S. & the different States.

Hutton's Tracts.

Arnott's Natural Philosophy.

Marshall's Life of Washington.

Wood & Bache's Dispensary.

Botta's American Revolution (until
Bancroft's is completed.)

Walsh's Appeal.

Kent's Commentaries.

Hallam's constitutional History.

Incidents of Travel in Egypt, Arabia & the Holy Land.

Vattel's Law of Nations.

*Bradford's Atlas.

A year in Spain.

Jacobson's Sea Laws.

Lives & Voyages of Drake, Cavendish & Dampier.

Gordons Digest, or Ingersoll's
abridgement of U.S. Laws.

Historical account of the Circumnavigation of the Globe &c.

Treaties with foreign Powers.

Federalist.

from the Voyage of Magellan to
the death of Cook.

Ledyard's Travels.

Astoria.

Plutarch's Lives.

Voyage of the Potomac.

Bible & Prayer book.

55 The readers listed include "Introduction to School Reader, Gradual Reader, Village Reader, First Class Reader, Sequel to Gradual Reader, Second Class Reader, Worcester's Book of Reading Lessons, Swan's District School Reader, American School Reader, Porter's Periodical Reader, National Reader, Grammar of the English Language, Brown's Grammar" (U.S. Steam Sloop *Narragansett*'s Circulation Library).

56. Chadwick, Chief of Bureau of Equipment, 19 June 1897, Congressional Information Service, *U.S. Executive Branch Documents, 1789–1909*, pt. 5, *Navy Department*.

57. James C. Osborn, second mate of the *Morgan*, recorded in the ship's log the list of books he read on his 1841–45 whaling voyage. The following is a transcription of fig. 1.1:

A List of Books that I have read on the Voyage.

1 vol. Goods' Book of Nature.	The American Longer	1 vol.
1 vol. Self Knowledg.	Benjm Heen	1 vol.
1 vol. Morrels Voyages.	Pelham Bulwer	2 vol.
2 vol. Madm De Lacy.	Rolans History	3 vol.
2 vol. Quadroon.	Napolians Anicdotes	1 vol.
2 vol. Pathfinder.	Bulwers Novels	12 vols.
1 vol. Pilot.	The Prince & Pedler	2 vols.
1 vol. Reunza or the Last of the Trybunes.	Jack Adams	1 vol.
1 vol. Numid of Pompei.	May you like it	1 vol.
1 vol. Book of Beauty.	Kings High way	2 vol.

1 vol. Tracks on Disapation.   The Young mans Guide   1 vol.
1 vol. Gray Ham's Lectures.
1 vol. Husbands Duty to Wife.
1 vol. Ladyes Medical Guide.
1 Madm Tusades History of the French Revolution.

James C Osborn at Sea Jan 6th 1841. 1842. 1843.
                                                Edgartown is my native place.
1 vol. Pamelia.
2 vol. Meriam Coffin.
1 vol. Ten Thousands a Year.
1 vol. Humphrey Clinker.

Journal of a Voyage to the Pacifick Ocean in the Good Ship Chas. W.
Morgan: Thomas A. Norton Master 1841. 1842. 1843. 1844. Arrived Jan
5th 1845.

2 vol. Bracebridge Hall.
1 vol. Travels in Egypt and Arabia Felix.
2 vol. Elizabeth de Bruce.
2 vol. Bravo.
2 vol. Repealers.
2 vol. Steam Voyage Down The Danube.
1 vol. Memoirs of Dr. Edward Young.
1 vol. Health Adviser.
1 vol. Female Wanderer.
1 vol. Female Horse Thief.
1 vol. Holdens Narritive.
1 vol. Rosamonds Narrative of the Roman Catholic Priests &c.
2 vol. Mercedes of Castile.
22 vol. of Marryatts Works.

58. Clark, "Diary of an Apprentice Cabinetmaker." I greatly profited from a semi-nar run by Robert Gross on Carpenter's journal at the American Antiquarian Society in June 2003. See also Zboray, "Antebellum Reading and the Ironies of Technological Innovation."

59. "Life at Sea," *Sheet Anchor*, 20 September 1845, 140.

60. *Life in a Man-of-War*, 108.

61. Ibid., 110.

62. Ibid., 107–8.

63. "Give the Sailor Good Books," *Sheet Anchor*, 20 September 1845, 140.

64. Marks, *Retrospect*, 32–33. This text was included in the list "No. 1 Sailor's Library, selected under the supervision of the American Seamen's Friend Society," 1843.

65. Ibid., 167.

66. Skallerup, *Books Afloat and Ashore*, 210.

67. Melville, *White-Jacket*, 169.

68. Henshaw, *Around the World*, 1:vii–viii.

69. Ibid., 1:ix.

70. *Life in a Man-of-War*, xv.

71. Barnard et al., *Narrative of the Sufferings and Adventures of Capt. Charles H. Barnard*, 39.

72. Hazen, *Five Years Before the Mast*, xi–xii (emphases in original).

73. Fabian does not discuss sailors in her analysis of the narratives of prisoners, soldiers, and slaves, among others.

74. Barnard et al., *Narrative of the Sufferings and Adventures of Capt. Charles H. Barnard*, 39.

75. Taylor, *Life on a Whaler*, xi.

76. Martingale [Sleeper], *Jack in the Forecastle*, preface (emphasis in original).

77. Harris, *Humbug*, 57, 79. Harris mentions maritime writing briefly when he notes, "Nowhere was the zest for operational description better satisfied than in the sea novels that figured prominently on American reading lists of the Jacksonian era. . . . The landlubber who wished to get through the novel [referring here to Dana's *Two Years before the Mast*] had, perforce, to learn the vocabulary and master the sets to follow the drama properly" (76). Harris's examples of sea novels include Melville's and Dana's, and his argument easily extends to the voluminous sailor writing not mentioned in *Humbug*.

78. Robbins, *Journal*, vi.

79. Qtd. in bookseller catalog, *Oliver S. Felt's Catalogue of Crosby and Nichols' Publications* (New York: Oliver S. Felt, n.d.).

80. Review of *An authentic Narrative of the loss of the American brig Commerce*, 389–90 (emphasis in original).

81. Ibid., 391.

82. Review of *Journal of a Cruise made to the Pacifick Ocean*, 274.

83. Ibid.

84. Review of *A Narrative of Voyages and Travels in the Northern and Southern Hemispheres*, 256–57.

CHAPTER 2

1. Dana, *Two Years before the Mast*, 38–39.

2. Riley, *Authentic Narrative of the Loss of the American Brig Commerce*, iii.

3. Ray, *Horrors of Slavery*, 69.

4. The consistent factor in this mobility was their labor knowledge, for as Marcus Rediker has observed, "Sailors circulated from ship to ship, even from merchant vessels to the Royal Navy, into privateering or piracy and back again, and found that the tasks performed and the skills required by each were essentially the same" (Rediker, *Between the Devil and the Deep Blue Sea*, 83).

5. The renegados operated in several Atlantic spheres, from the edges of the Mediterranean to the western coast of Africa to the Caribbean, the islands of which harbored many different pirates representing many different nationalities, not primarily European. Those European renegados who chose to serve with the Barbary pirates took Muslim names and converted to Islam as a condition of their service.

6. A note on terms: loosely speaking, the Algerine ruler in the seventeenth- and eighteenth-century height of piracy was called the "dey"; the Tripolitan ruler, the "bashaw" (an earlier version of the Turkish word "pasha"); the Tunisian, the "bey" (a Turkish term) or "dey"; and the Moroccan, the "emperor." These terms are often used interchangeably, though. Throughout this chapter I will use the narratives' preferred term "Algerine" rather than "Algerian" when referring to matters related to Algiers and its people. Used to describe these North African "Saracen" states, the term "Barbary" is a reference to the Berber natives of the region, as well as a suggestion of the "barbarity" that Europeans associated with North Africa. In their narratives, many sailors use the generic term "Turk," derived from the Ottoman Empire's long occupation of the region, to describe the residents of North Africa.

7. Information in this chapter regarding the Barbary pirates, the Barbary States, and the early American response is distilled from the sources that follow. On the centuries-long history of North African piracy: Bamford, *Barbary Pirates*; Clissold, *Barbary Slaves*; and Fisher, *Barbary Legend*. On the American military and diplomatic response: Barnby, *Prisoners of Algiers*; Carr, "John Adams and the Barbary Problem"; Chidsey, *Wars in Barbary*; Irwin, *Diplomatic Relations of the United States with the Barbary Powers*; Kitzen, *Tripoli and the United States at War*; Lambert, *Barbary Wars*; Leiner, *End of Barbary Terror*; London, *Victory in Tripoli*; Rojas, " 'Insults Unpunished' "; U.S. Office of Naval Records, *Naval Documents Related to the United States Wars with the Barbary Powers*; Whipple, *To the Shores of Tripoli*; and Zacks, *Pirate Coast*. On the American cultural response to captivity: Baepler, "Barbary Captivity Narrative in American Culture"; Carter, "Mathew Carey"; and Ebersole, *Captured by Texts*.

8. In an agrarian fantasy in his *Notes on the State of Virginia*, Jefferson wonders if "it might be better for us to abandon the ocean altogether, that being the element whereon we shall be principally exposed to jostle with other nations: to leave to others to bring what we shall want, and to carry what we can spare. This would make us invulnerable to Europe, by offering none of our property to their prize, and would turn all our citizens to the cultivation of the earth. . . . To aim at such a navy as the greater nations of Europe possess, would be a foolish and wicked waste of the energies of our countrymen" (175).

9. "Jefferson to Adams," 11 July 1786, in Adams, *Adams-Jefferson Letters*, 142.

10. "To James Madison," 1 September 1785, in Jefferson, *Writings*, 821.

11. "Adams to Jefferson," 3 July 1786, in Adams, *Adams-Jefferson Letters*, 139.

12. This phrase originates with the XYZ Affair but was marshaled to use in this case.

13. Cowdery, *American Captives in Tripoli*, 11.
14. Ibid.; Ray, *Horrors of Slavery*, 111.
15. Carey, *Short Account of Algiers*, 15–16, describes how new captives were processed:

> When an Algerine pirate takes a prize, he examines into the quality and circumstances of the prisoners. If he disbelieves the account they give of themselves, they are bastinadoed, till he has met with an agreeable answer. Having obtained what information he is able, he brings them on shore, after having stripped them almost naked. He carries them directly to the palace of the dey, where the European consuls assemble, to see if any of the prisoners belong to their respective nations, who are at peace with Algiers. In that case, they reclaim them, provided that they were only passengers; but if they have served on board of the ships of any people at war with "the mighty and invincible militia," they cannot be discharged without payment of the full ransom.
>
> Matters are thus settled between the dey and the consuls, what part of the prisoners are to be set at liberty, and what part are to be considered as slaves. The dey has next his choice of every eighth slave. He generally chuses the masters, surgeons, carpenters, and most useful hands belonging to the several prizes. Besides his eighth, he lays claim to all prisoners of quality, for whom a superior ransom is to be expected. The rest are left to the corsair and his owners. They are carried to the slave market; the crier proclaims their rank, profession, and circumstances, and the price set upon each of them. They are then led to the court before the palace of the dey, and there sold to the best bidder. If any sum is offered beyond the price first set upon them, it belongs to the government. The captors and owners have only that which was originally set upon the slaves.

16. Ray, *Horrors of Slavery*, 99.
17. Adams and Cock, *Narrative of Robert Adams*, 74.
18. Ray, *Horrors of Slavery*, 89–90, describes the experience of the bastinado:

> The instrument with which they prepare a man for torture, is called a bastone; It is generally about four or five feet long, and as thick in the middle as a man's leg, tapering to the ends. At equal distances from the centre, it is perforated in two places, and a rope incurvated, the ends passed through the holes, and knotted. This forms a loop. The person is then thrown on his back, his feet put through the loop, and a man at each end of the stick, both at once, twist it round, screw his feet and ancles tight together, and raise the soles of his feet nearly horizontal. A Turk sits on his back, and two men, with each a bamboo, or branch of the date tree, as large as a walking-staff, and about three feet in length, hard, and very heavy, strip or roll up their sleeves, and, with all their strength and fury, apply the bruising cudgel to the bottoms of the feet.

19. Ibid., 18.

20. Cathcart, *Captives*, 144–45. Cathcart further writes,

> O! America, could you see the miserable situation of your citizens in cap-
> tivity, who have shed their blood to secure you the liberty you now possess
> and enjoy; and who now have their misery augmented by the consideration
> that the country for which they fought is now free and in a flourishing
> condition, you are the first that set the example to the world, to shake off the
> yoke of tyranny, to expel despotism and injustice from the face of the earth.
> The negroes have even had a share in your deliberations, and have reaped the
> benefits arising from your wise and wholesome laws and regulations, and we,
> the very men who have assisted in all your laudable enterprises, are now cast
> off because we have been unfortunate; are denied the rights of our common
> country.

21. Foss, *Journal of the Captivity and Sufferings of John Foss*, 158.

22. Paddock, *Narrative of the Shipwreck of the Ship Oswego*, iii.

23. Ibid., 186.

24. Ray, *Horrors of Slavery*, 15.

25. This temporal limitation does not register for European sailors, for whom
    Barbary captivity was a threat for centuries. Europeans produced tales of their
    long-term vulnerability to captivity beginning in the Early Modern period;
    English examples include John Fox, "The Worthy Enterprise of John Fox, in
    Delivering 266 Christians Out of the Captivity of the Turks," in Richard
    Hakluyt, *Principal Navigations* (1589); John Rawlins, *The Famous and Wonderful
    Recovery of a Ship of Bristol, Called the Exchange, from the Turkish Pirates of Argier*
    (1622); *News from Sally of a Strange Delivery of Four English Captives from the
    Slavery of the Turks* (1642); and Thomas Phelps, *True Account of the Captivity of
    Thomas Phelps* (1685). Daniel Defoe's *Robinson Crusoe* is derived from this
    tradition, as is *Don Quixote*; Miguel de Cervantes himself spent five years in
    Algerine slavery.

26. See Baepler, "Barbary Captivity Narrative in Early America," "Barbary Cap-
    tivity Narrative in American Culture," and *White Slaves, African Masters*; Colley,
    "Going Native, Telling Tales"; Lewis, "Savages of the Seas"; Margulis, "Swar-
    thy Pirates and White Slaves"; Montgomery, "White Captives, African Slaves";
    Sieminski, "Puritan Captivity Narrative and the Politics of the American Rev-
    olution"; Snader, "Oriental Captivity Narrative and Early English Fiction."

27. An example of work that situates Rowson's play within a transnational context
    may be seen in Dillon's "Slaves in Algiers."

28. Many federal-era public figures were struck by the inversion of African slave/
    American captor and African captor/American slave. Benjamin Franklin, in
    one of his last publications before his death, exploited this homology to pointed
    satiric effect. As "Historicus," Franklin wrote a letter to the editor of the *Federal
    Gazette* that presented a fictional 100-year-old letter from an Algerian named

Sidi Mehemet Ibrahim. In the letter, Ibrahim ventriloquizes the defenses of slavery proposed by American southerners, only from an Algerian perspective:

> If we cease our Cruises against the Christians, how shall we be furnished with the Commodities their Countries produce, and which are so necessary for us? If we forbear to make Slaves of their People, who in this hot Climate are to cultivate our Lands? Who are to perform the common Labours of our City, and in our Families? Must we not then be our own Slaves? . . . If we then cease taking and plundering the Infidel Ships, and making Slaves of the Seamen and Passengers, our Lands will become of no Value for want of Cultivation; the Rents of Houses in the City will sink one half; and the Revenues of Government arising from its Share of Prizes be totally destroy'd!

Franklin's satire derives its effect from an assumption of public condemnation of Barbary captivity as well as of the rulers who sanction the practice of taking and keeping such captives. Yet its real thrust is aimed at American commercial interests, for whom Barbary piracy was so crippling. What Franklin suggests is that humanitarian concern for Barbary captives is wholly contingent on the fact that the humanitarian good, in this case, is also the commercial good. (The opposite was considered true for African slaves in America.) See Historicus [Franklin], "Sidi Mehemet Ibrahim on the Slave Trade," in Franklin, *Writings*, 1158.

29. Carey, *Short Account of Algiers*, 16.

30. Over fifty years later abolitionist Senator Charles Sumner would invoke the same "singular and suggestive comparison" in his *White Slavery in the Barbary States*. In it Sumner gave a historical account of the Barbary region, which he saw as "occupying nearly the same parallels with the Slave States of our Union. [Barbary] extends over nearly the same number of degrees of longitude with our Slave States, which seem now, alas! to stretch from the Atlantic Ocean to the Rio Grande. It is supposed to embrace about 700,000 square miles, which cannot be far from the space comprehended by what may be called the *Barbary States of America*" (11).

31. Montgomery, "White Captives, African Slaves," 617.

32. Tyler, *Algerine Captive*, 1:189. Underhill, like Robinson Crusoe, is serving aboard a slave ship when he himself is enslaved.

33. Davidson, *Revolution and the Word*, 206.

34. "American," *Humanity in Algiers*, 3–4.

35. Paddock, *Narrative of the Shipwreck of the Ship Oswego*, 137.

36. Riley, *Authentic Narrative of the Loss of the American Brig Commerce*, 394.

37. Ibid., 77. It should be noted that another of Riley's sailors, Archibald Robbins, like Clark, can feel little sympathy for African slaves: "These Africans, of every name and feature and complexion, take delight in enslaving each other; and although the slave trade, carried on by Christian merchants, on the coast of Africa, excites the just indignation of the Christian world, yet it can hardly be

expected that an American, who has for months and years been enslaved by them, can feel so much compassion towards a slave *here* as those do, who have always enjoyed the blessings of humanity and liberty" (Robbins, *Journal*, 77).

38. See, for example, Castiglia, *Bound and Determined*; Strong, *Captive Selves, Captivating Others*; Snader, *Caught between Worlds*; and Ebersole, *Captured by Texts*.

39. One of the only critical texts on Barbary narratives highlights the categorical differences between chattel slavery and captivity in its very title: Paul Baepler's well-researched anthology of captivity narratives, *White Slaves, African Masters*, sets up an odd dichotomy between the race of the slaves and the geographical origin of their masters. Even though Baepler's scholarly introduction to the narratives is careful to point out that "it would be wrong to equate [Barbary captivity] with institutionalized chattel slavery in the United States," his title could be seen to invite that very equation. The inverse racial dichotomy that Baepler invokes between this situation and that of the black Africans held in slavery by white Americans does not hold, though, in part because of the fact that the North "African masters" of Baepler's title are mostly Arabic in ethnic origin and culturally very different from the East and Central African targets of the Atlantic slave trade.

40. Foss, *Journal of the Captivity and Sufferings of John Foss*, 4.

41. Adams and Cock, *Narrative of Robert Adams*, xxi.

42. [Sparks], "Narrative of Robert Adams," 204.

43. [Sparks], "Interiour of Africa," 11.

44. [Sparks], "Narrative of Robert Adams," 204.

45. Review of *An authentic Narrative of the loss of the American brig Commerce*, 389–90 (emphasis in original).

46. [Sparks], "Narrative of Robert Adams," 221.

47. O'Brien, "[Extract of a letter]."

48. *Columbian Magazine* 1, no. 15 (November 1787): 108.

49. Cowdery, "Tripolitan Slavery." The same letter was reprinted by dozens of Middle Atlantic and New England newspapers in the days that followed.

50. Cowdery, *American Captives in Tripoli*, preface. The planned longer volume was never published; only Cowdery's *Journal in Miniature* survives in print.

51. "Literary," *Vermont Precursor*, 18 May 1807, 4.

52. Newman's argument, which as its text examines sailor tattoos and what they express politically, continues, "Sailors participated in the street politics of the early republic alongside laborers, mechanics, and other working men and women. . . . Their enthusiasm for the French Revolution, general dislike of Britain, and enduring loathing for the Royal Navy aroused their support for the Painite and Jeffersonian ideology of the Democratic-Republicans in distinctive ways. Seafarers' patriotic and political tattoos thus illustrate the tension between the distinctive experiences and goals of sailors and their membership and participation in communities and institutions on land" (Newman, "Reading the Bodies of Early American Seafarers," 79).

53. This model, part charitable and part municipal in its drive and advertisement, had been practiced by the Christian Mathurin order in France for several hundred years, in which the Mathurins successfully redeemed dozens of "Christian" prisoners in Africa. Thomas Jefferson, in fact, turned to the Mathurins as early intercessors on America's behalf, for as he explained to Adams, the "object of [their] institution is the begging of alms for the redemption of captives . . . and they redeem at a lower price than any other people can" ("Jefferson to Adams," 11 January 1787, in Adams, *Adams-Jefferson Letters*, 160).

54. Cathcart, *Captives*, 27–28.

55. Ibid., 152.

56. Carey, *Short Account of Algiers*, 36.

57. Cathcart, *Captives*, 27.

58. Ibid., 22.

59. Ibid., 41.

60. Paddock, *Narrative of the Shipwreck of the Ship Oswego*, advertisement.

61. Cochelet, *Narrative of the Shipwreck of the Sophia*, introduction.

62. Foss, *Journal of the Captivity and Sufferings of John Foss*, 3.

63. Riley, *Authentic Narrative of the Loss of the American Brig Commerce*, vii. Riley's account was easily the most popular Barbary narrative, with almost 1 million copies in print between 1817 and 1859 and such famous readers as Henry David Thoreau and Abraham Lincoln, who cited *Authentic Narrative* to be as influential on his thinking as Bunyan's *Pilgrim's Progress*.

64. Riley, *Authentic Narrative of the Loss of the American Brig Commerce*, 9.

65. Ibid., xv, 591, 599.

66. M'Lean, *Seventeen Years' History*.

67. Adams and Cock, *Narrative of Robert Adams*, xxi.

68. Paddock, *Narrative of the Shipwreck of the Ship Oswego*, 18.

69. Davis, *Narrative of Joshua Davis*.

70. Rediker, *Between the Devil and the Deep Blue Sea*, 87.

71. Paddock, *Narrative of the Shipwreck of the Ship Oswego*, 33.

72. It should be noted that the definition of a strike as a labor action came into use after Royal Naval sailors struck their sails—in the nautical meaning of "strike," to take down or put away—in protest of poor conditions and low wages, in the Spithead and Nore mutinies of 1797.

73. Ray, *Horrors of Slavery*, 131, 147. Ray records an earlier instance of captive sailors working for the collective nutritional good as well: "We found that we could sell our bread in market, for four paras a loaf. Three hundred of these paras make a dollar; and with the avails of one loaf, we could purchase as many vegetables as three men would eat at a meal, made into a soup, with bread and oil. We put ourselves into messes, as we chose, some of three or four men each, and thus, by sparing two loaves out of our day's rations, we could purchase carrots and scallions enough to make a handsome little pot of soup" (113).

74. Adams and Cock, *Narrative of Robert Adams*, xv.

75. Riley, *Authentic Narrative of the Loss of the American Brig Commerce*, v.

76. Foss, *Journal of the Captivity and Sufferings of John Foss*, 5–6.

77. Ibid., 178.

78. Colley, "Going Native, Telling Tales," 187. See also Colley, *Captives*.

CHAPTER 3

1. Philbrick, *James Fenimore Cooper and the Development of American Sea Fiction*, 3.

2. Most critics have followed Philbrick in tracing Cooper's own parallel transition from historical romance to a grittier form of realism, concluding that Cooper answered to market demands and a climate of reform in refashioning the focus of his novels, often unsuccessfully, both critically and commercially. Whereas literary and popular history have remembered Cooper more for his Leatherstocking tales, the five novels of the tracker Natty Bumppo set in the western frontier, his sea novels found enormous readership and special critical praise for their author.

3. Ames, *Mariner's Sketches*, 238–39.

4. The eleven sea novels are *The Pilot* (1823), *The Red Rover* (1828), *The Water-Witch* (1830), *Homeward Bound* (1838), *Mercedes of Castile* (1840), *The Two Admirals* (1842), *The Wing-and-Wing* (1842), *Afloat and Ashore* (1844), *The Crater* (1847), *Jack Tier* (1848), and *The Sea Lions* (1849). Cooper was also the author of naval histories, including *The History of the Navy of the United States of America* (1839), *The Battle of Lake Erie* (1843), and *Lives of Distinguished American Naval Officers* (1846), and a lengthy review included in the *Proceedings of the Naval Court Martial in the Case of Alexander Slidell Mackenzie* (1844).

5. Most nineteenth-century readers and reviewers saw Cooper emerging from the tradition of Scott and Smollett. Thomas Philbrick argues, however, that Cooper was the originator of the sea novel, not just its American incarnation, finding that Scott's and Smollett's novels cannot properly earn the generic distinction because the sea is not the primary textual emphasis. He explains: "No precedent existed for what he [Cooper] wished to write: a full-length novel in which the ocean formed the principal setting and in which seamen were the major characters. Among the previous literary treatments of nautical subjects, fragments which conceivably might be combined and ordered to form a useful prototype, few expressed the attitude toward seamen, ships, and the sea that was essential to his meaning" (Philbrick, *James Fenimore Cooper and the Development of American Sea Fiction*, 49–51).

6. When critical attention has turned to Cooper's maritime writing, the results have been historical studies of his works within the context of contemporary naval events and scandals. See, for example, the four brief papers on Cooper included in Dudley and Crawford, *Early Republic and the Sea*. Literary scholars have largely ignored Cooper's sea writing. Two exceptions are Philbrick's *James Fenimore Cooper and the Development of American Sea Fiction*, which provides an excellent overview of Cooper's nautical fiction, and Hugh McKeever Egan's

survey "Cooper and His Contemporaries" in Springer's 1995 collection *America and the Sea*. While the existing scholarship on Cooper's writing is able, it is not diverse; the scholars mentioned above—Philbrick, Dudley, and Egan—have provided the bulk of criticism on Cooper's sea fiction.

7. Philbrick, *James Fenimore Cooper and the Development of American Sea Fiction*, 43. Philbrick further specifies that "the sea novel as we know it owes its inception to the meeting of maritime nationalism and romanticism in the imagination of James Fenimore Cooper" (42).

8. Gardiner, review of *The Spy*, 250.

9. Cooper addressed this problem in terms of his female readership in the preface to his first historical novel, *The Spy*, in which he wrote, "We would not be understood as throwing the gauntlet to our fair countrywomen, by whose opinions it is that we expect to stand or fall; we only mean to say, that if we have got no lords and castles in the book, it is because there are none in the country" (x).

10. Gardiner, review of *The Spy*, 250.

11. The act of writing as a possessive practice has had a distinguished pedigree in American literary criticism, notably in Eric Cheyfitz's *Poetics of Imperialism* and Mary Louise Pratt's *Imperial Eyes*. What is worth noting in the matter of Cooper's novels, though, is how the ocean—a landscape that cannot be tangibly possessed or inscribed in the same way terrestrial ground can—presents challenges to the automatic presumption of sovereignty usual to such accounts.

12. Of course, the genre of historical romance was a form even newer than that of the American novel; many have credited it to Scott's *Waverly* (1814). Nina Baym has usefully defined the genre and has described the multiple ways the term "romance" was used in early American literary reviews; when speaking of the "historical romance," Baym makes a persuasive case for understanding the word "romance" in the phrase to mean "novel." She clarifies: "It would be false to this discourse to differentiate the historical fiction from the novel proper by defining it as a romance over against the novel" (Baym, *Novels, Readers, and Reviewers*, 235; see also 196–248).

13. Review of *The Pilot* (*North American Review*), 314.

14. Ibid., 328.

15. Letter to Carey & Lea, 30 December 1831, in Cooper, *Letters*, 2:169–70.

16. Cooper, *The Pilot*, 91. Future references to this Library of America volume will be included parenthetically within the text.

17. The great majority of Cooper's reviews, it must be said, take a decided pleasure in pointing out his literary sins. The index to a collection of contemporary criticism of his works has especially long entries for "detail, excessive," "dullness," "grammar (bad)," "improbabilities, inaccuracies, inconsistencies," "repetition of themes," and "taste, lack of." See index to Dekker and Williams, *James Fenimore Cooper*, 299–306. As Mark Twain's infamous *North American Review* analysis, "Fenimore Cooper's Literary Offences," puts it, "Cooper's art has some defects. In one place in *Deerslayer*, and in the restricted space of two thirds

of a page, Cooper has scored 114 offences against literary art out of a possible 115. It breaks the record" (2).

18. Ames, *Mariner's Sketches*, 238–39.

19. Ibid., 239.

20. Review of *The Pilot*, *New-York Mirror*, December 1824, 151.

21. Review of *Leisure Hours at Sea*, 454–55.

22. Leggett, *Naval Stories*, 12.

23. Review of *Nautical Reminiscences*.

24. *American Quarterly Review* 5, issue 342 (June 1829): 422.

25. Lounsbury, *James Fenimore Cooper*, 44.

26. Ibid., 45.

27. Philbrick, *James Fenimore Cooper and the Development of American Sea Fiction*, 61.

28. Cooper, *The Spy*, xi–xii.

29. In the passage in question (which originally appeared in *The Literary and Scientific Repository and Critical Review* in 1822), Cooper salutes Tyler's historicism with a nod to Henry Fielding:

> We say the historians—we do not mean to rank the writers of [fictional] tales, among the recorders of statutes, and battles, and party chronicles; but among those true historians which Dr. Moore says, are wanting, to give us just notions of what manner of men the ancient Greeks were, in their domestic affections, and retired deportment; and with whom Fielding classes himself, nearly in these words: "Those dignified authors who produce what are called true histories, are indeed writers of fictions, while I am a true historian, a describer of society as it exists, and of men as they are." (qtd. in Davidson, *Revolution and the Word*, 200)

30. To give a characteristic example, *Le Globe* of Paris singles out Tom Coffin as "a true masterpiece" of characterization. The review continues, "That sort of honesty and rude sensibility which Cooper excels in conveying, that singular love for his country the sea, that entire identification with his beloved schooner —all these make Long Tom an entirely engaging man" (qtd. in Dekker and Williams, *James Fenimore Cooper*, 130). In a rare exception to this laudatory reception, Nathaniel Ames thought that " 'Tom Coffin' is a *caricature* (and not a very good one) of an 'old salt,' but terribly strained and stiff" (Ames, *Mariner's Sketches*, 238). Toward the end of the nineteenth century, a British nautical writer and advocate for seamen concurred with Ames, writing of Coffin, "I will venture to say that if the like of such a man were at any period to have shipped aboard a vessel as able seaman, or in any other capacity, he would have been sent ashore by the captain as a lunatic" (Russell, "Sea Stories," 661).

31. After excerpting the whale-killing scene, the *North American Review* commented, "We will not say we do not know how a better description could have been given, since, but for the author, we should not know how it could have been given so well" (review of *The Pilot*, 321).

32. Dana, *Two Years before the Mast*, 39.
33. Ibid., 60.
34. Review of *Two Years before the Mast*, 57.
35. Dana, *Two Years before the Mast*, 462.
36. Review of *Two Years before the Mast*, 60.
37. According to Ezra Greenspan, Cooper "proved to be far less cooperative a partner than Irving had been; from their earliest negotiations he set tough conditions and crowded Putnam's room for maneuvering" (Greenspan, *George Palmer Putnam*, 228–30).
38. *The Water-Witch* reprint did not include a preface written explicitly for the Putnam edition. There is a second and final preface to the novel, but it was written for an 1833 London edition and therefore predates Dana's narrative and the literary historical changes it helped to effect.
39. "Notices of New Books," *United States Democratic Review* 25, issue 137 (November 1849): 476.
40. For a more extended discussion of Cooper's role in these maritime legal scandals, see Adams, "Cooper's Sea Fiction and *The Red Rover*"; Hugh McKeever Egan, "Enabling and Disabling the Lake Erie Discussion," in Dudley and Crawford, *Early Republic and the Sea*, 193–206; and Lounsbury, *James Fenimore Cooper*, 171–230.
41. Cooper, *The Red Rover*, 429. Future references to this Library of America volume will be included parenthetically within the text.
42. Letter to Rufus Wilmont Griswold, 10–18 January 1843, in Cooper, *Letters*, 4:341–43 (emphasis in original). The brackets around the phrase "could understand" indicate that Cooper originally wrote, and then struck out, the phrase.
43. This would become an enormous problem for Cooper in the following decade in the wake of the *Somers* mutiny, an infamous case of naval discipline that became the basis for Melville's *Billy Budd*. In the 1842 incident, Philip Spencer and two others were summarily hanged at sea (rather than tried in a naval court ashore) for allegedly plotting mutiny against *Somers* captain Alexander Slidell MacKenzie. The main point of controversy, about which Cooper wrote a lengthy commentary included in the published history of the case, was that the accused ringleader, Philip Spencer, was the son of the secretary of the navy. Cooper notoriously was one of the few defenders of Spencer, who was presumed to be influenced in his capital offense by reading the *Pirates Own Book*— and, crucially, Cooper's piracy novel *The Red Rover*. Cooper was involved in other personal and legal conflicts as a result of his naval historical writing about the War of 1812.
44. Hoxse, *Yankee Tar*, 7–8.
45. Dexter, *Narrative of the Loss of the Whaling Brig William and Joseph*, 45.
46. Delano, *Wanderings and Adventures*, 101.
47. In America in the 1830s, innovations in print technology helped fuel an explosion of magazines and cheap editions of books. By making bookmaking less

expensive and faster, these technological advancements allowed nonelites to enter the world of literary production. Ann Fabian has documented how the genre of the personal narrative was adapted in nineteenth-century America by beggars, convicts, slaves, and prisoners of war, and Ned Myers's own destitution places him in a similar category. Yet Fabian's account does not devote substantial attention to sailors and their narratives. This is perhaps because most sea writing did not emerge from seamen's state of pauperhood but from their conviction that their lives and adventures had cultural and monetary value. See Fabian, *Unvarnished Truth*.

48. See Little, *Life on the Ocean*, and Adams and Cock, *Narrative of Robert Adams*.

49. Cooper, *Ned Myers*, 278. Future references to this source will be included parenthetically within the text.

50. Qtd. in Dekker and Williams, *James Fenimore Cooper*, 121.

51. Review of *Ned Myers* (*Graham's Lady's and Gentleman's Magazine*).

52. Just a few examples of this one-upsmanship include Nicholas Isaacs's *Twenty Years Before the Mast* (1845), Samuel Leech's *Thirty Years from Home* (1843), and William Nevens's *Forty Years at Sea* (1845). The geometric growth of the number of years spent before the mast is not simply due to competitive increases, it must be noted. Dana's relatively scant "two years" expose him as a temporary sailor (despite his lowly shipboard status) rather than a lifetime tar. Therefore, sailors by trade could invoke their longevity at sea as a sign of the greater authenticity of their narratives.

53. Letter to Richard Henry Dana Sr., 15 October 1841, in Cooper, *Letters*, 4:181 (emphases in original).

54. Letter to Dana Sr., 30 October 1845, in ibid., 5:94.

55. Cooper, *Notions of the Americans*, 1:337 (note B).

56. Ames, *Mariner's Sketches*, 241.

57. Letter to George Bancroft, 5 June 1845, in Cooper, *Letters*, 5:36. The fuller elaboration of Cooper's advocacy stresses Ned's example to other seamen:

> I wrote a little book a year or two since called "Ned Myers." It contains an account of the real career of an old shipmate of mine, and of a man who is deserving of some rewards for his sufferings and conduct in the last war. I refer . . . you to the book itself for those services, of the truth of which I have the strongest corroborative proof in addition to Ned's own account of himself. Ned is an experienced seaman, and has often been chief mate of merchant vessels. . . . I think it would have a good effect on the morale of the service to give such a man some moderate preferment. If you have never seen the work, I would advise you to read it, less as an author, than as a brother litterateur. Its whole merit in a literary sense, is its truth, but the book can give you some notion of a common sailor's career.

58. Letter to William Bradford Shubrick, 6 October 1849, in ibid., 6:73–74.

59. The few critics who have devoted attention to *Ned Myers* agree that little can be

known about the specific form Cooper's and Myers's collaboration took in practice. It should be said that the structure of this collaboration is not a source of curiosity for such critics, generally speaking.

60. Philbrick, *James Fenimore Cooper and the Development of American Sea Fiction*, 129.

61. Letter to Richard Bentley, 18 July 1843, in Cooper, *Letters*, 4:391–92 (emphasis in original).

62. Review of *Ned Myers* (*Graham's Lady's and Gentleman's Magazine*) (emphasis in original).

63. Review of *Ned Myers* (*Editors' Table*) (emphasis in original).

64. In W. H. Gardiner's 1822 *North American Review* essay on Cooper's *The Spy*, Gardiner argues the problems facing American writers included uninspiring subject material, as the country and its inhabitants were presumed to be "utterly destitute of all sorts of romantic association." The traditional New England virtues of "cold uniformity and sobriety of character" combined to produce citizens who were "a downright, plain-dealing, inflexible, matter-of-fact sort of people" (250).

65. Letter to Susan Augusta Cooper, 14 January 1844, in Cooper, *Letters*, 6:332.

66. Letter from Shubrick to James Fenimore Cooper, 23 November 1843, in ibid., 4:431.

67. Letter to William Bradford Shubrick, 9 December 1843, in ibid., 4:428–29.

68. Lea & Blanchard had difficulty moving general literature during the years preceding the publication of *Ned Myers* anyway; as the press's historian notes, "The extreme business depression between 1839 and 1843 . . . rendered general literature less attractive. Large stocks of Cooper's novels bound in cloth were utterly unsalable and had to be stripped of their covers and done up in paper to find a market. General publishing began to center more and more in New York" (Bussy, *Two Hundred Years of Publishing*, 42).

69. A testimonial from *American Traveller* regarding this edition, quoted in the advertisement, praises Cooper's ability to give the subject "all the richness of romance, with the method and accuracy of strict history" (advertisement in *Ned Myers; or, A Life before the Mast* [Philadelphia: Lea & Blanchard, 1843]).

70. Letter to Richard Bentley, 25 September 1843, in Cooper, *Letters*, 4:415.

71. Letter to Richard Bentley, 9 January 1844, in ibid., 4:440–41.

72. Letter to Richard Bentley, 16 April 1844, in ibid., 4:456.

73. Letter from Richard Bentley to James Fenimore Cooper, 21 May 1844, in ibid., 4:456.

74. Letter to Richard Bentley, 9 January 1844, in ibid., 4:440–41.

CHAPTER 4

1. Bill Brown uses the phrase "materialist epistemology" on a few occasions in *A Sense of Things*, although he locates its meaning in a late-nineteenth-century context of retail and museology industries—a form of "object-based epistemol-

ogy," to use Steven Conn's formulation of museum culture (qtd. in Brown, *Sense of Things*, 83–84).

2. Bromell, *By the Sweat of the Brow*, 12; Weinstein, *Literature of Labor and the Labors of Literature*, 13.

3. Emerson, "Self-Reliance," in *Essays and Lectures*, 264.

4. That is, young men who may have shipped out in order to escape domestic responsibility found that maritime routine was subject to as much regulation and constriction as would be recommended by any treatise on domestic economy. See Druett, *Hen Frigates*; Creighton, *Rites and Passages*; and Creighton and Norling, *Iron Men, Wooden Women*.

5. Rediker, *Between the Devil and the Deep Blue Sea*, 185–86.

6. Conrad, *Heart of Darkness*, 106.

7. Ray, *Horrors of Slavery*, 19–20.

8. Leggett, *Naval Stories*, 15–18.

9. Ibid., 15.

10. Cooper, *The Pilot*, 238, 23.

11. Little, *Life on the Ocean*, 79.

12. Dana, *Two Years before the Mast*, 81. Ironically, Dana went to sea as a common sailor to ease an eye ailment he developed during study at Harvard. He presumes that a "long absence from books" will cure him, and yet while his vision is restored, Dana devotes a good portion of his narrative to descriptions of the books he reads, trades, and discusses with fellow sailors.

13. Gilman, *Letters Written Home*, 25–26.

14. *Life in a Man-of-War*, xv (emphases in original).

15. See, in particular, Dryden, "From the Piazza to the Enchanted Isles"; Reynolds, *Beneath the American Renaissance*; and Bercaw, *Melville's Sources*.

16. Melville, *Moby-Dick*, 72–73. Future references to this source will be included parenthetically within the text.

17. Taylor, *Life on a Whaler*, 2. Taylor further describes how he cedes his own vision to that of a more experienced sailor: "The man from the masthead shouted: 'Land O! Off the lee bow.' I remained on deck for sometime, gazing upon a dim outline which to my vision was nothing but a vast cloud; but the old tar was not to be deceived, and, trusting to his 'say-so', I went below for a four hours' nap with a light heart" (41).

18. Whitecar, *Four Years in a Whaleship*, 20–21.

19. Martingale [Sleeper], *Jack in the Forecastle*, 447–48, 449.

20. Ames, *Mariner's Sketches*, 225.

21. Henshaw, *Around the World*, 1:17–18.

22. Nevens, *Forty Years at Sea*, 13.

23. *Life in a Man-of-War*, xv (emphasis in original).

24. Robert Foulke calls this the "sea meditation" and locates its origins in Dana's *Two Years before the Mast*; see Foulke, *Sea Voyage Narrative*, 14.

25. Irving, *Sketch-Book*, 16.

26. Ibid., 17.

27. Browne, *Etchings of a Whaling Cruise*, 193, 194.

28. Martingale [Sleeper], *Jack in the Forecastle*, 27, 74.

29. Emerson, *Nature*, in *Essays and Lectures*, 10–11.

30. Descartes believed all motion resulted "from vortices of an impalpable ethereal fluid in which, he thought, all matter was embedded"; his theory of the vortex as a "machine," which Melville would have read about in Bayle's *Dictionary and Ephraim Chambers's Cyclopaedia: or, An Universal Dictionary of Arts and Sciences*, has been invoked in critical discussions of the whirlpool at the end of *Moby-Dick*. See Mancini, "Melville's 'Descartian Vortices' "; see also Leonard, "Descartes, Melville, and the Mardian Vortex." Although "Descartian vortices" are not specifically related to vision or optics, the model of vision offered by Descartes is useful in describing the sea eye's union of material and abstract knowledge. In his *Optics* Descartes describes how technical advancement, specifically the telescope, allows for an expanded understanding of nature. Yet Descartes is aware that an understanding of vision requires two levels of understanding, one theoretical, the other practical. He writes, "Carrying our vision much further than our forebears could normally extend their imagination, these telescopes seem to have opened the way for us to attain a knowledge of nature much greater and more perfect than they possessed. . . . And since the construction of the things of which I shall speak must depend on the skill of craftsmen, who usually have little formal education, I shall try to make myself intelligible to everyone." This passage suggests that one may know how to make a telescope and not know how to theorize with it, and inversely, one can interpret nature using a telescope whose construction would be a mystery. Descartes's understanding, his ideal of vision, involves a synthesis of both abilities, a fusion of mechanical and interpretive skills. See Descartes, *Philosophical Writings*, 152.

31. Marx, *Machine in the Garden*, 292.

32. Emerson, *Nature*, in *Essays and Lectures*, 10.

33. Franklin, *Discoverers, Explorers, Settlers*, 23; Poirier, *World Elsewhere*, 50; Jehlen, *American Incarnation*, 86. See also Pease, *Visionary Compacts*; Porter, *Seeing and Being*; Miller, *Empire of the Eye*; and New, *Line's Eye*.

34. Emerson, *Nature*, in *Essays and Lectures*, 33–34.

35. Crary, *Techniques of the Observer*, 7.

36. Ibid., 69. Jeannine DeLombard makes productive use of Crary's fascinating book in discussing the Emersonian eyeball in relationship to slave witnessing for Frederick Douglass. See DeLombard, " 'Eye-Witness to the Cruelty.' "

37. Dickinson, *Complete Poems*, 553.

38. Melville, "Thought on Book-Binding."

39. Ibid.

40. Groves, "Judging Literary Books by Their Covers," 75.

41. Melville, "Thought on Book-Binding."

42. Dana, *Two Years before the Mast*, 38–39.

43. Barnard et al., *Narrative of the Sufferings and Adventures of Capt. Charles H. Barnard*, 39.

44. Frank Shuffleton makes this observation most saliently in his article "Going Through the Long Vaticans."

45. Mark Bauerlein provides the most incisive discussion of "Etymology" and "Extracts" in arguing that the "opening indicates language's origin in the desire for ground and certainty *and* its inability to satisfy entirely and permanently that desire" ("Grammar and Etymology in *Moby-Dick*," 18). Betsy Hilbert usefully glosses what she calls the "Ballast Theory" of *Moby-Dick*, the idea that the whaling lore, in F. O. Matthiessen's words, "prevents the drama from gliding off into a world to which we would feel no normal tie whatever" (qtd. in Hilbert, "Truth of the Thing," 825. Furthermore, Christopher Sten sees the "bricolage" of the "Extracts" and "Etymology" sections as designed to "establish the epic stature" of the novel and predicts that their effect on the reader will be to produce "awe or wonder" (*Weaver God, He Weaves*, 138). See also Dillingham, *Melville's Later Novels*, and Dryden, *Melville's Thematics of Form*.

46. Weinstein, *Literature of Labor and the Labors of Literature*, 112.

47. Frank Shuffleton, in "Going Through the Long Vaticans," 528, astutely points out that both researchers are "buried" by the text.

48. Bauerlein makes a similar point in his sense that "Melville places his book on the margins of a philology" ("Grammar and Etymology in *Moby-Dick*," 21). An analogous observation has been made by Gert Morreel in his presentation " 'When Leviathan Is the Text.' "

49. In this sense I argue against David Reynolds, who in his *Beneath the American Renaissance* sees Melville transforming the popular, "low" material he reads into something new and improved.

50. In Samuel Otter's perceptive reading, Ishmael's tattoo is a reminder of the corporeality of the narrator himself. He notes that Ishmael's appearance is never described, and so "the fact that he has a tattoo, and even that he has a right arm, come as something of a surprise. . . . The cetacean dimensions on his arm give heft to his body" (Otter, *Melville's Anatomies*, 165).

51. Melville's interest in compelling readers to take an active role in shaping the material of his narratives is the subject of Chapter 5.

52. In this scene, Pip provides the final, synthetic reading when he recites lines he picked up from an old grammar book: "I look, you look, he looks; we look, ye look, they look." His seeming nonsense works on several levels: Pip's "I," the reader's "you," and the sailor's "he" all make a reading of the doubloon. What Pip's chant exposes more compellingly, however, is the various ways that looking (or seeing or reading) becomes shipboard practice. Among many commentators on Pip's role in this scene, Samuel Otter argues that "Pip's words do not emphasize distinct perspectives but, instead, define perception as a shared, structurally linked activity" (*Melville's Anatomies*, 170). Bauerlein, on the other

hand, links Pip's reading to the extracts and etymology, finding that Pip "articulates the systematic rules and arrangements that make meaning possible, leaving etymologists and other generic interpreters to determine what that meaning is" ("Grammar and Etymology in *Moby-Dick*," 26).

CHAPTER 5

1. Freeman, *Works of Charles Darwin*, 31–38. The same London printer, John Murray, published both Darwin's scientific works (including *The Origin of Species*) and the first British editions of Melville's South Sea narratives *Typee* and *Omoo*. See Melville, *Journals*, 290–91. See also Post-Lauria, *Correspondent Colorings*.
2. Sealts, *Melville's Reading*, 90.
3. "Cruise of the Essex," *Harper's New Monthly Magazine*, August 1859, 289–310.
4. Giant tortoises have a famously long life span; Harriet, a giant tortoise thought to have been taken from the Galapagos by Charles Darwin himself in 1835, died in June 2006 at the age of 175 years.
5. Colnett, *Voyage to the South Atlantic and Round Cape Horn*, 51.
6. Delano, *Narrative of Voyages and Travels*, 383. Of the islands' volcanic character, William Nevens also testifies, in language common to other sea narratives (including Melville's): "James' Island has the appearance of having been blown up from the bottom of the ocean by some convulsion of nature. The rocks have a singular appearance, and show very plainly the effects of fire, in many places having melted and run together" (Nevens, *Forty Years at Sea*, 221).
7. Nevens, *Forty Years at Sea*, 223.
8. Delano, *Wanderings and Adventures*, 44. See Chapter 6 for further discussion of Galapagos gravesites.
9. Nevens, *Forty Years at Sea*, 225. At one point in his narrative David Porter mocks one of the letters he finds in the post office, calling it a "rare specimen of orthography," and quotes it in full: "June 14th 1812. Ship Sukey John Macy 7½ Months out 150 Barrels 75 days from Lima No oil Since Leaving that Port. Spanyards Very Savage Lost on the Braziel Bank John Sealin Apprentice to Capt Benjamin Worth Fell from the fore top sail Yard in A Gale of Wind. Left Diana Capt paddock . . . 14 day Since 250 Barrels I Leave this port this Day With 250 Turpen 8 Boat Load Wood Yesterday Went Up to Patts Landing East Side. to the Starboard hand of the Landing 1½ Miles Saw 100 Turpen 20 Rods A part Road Very Bad. Yours Forevir, JOHN MACY" (Porter, *Voyage in the South Seas*, 153).
10. Delano, *Wanderings and Adventures*, 45.
11. Delano, *Narrative of Voyages and Travels*, 370. The works cited most frequently by mariners are Colnett, *Voyage to the South Atlantic and Round Cape Horn*; Burney, *Chronological History of the Discoveries in the South Sea or Pacific Ocean*; and Porter, *Voyage in the South Seas*.

12. Melville, "Encantadas," 311. Future references to this source will be included parenthetically within the text.

13. "Introductory," 1.

14. Ibid., 2–3.

15. On literary nativism in *Putnam's*, see Emery, " 'Benito Cereno' and Manifest Destiny," and Sundquist, *To Wake the Nations*.

16. Pratt, *Imperial Eyes*, 61.

17. Ibid., 51.

18. This model still holds an appeal; Putnam's "Literary Chronology" looks remarkably like the comparative tables included in present-day Norton anthologies.

19. Putnam, *World's Progress*, iii–iv.

20. *World's Progress* "not only centralized a great deal of information not previously easily accessible to the public but attached it to a narrative of American material and cultural productivity that became a central component of the developing American self-image at mid-century" (Greenspan, *George Palmer Putnam*, 134).

21. Putnam, "Scrapbook." In response to this solicitation, Ralph Waldo Emerson avowed that "nothing could be more agreeable" than this "American Magazine," while Erastus W. Ellesworth saw the magazine as a fine weapon against "foreign invasion" in the field of the "domestic arts."

22. "The Encantadas" was published under the byline "Salvator R. Tarnmoor," which most critics have seen as Melville's evocation of the seventeenth-century painter Salvator Rosa, whose ferocious, craggy landscapes typified popular conception of the romantic sublime. All of Melville's other contributions are anonymous. See Robillard, *Melville and the Visual Arts*, 52–54, and Furrow, "Terrible Made Visible." What makes "The Encantadas" compelling in the context of all the unsigned pieces in *Putnam's* is not just that it has a signature but the very fact that its concern with an individual's powers of imaginative creation appears under a constructed authorial name. When "The Encantadas" is collected and published in *The Piazza Tales*, Melville eliminates the pseudonym.

23. Putnam, *American Facts*, 11.

24. According to Putnam biographer Greenspan, the magazine "was based on the presumption of an underlying harmony of interests between authors and editors, publishers and readers, and the most encompassing of categories, Americans and Americans" (Greenspan, *George Palmer Putnam*, 305).

25. "Introductory," 2. The editorial devotion to "fact" influenced the magazine's contributors. For example, Julia Ward Howe wrote to Putnam that a poem she submitted "would please you, I think" because it is not "too metaphysical." Catharine Ledyard, another contributor, reports that she changed the ending of an article because she "could not endure the idea of winding up in such desperately sentimental fashion" (Putnam, "*Putnam's Monthly Magazine* Correspondence").

26. "Introductory," 2.

27. This was especially true for its writers (who were paid generously, even though

Putnam's circulation never approached that of *Harper's*). In another part of the "Introductory," the magazine sticks up for "copyright and justice to authors," noting that few readers care whether the publisher "may have broken the author's head or heart, to obtain the manuscript" (1). George Palmer Putnam himself was a strong advocate for international copyright. See Garwood, *American Periodicals from 1850 to 1860*, 70–71; Ljungquist, "Putnam's Monthly Magazine," 328–29; and Mott, *History of American Magazines*.

28. "Our Young Authors: Melville," *Putnam's Monthly Magazine*, February 1853, 157.
29. According to Sealts, *Melville's Reading*, 87, Melville "took profitable notice of what contemporary newspapers and magazines of the 1850's were carrying, and learned to pattern his own pieces accordingly, with respect to both form and content."
30. Poovey, *History of the Modern Fact*, xv, 1–15.
31. Darwin, *Journal of Researches*, 2:169.
32. See, for example, Smith, *Melville's Science*; Zimmerman, *Herman Melville*, 70–72; Dryden, "From the Piazza to the Enchanted Isles"; Dunphy, "Melville's Turning of the Darwinian Table in 'The Encantadas,'" 14; and Newman, *Reader's Guide to the Short Stories of Herman Melville*, 182.
33. Darwin, *Journal of Researches*, 1:145.
34. Melville, *Clarel*, 2.11.12–19.
35. Darwin, *Autobiography*, 138–39.
36. Poovey, *History of the Modern Fact*, 292.
37. Darwin, *Journal of Researches*, 2:171.
38. Ibid., 1:52.
39. "The National Inventory," *Putnam's Monthly Magazine*, January 1854, 16.
40. Ibid., 18.
41. Ibid.
42. "Introductory," 1.
43. Ibid.
44. "Islands of the Pacific," *Putnam's Monthly Magazine*, August 1856, 156.

CHAPTER 6

1. Ariès, *Western Attitudes toward Death*, 72.
2. Sears, *Sacred Places*, 100, 108.
3. *Life in a Man-of-War*, 78.
4. "The Sailor's Grave," *Sheet Anchor*, 4 October 1845, 145.
5. "Critical Notices," *United States Nautical Magazine*, 1 June 1845, 261.
6. Clark, *Lights and Shadows of Sailor Life*, viii. On the subject of Clark's amplification, it should be noted that on at least one occasion in *Lights and Shadows* Clark lifted passages from other seamen's narratives; I have identified several passages in Clark's narrative that were taken verbatim from Warriner's *Cruise of the Potomac*. The passages he borrows do not refer to Wilkes's expedition but to

features of South American towns commonly visited as ports. This practice has been noted in the sea writing of Herman Melville and Edgar Allan Poe; whatever judgment is to be made of these actions, they demonstrate the sailor's broader familiarity with sea narrative writing. And in titling his narrative *Lights and Shadows*, a phrase common to religious reform literature, Clark may be explicitly invoking broader, emblematic maritime experience.

7. Clark, *Lights and Shadows of Sailor Life*, ix (emphasis in original).

8. Ibid., vi.

9. Forbes [Bennet], *Appeal to Merchants and Ship Owners*, 7.

10. Stewart, *Visit to the South Seas*, 1:37.

11. Warriner, *Cruise of the Potomac*, 185–86. The copy of this narrative in the collection of the American Antiquarian Society features some provocative pencil annotations from an unidentified reader. The annotations appear in reference to an earlier discussion of death in the narrative, when Warriner remarks that the "death of a sailor is generally as little regarded on board ship as the fall of a leaf" (68). He continues, "Their life is a hard and a short one. . . . Many are yearly ingulfed [*sic*] amid the surges of the ocean, with no eye to witness their struggles, the waves alone their windingsheet, and their death prayer given to the winds" (69). In response to Warriner's claims about the special impact of death on sailors, a reader has responded with incredulity: "Why so more than to a landsman?"; "Fudge"; "Doubted"; "why? doubted." This reader's skepticism adds special pathos to sea narratives' repeated requests for sympathy.

12. Clark, *Lights and Shadows of Sailor Life*, 55.

13. Colton, *Deck and Port*, 52.

14. Ibid., 213–14.

15. Clark, *Lights and Shadows of Sailor Life*, 56.

16. Ibid., 61.

17. Ibid., 55. The full epitaph reads,

> To the memory of Thomas Hendrick, of the United States Ship of the Line North Carolina, who departed this life at Callao on the 13th, 1838, æt sixteen years.
>
> In vain had youth its flight impeded,
> And hope its passage had delayed;
> Death's mandate all has superseded,—
> The latest order Tom obeyed.

18. Warriner, *Cruise of the Potomac*, 68.

19. *Full Fadom Five*. These cenotaphs were not confined to those buried at sea; the following memorial is for a sailor buried on an African coastal island:

ERECTED
By the Officers and crew of the
Bark A. R. Tucker of New Bedford

> To the memory of CHARLES H. PETTY,
> of Westport, Mass.
> who died Dec. 14th 1863,
> in the 18th year of his age.
> His death occurred in nine hours
> after being bitten by a shark,
> while bathing near the ship,
> He was buried by his shipmates
> on the Island of De Loss, near the Coast of Africa.

20. Dana, *Two Years before the Mast*, 77.
21. Ibid., 158.
22. Melville, "Encantadas," 466. This passage is freely adapted from Porter's *Voyage in the South Seas* (see n. 23 below), as are many in Melville's sketch.
23. Melville, "Encantadas," 466. This verse is likewise a revision of text from Porter's narrative:

> Gentle reader, as you pass by,
> As you are now, so wonce was I;
> As now my body is in the dust,
> I hope in heaven my soul to rest.

Melville's version is more irreverent and humorous than the sober epitaph of Porter's account, which Porter transcribes "more on account of the extreme simplicity of the verse, and its powerful and flattering appeal to the feelings, than for its elegance, or the correctness of the composition" (Porter, *Voyage in the South Seas*, 191).

24. Dana, *Two Years before the Mast*, 463.
25. *Oxford English Dictionary*, 2nd ed. (1989).
26. Porter, *Voyage in the South Seas*, 219.
27. Ibid., 252–53. Cowan is killed on shore; his opponent in the duel is not known.
28. Ibid., 253.
29. Wilkes, *Narrative of the United States Exploring Expedition*, 4:93 (emphasis in original).
30. Ibid., 3:271.
31. Ibid., 3:273.
32. Ibid., 3:311–12.
33. "A Sailor's Burying Ground Discovered," *Sailor's Magazine, and Seamen's Friend*, November 1859, 96. The full notice reads,

> Captain Eldridge, of the Bark *Amazon* of Fairhaven, has recently discovered an island in the Pacific Ocean, several hundred miles from any land laid down on the charts. In a letter dated at sea, January 16th, 1859, he says of the island:
> "It is very low and dangerous, and is I expect the last resting place of the

crews of some of the ships that have been lost in years gone by. I ran along the lee, within pistol shot of the beach, but it was too rough to land, and, after convincing myself that there were no living people upon the island, I squared away again. On the highest part of this island is a house, apparently built from pieces of a wreck, with a flag-staff at one end, from which still dangles the halyard block. Near the house were several little hummocks, each with a tall upright stone upon it, undoubtedly the graves of the poor fellows who had escaped from the wreck of their vessel and died on this dreary spot, where perhaps, they had spent months in vainly looking for a passing sailor to relieve them from their weary prison."

34. Dana, *Two Years before the Mast*, 514.
35. Marin, *On Representation*, 273–74.
36. Clark, *Lights and Shadows of Sailor Life*, ix.
37. Ibid.
38. Martingale [Sleeper], *Jack in the Forecastle*, 361.
39. *Life in a Man-of-War*, 79; Colton, *Deck and Port*, 52.
40. Barthes, "Nautilus and the Drunken Boat," 65–66.
41. Qtd. in Newhall, *Adventures of Jack*, introduction. Herman Melville's *Moby-Dick* mockingly adapts the same passage from Byron.
42. Qtd. in Leggett, *Tales and Sketches*, 89.
43. Leech, *Thirty Years from Home*, 85–86.
44. Harrison, *Dominion of the Dead*, 14, 144.
45. Dana, *Two Years before the Mast*, 77 (emphases in original).
46. Harrison, *Dominion of the Dead*, 147.
47. Dennis, "Patriotic Remains," 137, 142.
48. Castronovo, *Necro Citizenship*.
49. Foucault, "Of Other Spaces," 27.
50. Casarino, *Modernity at Sea*, 13, 5–6.
51. Poe, *Narrative of Arthur Gordon Pym*, 1022. Future references to this source will be included parenthetically within the text.
52. Barthes, "Nautilus and the Drunken Boat," 65.
53. Gitelman, "Arthur Gordon Pym and the Novel Narrative of Edgar Allan Poe," 350–52. See also Poe, "South-Sea Expedition."
54. Dryden, *Monumental Melville*, 17.
55. Harrison, *Dominion of the Dead*, 14.
56. Melville, *Moby-Dick*, 478. Future references to this source will be included parenthetically within the text.
57. Brown, *Sense of Things*, 127.
58. Dryden, *Monumental Melville*, 20.
59. Casarino, *Modernity at Sea*, 107.
60. Martingale [Sleeper], *Jack in the Forecastle*, 361.

AFTERWORD

1. Russell, "Claim for American Literature," 149.

2. Ibid., 142.

3. Popular adventure narratives in the past decade have clustered around the topics of polar exploration; mountaineering stories (particularly ones that deal with the deadliest climbing day on record on Mt. Everest, in May 1996, which include Jon Krakauer's runaway best seller *Into Thin Air* [1997]); and nautical tales. Two books whose enormous commercial and critical successes helped reinvigorate the market for sea stories are Sebastian Junger's *The Perfect Storm* (1997) and Nathaniel Philbrick's *In the Heart of the Sea: The Tragedy of the Whaleship Essex* (2000), which won the National Book Award for nonfiction. The ongoing popularity of British novelist Patrick O'Brian's naval fictions and the cultural phenomenon (and unprecedented sales) generated by the film *Titanic* (1997) are two other notable confirmations of the appeal of sea stories to a new reading audience.

4. Russell, "Claim for American Literature," 138.

5. Emerson, *Journals*, 2 January 1833, 3. I am indebted to Max Cavitch for bringing this passage to my attention.

6. *Oxford English Dictionary*, 2nd. ed., 1989. The only citation in the entry for the noun form of "quiddle" is a different quotation from Emerson.

7. Chase et al., *Narrative*, 30–31.

8. The full title is *Narrative of the Most Extraordinary and Distressing Shipwreck of the Whale-ship Essex of Nantucket, Which Was Attacked & Finally Destroyed by a Large Spermaceti-Whale in the Pacific Ocean; with an Account of the Unparalleled Sufferings of the Captain and Crew during a Space of Ninety-Three Days at Sea, in Open Boats in the Years 1819 & 1820.*

9. Qtd. in Heffernan, *Stove by a Whale*, 143–44. The image of Chase secreting food also appears to evocative effect in Charles Olson's prologue to his meditation *Call Me Ishmael*.

10. Heffernan's scholarly study and edition *Stove by a Whale* provides a meticulous tally of all the versions of the story printed in the nineteenth century; see 171–82. In the twentieth century, the story of the *Essex* has been retold in Olson's study *Call Me Ishmael*, Carlisle's novel *Jonah Man*, and Philbrick's *In the Heart of the Sea*.

11. Qtd. in Heffernan, *Stove by a Whale*, 203–4.

BIBLIOGRAPHY

PRIMARY SOURCES

Periodicals

American Quarterly Review
Annual Reports of the American Seaman's Friend Society
Annual Reports of the Boston Seaman's Friend Society
Boston Commercial Gazette
Boston Mercantile Journal
Columbian Magazine
Editor's Table
Essex Register
Graham's Lady's and Gentleman's Magazine
Harper's New Monthly Magazine
The Life Boat
The Literary World
Monthly Nautical Magazine, and Quarterly Review
New England Magazine
New York American
New-York Mirror
New-York Spectator
North American Review
Putnam's Monthly Magazine
Sailor's Magazine
Sailor's Magazine and Naval Journal
The Sailor's Magazine, and Seamen's Friend
Sea Bird
Sheet Anchor
The United States Democratic Review
United States Nautical Magazine

U.S. Nautical Magazine and Naval Journal
Vermont Precursor
Worcester Magazine

Articles, Books, and Manuscripts

Adams, John. *The Adams-Jefferson Letters: The Complete Correspondence between Thomas Jefferson and Abigail and John Adams*. Edited by Lester J. Cappon. Chapel Hill: University of North Carolina Press, 1959.

Adams, Robert, and S. Cock. *The Narrative of Robert Adams, an American Sailor, who was wrecked on the Western coast of Africa, in the year 1810; was detained three years in slavery by the Arabs of the Great Desert, and resided several months in the city of Tombuctoo. With a Map, Notes and an Appendix*. Boston: Wells and Lilly, 1817.

"American." *Humanity in Algiers; or, The Story of Azem*. Troy: R. Moffit, 1801.

Ames, Nathaniel. *A Mariner's Sketches*. Rev. ed. Providence: Cory Marshall and Hammond, 1830.

Amory, John. *Almonuc*. Boston: J. B. Dow, 1840.

———. *The Young Rover*. Boston: J. B. Dow, 1836.

Anderson, Charles Roberts, Thomas ap Catesby Jones, and William H. Meyers. *Journal of a Cruise to the Pacific Ocean, 1842–1844, in the Frigate United States: With Notes on Herman Melville*. Durham: Duke University Press, 1937.

Averill, Charles E. *The Corsair King*. Boston: F. Gleason, 1848.

———. *The Secrets of the High Seas; or, The Mysterious Wreck in the Gulf Stream. A Tale of the Ocean's Exciting Incidents*. Boston: Williams, 1849.

Barnard, Charles H., et al. *A Narrative of the Sufferings and Adventures of Capt. Charles H. Barnard: In a Voyage Round the World, During the Years 1812, 1813, 1814, 1815, & 1816; Embracing an Account of the Seizure of His Vessel at the Falkland Islands*. New York: J. Lindon, 1829.

Beale, Thomas. *The Natural History of the Sperm Whale*. London: John Van Voorst, 1839.

Blunt, Edmund, ed. *New Practical Navigator*. Newburyport: Blunt, 1800.

———, ed. *Seamanship*. New York: Blunt, 1813.

Botsford, Edmund. *Spiritual Voyage*. Charleston, 1818.

Bourne, Benjamin Franklin. *The Captive in Patagonia; or, Life among the giants. A personal narrative*. Boston: Gould and Lincoln, 1853.

Bowditch, Nathaniel. *New American Practical Navigator*. New York: Blunt, 1817.

Browne, J. Ross. *Etchings of a Whaling Cruise*. New York: Harper, 1846.

Buntline, Ned [Edward C. Z. Judson]. *Seawaif; or, The Terror of the Coast. A tale of privateering in 1776*. New York: Frederic A. Brady, 1859.

Burney, James. *A Chronological History of the Discoveries in the South Sea or Pacific Ocean*. 4 vols. London: G. & W. Nicol, 1816.

Carey, Mathew. *A Short Account of Algiers, and of Its Several Wars against Spain, France, England, Holland, Venice, and Other Powers of Europe, from the Usurpation of Barba-*

rossa and the Invasion of the Emperor Charles V to the Present Time. With a Concise View of the Origin of the Rupture between Algiers and the United States. To Which Is Added, a Copious Appendix, Containing Letters from Captains Penrose, M'shane, and Sundry Other American Captives, with a Description of the Treatment Those Prisoners Experience. 2nd ed. Philadelphia: Carey, 1794.

Cathcart, James L., and Jane Bancker Newkirk. *Tripoli. First War with the United States*. LaPorte, Ind.: Herald Print, 1901.

Cathcart, James Leander. *The Captives: Eleven Years a Prisoner in Algiers*. La Porte, Ind.: Herald, 1899.

Chase, Owen, et al. *Narrative of the Most Extraordinary and Depressing Shipwreck of the Whale-ship Essex*. New York: Dover, 1989. Originally published in 1821 as *Narrative of the Most Extraordinary and Distressing Shipwreck of the Whale-ship Essex of Nantucket, Which Was Attacked & Finally Destroyed by a Large Spermaceti-Whale in the Pacific Ocean; with an Account of the Unparalleled Sufferings of the Captain and Crew during a Space of Ninety-Three Days at Sea, in Open Boats in the Years 1819 & 1820.*

Cheever, Henry T., Rev. *The Whale and his Captors; or, The whaleman's adventures, and the whale biography, as gathered on the homeward cruise of the "Commodore Preble."* New York: Harper, 1850.

Chetwood, W. R., et al. *The Voyages and Adventures of Captain Robert Boyle, in Several Parts of the World. Intermix'd with the Story of Mrs. Villars, an English Lady with Whom He Made His Surprizing Escape from Barbary; the History of an Italian Captive; and the Life of Don Pedro Aquilio, &C. Full of Various and Amazing Turns of Fortune. To Which Is Added, the Voyage, Shipwreck, and Miraculous Preservation, of Richard Castelman, Gent. With a Description of the City of Philadelphia, and the Country of Pennsylvania*. London: J. Watts, 1726.

Clark, Joseph G. *Lights and Shadows of Sailor Life, as exemplified in fifteen years' experience, including the more thrilling events of the U.S. Exploring Expedition, and reminisces of an eventful life on the "mountain wave."* Boston: Benjamin B. Mussey & Co., 1848.

Cleveland, Richard J. *A Narrative of Voyages and Commercial Enterprises*. 2 vols. Cambridge: John Owen, 1842.

Cloud, Enoch Carter, and Elizabeth McLean. *Enoch's Voyage: Life in a Whaleship 1851–1854*. 1st ed. Wakefield, R.I.: Moyer Bell, 1994.

Cochelet, Charles. *Narrative of the Shipwreck of the Sophia on the 30th of May, 1819, on the Western Coast of Africa, and of the Captivity of a Part of the Crew in the Desert of Sahara with Engravings*. London: Sir Richard Phillips, 1822.

Codman, John. *Sailors' Life and Sailors' Yarns*. New York: Francis & Co., 1847.

Colnett, James. *A Voyage to the South Atlantic and Round Cape Horn into the Pacific Ocean, for the Purpose of Extending the Spermaceti Whale Fisheries, and other objects of commerce, by ascertaining the ports, bays, harbours, and anchoring births, in certain islands and coasts in those seas at which the ships of the British merchants might be refitted*. London: W. Bennett, 1798.

Colton, Walter. *Deck and Port; or, Incidents of a Cruise in the United States frigate Congress to California.* New York: A. S. Barnes & Co., 1850.

Comer, George. *Manual of Instruction in Practical Navigation.* Boston: F. W. Lincoln, 1864.

Conrad, Joseph. *Heart of Darkness.* New York: Signet, 1983.

Cooper, James Fenimore. *The History of the Navy of the United States of America.* London: R. Bentley, 1839.

——. *Ned Myers; or, A Life before the Mast.* 1843. Rpt. Annapolis, Md.: Naval Institute Press, 1989.

——. *Notions of the Americans: Picked up by a Travelling Bachelor.* Philadelphia: Carey Lea & Blanchard, 1838.

——. *The Pilot: A Tale of the Sea.* 1823. Reprinted in *Sea Tales.* New York: Library of America, 1990.

——. *The Red Rover.* 1828. Reprinted in *Sea Tales.* New York: Library of America, 1990.

——. *The Spy: A Tale of the Neutral Ground.* New York: Wiley and Halstead, 1821.

——. *The Wing-and-Wing; or, Le Feu-Follet.* Edited by Thomas Philbrick. Heart of Oak Sea Classics. New York: Henry Holt, 1998.

Cooper, James Fenimore. *The Letters and Journals of James Fenimore Cooper.* Edited by James Franklin Beard. 6 vols. Cambridge: Harvard University Press, 1960.

Cooper, James Fenimore, and Susan Fenimore Cooper. *The Works of J. Fenimore Cooper.* Boston: Houghton Mifflin, 1880.

Cowdery, [Dr.]. *American Captives in Tripoli; or, Dr. Cowdery's Journal in Miniature; Kept During His Late Captivity in Tripoli.* Boston: Belcher & Armstrong, 1806.

——. "Tripolitan Slavery." *New-York Spectator*, 31 July 1804, 2.

Dampier, William. *A New Voyage Round the World. Describing particularly, The Isthmus of America, several Coasts and Islands in the West Indies, the Isles of Cape Verd, the Passage by Terra del Fuego, the South Sea Coasts of Chili, Peru, and Mexico; the Isle of Guam one of the Ladrones, Mindanao, and other Philippine and East-India Islands near Cambodia, China, Formosa, Luconia, Celebes, &c. New Holland, Sumatra, Nicobar Isles; the Cape of Good Hope, and Santa Hellena. THEIR Soil, Rivers, Harbours, Plants, Fruits, Animals, and Inhabitants. THEIR Customs, Religion, Government, Trade, &c. Illustrated with Particular Maps and Draughts.* London: James Knapton, 1697.

Dana, Richard Henry, Jr. *The Seaman's Friend.* 1851. Rpt. Delmar, N.Y.: Scholars' Facsimiles and Reprints, 1979.

——. *Two Years before the Mast.* 1840. Rpt. New York: Penguin, 1981.

Darwin, Charles. *The Autobiography of Charles Darwin.* Edited by Nora Barlow. New York: Harcourt Brace, 1958.

——. *Journal of Researches into the Natural History and Geology of the Countries Visited During the Voyage of H.M.S. Beagle Round the World, under the Command of Capt. Fitz Roy, R.N.* New York: Harper, 1846.

Davis, Joshua. *A Narrative of Joshua Davis, an American Citizen, Who Was Pressed and*

Served on Board Six Ships of the British Navy. He Was in Seven Engagements, Once Wounded, Five Times Confined in Irons, and Obtained His Liberty by Desertion: The Whole Being an Interesting and Faithful Narrative of the Discipline, Various Practices and Treatment of Pressed Seamen in the British Navy, and Containing Information That Never Was before Presented to the American People. Boston: B. True, 1811.

Delano, Amasa. *A Narrative of Voyages and Travels, in the Northern and Southern Hemispheres: Comprising Three Voyages Round the World; Together with a Voyage of Survey and Discovery, in the Pacific Ocean and Oriental Islands.* Boston: E. G. House, 1817.

Delano, Reuben. *Wanderings and Adventures of Reuben Delano, Being a Narrative of twelve years Life in a Whale Ship!* Worcester: Thomas Drew, Jr., 1846.

Dexter, Elisha. *Narrative of the Loss of the Whaling Brig William and Joseph, of Martha's Vineyard, and the sufferings of her crew for seven days, a part of the time on a raft in the Atlantic ocean; with an appendix, containing some remarks on the whaling business, and descriptions of the mode of killing and taking care of whales.* Boston: Charles C. Mead, 1848.

Dickinson, Emily. *The Complete Poems of Emily Dickinson.* Edited by Thomas H. Johnson. Boston: Little, Brown, 1960.

Dumont, P. J. *Narrative of Thirty-Four Years Slavery and Travels in Africa.* London: Richard Phillips, 1819.

Duncan, Archibald. *Mariner's Chronicle.* New Haven: Durrie and Peck, 1834.

Ellis, William. *Polynesian Researches.* New York: J. & J. Harper, 1833.

Ellms, Charles, comp. *Pirate's Own Book.* New York: A. & C. B. Edwards, 1842.

Emerson, Ralph Waldo. *Essays and Lectures.* New York: Library of America, 1983.

———. *Journals.* Edited by Edward Waldo Emerson and Waldo Emerson Forbes. Vol. 3. Cambridge: Riverside Press, 1909.

Equiano, Olaudah. *The Interesting Narrative of the Life of Olaudah Equiano; or, Gustavus Vassa, the African, Written by Himself.* Edited by Werner Sollors. New York: Norton, 2001.

Forbes, R. B. [Robert Bennet]. *An Appeal to Merchants and Ship Owners on the subject of Seamen. A lecture delivered at the request of the Boston marine society, March 7, 1854.* Boston: Sleeper & Rogers, 1854.

Foss, John. *A Journal of the Captivity and Sufferings of John Foss; Several Years a Prisoner at Algiers: Together with Some Account of the Treatment of Christian Slaves When Sick:—and Observations on the Manners and Customs of the Algerines.* Newburyport, Mass.: Angier March, 1798.

Franklin, Benjamin. *Writings.* New York: Library of America, 1987.

Full Fadom Five: Memorials in the Seaman's Bethel, New Bedford. Sharon, Mass.: Priceless Pearl, 1968.

Gardiner, W. H. Review of *The Spy. North American Review* 15, issue 36 (July 1822): 250–83.

Gilman, William Henry. *Letters Written Home.* Exeter, N.H.: 1911.

Glascock, William Nugent. *Naval Sketch-Book.* 1835. Rpt. London: Henry Colburn, 1836.

Gringo, Harry [Henry Augustus Wise]. *Tales for the Marines.* Boston: Phillips, Sampson, & Company, 1855.

Haley, Nelson. *Whale Hunt: Narrative of a Voyage.* 1854. Rpt. New York: Ives, Washburn, 1948.

Haley, William D. *Words for the Workers; in a series of lectures to workingmen, mechanics, and apprentices.* Boston: Crosby, Nichols and Co., 1855.

Halyard, Harry. *The Rover of the Reef.* Boston: F. Gleason, 1848.

——. *Wharton the Whale-Killer.* Boston: F. Gleason, 1848.

Hawthorne, Nathaniel. "The Custom House." In *The Scarlet Letter.* 1850. Rpt. Oxford: Oxford University Press, 1990.

Hazen, Jacob A. *Five Years Before the Mast; or, Life in the Forecastle, aboard a whaler and man-of-war.* 1853. Rpt. New York: World Publishing House, 1876.

Henshaw, J. Sidney. *Around the World: A narrative of a voyage in the East India Squadron, under Commodore George C. Read. By an officer of the U.S. Navy.* 2 vols. New York: Charles S. Francis, 1840.

Holden, Horace. *A Narrative of the Shipwreck, Captivity and Sufferings of Horace Holden and Benj. H. Nute; who were cast away in the American ship mentor, on the Pelew Islands, in the year 1832; and for two years afterward were subjected to unheard of sufferings among the barbarous inhabitants of Lord North's Island.* Boston: Russell, Shattuck, and Co. 1836.

Hoxse, John. *The Yankee Tar. An authentic narrative of the voyages and hardships of John Hoxse, and the cruises of the US Frigate Constellation, and her engagements with the French frigates Le Insurgente and Le Vengeance, in the latter of which the author loses his right arm, and severely wounded in the side.* Northampton: printed by John Metcalf, for the author, 1840.

Ingraham, Joseph H. *The Cruiser of the Mist.* New York: Burgess, Stringer, 1845.

——. *The Hunted Slaver; or, Wrecked in Port.* 1844.

"Introductory." *Putnam's Monthly Magazine,* January 1853, 1–3.

Irving, Washington. *The Sketch-Book of Geoffrey Crayon, Gent.* 1819–20. Rpt. New York: Signet, 1981.

Isaacs, Nicholas Peter. *Twenty Years Before the Mast; or, Life in the Forecastle.* New York: J. P. Beckwith, 1845.

Jefferson, Thomas. *Notes on the State of Virginia.* Edited by William Peden. Chapel Hill: University of North Carolina Press, 1955.

——. *Writings.* New York: Library of America, 1984.

Jewitt, John R. *Narrative of the Adventures and Sufferings of John R. Jewitt; only survivor of the crew of the ship Boston, during a captivity of nearly three years among the savages of Nootka sound: with an account of the manners, mode of living, and religious opinions of the natives.* New York, 1815.

Judson, Edward Z. C. [Ned Buntline, pseud.] *Cruisings, Afloat and Ashore, from the Private Log of Ned Buntline.* New York: Beadle and Adams, 1848.

Knapp, Andrew, ed. *Newgate Calendar.* London: J. Robins, 1824–28.

Lawrence, Mary Chipman, and Stanton Garner. *The Captain's Best Mate: The Journal* of Mary Chipman Lawrence on the Whaler Addison, 1856–1860. Hanover, N.H.: University Press of New England, 1986.

Leech, Samuel. *Thirty Years from Home; or, A Voice from the Main Deck.* Boston: Tappan and Dennet, 1843.

Leggett, William. *Naval Stories.* New York: G. & C. & H. Carvill, 1834.

——. *Tales and Sketches, By a Country Schoolmaster.* New York: J. & J. Harper, 1829.

Life in a Man-of-War; or, Scenes in "Old Ironsides" during her cruise in the Pacific. Philadelphia: Lydia R. Bailey, 1841.

"Literary Pursuits of Sailors." In *The Mariner's Library or Voyager's Companion. Containing narratives of the most popular voyages, from the time of Columbus to the present day; with accounts of remarkable shipwrecks, naval adventures, the whale fishery, &c.* Boston: Lilly, Wait, Colman and Holden, 1833.

Little, George. *American Cruiser.* Boston: Waite, Pierce, 1846.

——. *Life on the Ocean; or, Twenty years at sea.* 1843. Rpt. Boston: Waite, Peirce and Company, 1845.

Log 143. Logbook, 1841–1845, *Charles W. Morgan* (Ship: 1841). G. W. Blunt White Library, Mystic Seaport, Mystic, Conn.

Log 832. Lexington, from Nantucket, Master Peter C. Brock, logkeeper Edward C. Luce, Dec. 11, 1853–Nov. 15, 1854; Log 832 *Louisa Sears* (Bark). Journal 1856–58, kept by Edward C. Luce on board bark *Louisa Sears* of Edgartown, MA. Edward Mayhew, master, for a voyage to the Atlantic Ocean whaling grounds. G. W. Blunt White Library, Mystic Seaport, Mystic, Conn.

Log 850. JOHN Q ADAMS (ship). Journal, 1852–1853, kept on board ship JOHN Q ADAMS of Boston, Mass., Howes, master, for a coastwise and South American trading voyage. Photocopy. G. W. Blunt White Library, Mystic Seaport, Mystic, Conn.

Log 961. Mary C. Ames (schooner). Journal, June 1–Aug. 30 1847, aboard Sch. *Mary C. Ames* of Newburyport, MA, Bailey, Master, for a cod fishing voyage in Newfoundland waters (ends at sea). G. W. Blunt White Library, Mystic Seaport, Mystic, Conn.

London, Jack. *Martin Eden.* New York: Penguin, 1984.

——. *The Sea Wolf.* New York: Bantam, 1991.

Mackenzie, Alexander Slidell, James Fenimore Cooper, and United States Navy. *Proceedings of the Naval Court Martial in the Case of Alexander Slidell Mackenzie, a Commander in the Navy of the United States, &C.: Including the Charges and Specifications of Charges, Preferred against Him by the Secretary of the Navy. To Which Is Annexed, an Elaborate Review.* New York: H. G. Langley, 1844.

Marks, Richard. *The Retrospect; or, Review of Providential Mercies; with Anecdotes of Various Characters, and an Address to Naval Officers.* Boston: S. T. Armstrong and Crocker and Brewster, 1822.

Martingale, Hawser [John Sherburne Sleeper]. *Jack in the Forecastle; or, Incidents in the Early Life of Hawser Martingale.* 1860. Rpt. Boston: Crosby and Nichols, 1865.

——. *Salt Water Bubbles; or, Life on the Wave.* Boston: W. J. Reynolds, 1854.

McNairn, Alan D., ed. *Life Aboard: The Journals of William N. and George F. Smith.* Saint John, Calif.: New Brunswick Museum, 1988.

McNally, William. *Evils and Abuses in the Naval and Merchant Service, Exposed.* Boston: Cassady and March, 1839.

Melville, Herman. *Billy Budd and Other Stories.* New York: Penguin, 1986.

——. *Clarel, a Poem and Pilgrimage in the Holy Land.* Evanston, Ill.: Northwestern-Newberry, 1991.

——. *Correspondence.* Edited by Harrison Hayford, Hershel Parker, and G. Thomas Tanselle. Evanston, Ill.: Northwestern-Newberry, 1993.

——. "The Encantadas, or Enchanted Isles." *Putnam's Monthly Magazine*, March 1854, 311–19; April 1854, 345–45; May 1854, 460–66.

——. *Journals.* Evanston, Ill.: Northwestern-Newberry, 1989.

——. *Mardi.* Evanston, Ill.: Northwestern-Newberry, 1970.

——. *Moby-Dick.* Evanston, Ill.: Northwestern-Newberry, 1988.

——. *Omoo.* Evanston, Ill.: Northwestern-Newberry, 1968.

——. *Redburn: His First Voyage.* Evanston, Ill.: Northwestern-Newberry, 1972.

——. "A Thought on Book-Binding." *Literary World*, 16 March 1850, 277.

——. *Typee.* Evanston, Ill.: Northwestern-Newberry, 1968.

——. *White-Jacket; or, The World in a Man-of-War.* Evanston, Ill.: Northwestern-Newberry, 1970.

Millet, Samuel. *A Whaling Voyage in the Bark "Willis," 1849–1850.* Boston: privately printed, 1924.

M'Lean, James. *Seventeen Years' History, of the Life and Sufferings of James M'lean, an Impressed American Citizen & Seaman, Embracing but a Summary of What He Endured, While Detained in the British Service, During That Long and Painful Period.* Hartford: B. & J. Russell, 1814.

Moore, Thomas. *Prose and Verse: Humorous, Satirical, and Sentimental.* London: Chatto and Windus, 1878.

Morell, Benjamin, Jr. *A Narrative of Four Voyages to the South Sea, North and South Pacific Ocean, Chinese Sea, Ethiopic and Southern Atlantic Ocean, Indian and Antarctic ocean. From the year 1822 to 1831. Comprising critical surveys of coasts and islands, with sailing directions. And an account of some new and valuable discoveries, including the Massacre islands, where thirteen of the author's crew were massacred and eaten by cannibals.* New York: Harper's, 1832.

Munger, James F. *Two Years in the Pacific and Arctic Oceans and China, being a journal of every day life on board ship, interesting information in regard to the inhabitants of different countries, and the exciting events peculiar to a whaling voyage.* Vernon, N.Y.: JR Howlett, 1852.

Myers, Ned, and James Fenimore Cooper. *Ned Myers; or, A Life before the Mast.* Classics of Naval Literature. Annapolis, Md.: Naval Institute Press, 1989.

Nevens, William. *Forty Years at Sea; or, A narrative of the adventures of William Nevens.* Portland, Maine: Thurston, Fenley & Co., 1846.

Newhall, Charles Lyman. *The Adventures of Jack; or, A Life on the Wave.* Southbridge, Mass.: Printed by the author, 1859.

Nickerson, Thomas, Owen Chase, and others. *The Loss of the Ship "Essex," Sunk by a Whale.* Edited by Nathaniel Philbrick and Thomas Philbrick. New York: Penguin, 2000.

Noah, M. M. *Address delivered at the re-opening of the Apprentices' Library, and reading rooms, at the Mechanics' Hall.* New York: Van Norden and Amerman, 1850.

O'Brien, Richard. "[Extract of a Letter from Capt. O'Brien, an American Prisoner at Algiers, Dated January 26, 1786]." *Worcester Magazine,* June 1786, 102.

Olmsted, Francis Allyn. *Incidents of a Whaling Voyage: To Which Are Added Observations on the Scenery, Manners and Customs, and Missionary Stations of the Sandwich and Society Islands.* New York: D. Appleton and Co., 1841.

Paddock, Judah. *A Narrative of the Shipwreck of the Ship Oswego, on the Coast of South Barbary, and of the Sufferings of the Master and the Crew While in Bondage among the Arabs; Interspersed with Numerous Remarks Upon the Country and Its Inhabitants, and Concerning the Peculiar Perils of That Coast.* New York: Collins & Co., 1818.

Peterson, Charles. *Cruising in the Last War.* Philadelphia: T. B. Peterson, 1850.

Pirates Own Book: Authentic Narratives of the Most Celebrated Sea Robbers. Marine Research Society. New York: Dover, 1993.

Pitts, Joseph. *Narrative of the Captivity of Joseph Pitts, among the Algerines, and of His Fortunate Escape from the Mahometans.* Frederick-Town, Md.: Hardt and Cross, 1815.

Poe, Edgar Allan. "A Descent into the Maelstrom." 1841. In *Complete Tales and Poems,* 127–40. New York: Vintage, 1975.

———. "MS Found in a Bottle." 1833. In *Complete Tales and Poems,* 118–26. New York: Vintage, 1975.

———. *The Narrative of Arthur Gordon Pym.* In *Poetry and Tales,* 1003–1182. New York: Library of America, 1984.

———. "South-Sea Expedition." *Southern Literary Messenger* 3, no. 1 (January 1937): 68.

Porter, David. *A Voyage in the South Seas, in the Years 1812, 1813, and 1814 with Particular Details of the Gallipagos and Washington Islands.* London: Phillips & Co., 1823.

Porter, David, R. D. Madison, and Karen Hamon. *Journal of a Cruise.* Classics of Naval Literature. Annapolis, Md.: Naval Institute Press, 1986.

Putnam, George Palmer. *American Facts. Notes and Statistics Relative to the Government, Resources, Engagements, Manufactures, Commerce, Religion, Education, Literature, Fine Arts, Manners and Customs of the United States of America.* London: Wiley and Putnam, 1845.

———. "*Putnam's Monthly Magazine* Correspondence." Box 1, folder 63; box 5, folders 35, 59. George Palmer Putnam Collection. Manuscript Division. Department of Rare Books and Special Collections. Princeton University Libraries, Princeton, N.J.

———. "Scrapbook 1813–1888." Box 11, folder 1. George Palmer Putnam Collection. Manuscript Division. Department of Rare Books and Special Collections. Princeton University Libraries, Princeton, N.J.

——. *The World's Progress: A Dictionary of Dates. With Tabular Views of General History.* New York: G. P. Putnam, 1850.

Ray, William. *Horrors of Slavery; or, The American Tars in Tripoli. Containing an Account of the Loss and Capture of the United States Frigate Philadelphia; Treatment and Sufferings of the Prisoners; Description of the Place; Manners, Customs, &C. Of the Tripolitans; Public Transactions of the United States with That Regency, Including Gen. Eaton's Expedition; Interspersed with Interesting Remarks, Anecdotes, and Poetry, on Various Subjects / Written During Upwards of Nineteen Months' Imprisonment and Vassalage among the Turks.* Troy, N.Y.: Oliver Lyon, 1808.

Review of *An authentic Narrative of the loss of the American brig Commerce*, by James Riley. *North American Review* 5, issue 15 (September 1817): 389–409.

Review of *Journal of a Cruise made to the Pacifick Ocean*, by Captain David Porter. *North American Review* 1, issue 2 (July 1815): 274–47.

Review of *Leisure Hours at Sea*, by a Midshipman of the United States Navy [William Leggett]. *North American Review* 22, issue 51 (April 1826): 453–55.

Review of *A Narrative of Voyages and Travels in the Northern and Southern Hemispheres*, by Amasa Delano. *North American Review* 5, issue 14 (July 1817): 244–57.

Review of *Nautical Reminiscences*, by Nathaniel Ames. *New England Magazine*, April 1832, 356.

Review of *Ned Myers; or, A Life Before the Mast. Editors' Table*, January 1844, 155.

Review of *Ned Myers; or, A Life Before the Mast. Graham's Lady's and Gentleman's Magazine*, January 1844, 46.

Review of *The Pilot, a Tale of the Sea. North American Review* 18, issue 43 (April 1824): 314–28.

Review of *Two Years before the Mast. North American Review* 52, issue 110 (January 1841): 56–75.

Riley, James. *An Authentic Narrative of the Loss of the American Brig Commerce, Wrecked on the Western Coast of Africa, in the Month of August, 1815. With an Account of the Sufferings of Her Surviving Officers and Crew, Who Were Enslaved by the Wandering Arabs on the Great African Desert, or Zahahrah; and Observations Historical, Geographical, &C. Made During the Travels of the Author, While a Slave to the Arabs, and in the Empire of Morocco.* New York: Collins & Co., 1818.

Robbins, Archibald. *A Journal, Comprising an Account of the Loss of the Brig Commerce,: of Hartford, (Con.) James Riley, master, upon the western coast of Africa, August 28th, 1815; also of the slavery and sufferings of the author and the rest of the crew, upon the desert of Zahara, in the years 1815, 1816, 1817; with accounts of the manners, customs, and habits of the wandering Arabs; also, a brief historical and geographical view of the continent of Africa.* Hartford: F. D. Bolles, 1817.

Russell, W. Clark. "A Claim for American Literature." *North American Review* 154, issue 423 (February 1892): 138–49.

——. "Sea Stories." *The Eclectic Magazine of Foreign Literature*, November 1884, 654–69.

Scott, Michael. *Tom Cringle's Log.* Heart of Oak Sea Classics. New York: Henry Holt, 1999.

Slocum, Joshua. *Sailing Alone Around the World*. New York: The Adventure Library, 1995.

Smith, Charles Edward, and Charles Edward Smith Harris. *From the Deep of the Sea: Being the Diary of the Late Charles Edward Smith*. New York: Macmillan, 1923.

Smith, G. C., ed. *Boatswain's Mate*. New York: Gallaudet, 1818.

Smith, Thomas W. *A Narrative of the Life, Travels and Sufferings of Thomas W. Smith: Comprising an account of his early life, adoptions by the Gipsys; his travels during eighteen voyages to various parts of the world, during which he was five times shipwrecked; thrice on a desolate island and near the south pole, one on the coast of England, and once on the coast of Africa*. Boston: Wm. C. Hill, 1844.

Smollett, Tobias. *The Adventures of Roderick Random*. New York: Signet, 1964.

[Sparks, Jared.] "Interiour of Africa." *North American Review* 5, issue. 13 (May 1817): 11–26.

——. "Narrative of Robert Adams." *North American Review* 5, no. 14 (July 1817): 204–24.

Stevens, William Lord. *Ship Trescott: The Voyage of a Forty-niner. A journal in verse*. Stonington, Conn., 1849.

Stewart, C. S. *Private Journal of a Voyage to the Pacific Ocean, and residence at the Sandwich Islands, in the years 1822, 1823, 1824, and 1825*. New York: John P. Haven, 1828.

——. *A Visit to the South Seas, in the US Ship Vincennes, during the years 1829 and 1830*. 2 vols. New York: John P. Haven, 1831.

Sullivan, William V. *Scarcity of Seamen*. Boston, 1853.

Sumner, Charles. *White Slavery in the Barbary States*. Boston: J. P. Jewett and Company, 1853.

Taylor, Nathaniel W. *Life on a Whaler; or, Antarctic Adventures in the Isle of Desolation*. 1858. Rpt. New London County Historical Society, 1929.

Thoreau, Henry David. *Walden: A Week, Walden, the Maine Woods, Cape Cod*. New York: Library of America, 1985.

——. *The Writings of Henry David Thoreau*. Edited by F. B. Sanborn. 20 vols. New York: Houghton Mifflin, 1906.

Torrey, William. *Torrey's Narrative; or, The Life and Adventures of William Torrey. Who for the space of 25 months, within the years 1835, '36, and '37, was held a captive by the cannibals of the Marquesas, (a group of islands in the south sea,) among whom he was cast from the wreck of the Brig Doll, Capt. ——, of Otaheite, of which wreck himself, and one shipmate, can alone tell the sad tale. Also, for many years served in the several capacities requisite for seamen, on both English and American merchants' ships*. Boston: Press of A. J. Wright, 1848.

Tyng, Charles. *Before the Wind: The Memoir of an American Sea Captain, 1808–1833*. Edited by Susan Fels. New York: Viking, 1999.

Tudor, William. "Books Relating to America." *North American Review* 1, issue 1 (May 1815): 1–13.

Twain, Mark. "Fenimore Cooper's Literary Offences." *North American Review* 161, issue 464 (July 1895): 1–12.

Tyler, Royall. *The Algerine Captive; or, The Life and Adventures of Doctor Updike Underhill, Six Years a Prisoner among the Algerines*. Walpole, N.H., 1797.

U.S. Office of Naval Records and Library and Dudley Wright Knox. *Naval Documents Related to the United States Wars with the Barbary Powers . . . : Naval Operations Including Diplomatic Background . . . Published under Direction of The . . . Secretary of the Navy*. Washington, D.C.: U.S. Govt. Print. Off., 1939.

Waddel, Charles. *The Lady of the Green and Blue*. Boston: George H. Williams, 1848.

Wallace, J. *New Treatise on the Use of the Globes and Practical Astronomy*. New York: Smith and Forman, 1822.

Warriner, Francis. *Cruise of the United States Frigate Potomac round the world, during the years 1831–34. Embracing the attack on Quallah Battoo, with notices of scenes, manners, etc., in different parts of Asia, South America, and the islands of the Pacific*. New York: Leavitt, Lord & Co., 1835.

Whitcomb, Samuel, Jr. *An Address before the Working-Men's Society of Dedham*. Dedham, Mass.: L. Powers, 1831.

Whitecar, William B., Jr. *Four Years in a Whaleship. Embracing cruises in the Pacific, Atlantic, Indian, and Antarctic Oceans, in the years 1855, '6, '7, '8, '9*. Philadelphia: J. B. Lippincott, 1860.

Wilkes, Charles. *Narrative of the United States Exploring Expedition, During the years 1838, 1839, 1840, 1841, 1842*. 5 vols. and an atlas. Philadelphia: Lea & Blanchard, 1845.

——. *Voyage Round the World, Embracing the Principal Events of the Narrative of the United States Exploring Expedition*. New York: G. P. Putnam, 1851.

SECONDARY SOURCES

Adams, Charles H. "Cooper's Sea Fiction and *The Red Rover*." *Studies in American Fiction* 16, no. 2: 155–68.

Allison, Robert J. Review of *White Slaves, African Masters: An Anthology of American Barbary Captivity Narratives*, edited by Paul Baepler. *William and Mary Quarterly*, 3rd ser., 57, no. 2 (April 2000): 459–61.

Amory, Hugh, and David D. Hall. *A History of the Book in America*. Vol. 1, *The Colonial Book in the Atlantic World*. Cambridge: Cambridge University Press, 2000.

Anderson, Benedict. *Imagined Communities: Reflections on the Origin and Spread of Nationalism*. London: Verso, 1991.

Andrews, William L. *To Tell a Free Story: The First Century of Afro-American Autobiography, 1760–1865*. Champaign: University of Illinois Press, 1997.

Appleton, J. H. *The Experience of Landscape*. London: Wiley, 1974.

Arac, Jonathan. *The Emergence of American Literary Narrative, 1820–1860*. Cambridge: Harvard University Press, 2005.

Ariès, Philippe. *Western Attitudes toward Death: From the Middle Ages to the Present*. Baltimore: Johns Hopkins University Press, 1974.

Armitage, David, and Michael J. Braddick. *The British Atlantic World, 1500–1800*. Hampshire: Palgrave Macmillan, 2002.

Auerbach, Jonathan. *Male Call: Becoming Jack London*. Durham: Duke University Press, 1996.

Augst, Thomas. *The Clerk's Tale: Young Men and Moral Life in Nineteenth-Century America*. Chicago: University of Chicago Press, 2001.

Baepler, Paul. "The Barbary Captivity Narrative in American Culture." *Early American Literature* 39, no. 2 (2004): 217–46.

———. "The Barbary Captivity Narrative in Early America." *Early American Literature* 30, no. 2 (1995): 95–120.

———. *White Slaves, African Masters: An Anthology of American Barbary Captivity Narratives*. Chicago: University of Chicago Press, 1999.

Bailyn, Bernard. *Atlantic History: Concept and Contours*. Cambridge: Harvard University Press, 2005.

Baker, Margaret. *Folklore of the Sea*. London: David & Charles, 1979.

Barrell, John. *The Idea of Landscape and the Sense of Place*. Cambridge: Cambridge University Press, 1972.

Barthes, Roland. "The Nautilus and the Drunken Boat." In *Mythologies*, 65–67. New York: Hill and Wang, 1983.

Bamford, Paul W. *The Barbary Pirates: Victims and the Scourge of Christendom*. Minneapolis: Associates of the James Ford Bell Library, University of Minnesota, 1972.

Bank, Stanley. *American Romanticism: A Shape for Fiction*. New York: Putnam, 1969.

Barnby, H. G. *The Prisoners of Algiers: An Account of the Forgotten American-Algerian War, 1785–1797*. London: Oxford University Press, 1966.

Bate, Jonathan. *Romantic Ecology*. London: Routledge, 1991.

Bauerlein, Mark. "Grammar and Etymology in *Moby-Dick*." *Arizona Quarterly* 46, no. 3 (Fall 1990): 17–32.

Baym, Nina. *Novels, Readers, and Reviewers: Responses to Fiction in Antebellum America*. Ithaca: Cornell University Press, 1984.

Beck, Horace Palmer, and Marine Historical Association. *Folklore and the Sea*. Middletown, Conn.: Wesleyan University Press, 1973.

Beer, Gillian. *Darwin's Plots: Evolutionary Narrative in Darwin, George Eliot, and Nineteenth-Century Fiction*. Cambridge: Cambridge University Press, 2000.

———. *Open Fields: Science in Cultural Encounter*. Oxford: Oxford University Press, 1996.

Bender, Bert. *The Descent of Love: Darwin and the Theory of Sexual Selection in American Fiction, 1871–1926*. Philadelphia: University of Pennsylvania Press, 1996.

———. *Sea-Brothers: The Tradition of American Sea Fiction from "Moby-Dick" to the Present*. Philadelphia: University of Pennsylvania Press, 1988.

Benesch, Klaus, Jon-K Adams, and Kerstin Schmidt, eds. *The Sea and the American Imagination*. Tübingen: Stauffenburg Verlag, 2004.

Bennett, Michael J. *Union Jacks: Yankee Sailors in the Civil War*. Chapel Hill: University of North Carolina Press, 2004.

Bercaw, Mary K. *Melville's Sources*. Evanston, Ill.: Northwestern University Press, 1987.

Bercovitch, Sacvan. *The American Jeremiad*. Madison: University of Wisconsin Press, 1978.

Bercovitch, Sacvan, and Myra Jehlen. *Ideology and Classic American Literature*. Cambridge: Cambridge University Press, 1986.

Berry, Robert. *Yankee Stargazer*. New York: McGraw-Hill, 1941.

Blanchot, Maurice. *The Space of Literature*. Lincoln: University of Nebraska Press, 1982.

Bloom, Clive. *Reading Poe, Reading Freud: The Romantic Imagination in Crisis*. Basingstoke: Macmillan, 1988.

Blum, Hester. "Atlantic Trade." In *A Companion to Herman Melville*, edited by Wyn Kelley, 113–28. Oxford: Blackwell, 2006.

Boime, Albert. *The Magisterial Gaze*. Washington, D.C.: Smithsonian, 1971.

Bolster, W. Jeffrey. *Black Jacks: African American Seamen in the Age of Sail*. Cambridge: Harvard University Press, 1997.

Bonaparte, Marie. *The Life and Works of Edgar Allan Poe: A Psycho-Analytic Interpretation*. London: Imago, 1949.

Bonner, Willard H. *Harp on the Shore: Thoreau and the Sea*. Albany: SUNY Press, 1985.

Boone, Joseph, and Michael Cadden, eds. *Engendering Men*. New York: Routledge, 1990.

Brodhead, Richard. *Cultures of Letters: Scenes of Reading and Writing in Nineteenth-Century America*. Chicago: University of Chicago Press, 1993.

Bromell, Nicholas. *By the Sweat of the Brow: Literature and Labor in Antebellum America*. Chicago: University of Chicago Press, 1993.

Brown, Bill. *The Material Unconscious: American Amusement, Stephen Crane, and the Economies of Play*. Cambridge: Harvard University Press, 1996.

———. *A Sense of Things: The Object Matter of American Literature*. Chicago: University of Chicago Press, 2003.

Buell, Lawrence. *The Environmental Imagination: Thoreau, Nature Writing, and the Formation of American Culture*. Cambridge: Harvard University Press, 1995.

———. *Literary Transcendentalism: Style and Vision in the American Renaissance*. Ithaca: Cornell University Press, 1973.

Busch, Briton. *"Whaling Will Never Do For Me."* Lexington: University Press of Kentucky, 1986.

Bussy, R. Kenneth. *Two Hundred Years of Publishing: A History of the Oldest Publishing Company in the United States, Lea & Febiger, 1785–1985*. Philadelphia: Lea & Febiger, 1985.

Cameron, Sharon. *Writing Nature: Henry Thoreau's Journal*. New York: Oxford University Press, 1985.

Carlisle, Henry. *The Jonah Man*. New York: Knopf, 1984.

Carlson, Patricia Ann, ed. *Literature and Lore of the Sea*. Amsterdam: Rodopi, 1986.

Carney, Beth, and Maureen Dezell. "Names and Faces: Indies Uniting at Nantucket Fest." *Boston Globe*, 20 June 1998, C2.

Carr, James A. "John Adams and the Barbary Problem: The Myth and the Record." *American Neptune* 26, no. 4 (1966): 231–57.

Carretta, Vincent. *Equiano the African: Biography of a Self-Made Man*. Athens: University of Georgia Press, 2005.

Carter, Edward C. "Mathew Carey, Advocate of American Naval Power, 1785–1814." *American Neptune* 23, no. 3 (1966): 177–88.

Casarino, Cesare. *Modernity at Sea: Melville, Marx, Conrad in Crisis*. Minneapolis: University of Minnesota Press, 2002.

Casper, Scott E., Joanne D. Chaison, and Jeffrey D. Groves. *Perspectives on American Book History: Artifacts and Commentary*. Amherst: University of Massachusetts Press, 2002.

Castiglia, Christopher. *Bound and Determined: Captivity, Culture-Crossing, and White Womanhood from Mary Rowlandson to Patty Hearst*. Chicago: University of Chicago Press, 1996.

Castronovo, Russ. *Necro Citizenship: Death, Eroticism, and the Public Sphere in the Nineteenth-Century United States*. Durham: Duke University Press, 2001.

Charvat, William. *Literary Publishing in America, 1790–1850*. Amherst: University of Massachusetts Press, 1993.

———. *The Profession of Authorship in America, 1800–1870: The Papers of William Charvat*. Columbus: Ohio State University Press, 1968.

Cheyfitz, Eric. *The Poetics of Imperialism: Translation and Colonization from the Tempest to Tarzan*. New York: Oxford University Press, 1991.

Chidsey, Donald Barr. *The Wars in Barbary: Arab Piracy and the Birth of the United States Navy*. New York: Crown, 1971.

Clark, Christopher. "The Diary of an Apprentice Cabinetmaker: Edward Jenner Carpenter's 'Journal,' 1844–45." *Proceedings of the American Antiquarian Society* 98 (1988): 303–394.

Clissold, Stephen. *The Barbary Slaves*. New York: Barnes and Noble, 1992.

Cohen, Margaret. "Traveling Genres." *New Literary History* 34, no. 3 (Summer 2003): 481–99.

Colley, Linda. *Captives: Britain, Empire, and the World, 1600–1850*. London: Pimlico, 2003.

———. "Going Native, Telling Tales: Captivity, Collaborations and Empire." *Past and Present*, August 2000, 170–93.

Colonial Society of Massachusetts. *Seafaring in Colonial Massachusetts: A Conference Held by the Colonial Society of Massachusetts, November 21 and 22, 1975*. Boston: Colonial Society of Massachusetts, 1980.

Corbin, Alain. *The Lure of the Sea: The Discovery of the Seaside in the Western World, 1750–1840*. Cambridge: Polity Press, 1994.

Cotter, Charles. *History of Nautical Astronomy*. New York: American Elsevier, 1968.

Crary, Jonathan. *Techniques of the Observer: On Vision and Modernity in the Nineteenth Century*. Cambridge: MIT Press, 1990.

Creighton, Margaret S. *Rites and Passages: The Experience of American Whaling, 1830–1870*. Cambridge: Cambridge University Press, 1995.

Creighton, Margaret S., and Lisa Norling, eds. *Iron Men, Wooden Women: Gender and Seafaring in the Atlantic World, 1700–1920*. Baltimore: Johns Hopkins University Press, 1996.

Cremin, Lawrence. "Reading, Writing, and Literacy." *Review of Education* 1 (November 1975): 517–21.

Davidson, Cathy N. *Reading in America: Literature and Social History*. Baltimore: Johns Hopkins University Press, 1989.

———. *Revolution and the Word: The Rise of the Novel in America*. New York: Oxford University Press, 1986.

Dekker, George. *James Fenimore Cooper: The American Scott*. New York: Barnes and Noble, 1967.

Dekker, George, and John P. Williams, eds. *James Fenimore Cooper: The Critical Heritage*. London: Routledge, 1973.

DeLombard, Jeannine. "'Eye-Witness to the Cruelty': Southern Violence and Northern Testimony in Frederick Douglass's 1845 Narrative." *American Literature* 73, no. 2 (2001): 245–75.

Denning, Michael. *Mechanic Accents: Dime Novels and Working-Class Culture America*. London: Verso, 1987.

Dennis, Ian. *Nationalism and Desire in Early Historical Fiction*. New York: St. Martin's, 1997.

Dennis, Matthew. "Patriotic Remains: Bones of Contention in the Early Republic." In *Mortal Remains: Death in Early America*, edited by Nancy Isenberg and Andrew Burstein, 136–48. Philadelphia: University of Pennsylvania Press, 2003.

Descartes, René. *The Philosophical Writings of Descartes*. Translated by John Cottingham, Robert Stoothoff, and Dugald Murdoch. Cambridge: Cambridge University Press, 1985.

Dillingham, William. *Melville's Later Novels*. Athens: University of Georgia Press, 1986.

Dillon, Elizabeth Maddock. "Slaves in Algiers: Race, Republican Genealogies, and the Global Stage." *American Literary History* 16, no. 3 (2004): 407–36.

Dimock, Wai-chee. *Empire for Liberty: Melville and the Poetics of Individualism*. Princeton: Princeton University Press, 1988.

Dorsey, Bruce. *Reforming Men and Women: Gender in the Antebellum City*. Ithaca: Cornell University Press, 2002.

Douglas, Ann. "Heaven Our Home: Consolation Literature in the Northern United States, 1830–1880." In *Death in America*, edited by David E. Stannard, 49–68. Philadelphia: University of Pennsylvania Press, 1975.

Dow, George. *Whale Ships and Whaling*. New York: Argosy Antiquarian, 1967.

Druett, Joan. *Hen Frigates: Wives of Merchant Captains under Sail*. New York: Simon and Schuster, 1998.

Dryden, Edgar A. "From the Piazza to the Enchanted Isles: Melville's Textual

Rovings." In *After Strange Texts: The Role of Theory in the Study of Literature*, edited by Gregory S. Jay and David Lee Miller, 46–68. University: University of Alabama Press, 1985.

——. *Melville's Thematics of Form: The Great Art of Telling the Truth*. Baltimore: Johns Hopkins University Press, 1968.

——. *Monumental Melville: The Formation of a Literary Career*. Palo Alto: Stanford University Press, 2004.

Dudley, William S., and Michael Crawford, eds. *The Early Republic and the Sea: Essays on the Naval and Maritime History of the Early United States*. Dulles, Va.: Potomac Books, 2001.

Dulles, Foster. *Lowered Boats*. New York: Harcourt Brace, 1933.

Dunphy, Mark. "Melville's Turning of the Darwinian Table in 'The Encantadas.' " *Melville Society Extracts* 79 (November 1989): 14.

Dye, Ira. "Early American Merchant Seafarers." *Proceedings of the American Philosophical Society* 120, no. 5 (October 1976): 331–60.

Ebersole, Gary L. *Captured by Texts: Puritan to Postmodern Images of Indian Captivity*. Charlottesville: University Press of Virginia, 1995.

Edwards, Philip. *The Story of the Voyage: Sea-Narratives in Eighteenth-Century England*. Cambridge: Cambridge University Press, 1994.

Egan, Hugh McKeever. "Gentlemen-Sailors: The First-Person Sea Narratives of Dana, Cooper, and Melville." Ph.D. diss., University of Iowa, 1983.

Elkins, James. *The Poetics of Perspective*. Ithaca: Cornell University Press, 1994.

Ellis, Richard. *Men and Whales*. New York: Knopf, 1991.

Emery, Allan Moore. " 'Benito Cereno' and Manifest Destiny." *Nineteenth-Century Fiction* 39, no. 1 (June 1984): 48–68.

Fabian, Ann. *The Unvarnished Truth: Personal Narratives in Nineteenth-Century America*. Berkeley: University of California Press, 2000.

Fender, Stephen. *Sea Changes*. Cambridge: Cambridge University Press, 1992.

Fiedler, Leslie A. *Love and Death in the American Novel*. Rev. ed. New York: Stein and Day, 1966.

Fisher, Godfrey. *Barbary Legend: War, Trade, and Piracy in North Africa, 1415–1830*. Oxford: Clarendon, 1957.

Fisher, Philip. *Hard Facts: Setting and Form in the American Novel*. New York: Oxford University Press, 1985.

——. *Still the New World: American Literature in a Culture of Creative Destruction*. Cambridge: Harvard University Press, 1999.

——. *Wonder, the Rainbow, and the Aesthetics of Rare Experiences*. Cambridge: Harvard University Press, 1998.

Foucault, Michel. "Of Other Spaces." *Diacritics*, Spring 1986, 22–27.

Foulke, Robert. *The Sea Voyage Narrative*. London: Routledge, 1997.

Franklin, Wayne. *Discoverers, Explorers, Settlers: The Diligent Writers of Early America*. Chicago: University of Chicago Press, 1979.

——. *The New World of James Fenimore Cooper*. Chicago: University of Chicago Press, 1982.

Franklin, Wayne, and Michael Steiner. *Mapping American Culture*. Iowa City: University of Iowa Press, 1992.

Freedgood, Elaine. *Victorian Writing about Risk: Imagining a Safe England in a Dangerous World*. Cambridge: Cambridge University Press, 2000.

Freeman, R. B. *The Works of Charles Darwin: An Annotated Bibliographical Handlist*. Hamden, Conn.: Archon, 1977.

Furrow, Sharon. "The Terrible Made Visible: Melville, Salvator Rosa, and Piranesi." *ESQ* 19, no. 4 (1973): 237–49.

Garvey, T. Gregory. *Creating the Culture of Reform in Antebellum America*. Athens: University of Georgia Press, 2006.

Garwood, Irving. *American Periodicals from 1850 to 1860*. Macomb, Ill., 1931.

Gates, Henry Louis, Jr., and William L. Andrews, eds. *Pioneers of the Black Atlantic: Five Slave Narratives from the Enlightenment, 1772–1815*. Washington, D.C.: Civitas, 1998.

Gilje, Paul A. *Liberty on the Waterfront: American Maritime Culture in the Age of Revolution*. Philadelphia: University of Pennsylvania Press, 2004.

Gilmore, Michael. *American Romanticism and the Marketplace*. Chicago: University of Chicago Press, 1985.

Gilroy, Paul. *The Black Atlantic: Modernity and Double Consciousness*. Cambridge: Harvard University Press, 1995.

Ginzberg, Lori. *Women and the Work of Benevolence: Morality, Politics, and Class in the Nineteenth-Century United States*. New Haven: Yale University Press, 1990.

Gitelman, Lisa. "Arthur Gordon Pym and the Novel Narrative of Edgar Allan Poe." *Nineteenth-Century Literature* 47, no. 3 (December 1992): 349–61.

Glenn, Myra C. *Campaigns against Corporal Punishment: Prisoners, Sailors, Women, and Children in Antebellum America*. Albany: SUNY Press, 1984.

Goetzmann, William H. *Exploration and Empire: The Explorer and the Scientist in the Winning of the American West*. Fred H. and Ella Mae Moore Texas History Reprint Series. Austin: Texas State Historical Association, 1993.

———. *New Lands, New Men: America and the Second Great Age of Discovery*. Austin: Texas State Historical Association, 1995.

Gombrich, E. H. *The Image and the Eye: Further Studies in the Psychology of Pictorial Representation*. Oxford: Phaidon, 1982.

Greenfield, Bruce Robert. *Narrating Discovery: The Romantic Explorer in American Literature, 1790–1855*. New York: Columbia University Press, 1992.

Greenspan, Ezra. *George Palmer Putnam: Representative American Publisher*. University Park: Pennsylvania State University Press, 2000.

Groves, Jeffrey D. "Judging Literary Books by Their Covers: House Styles, Ticknor and Fields, and Literary Promotion." In *Reading Books: Essays on the Material Text and Literature in America*, edited by Michele Moylan and Lane Stiles, 75–100. Amherst: University of Massachusetts Press, 1996.

Habermas, Jurgen. *The Structural Transformation of the Public Sphere: An Inquiry into a Category of Bourgeois Society*. Cambridge: MIT Press, 1989.

Hall, David D. *Cultures of Print: Essays in the History of the Book*. Studies in Print Culture and the History of the Book. Amherst: University of Massachusetts Press, 1996.

Hardwick, Elizabeth. *Herman Melville*. Penguin Lives Series. New York: Viking, 2000.

Harris, Neil. *Humbug: The Art of P. T. Barnum*. Chicago: University of Chicago Press, 1981.

Harrison, Robert Pogue. *The Dominion of the Dead*. Chicago: University of Chicago Press, 2003.

Hayes, Kevin J. *Melville's Folk Roots*. Kent, Ohio: Kent State University Press, 1999.

Hayes, Kevin J., Hershel Parker, and Steven Mailloux. *Checklist of Melville Reviews*. Evanston, Ill.: Northwestern University Press, 1991.

Heffernan, Thomas Farel. *Stove by a Whale: Owen Chase and the Essex*. New York: Columbia University Press, 1981.

Henningsen, Henning. *Crossing the Equator*. Copenhagen: Munksgaard, 1961.

Higgins, Brian, and Hershel Parker, eds. *Critical Essays on Herman Melville's Moby Dick*. New York: Macmillan, 1992.

———. *Herman Melville: The Contemporary Reviews*. American Critical Archives 6. Cambridge: Cambridge University Press, 1995.

Hilbert, Betsy. "The Truth of the Thing: Nonfiction in *Moby-Dick*." *College English* 48, no. 8 (December 1986): 824–31.

Himmelfarb, Gertrude. *Darwin and the Darwinian Revolution*. New York: Norton, 1968.

Hoffman, Daniel. *Poe Poe Poe Poe Poe Poe Poe*. Garden City, N.Y.: Doubleday, 1972.

Hohman, Elmo. *The American Whaleman*. New York: Longmans, Green, 1928.

Hovde, David M. "Sea Colportage: The Loan Library System of the American Seamen's Friend Society, 1859–1967." *Libraries and Culture* 29, no. 4 (Fall 1994): 389–414.

Howse, Derek. *Greenwich Time and the Longitude*. London: Phillip Wilson, 1997.

Huggan, Graham. "Decolonizing the Map: Post-Colonialism, Post-Structuralism and the Cartographic Connection." In *Past the Last Post*, edited by Ian Adam and Helen Tiffin, 125–38. Winnipeg: University of Calgary Press, 1990.

Irwin, Ray W. *The Diplomatic Relations of the United States with the Barbary Powers, 1776–1816*. Chapel Hill: University of North Carolina Press, 1931.

Jackson, Charles O. *Passing: The Vision of Death in America*. Westport, Conn.: Greenwood Press, 1977.

Jacobson, Kristin. "Desiring Natures: The American Adrenaline Narrative." *Genre* 35, no. 2 (Summer 2002): 355–82.

James, C. L. R. *Mariners, Renegades, and Castaways: The Story of Herman Melville and the World We Live In*. New York: Schocken Books, 1985.

Jehlen, Myra. *American Incarnation: The Individual, the Nation, and the Continent*. Cambridge: Harvard University Press, 1986.

Johnson, Donald S. *Phantom Islands of the Atlantic*. Fredericton, New Brunswick: Goose Lane, 1994.

Kazanjian, David. *The Colonizing Trick: National Culture and Imperial Citizenship in Early America*. Minneapolis: University of Minnesota Press, 2003.

Kennedy, J. Gerald. *The Narrative of Arthur Gordon Pym and the Abyss of Interpretation*. New York: Twayne, 1995.

———. "Poe and Magazine Writing on Premature Burial." *Studies in the American Renaissance* (1977): 195–78.

———. *Poe, Death, and the Life of Writing*. New Haven: Yale University Press, 1987.

Kitzen, Michael L. S. *Tripoli and the United States at War: A History of American Relations with the Barbary States, 1785–1805*. Jefferson, N.C.: McFarland, 1993.

Klein, Bernhard, ed. *Fictions of the Sea: Critical Perspectives on the Ocean in British Literature and Culture*. Brookfield, Vt.: Ashgate, 2002.

Klein, Bernhard, and Gesa MacKenthun, eds. *Sea Changes: Historicizing the Ocean*. London: Routledge, 2003.

Korty, Margaret Barton. "Benjamin Franklin and Eighteenth-Century American Libraries." *Transactions of the American Philosophical Society*, new ser., vol. 55, pt. 9. Philadelphia: American Philosophical Society, 1965.

Labaree, Benjamin Woods. *America and the Sea: A Maritime History*. American Maritime Library, vol. 15. Mystic, Conn.: Mystic Seaport, 1998.

Lamb, Jonathan. *Preserving the Self in the South Seas, 1680-1840*. Chicago: University of Chicago Press, 2001.

Lambert, Frank. *The Barbary Wars: American Independence in the Atlantic World*. New York: Hill and Wang, 2005.

Lawson-Peebles, Robert. *Landscape and Written Expression in Revolutionary America*. Cambridge: Cambridge University Press, 1988.

———. *Views of American Landscapes*. Cambridge: Cambridge University Press, 1989.

Lee, Grace Farrell. "Pym and Moby-Dick." *American Transcendental Quarterly* 37 (Winter 1978): 73–86.

Leiner, Frederick C. *The End of Barbary Terror: America's 1815 War against the Pirates of North Africa*. Cambridge: Oxford University Press, 2006.

———. *Millions for Defense: The Subscription Warships of 1798*. Annapolis, Md.: Naval Institute Press, 2000.

Lemisch, Jesse. *Jack Tar vs. John Bull: The Role of New York's Seamen in Precipitating the Revolution*. New York: Garland, 1997.

Leonard, David Charles. "Descartes, Melville, and the Mardian Vortex." *South Atlantic Bulletin* 45, no. 2 (May 1980): 13–25.

Lewis, James R. "Savages of the Seas: Barbary Captivity Tales and Images of Muslims in the Early Republic." *Journal of American Culture* 13, no. 2 (1990): 75–84.

Lewis, R. W. B. *The American Adam: Innocence, Tragedy, and Tradition in the Nineteenth Century*. Chicago: University of Chicago Press, 1958.

Leyland, John. *The British Tar in Fact and Fiction: The Poetry, Pathos, and Humour of the Sailor's Life*. New York: Harper, 1909.

Linebaugh, Peter, and Marcus Buford Rediker. *The Many-Headed Hydra: The Hidden History of the Revolutionary Atlantic*. Boston: Beacon Press, 2000.

Ljungquist, Kent. "Putnam's Monthly Magazine." In *American Literary Magazines: The Eighteenth and Nineteenth Centuries*, edited by Edward E. Chielens, 328–33. New York: Greenwood Press, 1986.

Lockridge, Kenneth A. *Literacy in Colonial New England: An Enquiry into the Social Context of Literacy in the Early Modern West*. New York: Norton, 1974.

London, Joshua E. *Victory in Tripoli: How America's War with the Barbary Pirates Established the U.S. Navy and Built a Nation*. Hoboken, N.J.: Wiley, 2005.

Lounsbury, Thomas Raynesford. *James Fenimore Cooper*. New York: Houghton Mifflin, 1883.

Loxley, Diana. *Problematic Shores: The Literature of Islands: Discourses of Nineteenth-Century Imperial Ideology*. Basingstoke: Macmillan, 1990.

Lydenberg, Harry Miller. *Crossing the Line*. New York: New York Public Library, 1957.

Mancini, Matthew. "Melville's 'Descartian Vortices.'" *ESQ* 36, no. 4 (1990): 315–27.

Margulis, Jennifer. "Swarthy Pirates and White Slaves: Barbary Captivity in the American Literary Imagination." Ph.D. diss., Emory University, 1999.

Marin, Louis. *On Representation*. Stanford: Stanford University Press, 2001.

Martin, Robert K. *Hero, Captain, and Stranger: Male Friendship, Social Critique, and Literary Form in the Sea Novels of Herman Melville*. Chapel Hill: University of North Carolina Press, 1986.

Martin, Ronald E. *American Literature and the Destruction of Knowledge: Innovative Writing in the Age of Epistemology*. Durham: Duke University Press, 1991.

Marx, Leo. *The Machine in the Garden: Technology and the Pastoral Ideal in America*. New York: Oxford University Press, 1964.

Mason, John B. "The North American Review." In *American Literary Magazines: The Eighteenth and Nineteenth Centuries*, edited by Edward E. Chielens, 289–300. New York: Greenwood Press, 1986.

Matteson, John T. "Grave Discussions: The Image of the Sepulchre in Webster, Emerson, and Melville." *New England Quarterly* 74, no. 3 (September 2001): 419–46.

Matthiessen, F. O. *American Renaissance: Art and Expression in the Age of Emerson and Whitman*. London: Oxford University Press, 1968.

Mead, Joan Tyler. "Poe's 'Manual of "Seamanship."'" In *Poe's "Pym": Critical Explorations*, edited by Richard Kopley, 20–32. Durham: Duke University Press, 1992.

Mencken, August. *First-Class Passenger: Life at Sea as Experienced and Recorded by Voyaging Landlubbers of the Past*. New York: Knopf, 1938.

Michaels, Walter Benn, and Donald E. Pease. *The American Renaissance Reconsidered*. Baltimore: Johns Hopkins University Press, 1985.

Miller, Angela. *The Empire of the Eye*. Ithaca: Cornell University Press, 1993.

Miller, David, ed. *American Iconology*. New Haven: Yale University Press, 1993.

Miller, Perry. *The Raven and the Whale: The War of Words and Wits in the Era of Poe and Melville*. New York: Harcourt Brace, 1956.

Milne, Gordon. *Ports of Call: A Study of the American Nautical Novel.* Lanham, Md.: University Press of America, 1986.

Mitford, Jessica. *The American Way of Death.* New York: Simon and Schuster, 1963.

Montgomery, Benilde. "White Captives, African Slaves: A Drama of Abolition." *Eighteenth-Century Studies* 27, no. 4 (Summer 1994): 617.

Moore, Richard S. *That Cunning Alphabet: Melville's Aesthetics of Nature.* Amsterdam: Rodopi, 1982.

Morreel, Gert. " 'When Leviathan Is the Text': Encyclopedism and the Limits of Representation in *Moby-Dick*." Melville's Use of Language Panel, Melville and the Sea, Convention of the Melville Society, Mystic Seaport, Mystic, Conn., 18 June 1999.

Morrison, Toni. *Playing in the Dark: Whiteness and the Literary Imagination.* New York: Vintage, 1992.

Mott, Frank Luther. *A History of American Magazines, 1850–1865.* Cambridge: Harvard University Press, 1938.

Moylan, Michele, and Lane Stiles. *Reading Books: Essays on the Material Text and Literature in America.* Studies in Print Culture and the History of the Book. Amherst: University of Massachusetts Press, 1996.

Muller, John P., and William J. Richardson. *The Purloined Poe: Lacan, Derrida, and Psychoanalytic Reading.* Baltimore, Md.: Johns Hopkins University Press, 1988.

Nash, Roderick. *Wilderness and the American Mind.* New Haven: Yale University Press, 1982.

Neill, Peter. *American Sea Writing: A Literary Anthology.* New York: Library of America, 2000.

Nevius, Blake. *Cooper's Landscapes.* Berkeley: University of California Press, 1976.

New, Elisa. "Beyond the Romance Theory of American Vision: Beauty and the Qualified Will in Edwards, Jefferson, and Audubon." *American Literary History* 7, no. 3 (1995): 381–414.

———. *The Line's Eye: Poetic Experience, American Sight.* Cambridge: Harvard University Press, 1998.

Newman, Lea Bertani Vozar. *A Reader's Guide to the Short Stories of Herman Melville.* Boston: G. K. Hall, 1986.

Newman, Simon P. "Reading the Bodies of Early American Seafarers." *William and Mary Quarterly*, 3rd ser., 55, no. 1 (January 1998): 79.

Novak, Barbara. *American Painting of the Nineteenth Century: Realism, Idealism, and the American Experience.* New York: Harper and Row, 1979.

———. *Nature and Culture: American Landscape and Painting, 1825–1875.* New York: Oxford University Press, 1995.

Nunis, Doyce B. "Books in Their Sea Chests." *American West* 2, no. 3 (Summer 1965): 74–79.

Olson, Charles. *Call Me Ishmael.* New York: Grove Press, 1958.

Otter, Samuel. *Melville's Anatomies.* Berkeley: University of California Press, 1999.

Panofsky, Erwin. *Perspective as Symbolic Form.* Cambridge: MIT Press, 1991.

Parker, Hershel. *Flawed Texts and Verbal Icons: Literary Authority in American Fiction.* Evanston, Ill.: Northwestern University Press, 1984.

——. *Herman Melville: A Biography.* 2 vols. Baltimore: Johns Hopkins University Press, 1996, 2002.

Parker, Hershel, and Harrison Hayford. *Moby-Dick as Doubloon: Essays and Extracts, 1851–1970.* New York: Norton, 1970.

Pease, Donald E. *Visionary Compacts: American Renaissance Writings in Cultural Context.* Madison: University of Wisconsin Press, 1987.

Peck, H. Daniel. *A World by Itself: The Pastoral Moment in Cooper's Fiction.* New Haven: Yale University Press, 1977.

Peck, H. Daniel, and Henry David Thoreau. *Thoreau's Morning Work: Memory and Perception in a Week on the Concord and Merrimack Rivers, the Journal, and Walden.* New Haven: Yale University Press, 1990.

Peck, John. *Maritime Fiction: Sailors and the Sea in British and American Novels, 1719– 1917.* New York: St. Martin's, 2000.

Philbrick, Nathaniel. *In the Heart of the Sea: The Tragedy of the Whaleship Essex.* New York: Viking Penguin, 2000.

——. *Mayflower: A Story of Courage, Community, and War.* New York: Viking Penguin, 2006.

——. *Sea of Glory: America's Voyage of Discovery—the U.S. Exploring Expedition, 1838– 1842.* New York: Viking Penguin, 2003.

Philbrick, Thomas. *James Fenimore Cooper and the Development of American Sea Fiction.* Cambridge: Harvard University Press, 1961.

Phillips, Richard. *Mapping Men and Empire.* London: Routledge, 1996.

Poirier, Richard. *A World Elsewhere: The Place of Style in American Literature.* New York,: Oxford University Press, 1966.

Poovey, Mary. *A History of the Modern Fact: Problems of Knowledge in the Sciences of Wealth and Society.* Chicago: University of Chicago Press, 1998.

Porte, Joel. *The Romance in America: Studies in Cooper, Poe, Hawthorne, Melville, and James.* Middletown, Conn.: Wesleyan University Press, 1969.

Porter, Carolyn. *Seeing and Being: The Plight of the Participant Observer in Emerson, James, Adams, and Faulkner.* Middletown, Conn.: Wesleyan University Press, 1985.

Post-Lauria, Sheila. *Correspondent Colorings: Melville in the Marketplace.* Amherst: University of Massachusetts Press, 1996.

Pratt, Mary Louise. *Imperial Eyes.* London: Routledge, 1992.

Raban, Jonathan. *The Oxford Book of the Sea.* Oxford: Oxford University Press, 1992.

Rediker, Marcus. *Between the Devil and the Deep Blue Sea: Merchant Seamen, Pirates, and the Anglo-American Maritime World, 1700–1750.* Cambridge: Cambridge University Press, 1987.

Reynolds, David S. *Beneath the American Renaissance: The Subversive Imagination in the Age of Emerson and Melville.* New York: Random House, 1988.

Ringe, Donald A. *James Fenimore Cooper*. Twayne's United States Authors Series. Boston: Twayne, 1988.

——. *The Pictorial Mode; Space and Time in the Art of Bryant, Irving, and Cooper*. Lexington: University Press of Kentucky, 1971.

Ringle, Ken. "Publishers Fathom the Deep Blue Sea: Nautical Adventure Tales Put the Wind in Book Sales." *Washington Post*, 8 October 1998, D1.

Robertson, Robert Blackwood. *Of Whales and Men*. New York: Knopf, 1954.

Robillard, Douglas. *Melville and the Visual Arts: Ionian Form, Venetian Tint*. Kent, Ohio: Kent State University Press, 1997.

Rogin, Michael Paul. *Subversive Genealogy: The Politics and Art of Herman Melville*. New York: Knopf, 1983.

Rojas, Martha Elena. " 'Insults Unpunished': Barbary Captives, American Slaves, and the Negotiation of Liberty." *Early American Studies* 1, no. 2 (Fall 2003): 159–86.

Ross, W. Gillies. *Arctic Whalers, Icy Seas: Narratives of the Davis Strait Whale Fishery*. Toronto, Canada: Irwin, 1985.

Rowe, John Carlos. "Writing and Truth in the Narrative of Arthur Gordon Pym." *Glyph* 2 (1977): 102–21.

St. George, Robert Blair. *Material Life in America, 1600–1860*. Boston: Northeastern University Press, 1988.

Samson, John. *White Lies: Melville's Narratives of Facts*. Ithaca: Cornell University Press, 1989.

Saum, Lewis O. "Death in the Popular Mind of Pre–Civil War America." In *Death in America*, edited by David E. Stannard, 30–48. Philadelphia: University of Pennsylvania Press, 1975.

Scammell, Geoffrey Vaughn. *Ships, Oceans, and Empire: Studies in European Maritime and Colonial History, 1400–1750*. Brookfield, Vt.: Ashgate, 1995.

Scarry, Elaine. *The Body in Pain: The Making and Unmaking of the World*. New York: Oxford University Press, 1985.

——. *Dreaming by the Book*. New York: Farrar Straus and Giroux, 1999.

Schama, Simon. *Landscape and Memory*. New York: Knopf, 1995.

Sealts, Merton M. *Melville's Reading: A Check-List of Books Owned and Borrowed*. Madison: University of Wisconsin Press, 1966.

Sears, John F. *Sacred Places: American Tourist Attractions in the Nineteenth Century*. New York: Oxford University Press, 1989.

Seelye, John. *Prophetic Waters*. New York: Oxford University Press, 1977.

Seidel, Michael. *Robinson Crusoe: Island Myths and the Novel*. Boston: Twayne, 1991.

Shuffleton, Frank. "Going Through the Long Vaticans: Melville's 'Extracts' in *Moby-Dick*." *Texas Studies in Literature and Language* 25, no. 4 (Winter 1983): 528–40.

Sieminski, Greg. "The Puritan Captivity Narrative and the Politics of the American Revolution." *American Quarterly* 42, no. 1 (March 1990): 35–56.

Skallerup, Harry R. *Books Afloat and Ashore: A History of Books, Libraries, and Reading among Seamen during the Age of Sail*. Hamden, Conn: Archon, 1974.

Skelton, R. A. *Explorers' Maps.* London: Routledge, 1958.

Slotkin, Richard. *Fatal Environment.* New York: Athaneum, 1985.

——. *Regeneration through Violence.* Middletown, Conn.: Wesleyan University Press, 1973.

Smith, Henry Nash. *Virgin Land.* Cambridge: Harvard University Press, 1970.

Smith, Richard Dean. *Melville's Science: "Devilish Tantalization of the Gods!"* New York: Garland, 1993.

Snader, Joe. *Caught between Worlds: British Captivity Narratives in Fact and Fiction.* Lexington: University Press of Kentucky, 2000.

——. "The Oriental Captivity Narrative and Early English Fiction." *Eighteenth-Century Fiction* 9, no. 3 (April 1997): 267–98.

Spengemann, William C. *The Adventurous Muse: The Poetics of American Fiction, 1789–1900.* New Haven: Yale University Press, 1977.

Spiller, Robert. *The American Literary Revolution, 1783–1837.* Documents in American Civilization Series. Garden City, N.Y.: Anchor Books, 1967.

Springer, Haskell S., ed. *America and the Sea: A Literary History.* Athens: University of Georgia Press, 1995.

Spufford, Margaret. *Contrasting Communities: English Villagers in the Sixteenth and Seventeenth Centuries.* London: Cambridge University Press, 1974.

Stein, Roger. *Seascape and the American Imagination.* New York: CN Potter, 1975.

Sten, Christopher. *The Weaver God, He Weaves: Melville and the Poetics of the Novel.* Kent, Ohio: Kent State University Press, 1996.

Streeby, Shelley. *American Sensations: Class, Empire, and the Production of Popular Culture.* Berkeley: University of California Press, 2002.

Strong, Pauline Turner. *Captive Selves, Captivating Others: The Politics and Poetics of Colonial American Captivity Narratives.* Boulder, Colo.: Westview Press, 1999.

Sundquist, Eric J. *Home as Found.* Baltimore: Johns Hopkins University Press, 1979.

——. *To Wake the Nations: Race in the Making of American Literature.* Cambridge: Harvard University Press, 1993.

Thrower, Nathan. *Maps and Civilization.* Chicago: University of Chicago Press, 1996.

Tolchin, Neal L. *Mourning, Gender, and Creativity in the Art of Herman Melville.* New Haven: Yale University Press, 1988.

Tomkins, Jane. *Sensational Designs.* New York: Oxford University Press, 1985.

Turner, Frederick W. *Beyond Geography: The Western Spirit against the Wilderness.* New Brunswick, N.J.: Rutgers University Press, 1992.

Tyacke, Sarah. "Describing Maps." In *The Book Encompassed*, edited by Peter Davison, 130–41. Cambridge: Cambridge University Press, 1992.

Viola, Herman J., and Carolyn Margolis. *Magnificent Voyagers: The U.S. Exploring Expedition, 1838–1842.* Washington, D.C.: Smithsonian Institution Press, 1985.

Wallace, James D. *Early Cooper and His Audience.* New York: Columbia University Press, 1986.

Warner, Michael. *The Letters of the Republic: Publication and the Public Sphere in Eighteenth-Century America.* Cambridge: Harvard University Press, 1990.

Weinstein, Cindy. *The Literature of Labor and the Labors of Literature: Allegory in Nineteenth-Century American Fiction.* Cambridge: Cambridge University Press, 1995.

Whipple, A. B. C. *To the Shores of Tripoli: The Birth of the U.S. Navy and Marines.* New York: William Morrow, 1991.

Williams, Julie Hedgepeth. *The Significance of the Printed Word in Early America: Colonists' Thoughts on the Role of the Press.* Contributions to the Study of Mass Media and Communications, no. 55. Westport, Conn.: Greenwood Press, 1999.

Wilmerding, John. *American Marine Painting.* Princeton: Princeton University Press, 1991.

———. *American Views.* New York: Abrams, 1987.

Wilson, Peter Lamborn. *Pirate Utopias: Moorish Corsairs and European Renegadoes.* Brooklyn: Autonomedia, 1995.

Wood, James Playsted. *Magazines in the United States.* New York: Ronald Press, 1971.

Wright, Lyle Henry. *American Fiction, 1774–1850: A Contribution toward a Bibliography.* Huntington Library Publications. 2nd rev. ed. San Marino, Calif.: Huntington Library, 1969.

Zacks, Richard. *The Pirate Coast: Thomas Jefferson, the First Marines, and the Secret Mission of 1805.* New York: Hyperion, 2005.

Zboray, Ronald J. "Antebellum Reading and the Ironies of Technological Innovation." *American Quarterly* 40, no. 1 (March 1988): 65–82.

Zimmerman, Brett. *Herman Melville: Stargazer.* Montreal: McGill-Queen's University Press, 1998.

INDEX

88–89, 95, 96–97, 186–87, 191; in
maritime narratives, 39, 40–41, 43,
58, 61–62, 218 (n. 52)
*Authentic Narrative of the Loss of the
American Brig Commerce, An* (Riley),
66; Arabic alphabet and vocabulary
list in, 60 (ill.); map from, 59 (ill.)

Ballads, 5, 9, 201–2 (n. 3)
Bancroft, George, 98
Banks, Sir Joseph, 62
Barbary captives, 28, 29, 41, 42–43,
44–45, 48–52, 58, 61, 66–67; causes
of, 8, 48; comparison of to African
slaves, 54–55, 56–57, 210–11
(n. 28), 211 (n. 30), 211–12 (n. 37);
comparison of to American Indians,
54; comparison of to British impressment, 67; economic value of,
57–58, 209 (n. 15); ethnic diversity
of, 58; Europeans as, 210 (n. 25); labor performed by, 51; and name
origin of Barbary, 208 (n. 6); number
of, 49; poems by, 63; ransoming of,
49–50, 57, 63, 64, 213 (n. 53); religious conversion of, 28, 58, 63, 208
(n. 5); treatment of, 51, 56–57, 63,
65, 68–69, 209 (nn. 15, 18), 213
(n. 73). *See also* Barbary captivity
narratives
Barbary captivity narratives, 46–70, 75;
audience for, 46–47, 53, 58, 63–64,
66–70, 74; British, 57, 69; most popular, 213 (n. 63); by nonwhite American, 58, 61; scholarly study of, 212
(n. 39); third-person, 61–62; as
warning to other sailors, 12, 46, 58,
66–67
Barnard, Charles, 39–40, 41
Barnum, P. T., 41
Barthes, Roland, 176–77
Bastinado (torture method), 51, 57, 65,
209 (nn. 15, 18)

Bathurst, Lord, 62
Baym, Nina, 215 (n. 12)
"Before the mast": meaning of, 10
"Benito Cereno" (Melville), 134, 138
Bennett, Michael J., 25
Bentley, Richard, 100, 101, 104–6
Betsey (ship), 50
Bible, 5, 21, 27, 29, 30, 32, 99; Mount
Pisgah referenced in, 156; parodied,
37; whales referenced in, 127
Biographies: compared to personal narratives, 94, 101
Black Atlantic studies, 12, 200–201
(n. 35)
Black sailors, 8, 199 (n. 25), 203 (n. 35)
Books: appendixes in, 66–67; author
portraits in, 62; binding of, 124–25;
and cheap literature, 9–10, 37; com-
pared to whales, 130; cost of, 21, 30,
160; endnotes in, 174, 175, 183,
186–87, 190–92; epilogues in, 187,
190; as metaphors for ships, 114–15,
123–24; production of, 5, 9, 21, 42,
43, 44, 103–5, 114–16, 124–25, 160,
217–18 (n. 47); subversive, 34–35;
title pages of, 42, 62, 101; traded, 5,
21, 27. *See also* Prefaces
Boston Commercial Gazette, 33
Boston Seaman's Friend Society, 31
Bowditch, Nathaniel, 119, 131
Boyle, Robert, 28
Bradford, William, 76, 199 (n. 23)
Briggs, Frederick, 145
British: impressment, 12, 37, 47, 48,
67–68; maritime narratives, 8, 69;
slave trade, 55; whaling fleet, 167–69
Broadsides, 5, 9, 198 (n. 7), 199
(n. 23)
Bromell, Nicholas K., 110
Brown, Bill, 188–89, 219–20 (n. 1)
Browne, J. Ross, 21–22, 120–21
Bulwer-Lytton, Edward, 20, 22, 34, 35
Buntline, Ned, 9, 10, 200 (n. 32)

Burial grounds. *See* Cemeteries; Gravesites

Burial memorials, 160, 161, 165; sea narratives as, 187. *See also* Cenotaphs

Burials, sailor: anonymous, 174; effect of on crew, 164, 178; in foreign lands, 158, 159, 162–70, 172; in hammock, 188; methods of, 158; ocean as cemetery, 175–76, 177; at sea, 158–59, 161–62, 164, 175–82; secret, 161, 172. *See also* Burial memorials; Corpses; Gravesites

Byron, Lord, 4, 81–82; on death, 177

Cannibalism: Malolo, Fiji Islands, 172; by sailors, 195

Captains: burial of at sea, 175–76; tyranny of, 25, 110–11

Carey, Mathew, 54–55, 64

Carey & Lea (publishing house), 77

Carpenter, Edward Jenner, 34

Carretta, Vincent, 199 (n. 25)

Casarino, Cesare, 181–82, 188, 189, 197 (n. 3), 200–201 (n. 35)

Castronovo, Russ, 180

Cathcart, James Leander, 50, 52, 63, 64, 65, 210 (n. 20)

Catholics: gravesites of, 161; Spaniards as, 65

Cemeteries, 158, 164–65; as a heterotopia, 180, 182; Mount Auburn, 172, 173 (ill.); name origin of, 158; as parks, 158, 166; as places for meditation, 158; Protestant, 163; rural cemetery movement, 158, 165, 166, 167, 182

Cenotaphs, 165, 173 (ill.), 174–75; for interred sailor, 226–27 (n. 19)

Chanteys, sea, 5, 9, 197 (n. 2)

Charles W. Morgan (ship), 22, 34; logbook page, 24 (ill.)

Chase, Owen, 194–95

Christian organizations, 27, 29–30, 32

Circulating libraries, 29, 30–35; rules and regulations of, 38 (ill.)

Civil War, U.S., 25, 153

"Claim for American Literature, A" (Russell), 193

Clarel (Melville), 148–49

Clark, Joseph: as member of the United States Exploring Expedition (1838–42), 159–61, 162, 164, 169, 174–75; and plagiarism, 225–26 (n. 6)

Classification and taxonomies: in *Moby-Dick*, 127, 129, 130, 131; Pratt on, 138–39; "tabular histories," 139, 140–43 (ill.), 144, 146; as a way to view the world, 139. *See also* Population charts

Cochelet, Charles, 66

Coffins, symbolic, 182–92; as canoe, 188–89; as grave marker, 189–90; as life buoy, 187, 188, 189; as living space, 183, 185–86; as locker, 188; premature burial in, 184–85; text imprinted on, 188–90

Cohen, Margaret, 200–201 (n. 35)

Collectivity, 64–65; of knowledge, 114; of maritime labor, 39, 111–12, 116; of reading, 21

Colley, Linda, 69

Colnett, James, 133, 134, 135, 146

Colton, Walter, 32, 163

Columbian Magazine, 63

Columbus, Christopher, 137, 138

Commerce: importance of maritime industry, 25, 44, 71, 181, 197 (n. 6)

Commonplace books, 116, 129, 131

Conrad, Joseph, 112, 181

Constitution (ship), 19–20

Continental navy, 48, 49

Cook, James, 169; gravesite of, 161, 169–70, 171 (ill.)

Cooper, James Fenimore, 71–106, 159–60; as amanuensis, 93–95, 99, 100–102, 218–19 (n. 59); as "the

American Scott," 77; audience of, 20, 34, 35, 72, 79, 82–84, 89, 91–92, 104, 125–26, 215 (n. 9); biographies on, 81; on copyright law, 104; critiqued by sailors, 72–73, 78–79, 80; and depiction of common sailors, 97; and depiction of female characters, 84–85; first American sea novels of, 9, 11, 71, 75, 199 (n. 27), 214 (n. 5); on flogging, 97; and focus on nautical hierarchies, 72–73, 74, 92, 99; geographical settings in works of, 77–78; and historical fiction, 9, 82–83, 91–92; and interest in book production, 43, 103–5; and involvement in mutiny case, 217 (n. 43); Leatherstocking tales of, 75, 87, 214 (n. 2); and libel lawsuits, 89; and logbooks as metaphor, 94, 102–4; maritime career of, 5, 72, 74, 77, 93, 99; maritime nationalism of, 75; on mortality, 103; and nautical realism, 72–73, 88–89, 91–92, 94–95, 96–97, 103–4, 105–6, 214 (n. 2); and rejection of gothic mode, 77–78; reprints of works issued, 73–74, 81, 87–92, 100, 124–25; reviews of work of, 215–16 (n. 17); scholarly study of, 214–15 (n. 6). See also *History of the Navy* (Cooper); *Ned Myers; or, A Life before the Mast* (Cooper); *Pilot, The* (Cooper); *Red Rover, The* (Cooper); *Spy, The* (Cooper); *Water-Witch, The* (Cooper)

Copyright law, 104, 224–25 (n. 27)

Corporal punishment: flogging, 10, 25, 30, 51, 96–97, 111; whipping, 63. *See also* Torture

Corpses: cannibalism of, 172, 195; decomposition of, 192; disposal of, 161–62, 164, 188, 192; as metaphor for ships, 163

Corsair, The (Byron), 81–82

Corsairs. *See* Barbary captives; Barbary captivity narratives; Piracy

Country of the Pointed Firs (Jewett), 11

Cowan, John S., 168, 169, 227 (n. 27)

Cowdery, Jonathan, 63

Crary, Jonathan, 123

Crime: genre, 21–22, 47, 53, 97, 128; murders, 161, 169, 170, 172

Criticism, literary, 12; of sea narratives, 40, 42–43, 61, 75

Cropsy, Peter C., 165

Curtis, G. W., 145

Daboll, Nathan, 131

Dampier, William, 133

Dana, Richard Henry, Jr., 21, 100, 187, 189; authorship of questioned, 95–96; in California, 165–66, 174, 175; death of, 193; loss of journals of, 119; naval career of, 10, 199 (n. 30), 218 (n. 52); on "plain matters of fact," 3, 46; "Twenty-Four Years After," 174, 175; viewed posthumously, 193–94. See also *Two Years before the Mast* (Dana)

Dana, Richard Henry, Sr., 95–96, 199 (n. 30)

Darwin, Charles: Galapagos travels of, 133, 134; on poetry, 149; South American travels of, 151–52. See also *Voyage of the Beagle* (Darwin)

Dauphin (ship), 50

Davidson, Cathy, 29, 56, 82

Davis, Joshua, 67–68

Davy Jones's locker, 176–77, 189

Death, maritime, 160–62; disorienting nature of, 178–81; by drowning, 110, 178–79; by duel, 168, 227 (n. 27); by hanging, 217 (n. 43); impermanence of life considered, 159, 162; as metaphor, 177; murders, 161, 169, 170, 172; narrative response to, 158–59, 162, 165, 174, 175–92;

place of in the maritime world, 169–
70, 172, 174–75; poetry on, 177; by
suicide, 168; "vacancy" created by,
165, 179, 189. *See also* Mortality

Decatur, Stephen, 50

Deck and Port (Colton), 32

Defoe, Daniel, 8, 199 (n. 24). See also
Robinson Crusoe (Defoe)

Delano, Amasa, 43–44, 133, 134, 135,
138, 146

Delano, Reuben, 93, 134–35

Denning, Michael, 6

Dennis, Matthew, 179–80

"Descartian vortices," 121, 221 (n. 30)

Desertion, 49, 67, 98

Dexter, Elisha, 93

Dibdin, Charles, 197 (n. 2)

Dickinson, Emily, 123

Dimond, William, 177

Discovery narratives, 122

Doggerel verse, 159, 162–69, 227
(n. 23). *See also* Poetry

Dryden, Edgar A., 187, 189

Duels, 168, 227 (n. 27)

Dye, Ira, 26, 203 (n. 35)

Economy. *See* Commerce

Education, 27–28, 29, 44

Edwards, William, 164

Emerson, Ralph Waldo, 110, 121, 193;
on visual perspective, 2–3, 122–23,
221 (n. 36)

Emersonian eyeball, 2, 121–22, 221
(n. 36)

"Encantadas, or Enchanted Isles, The"
(Melville), 131–32; audience of,
135–36; documenting the existence
of places, 152; epistemology explored in, 135, 146, 147; gravesite
noted in, 166, 167; maritime death
in, 162; population charts in, 136–
37, 146, 147–48, 149 (ill.), 150, 151,
152; pseudonym used in, 139, 224

(n. 22); publication of, 133, 135,
136–39, 145–47; reader's textual experience of, 136, 146–47, 150–51,
154–56; "seeing" the islands, 146–
47, 154–57; source material for,
133–35, 136–37, 146, 147–49

Enlisted men, 34, 97

Epistemology, maritime, 2–4; on
death, 159, 161–62, 178, 182, 187;
union of manual and mental labor, 1,
2, 3–4, 110, 112–13, 116, 117–18,
119, 120–22, 123, 129–31, 159, 178,
180–81. *See also* "Sea eye"

Epitaphs, sailor, 161, 162–70, 171 (ill.),
227 (n. 23); referencing maritime labor, 163, 164; subversive nature of,
164. *See also* Doggerel verse

Equiano, Olaudah, 8, 199 (n. 25)

Essex (ship), 135, 166, 194–95; War of
1812, 167–69

Etchings of a Whaling Cruise (Browne),
120–21

Etymologies: in *Moby-Dick*, 127–28

Europeans: as Barbary captives, 210
(n. 25); as colonizers, 8; as renegados,
57

Evolution, theory of, 133, 134

Eye. *See* Emersonian eyeball; "Sea
eye"

Fabian, Ann, 40, 73, 101, 217–18
(n. 47)

Fiction, maritime, 20, 34, 35, 47; on
death, 159, 176–77, 179, 182–92;
first American, 9, 11, 71, 75, 199
(n. 27), 214 (n. 5); focus on working
sailors in, 74, 87, 181; as manifestation of heterotopia, 181; popular, 6,
9–10; shift from romance to realism
in, 10–11, 72, 214 (n. 2); in shipboard libraries, 34; technical specificity of, 81, 82–84, 85–86, 186. *See
also* Historical romance

Madison, James, 139

Maldonado, Uruguay, 151–52

Manuals: conduct, 20, 22, 34; how-to, 41

Maps: Galapagos Islands, 133; illustrating narratives, 42–43, 58, 62; Northwest Africa, 59 (ill.); used by Darwin, 151–52

Mardi (Melville), 126

Maria (ship), 50, 63

Marin, Louis, 174, 175

"Mariner's Dream, A" (Dimond), 177

Mariner's Sketches, A (Ames), 32, 78, 97, 118

Marines, 50

Maritime narratives. *See* Narratives, maritime

Marks, Richard, 37

Marryat, Frederick, 19–20, 34, 35

Martingale, Hawser, 4, 6, 41; on death, 175–76, 177, 187. See also *Jack in the Forecastle*

Marx, Leo, 121–22

Massachusetts: burial memorials in, 164–65, 172, 173 (ill.)

Masthead, 3; life "before the mast," 10; lookout duty from, 1, 118, 119–22

Melville, Herman, 43, 116, 181; analyzed by *Putnam's*, 145, 225 (n. 29); on Cooper, 124–26, 127; death of, 193; endnotes in works of, 183; genealogy of, 120; maritime career of, 5, 133, 195; on maritime death, 159, 182–83, 187–90, 192; and plagiarism, 225–26 (n. 6); prefaces in works of, 126, 183; reference by to Columbus, 138; and relationship between fact and imagination, 1, 136–37, 145–52, 157; "sea eye" explored, 127, 131, 135, 221 (n. 30); viewed posthumously, 193–94. *See also* "Benito Cereno" (Melville); *Clarel* (Melville); "Encantadas, or En-chanted Isles, The" (Melville); *Moby-Dick* (Melville); *White Jacket* (Melville)

Merchant Seamen's Bible Society, 29, 198 (n. 12)

Merchant ships: libraries on, 27, 34; safety of, 48, 49

Midshipman Easy (Marryat), 20

M'Lean, James, 67

Moby-Dick (Melville), 116, 181; Ahab, 127, 189; burial memorials referenced in, 164; coffin used symbolically in, 182–83, 187–90; epilogue, 187, 190; epistemology explored in, 130–31; "Etymology" and "Extracts" sections, 116, 126–29, 190, 222 (n. 45), 222–23 (n. 52); Ishmael, 117, 130, 182, 187–90, 192, 222 (n. 50); on lookout duty, 1, 119, 120, 121–22; metaphysical concerns in, 1, 120; monotony of the sea in, 117; narrative structure of, 190; *Pequod*, 130–31, 187, 188, 189; prefaces and endnotes, 183; Queequeg, 182, 183, 187–90, 192; as a repository of sailor writing, 129; "sea eye" in, 131, 221 (n. 30); Stubb, 130–31; sub-sub librarian, 128–29; tattoos in, 130, 188–90, 222 (n. 50); taxonomies and classification in, 127, 129, 130, 131, 138; Usher, 126, 127–29; white whale, 195

Modernism: maritime literature and, 181, 188–89

Monsters, sea, 4, 199 (n. 23)

Montgomery, Benilde, 55

Moore, Thomas, 201–2 (n. 3)

Morell, Benjamin, Jr., 1, 197 (n. 2)

Morocco: as a Barbary State, 48, 208 (n. 6); enslavement in, 47, 56–57; settlement treaty with, 50

Mortality: Cooper on, 103; Melville on, 127–28; shipboard dangers and, 110. *See also* Death

vs. Barbary, 49. *See also* Barbary captives; Barbary captivity narratives; Renegados (pirates)

Pirate, The (Scott), 81, 84, 88–89

Pirates Own Book, 5, 35, 47

Plagiarism, 186, 225–26 (n. 6)

Poe, Edgar Allan, 181; interest of in premature burials, 184–85; lack of maritime experience of, 186; on maritime death, 59, 182–92; only novel by, 184; and plagiarism, 186, 225–26 (n. 6). See also *Narrative of Arthur Gordon Pym, The* (Poe)

Poetry, 8–9, 79–80; by Barbary captives, 53, 63; on death, 177; importance of to Dana, 165–66; by Leggett, 79–80, 177; on the sea, 79–80; by Shelley, 148–49. *See also* Doggerel verse

Poirier, Richard, 122

Polar exploration, 184, 186, 229 (n. 3)

Poovey, Mary, 147–48, 150, 153

Population charts: American census report, 146, 152–53, 154 (ill.); Galapagos Islands, 136–37, 146, 147, 149 (ill.), 150, 151, 152; Pacific islands, 152; racial vs. geographical, 153

Pornography, 37

Port, 7, 30, 113. *See also* Shore leave

Porter, David: narratives of, 43, 133–34, 146, 162, 167–69; naval career, 134–35, 167–69

Practical Navigator (Bowditch), 119, 131

Pratt, Mary Louise, 138–39

Prefaces. *See* Apologia; Melville, Herman: prefaces in works of; *Moby Dick* (Melville): prefaces and endnotes; *Narrative of Arthur Gordon Pym, The* (Poe): prefaces and endnotes; *Ned Myers; or, A Life before the Mast* (Cooper): preface; *Pilot, The* (Cooper): preface; *Red Rover, The* (Cooper): preface; *Spy, The*

(Cooper): preface; *Two Years before the Mast* (Dana): preface

"Premature Burial" (Poe), 184

Presbyterian Board of Publication, 32

Privateers, 52

Proprioceptive sea eye: advice on acquiring, 154–56; *Putnam's Monthly* on, 156–57; in "The Encantadas," 146–47, 154–57

Protection. *See* Tribute payments (extortion)

Protestants: gravesites and cemeteries of, 161, 163

Putnam, G. P. (publishing house): and reissues of Cooper, 73–74, 81, 87–90, 124–25. See also *Putnam's Monthly Magazine of American Literature, Science, and Art*

Putnam, George Palmer, 139; and copyright advocacy, 224–25 (n. 27); statistical works authored by, 139, 140–43 (ill.), 144, 146, 153. *See also* G. P. Putnam (publishing house); *Putnam's Monthly Magazine of American Literature, Science, and Art*

Putnam's Monthly Magazine of American Literature, Science, and Art, 131–32, 133, 135, 136–37; authors published anonymously in, 139; circulation of, 224–25 (n. 27); "The Encantadas" published in, 133, 135, 136–39, 145–47, 157; length of run of, 144; Melville discussed in, 145; mission of, 137–38, 139, 144–45, 156, 224 (n. 25); national census report in, 137, 146, 152–53, 154 (ill.); "Our Young Authors" series, 145; publisher of, 139

Qaramanli, Yusuf, 50

Ray, William, 122; on captivity, 53, 63, 68–69; and comparison of naval service to enslavement, 25, 51–52; on labor, 47–48, 113

Reading: Sailor's Reading Room, 9; symbolic use of, 185–86; while on duty, 78, 118. *See also* Literacy

Redburn (Melville), 126

Rediker, Marcus: on class status, 25; on labor, 68, 111–12, 123, 207 (n. 4); on literacy, 26, 28–29

Red Rover, The (Cooper), 11, 35, 73–74, 78–79; genealogy of, 81; · Melville on, 124–26, 127; preface, 73–74, 87, 89–90, 91–92, 103

Reform movements, antebellum, 4, 5, 10, 22, 23, 27, 29–32, 44, 71, 97, 111, 203 (n. 38); and lack of concern for material needs of sailors, 160

Reid, Midshipman: cenotaph memorializing, 173 (ill.)

Religious tracts, 9, 21, 22, 30–31, 32, 34, 160

Renegados (pirates), 28, 49, 57, 208 (n. 5)

Revolutionary War, U.S.: heroes of fictionalized, 82; and postwar navy, 8, 48; sailors in, 25

Reynolds, Jeremiah, 186

Riley, James, 8, 42–43, 47, 56–57, 62, 66, 69, 213 (n. 63); Arabic alphabet and vocabulary list used by, 60 (ill.); map showing overland journey of, 59 (ill.)

Robbins, Archibald, 41–42, 211–12 (n. 37)

Robinson Crusoe (Defoe), 6, 8; original title of, 199 (n. 24)

Roderick Random (Smollett), 84, 90, 91

Rosa, Salvator, 224 (n. 22)

Rowson, Susanna, 8–9, 54, 55–56

Rural cemetery movement, 158, 165, 166, 167, 182

Russell, W. Clark: on Melville and Dana, 193–94

Sailors: ambition of, 22, 28, 30, 31, 44; class status of, 25–26, 40, 160, 174–75; destitution of, 92–93, 101, 217–18 (n. 47); emptiness of the sea first experienced by, 6, 117; intellectual abilities of, 23; international status of, 12, 48, 168; and leisure at sea, 2, 5, 19, 111; on liberty, 23, 25, 51–52; literary tastes of, 9–10, 20, 34–35, 37, 78; mobility of, 52–53, 68, 102, 207 (n. 4); and need for order, 111, 112, 117; novices initiated, 7; participation of in literary culture, 2, 5, 12, 19–45, 75, 96; punning, 35, 40; self-definition of, 26, 53–54; vices, 29, 30, 31, 32, 78–79, 97, 113; wages of, 2, 4, 111, 181

Sailor's Magazine, 30; report in, 172, 174

Sandwich Islands (Hawaii): Captain Cook gravesite, 161, 169–70, 171 (ill.)

School readers, 34, 205 (n. 55)

Scientific expression: nineteenth-century reevaluation of, 136, 147

Scott, Walter, 90, 91, 92; *The Pirate*, 81, 84, 88–89; and popularization of historical romance, 76; read by sailors, 20, 34, 35, 75, 78

"Scribbler's itch," 201 (n. 2)

"Sea eye," 3–4; commonplace books a product of, 129; and dangers of contemplation, 119, 120–22; and "Descartian vortices," 221 (n. 30); development of, 109–10, 113–14, 116; in "The Encantadas" 135; illustrated by weather forecasting, 113–14; in *Moby-Dick*, 131, 221 (n. 30); proprioceptive, 146–47, 154–57. *See also* Labor, maritime: union of manual and mental labor; Visual perspective

"Sea legs," 7